Conquer yourself rather than the world!

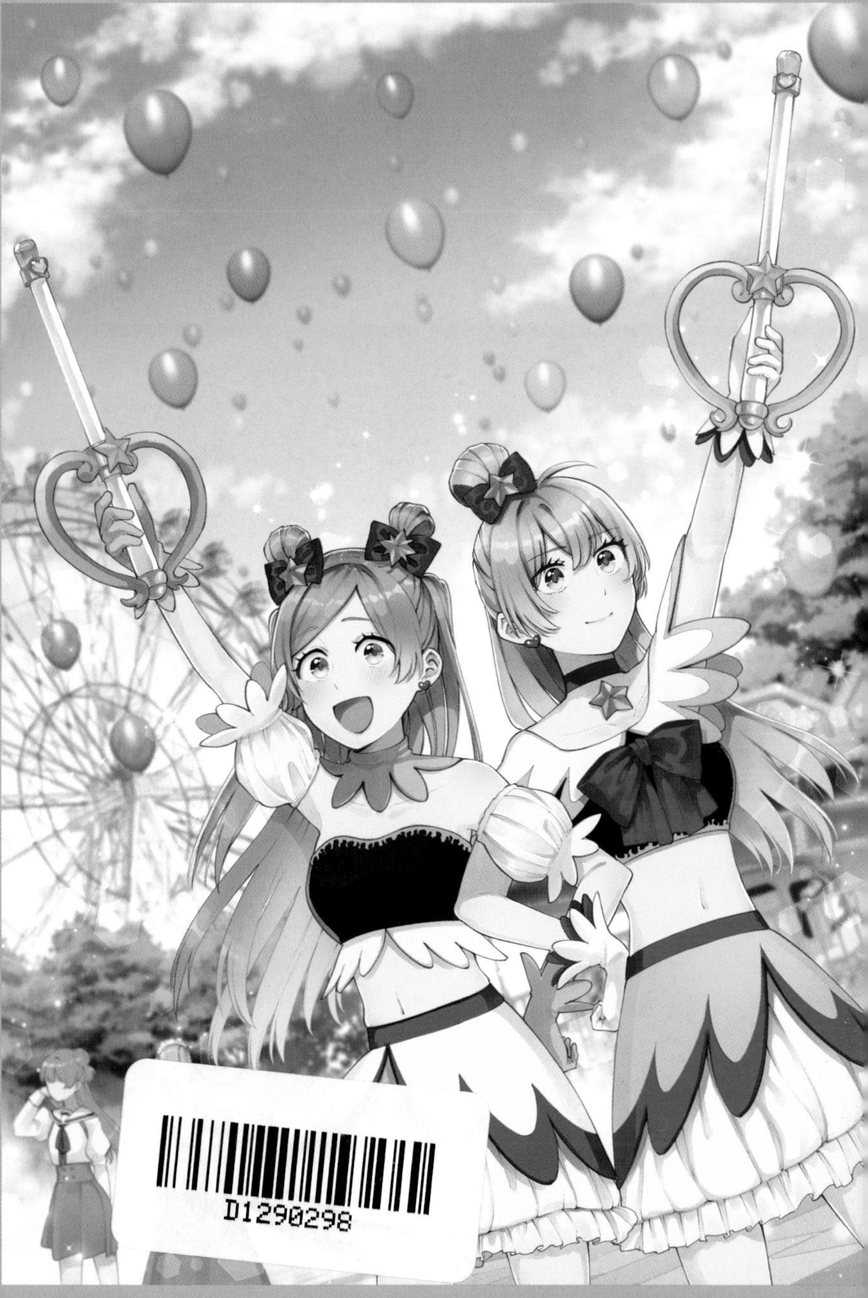

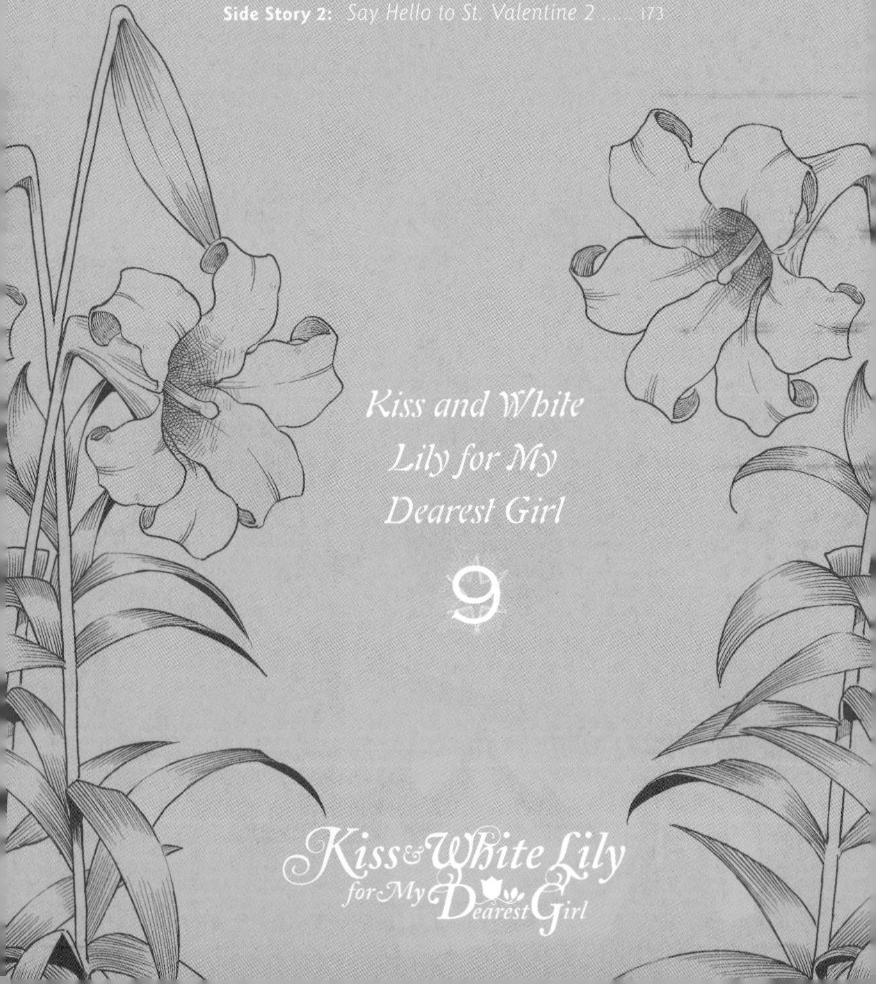

Kiss and White Lily for My Dearest Girl

9

Kiss & White Lily for My Dearest Girl

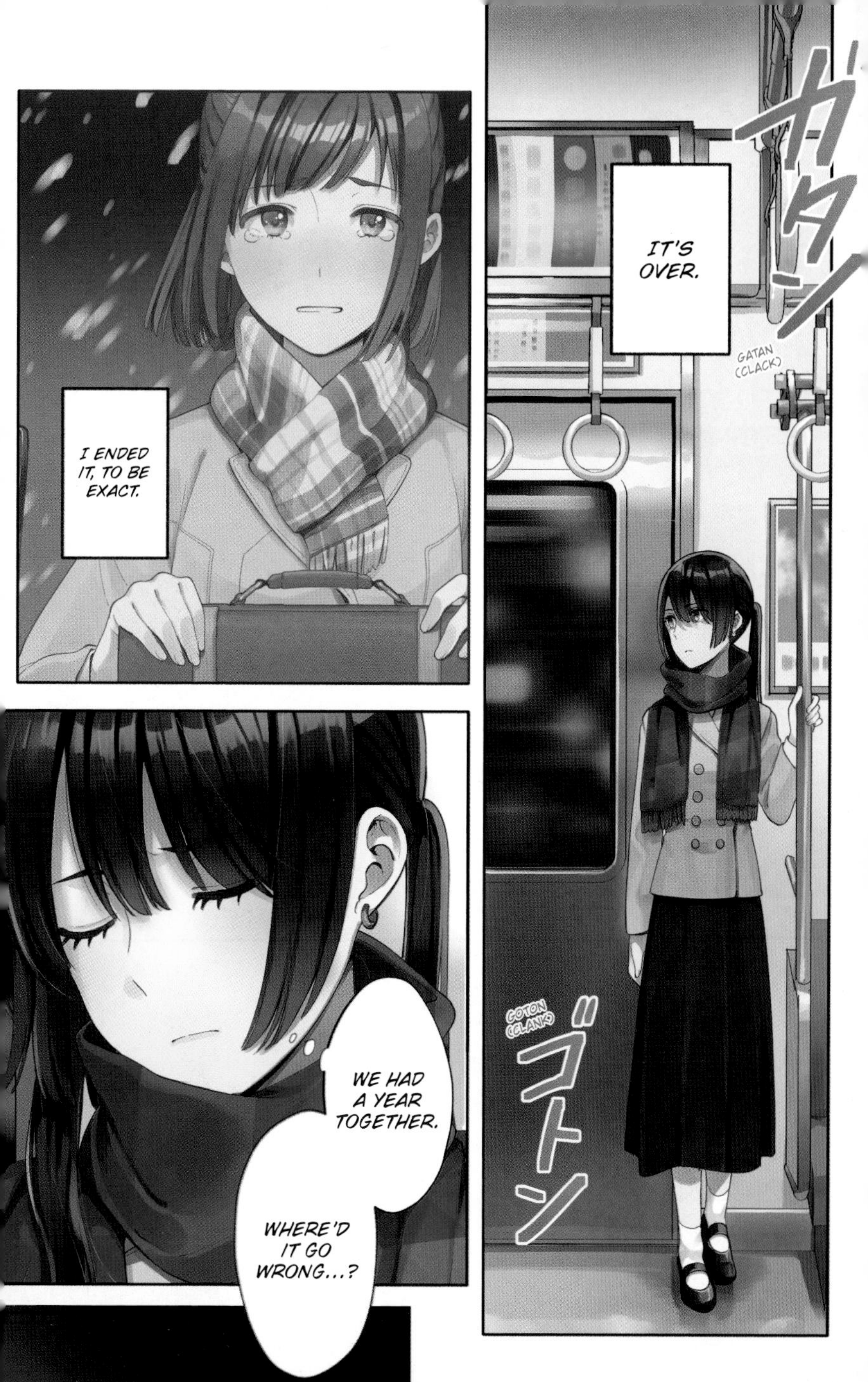
IT'S OVER.
ガタン
GATAN (CLACK)
ゴトン
GOTON (CLANK)
I ENDED IT, TO BE EXACT.
WE HAD A YEAR TOGETHER.
WHERE'D IT GO WRONG...?

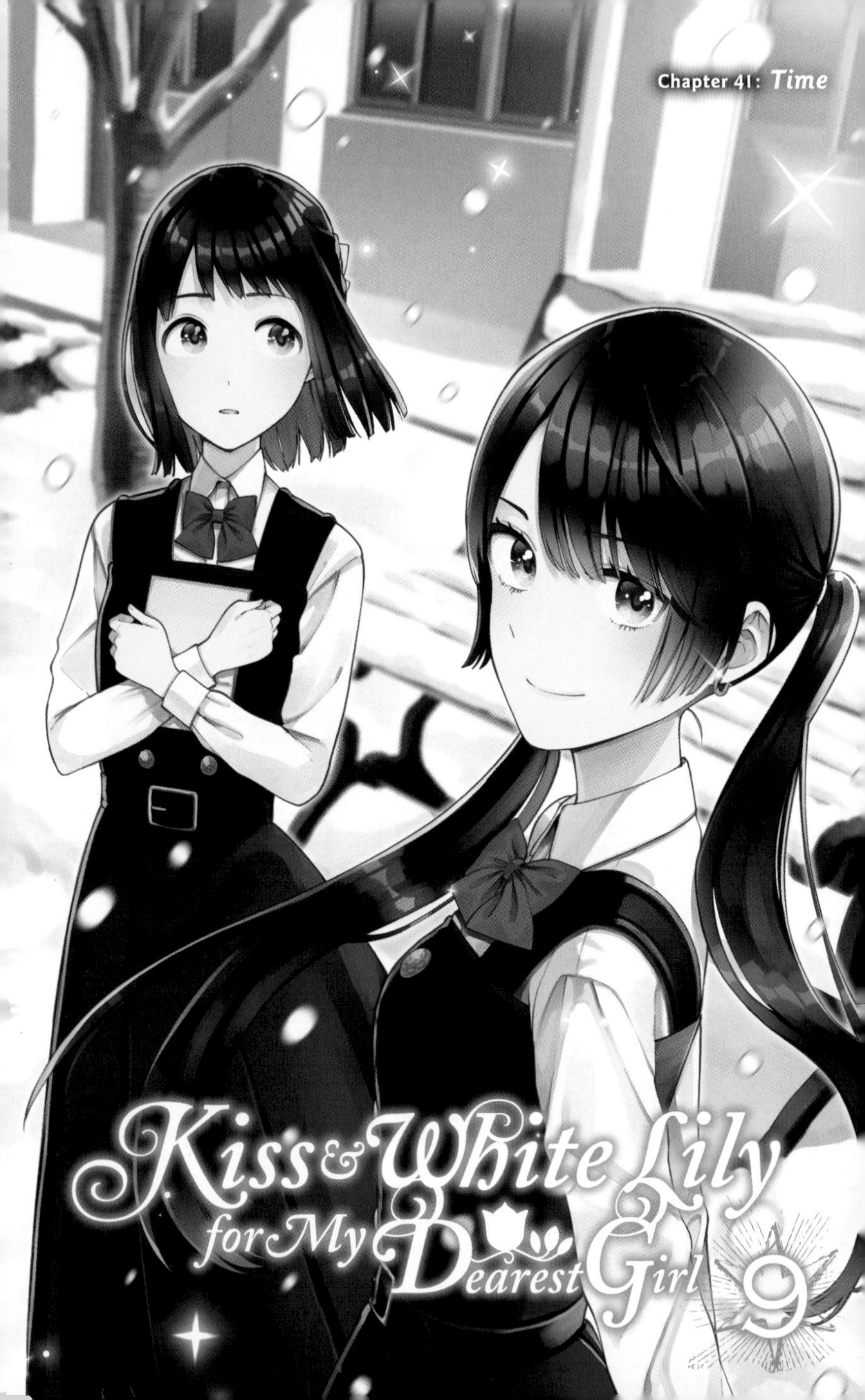
Chapter 41: Time
Kiss & White Lily for My Dearest Girl
9

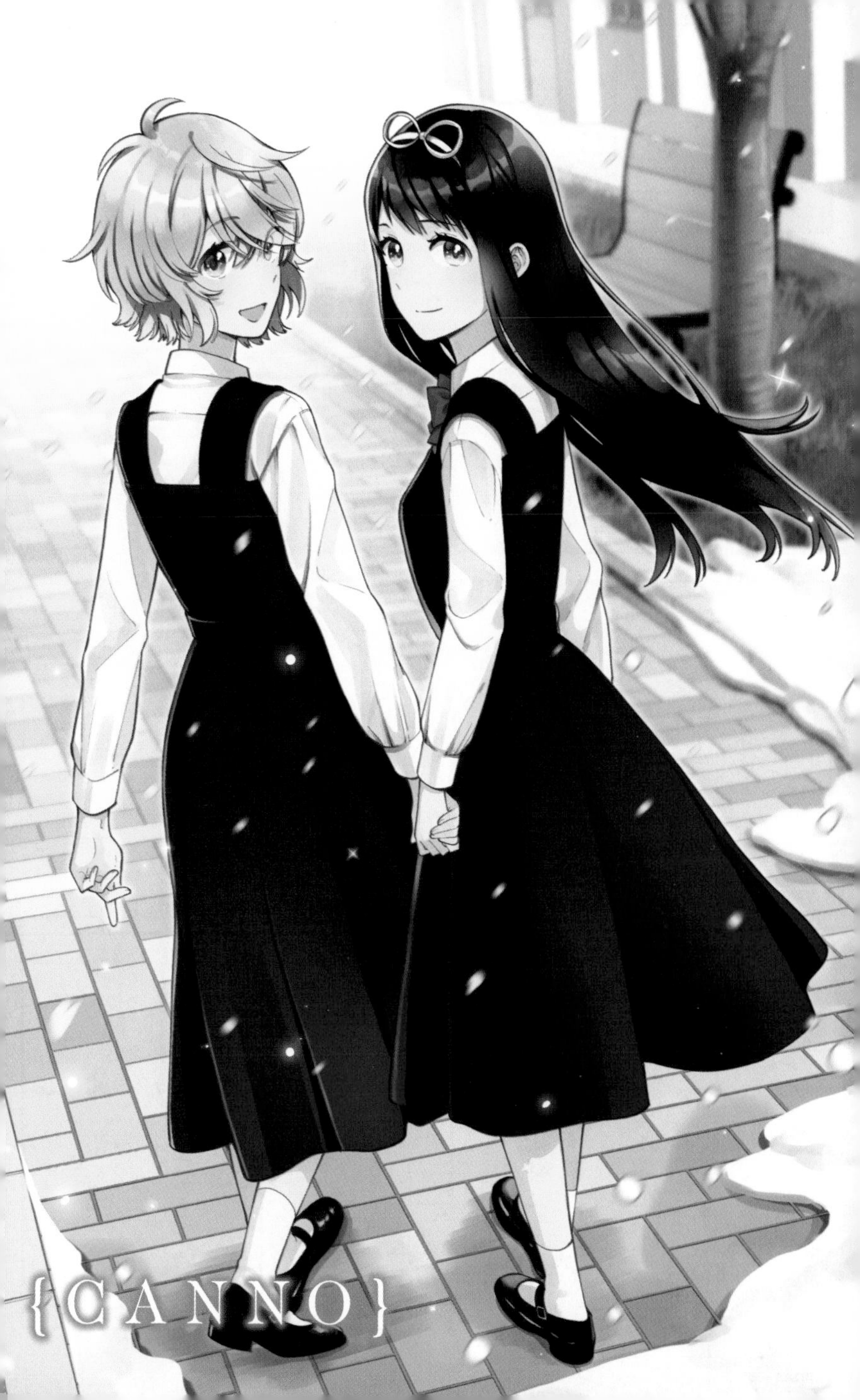
{CANNO}

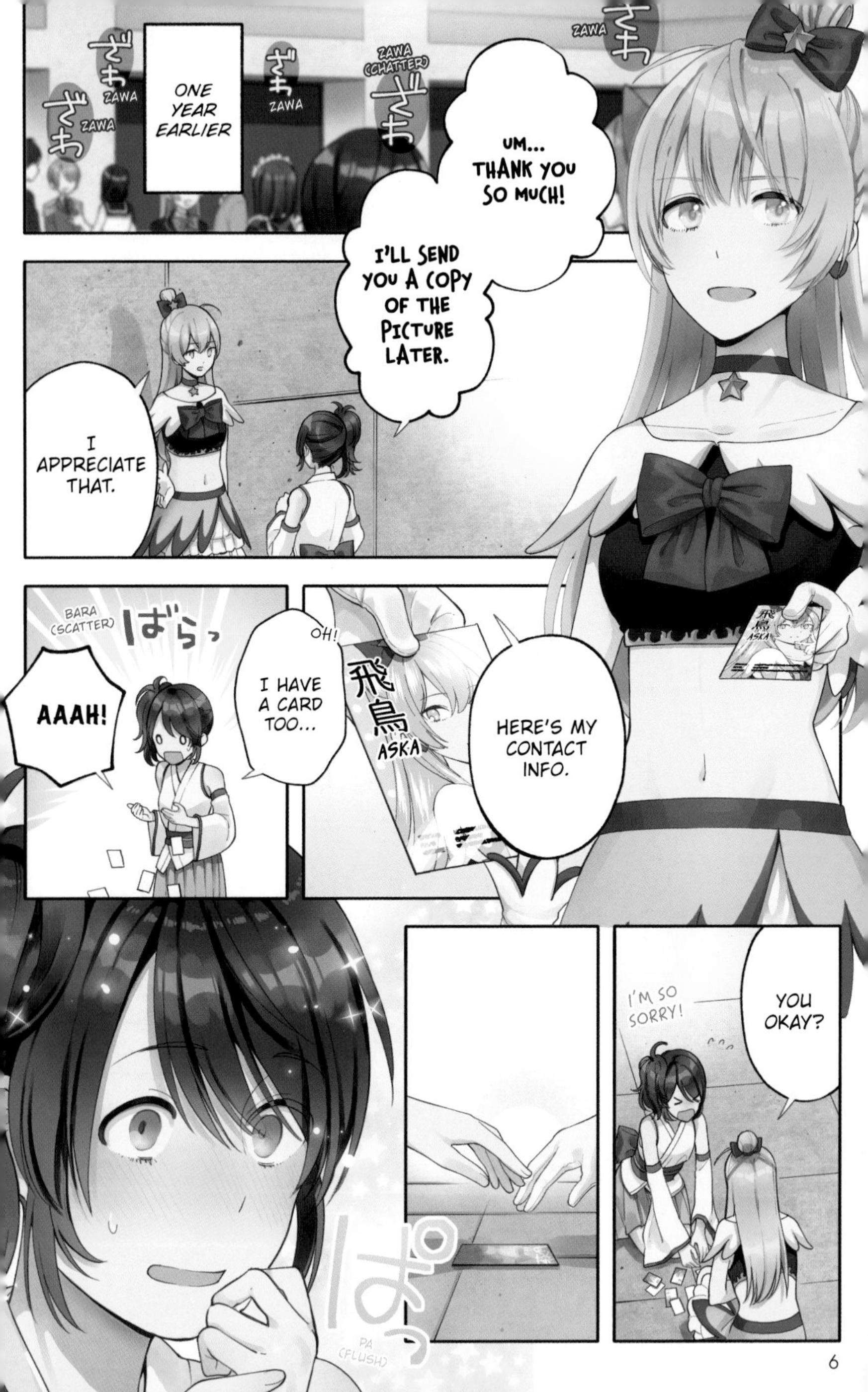
ZAWA
ざわ
ZAWA (CHATTER)
ざわ
ZAWA
ざわ
ONE YEAR EARLIER
ざわ
ZAWA
ざわ
ZAWA
UM... THANK YOU SO MUCH!
I'LL SEND YOU A COPY OF THE PICTURE LATER.
I APPRECIATE THAT.
HERE'S MY CONTACT INFO.
飛鳥
ASKA
OH!
I HAVE A CARD TOO...
BARA (SCATTER)
ばらっ
AAAH!
YOU OKAY?
I'M SO SORRY!
ぱっ
PA (FLUSH)

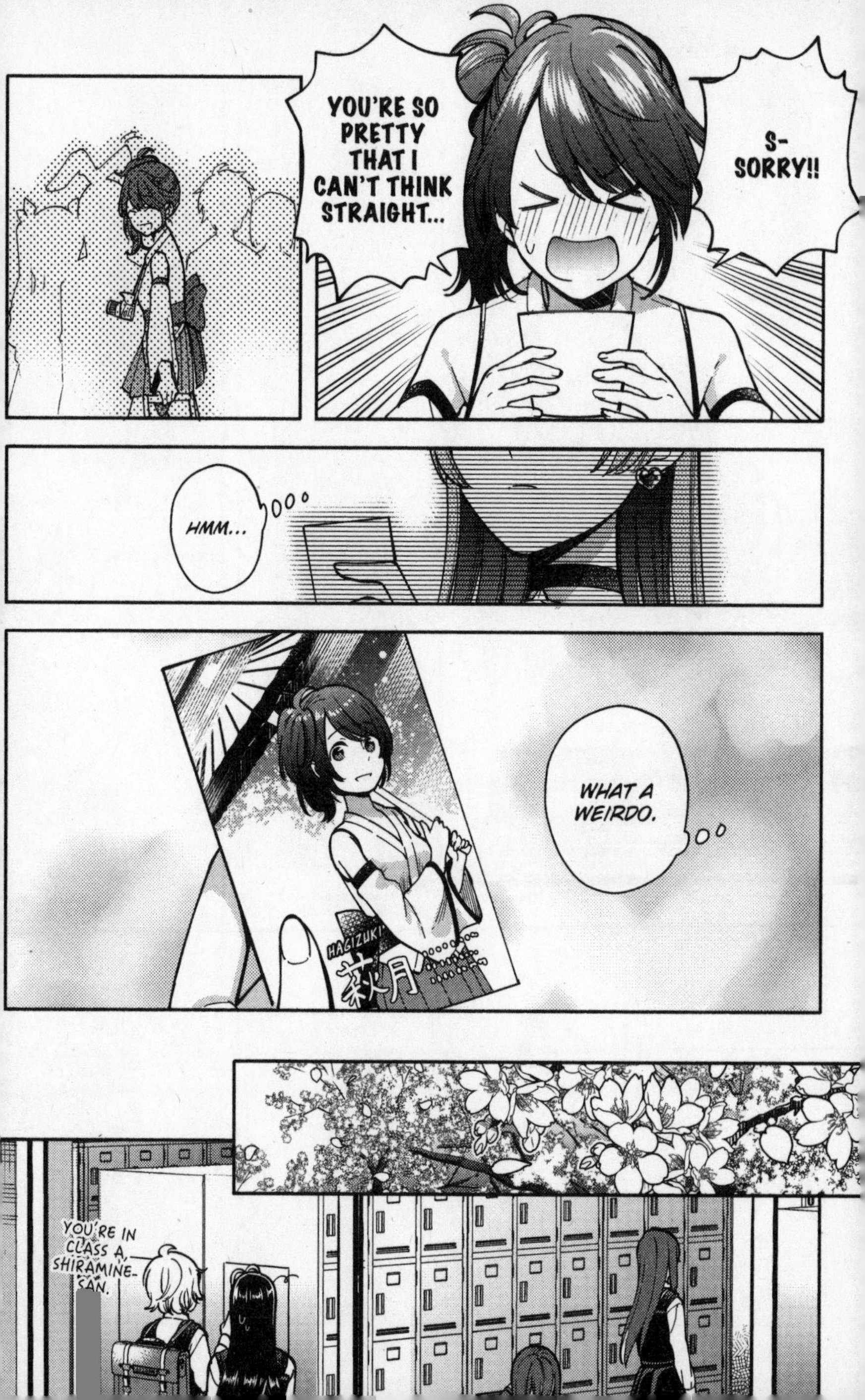
S-SORRY!!
YOU'RE SO PRETTY THAT I CAN'T THINK STRAIGHT...
HMM...
WHAT A WEIRDO.
HAGIZUKI
萩月
YOU'RE IN CLASS A, SHIRAMINE-SAN.

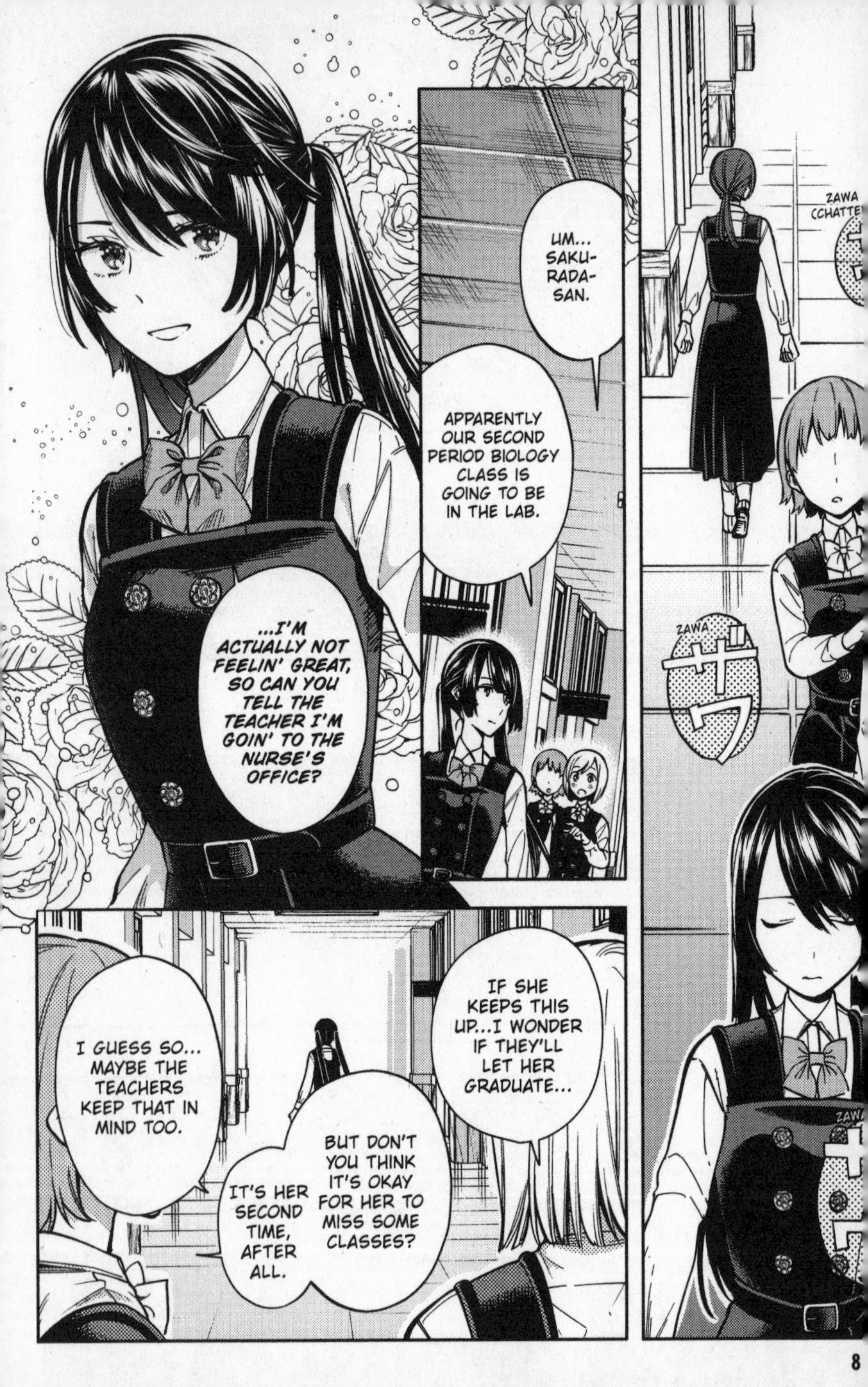
ZAWA (CHATTE
ZAWA
ZAWA
UM... SAKURADA-SAN.
APPARENTLY OUR SECOND PERIOD BIOLOGY CLASS IS GOING TO BE IN THE LAB.
...I'M ACTUALLY NOT FEELIN' GREAT, SO CAN YOU TELL THE TEACHER I'M GOIN' TO THE NURSE'S OFFICE?
IF SHE KEEPS THIS UP...I WONDER IF THEY'LL LET HER GRADUATE...
IT'S HER SECOND TIME, AFTER ALL.
BUT DON'T YOU THINK IT'S OKAY FOR HER TO MISS SOME CLASSES?
I GUESS SO... MAYBE THE TEACHERS KEEP THAT IN MIND TOO.

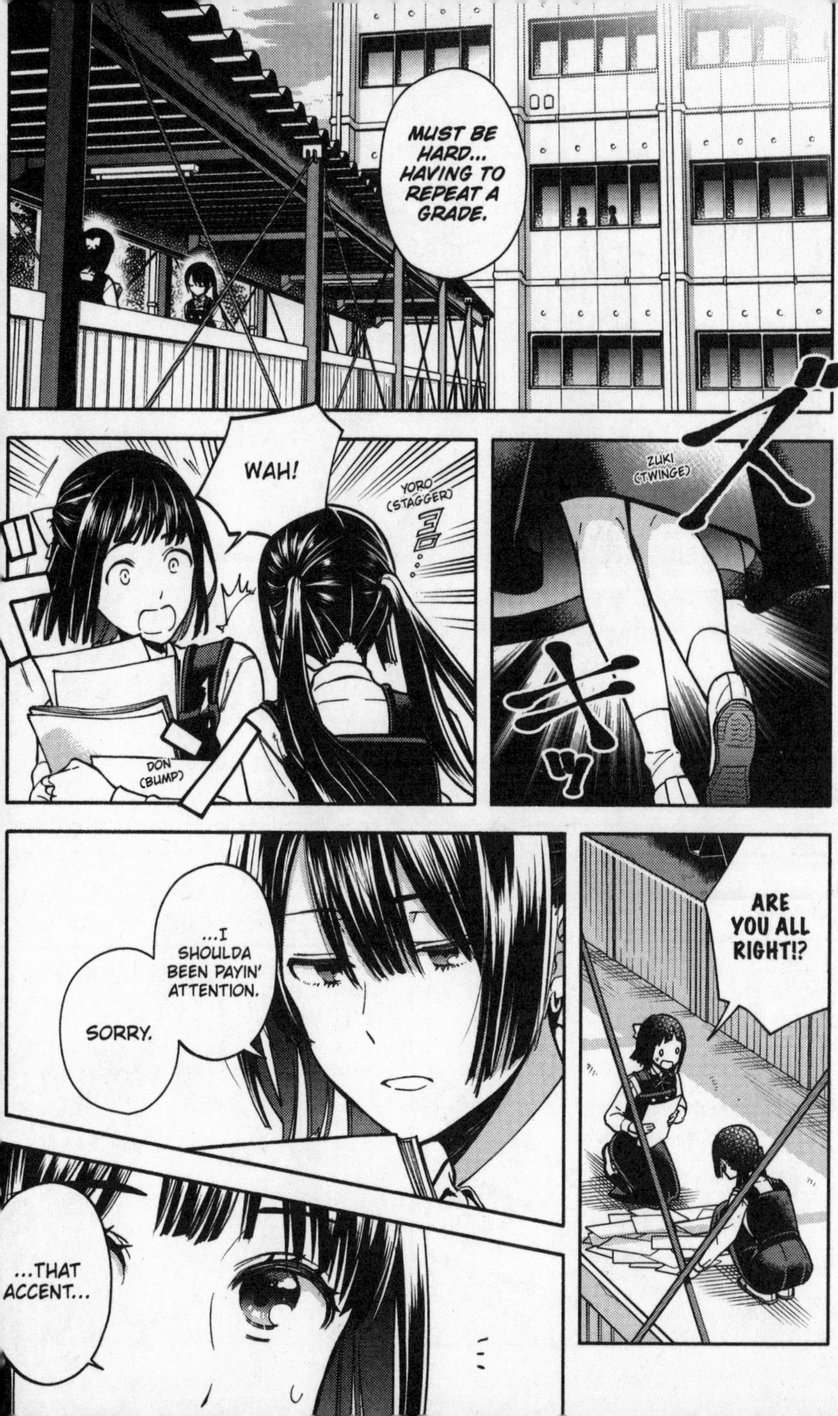
MUST BE HARD... HAVING TO REPEAT A GRADE.
ZUKI (TWINGE)
WAH!
YORO (STAGGER)
DON (BUMP)
ARE YOU ALL RIGHT!?
...I SHOULDA BEEN PAYIN' ATTENTION.
SORRY.
...THAT ACCENT...

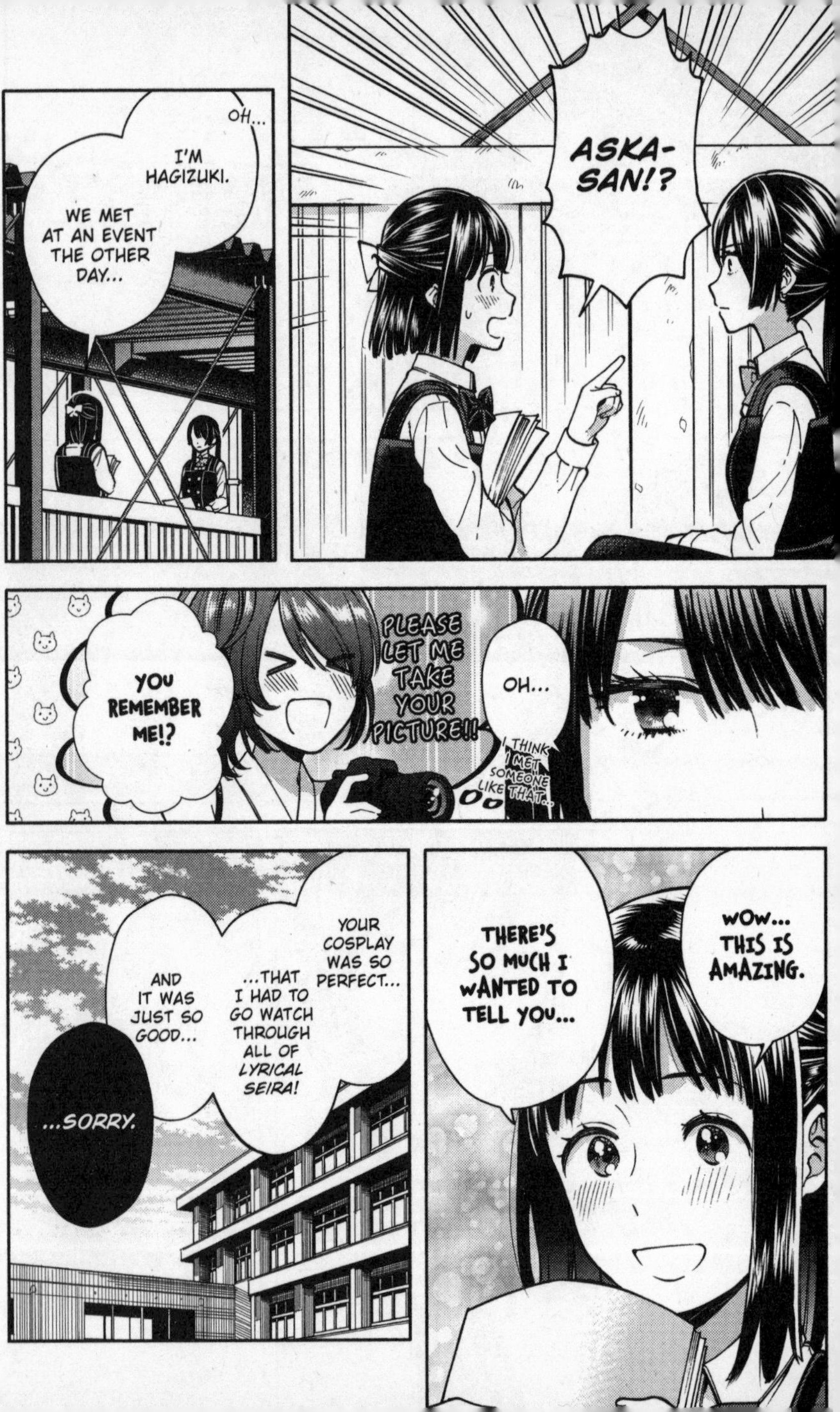
ASKA-SAN!?
OH...
I'M HAGIZUKI.
WE MET AT AN EVENT THE OTHER DAY...
OH...
I THINK I MET SOMEONE LIKE THAT...
PLEASE LET ME TAKE YOUR PICTURE!!
YOU REMEMBER ME!?
WOW... THIS IS AMAZING.
THERE'S SO MUCH I WANTED TO TELL YOU...
YOUR COSPLAY WAS SO PERFECT...
...THAT I HAD TO GO WATCH THROUGH ALL OF LYRICAL SEIRA!
AND IT WAS JUST SO GOOD...
...SORRY.

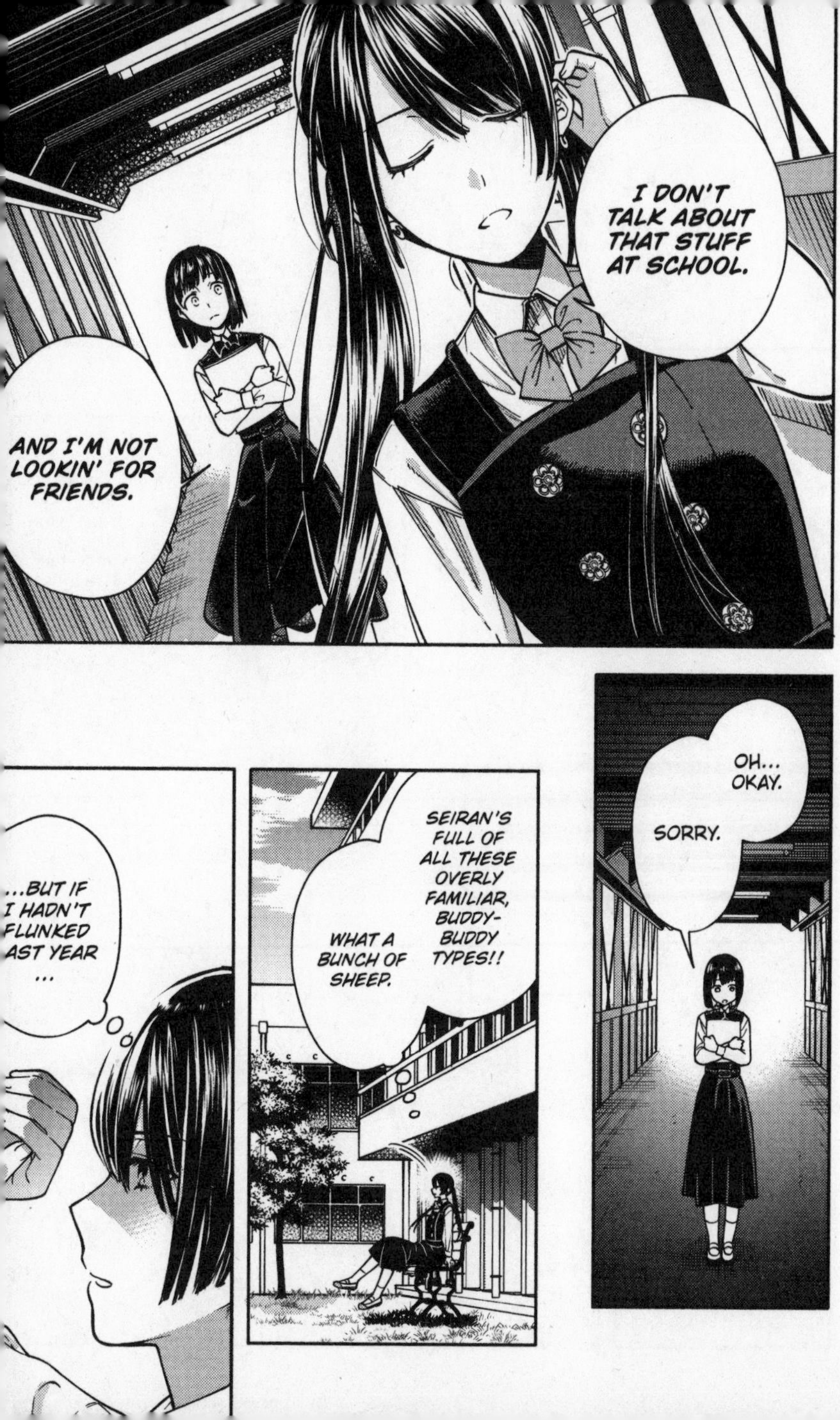
I DON'T TALK ABOUT THAT STUFF AT SCHOOL.
AND I'M NOT LOOKIN' FOR FRIENDS.
OH... OKAY.
SORRY.
SEIRAN'S FULL OF ALL THESE OVERLY FAMILIAR, BUDDY-BUDDY TYPES!!
WHAT A BUNCH OF SHEEP.
...BUT IF I HADN'T FLUNKED AST YEAR ...

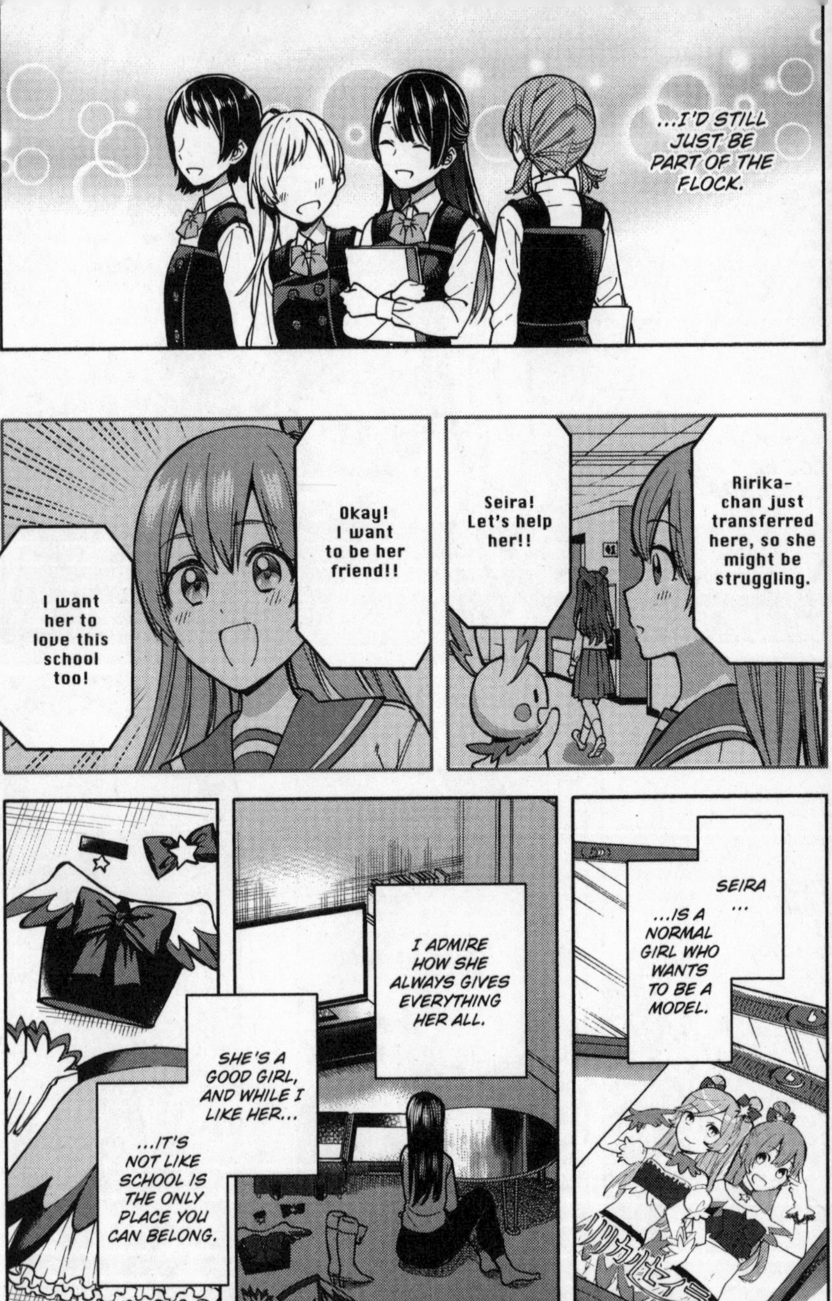
...I'D STILL JUST BE PART OF THE FLOCK.
Ririka-chan just transferred here, so she might be struggling.
Seira! Let's help her!!
Okay! I want to be her friend!!
I want her to love this school too!
SEIRA ...
...IS A NORMAL GIRL WHO WANTS TO BE A MODEL.
I ADMIRE HOW SHE ALWAYS GIVES EVERYTHING HER ALL.
SHE'S A GOOD GIRL, AND WHILE I LIKE HER...
...IT'S NOT LIKE SCHOOL IS THE ONLY PLACE YOU CAN BELONG.

BOX: LYRICAL SEIRA 1

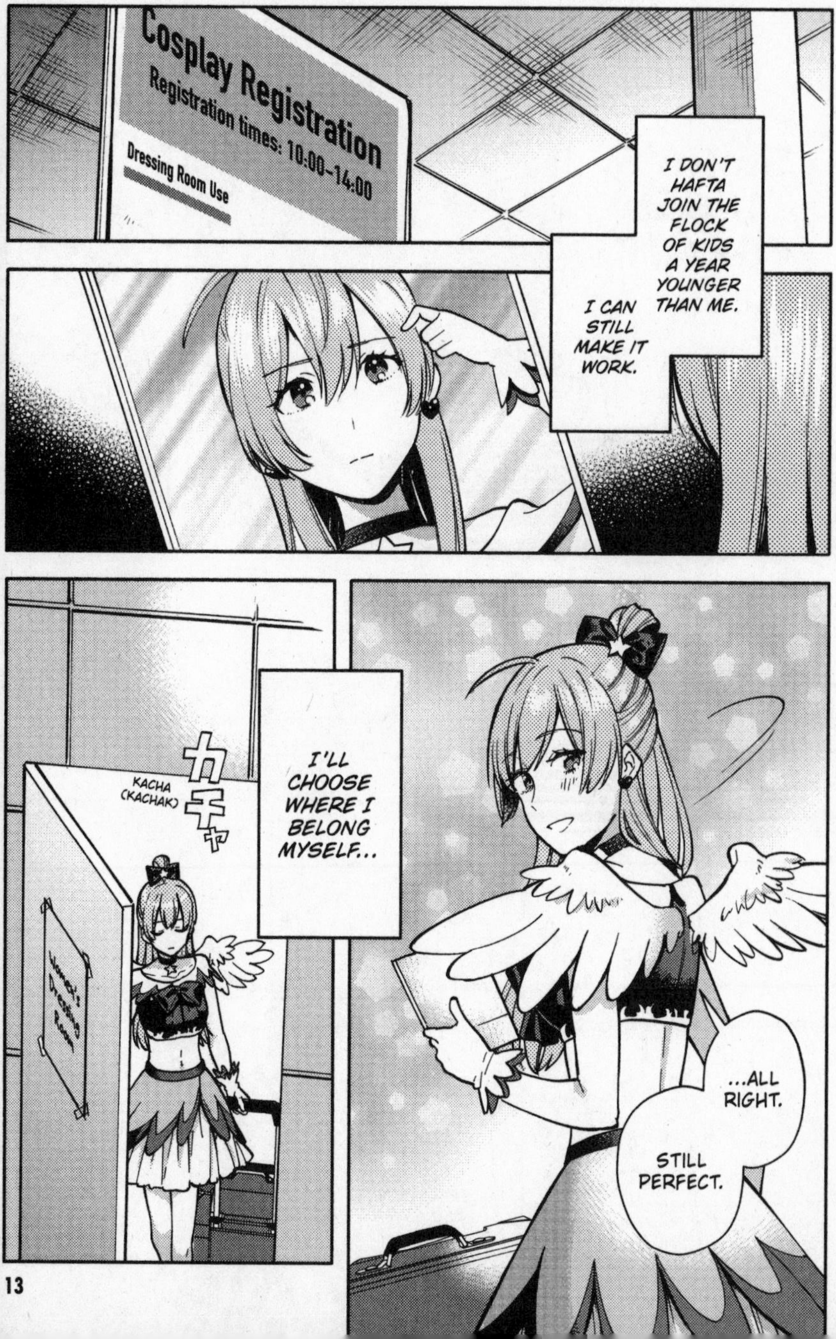
Cosplay Registration
Registration times: 10:00-14:00
Dressing Room Use
I DON'T HAFTA JOIN THE FLOCK OF KIDS A YEAR YOUNGER THAN ME.
I CAN STILL MAKE IT WORK.
...ALL RIGHT.
STILL PERFECT.
I'LL CHOOSE WHERE I BELONG MYSELF...
カチャ
KACHA (KACHAK)
Women's Dressing Room

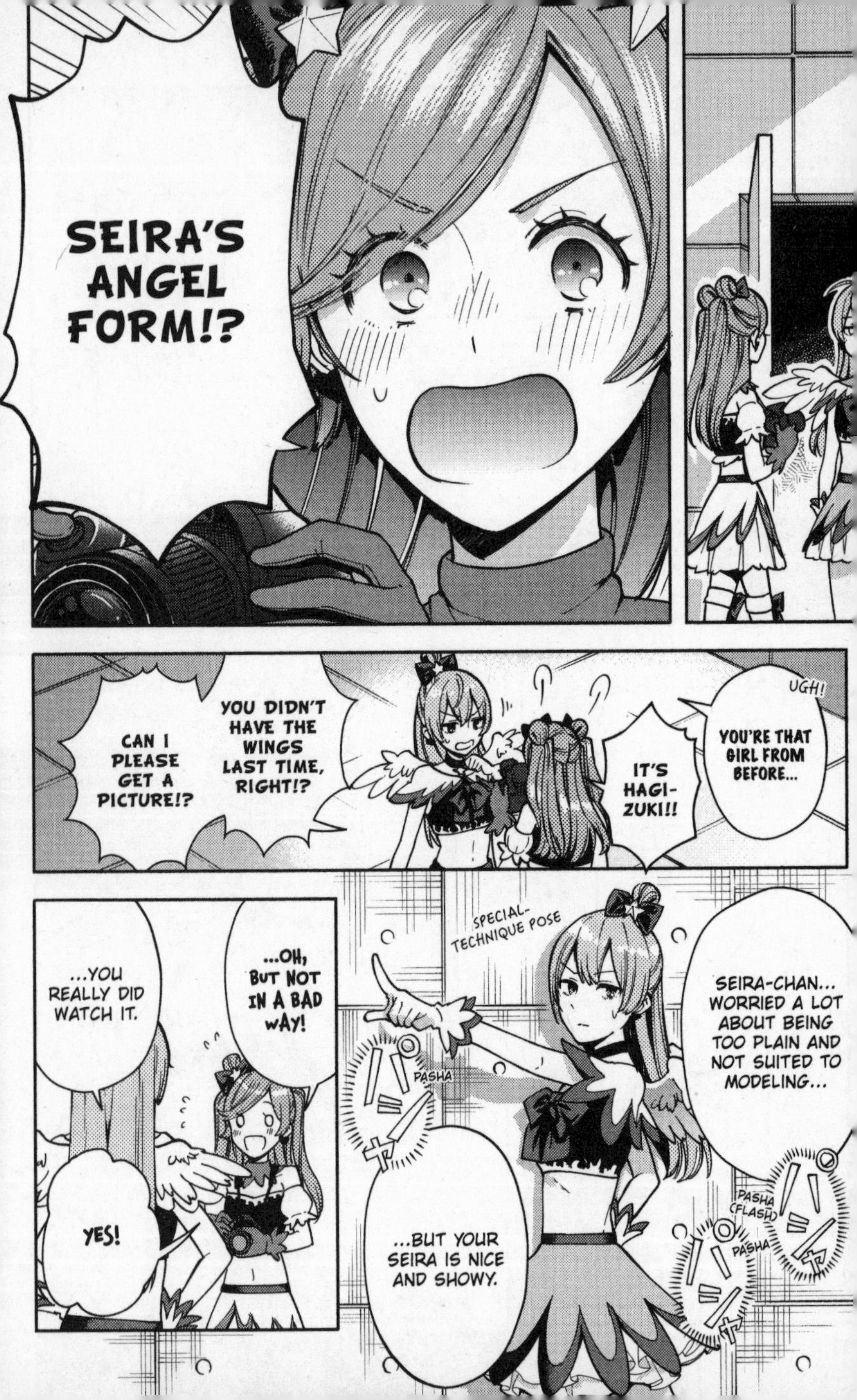
SEIRA'S ANGEL FORM!?
UGH!
YOU'RE THAT GIRL FROM BEFORE...
IT'S HAGI-ZUKI!!
YOU DIDN'T HAVE THE WINGS LAST TIME, RIGHT!?
CAN I PLEASE GET A PICTURE!?
SEIRA-CHAN... WORRIED A LOT ABOUT BEING TOO PLAIN AND NOT SUITED TO MODELING...
SPECIAL-TECHNIQUE POSE
PASHA (FLASH)
PASHA
PASHA
...BUT YOUR SEIRA IS NICE AND SHOWY.
...OH, BUT NOT IN A BAD wAY!
...YOU REALLY DID WATCH IT.
YES!

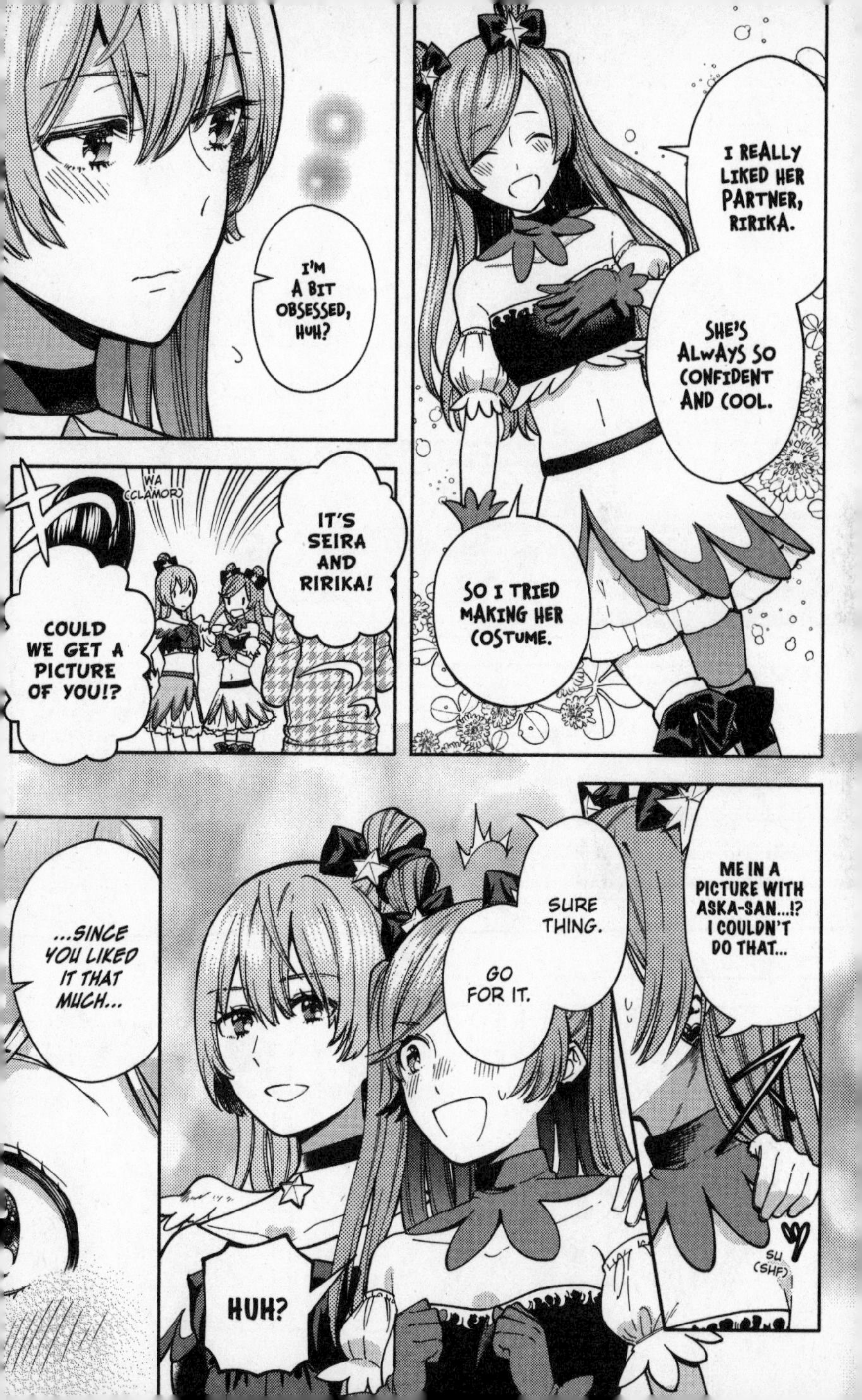
I REALLY LIKED HER PARTNER, RIRIKA.
SHE'S ALWAYS SO CONFIDENT AND COOL.
SO I TRIED MAKING HER COSTUME.
I'M A BIT OBSESSED, HUH?
IT'S SEIRA AND RIRIKA!
WA (CLAMOR)
COULD WE GET A PICTURE OF YOU!?
ME IN A PICTURE WITH ASKA-SAN...!? I COULDN'T DO THAT...
SURE THING.
GO FOR IT.
SU (SHF)
HUH?
...SINCE YOU LIKED IT THAT MUCH...

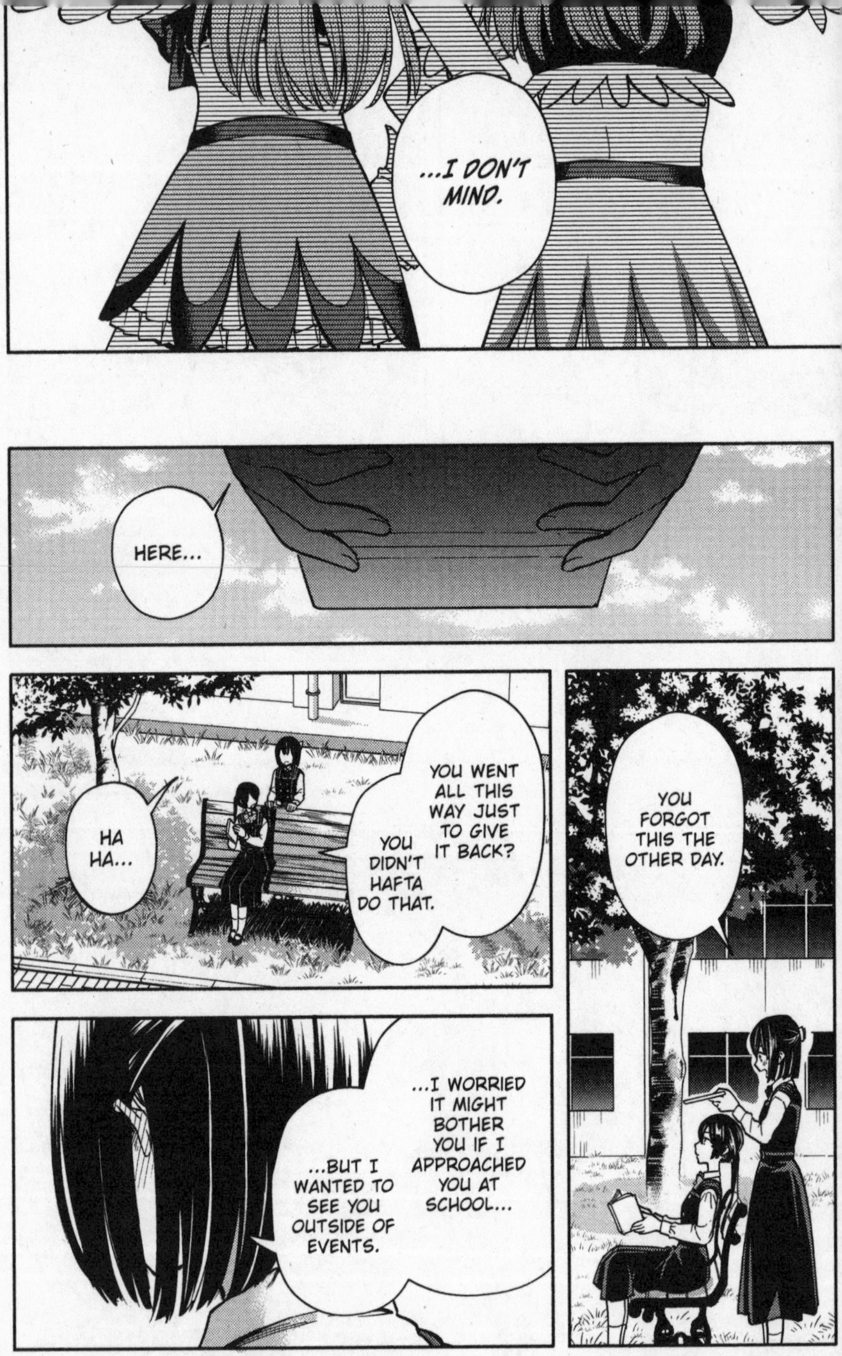
...I DON'T MIND.
HERE...
YOU FORGOT THIS THE OTHER DAY.
YOU WENT ALL THIS WAY JUST TO GIVE IT BACK?
YOU DIDN'T HAFTA DO THAT.
HA HA...
...I WORRIED IT MIGHT BOTHER YOU IF I APPROACHED YOU AT SCHOOL...
...BUT I WANTED TO SEE YOU OUTSIDE OF EVENTS.

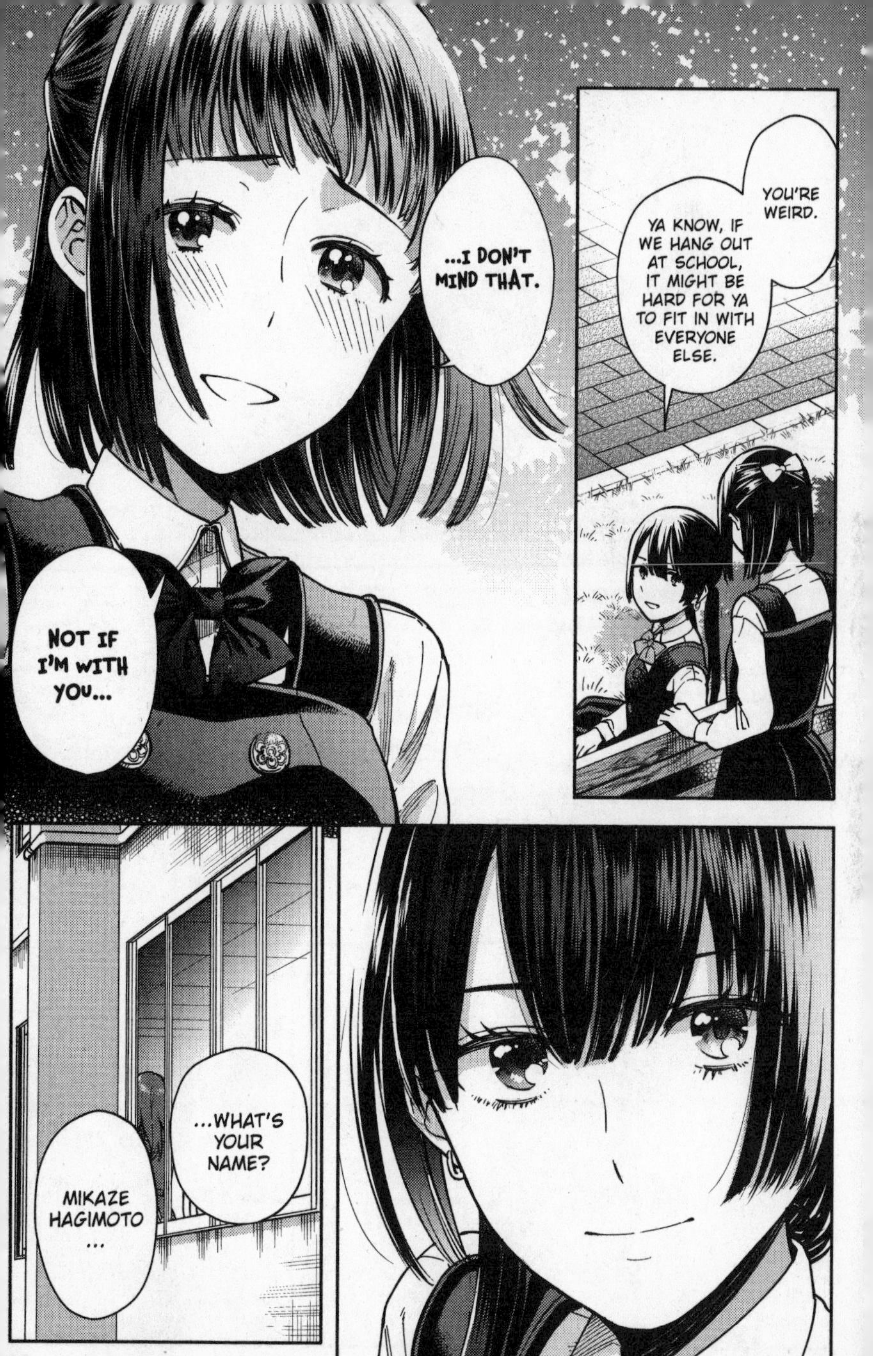
YOU'RE WEIRD.
YA KNOW, IF WE HANG OUT AT SCHOOL, IT MIGHT BE HARD FOR YA TO FIT IN WITH EVERYONE ELSE.
...I DON'T MIND THAT.
NOT IF I'M WITH YOU...
...WHAT'S YOUR NAME?
MIKAZE HAGIMOTO ...

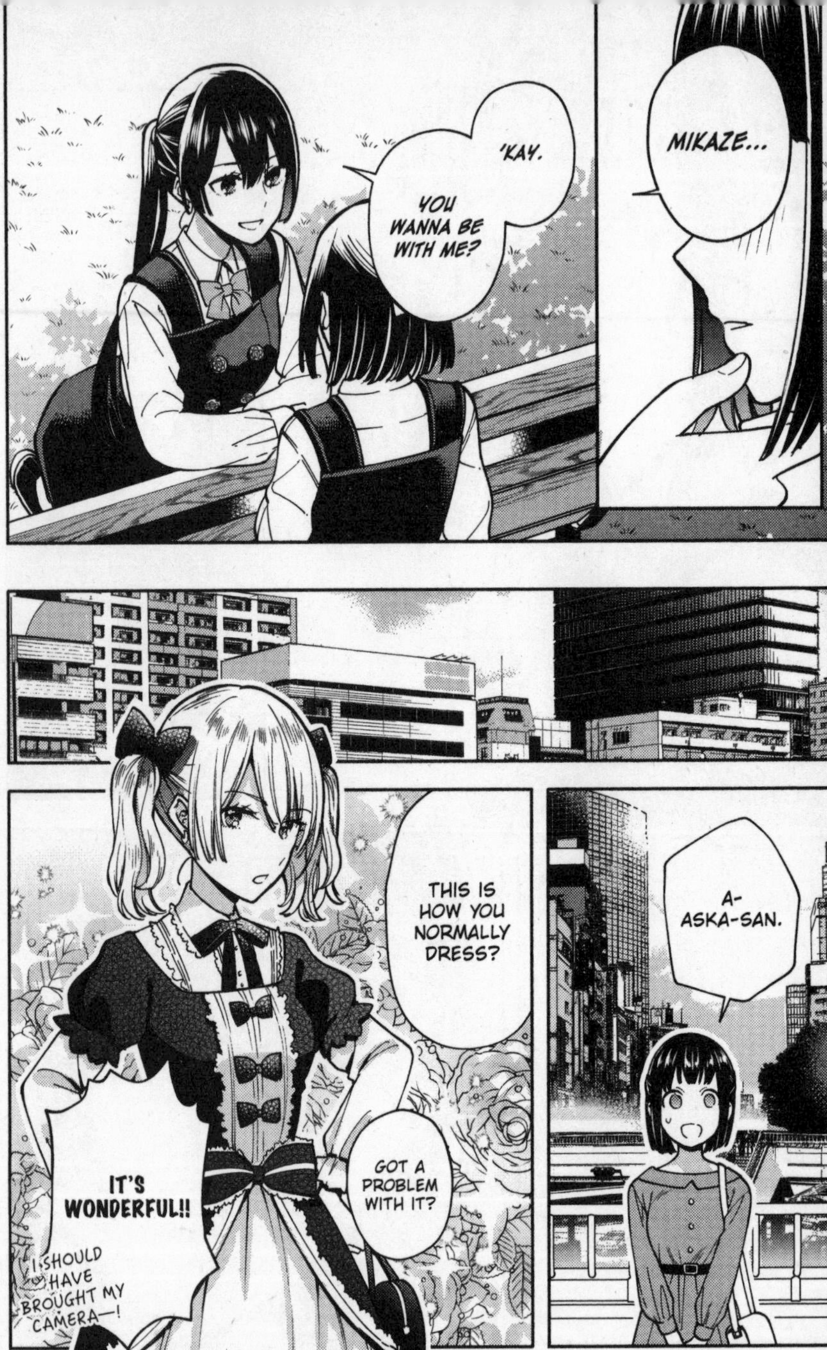
MIKAZE...
'KAY.
YOU WANNA BE WITH ME?
A- ASKA-SAN.
THIS IS HOW YOU NORMALLY DRESS?
GOT A PROBLEM WITH IT?
IT'S WONDERFUL!!
I SHOULD HAVE BROUGHT MY CAMERA—!

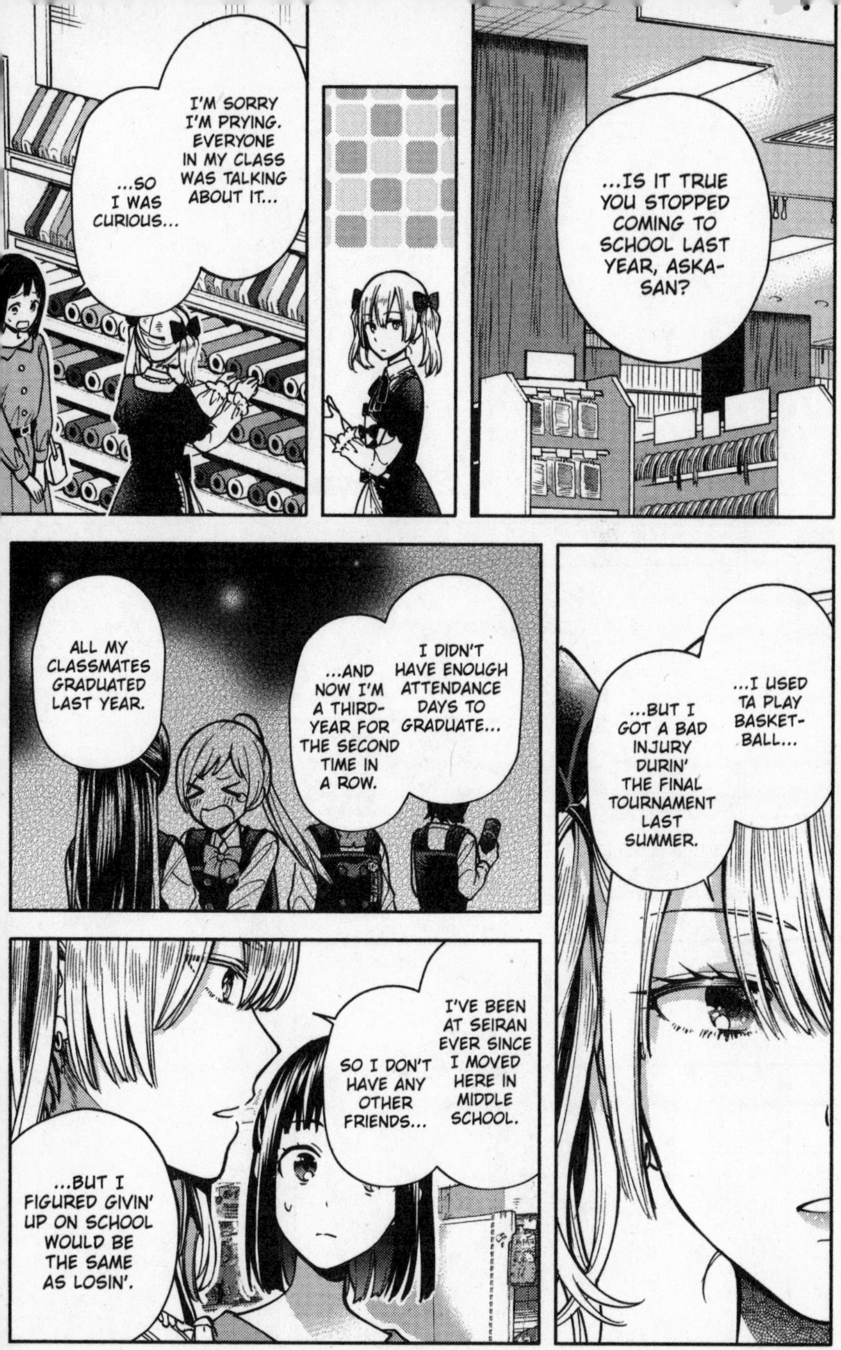
...IS IT TRUE YOU STOPPED COMING TO SCHOOL LAST YEAR, ASKA-SAN?
I'M SORRY I'M PRYING. EVERYONE IN MY CLASS WAS TALKING ABOUT IT...
...SO I WAS CURIOUS...
...I USED TA PLAY BASKET-BALL...
...BUT I GOT A BAD INJURY DURIN' THE FINAL TOURNAMENT LAST SUMMER.
I DIDN'T HAVE ENOUGH ATTENDANCE DAYS TO GRADUATE...
...AND NOW I'M A THIRD-YEAR FOR THE SECOND TIME IN A ROW.
ALL MY CLASSMATES GRADUATED LAST YEAR.
I'VE BEEN AT SEIRAN EVER SINCE I MOVED HERE IN MIDDLE SCHOOL.
SO I DON'T HAVE ANY OTHER FRIENDS...
...BUT I FIGURED GIVIN' UP ON SCHOOL WOULD BE THE SAME AS LOSIN'.

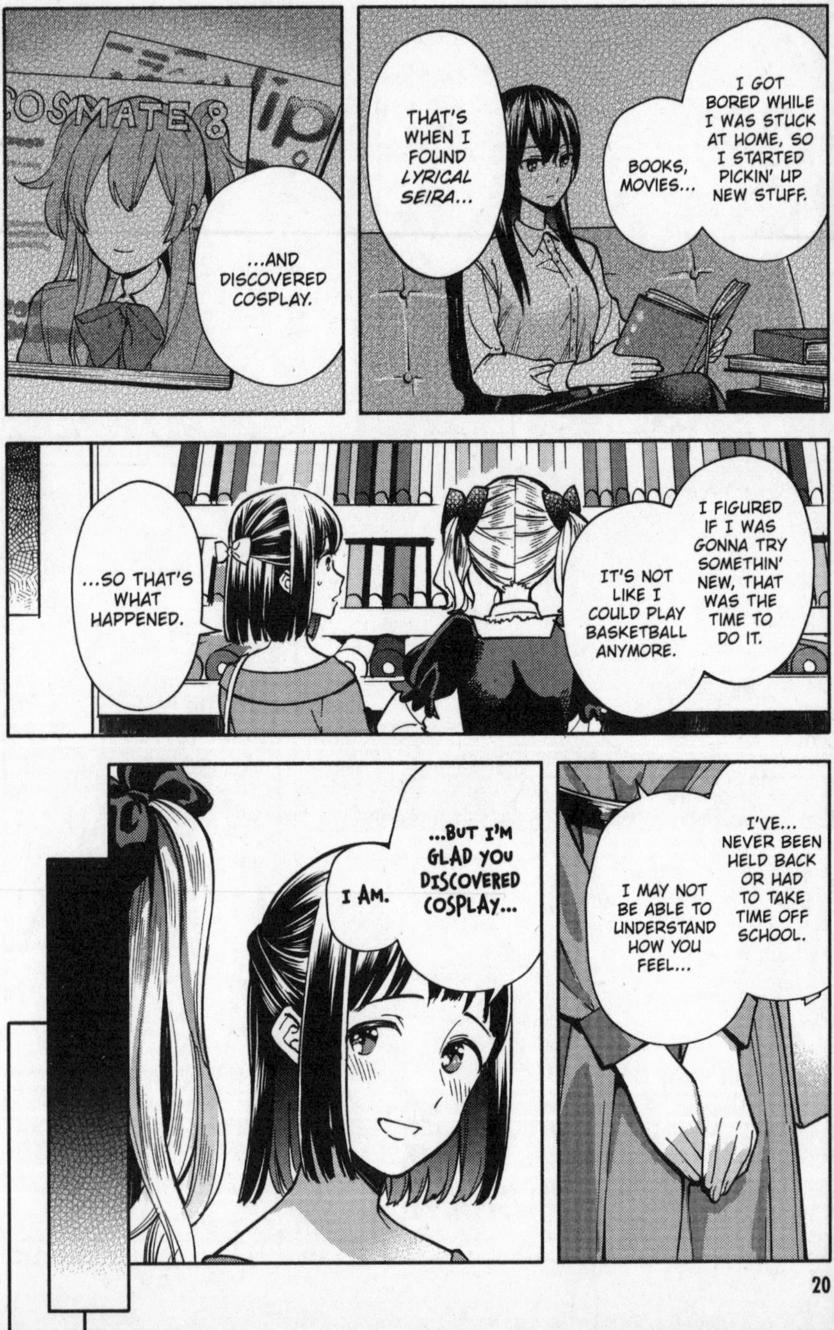
I GOT BORED WHILE I WAS STUCK AT HOME, SO I STARTED PICKIN' UP NEW STUFF.
BOOKS, MOVIES...
THAT'S WHEN I FOUND *LYRICAL SEIRA*...
COSMATE 8
...AND DISCOVERED COSPLAY.
I FIGURED IF I WAS GONNA TRY SOMETHIN' NEW, THAT WAS THE TIME TO DO IT.
IT'S NOT LIKE I COULD PLAY BASKETBALL ANYMORE.
...SO THAT'S WHAT HAPPENED.
I'VE... NEVER BEEN HELD BACK OR HAD TO TAKE TIME OFF SCHOOL.
I MAY NOT BE ABLE TO UNDERSTAND HOW YOU FEEL...
...BUT I'M GLAD YOU DISCOVERED COSPLAY...
I AM.

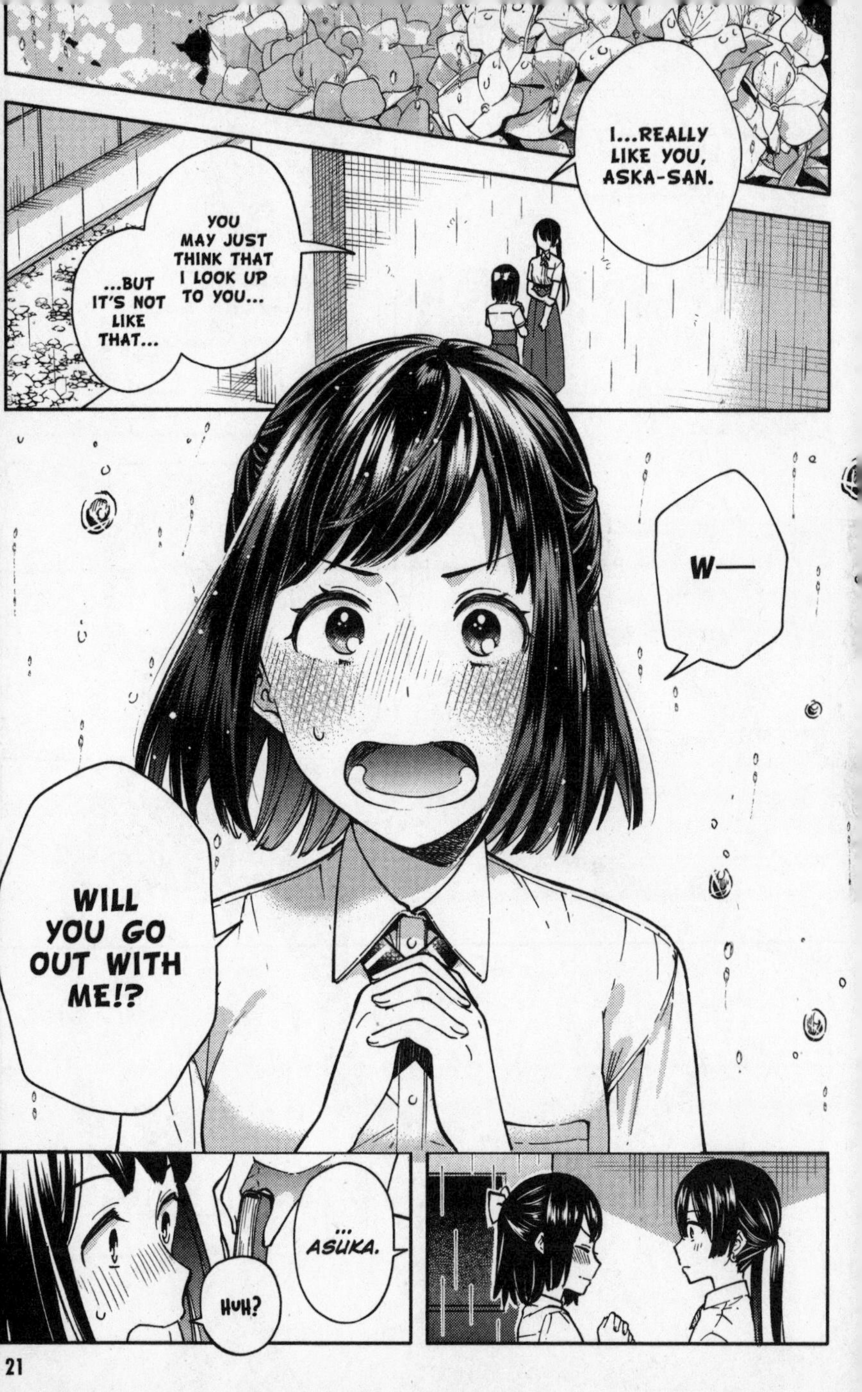

I...REALLY LIKE YOU, ASKA-SAN.
YOU MAY JUST THINK THAT I LOOK UP TO YOU...
...BUT IT'S NOT LIKE THAT...
W—
WILL YOU GO OUT WITH ME!?
...ASUKA.
HUH?

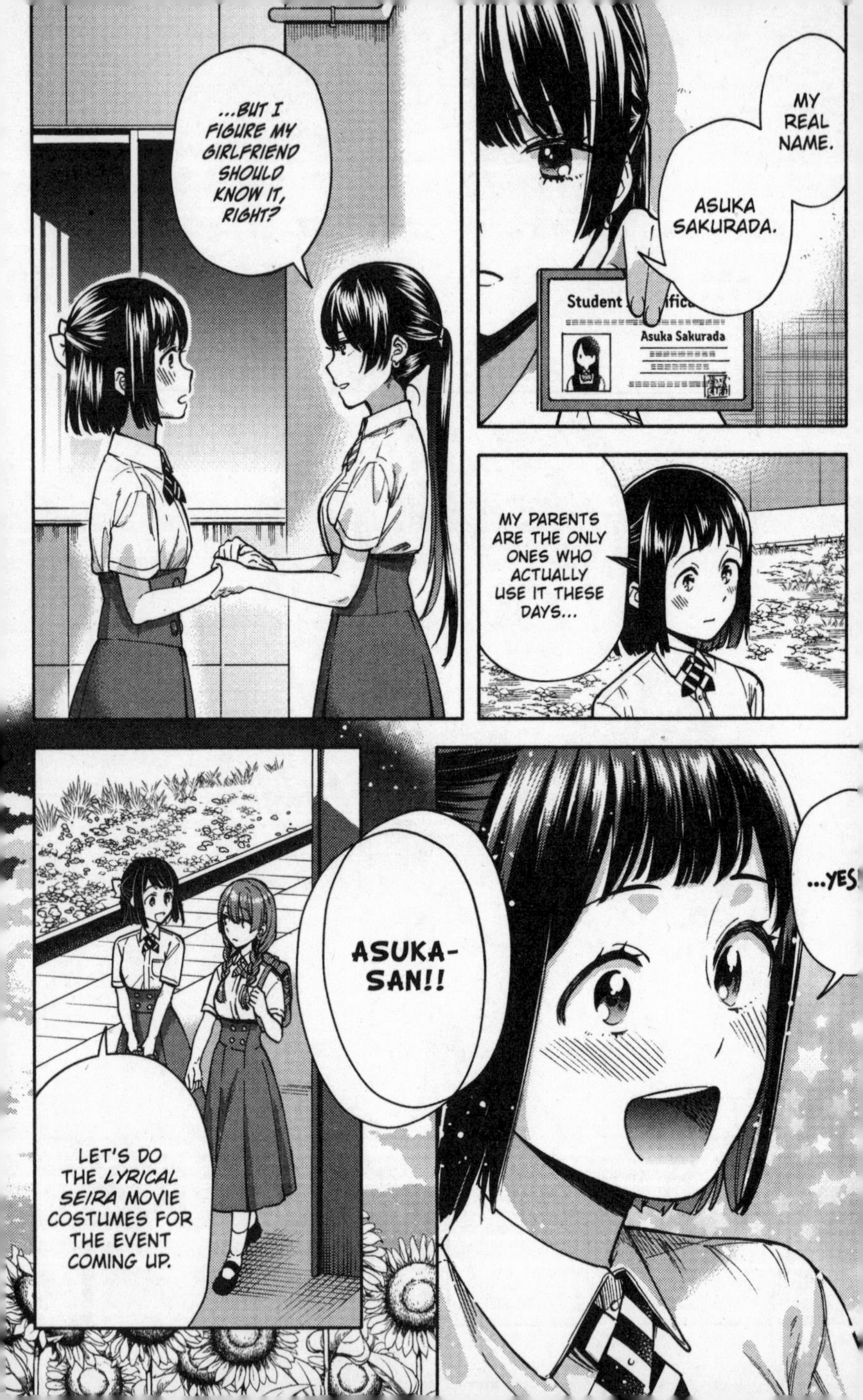
MY REAL NAME.
ASUKA SAKURADA.
Student
Asuka Sakurada
MY PARENTS ARE THE ONLY ONES WHO ACTUALLY USE IT THESE DAYS...
...BUT I FIGURE MY GIRLFRIEND SHOULD KNOW IT, RIGHT?
...YES
ASUKA-SAN!!
LET'S DO THE LYRICAL SEIRA MOVIE COSTUMES FOR THE EVENT COMING UP.

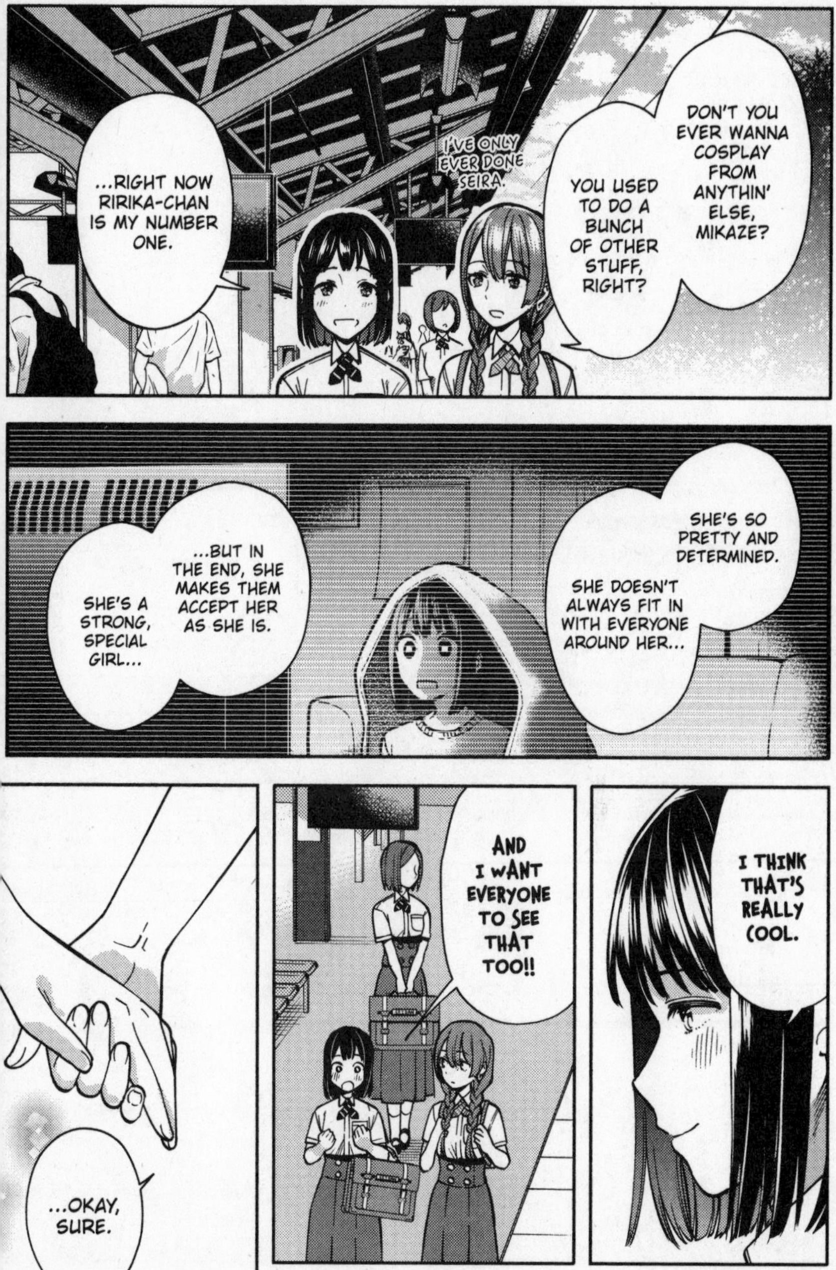
DON'T YOU EVER WANNA COSPLAY FROM ANYTHIN' ELSE, MIKAZE?
YOU USED TO DO A BUNCH OF OTHER STUFF, RIGHT?
I'VE ONLY EVER DONE SEIRA.
...RIGHT NOW RIRIKA-CHAN IS MY NUMBER ONE.
SHE'S SO PRETTY AND DETERMINED.
SHE DOESN'T ALWAYS FIT IN WITH EVERYONE AROUND HER...
...BUT IN THE END, SHE MAKES THEM ACCEPT HER AS SHE IS.
SHE'S A STRONG, SPECIAL GIRL...
I THINK THAT'S REALLY COOL.
AND I WANT EVERYONE TO SEE THAT TOO!!
...OKAY, SURE.

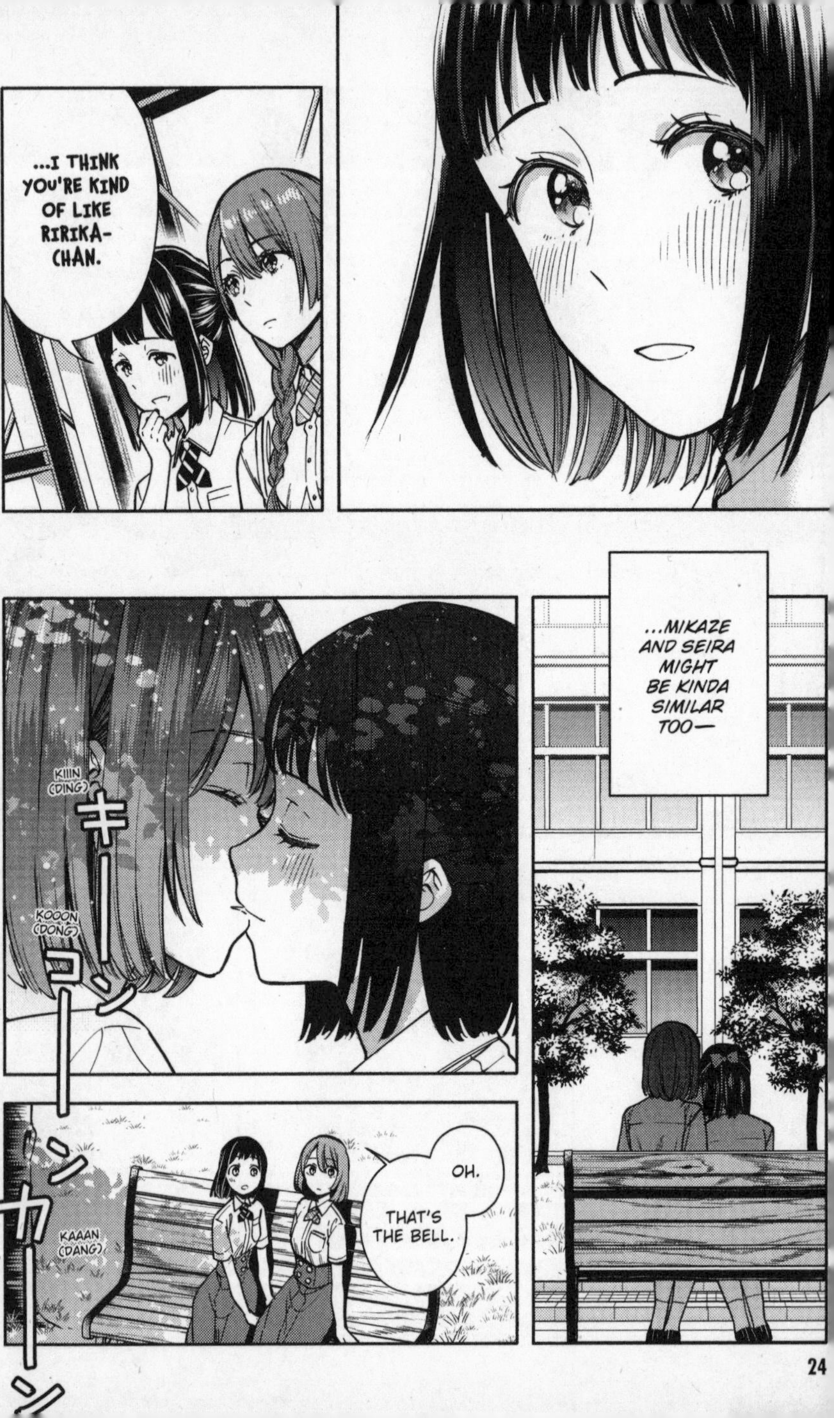
...I THINK YOU'RE KIND OF LIKE RIRIKA-CHAN.
...MIKAZE AND SEIRA MIGHT BE KINDA SIMILAR TOO—
KIIIN (DING)
キー
KOOON (DONG)
コン
KAAAN (DANG)
カーン
OH.
THAT'S THE BELL.

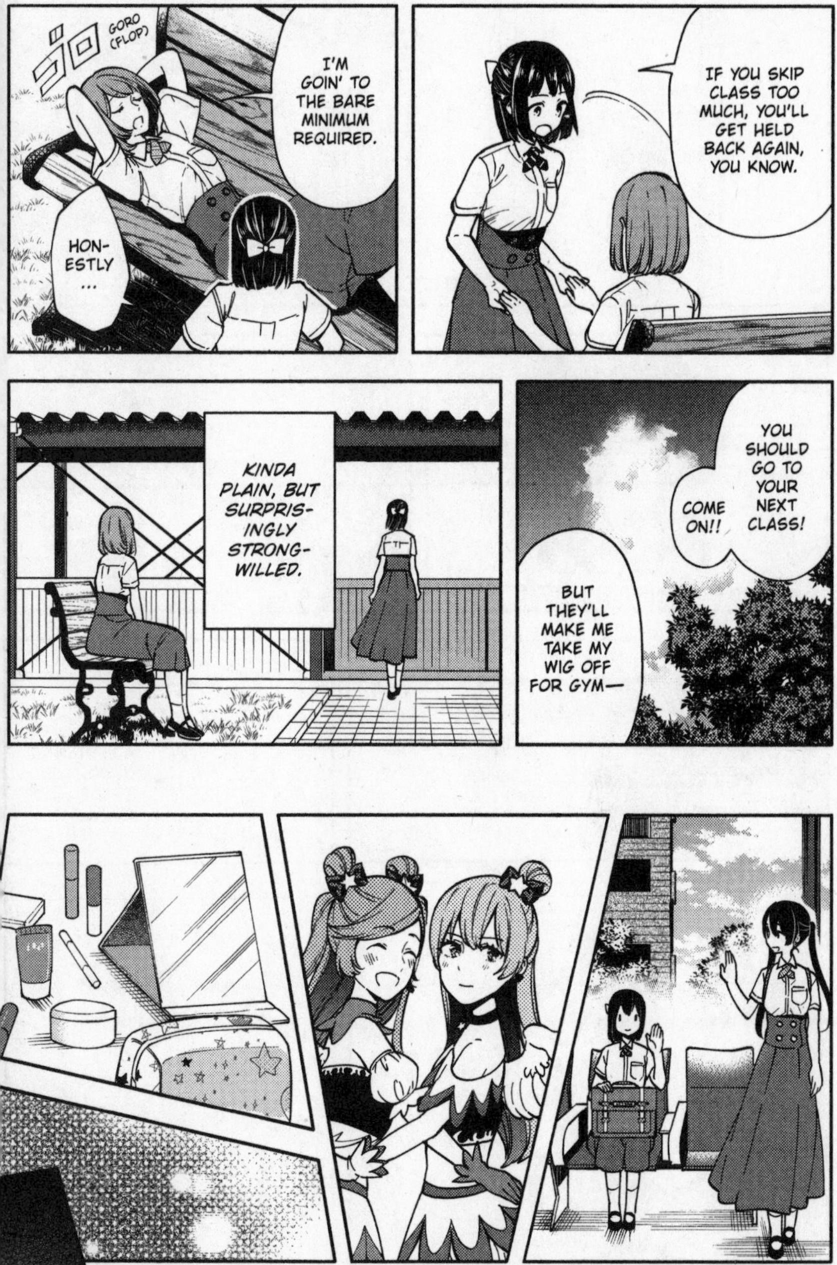
IF YOU SKIP CLASS TOO MUCH, YOU'LL GET HELD BACK AGAIN, YOU KNOW.
I'M GOIN' TO THE BARE MINIMUM REQUIRED.
ゴロ GORO (FLOP)
HON-ESTLY...
YOU SHOULD GO TO YOUR NEXT CLASS!
COME ON!!
BUT THEY'LL MAKE ME TAKE MY WIG OFF FOR GYM—
KINDA PLAIN, BUT SURPRIS-INGLY STRONG-WILLED.

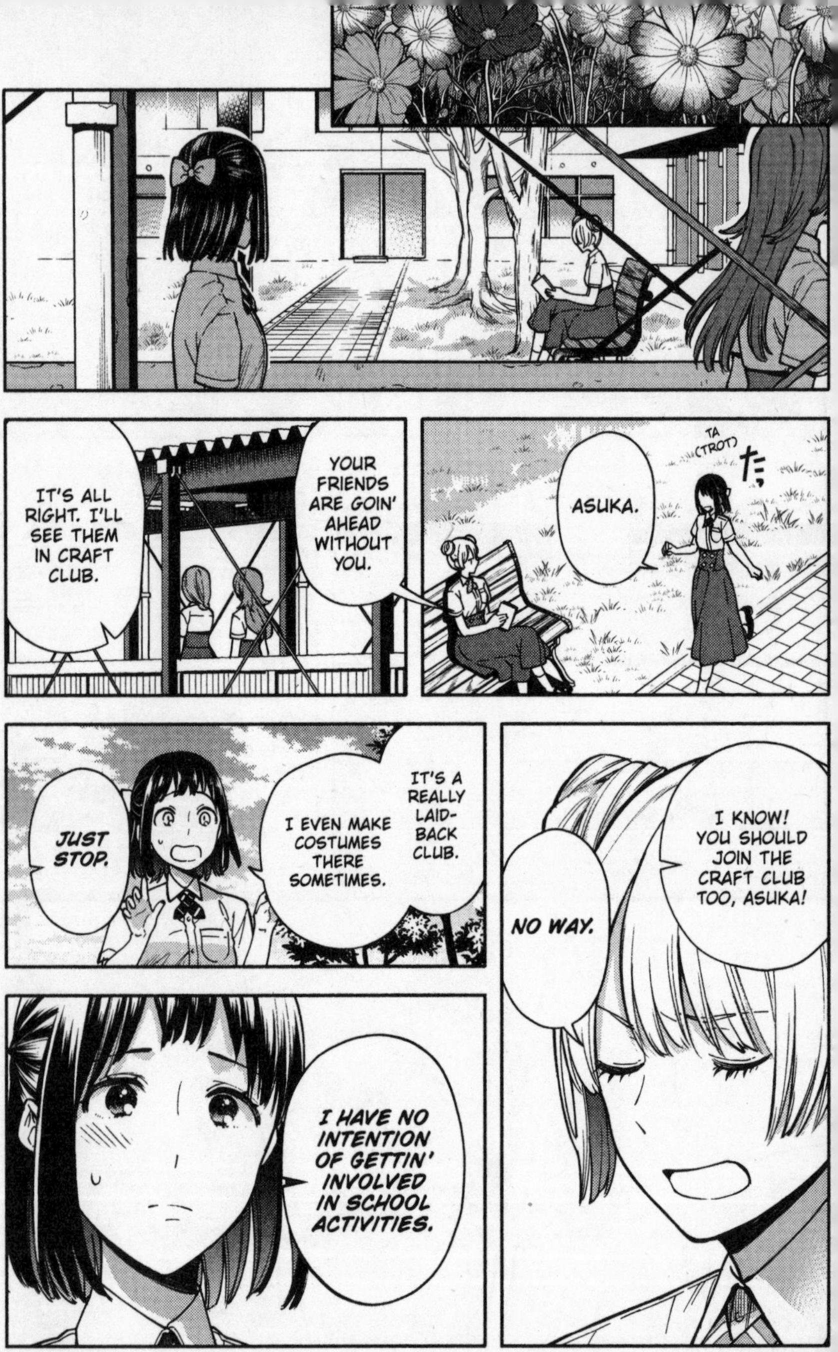
TA (TROT)
ASUKA.
YOUR FRIENDS ARE GOIN' AHEAD WITHOUT YOU.
IT'S ALL RIGHT. I'LL SEE THEM IN CRAFT CLUB.
I KNOW! YOU SHOULD JOIN THE CRAFT CLUB TOO, ASUKA!
NO WAY.
IT'S A REALLY LAID-BACK CLUB.
I EVEN MAKE COSTUMES THERE SOMETIMES.
JUST STOP.
I HAVE NO INTENTION OF GETTIN' INVOLVED IN SCHOOL ACTIVITIES.

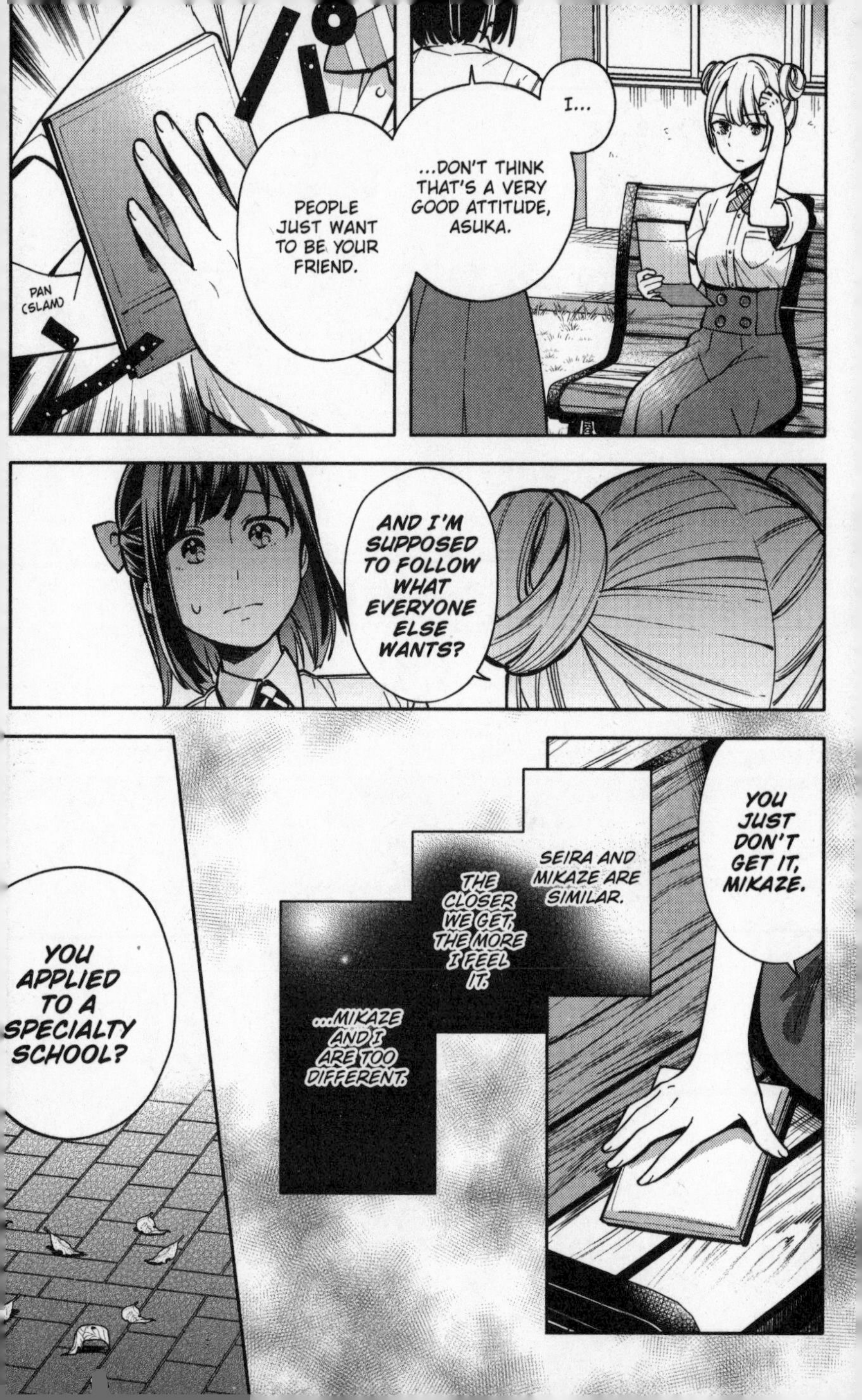

I...
...DON'T THINK THAT'S A VERY GOOD ATTITUDE, ASUKA.
PEOPLE JUST WANT TO BE YOUR FRIEND.
PAN (SLAM)
AND I'M SUPPOSED TO FOLLOW WHAT EVERYONE ELSE WANTS?
YOU JUST DON'T GET IT, MIKAZE.
SEIRA AND MIKAZE ARE SIMILAR.
THE CLOSER WE GET, THE MORE I FEEL IT.
...MIKAZE AND I ARE TOO DIFFERENT.
YOU APPLIED TO A SPECIALTY SCHOOL?

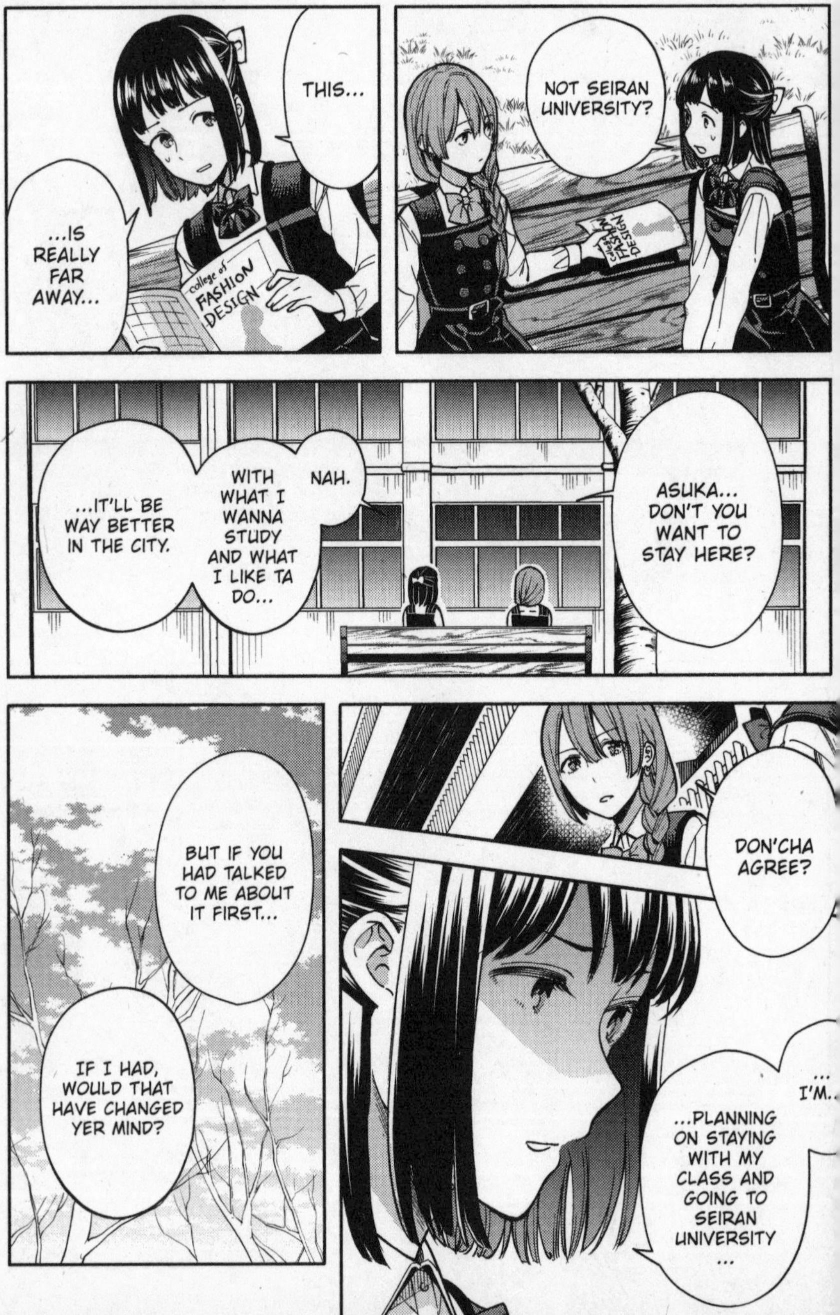
NOT SEIRAN UNIVERSITY?
THIS...
...IS REALLY FAR AWAY...
college of FASHION DESIGN
ASUKA... DON'T YOU WANT TO STAY HERE?
NAH.
WITH WHAT I WANNA STUDY AND WHAT I LIKE TA DO...
...IT'LL BE WAY BETTER IN THE CITY.
DON'CHA AGREE?
... I'M...
...PLANNING ON STAYING WITH MY CLASS AND GOING TO SEIRAN UNIVERSITY ...
BUT IF YOU HAD TALKED TO ME ABOUT IT FIRST...
IF I HAD, WOULD THAT HAVE CHANGED YER MIND?

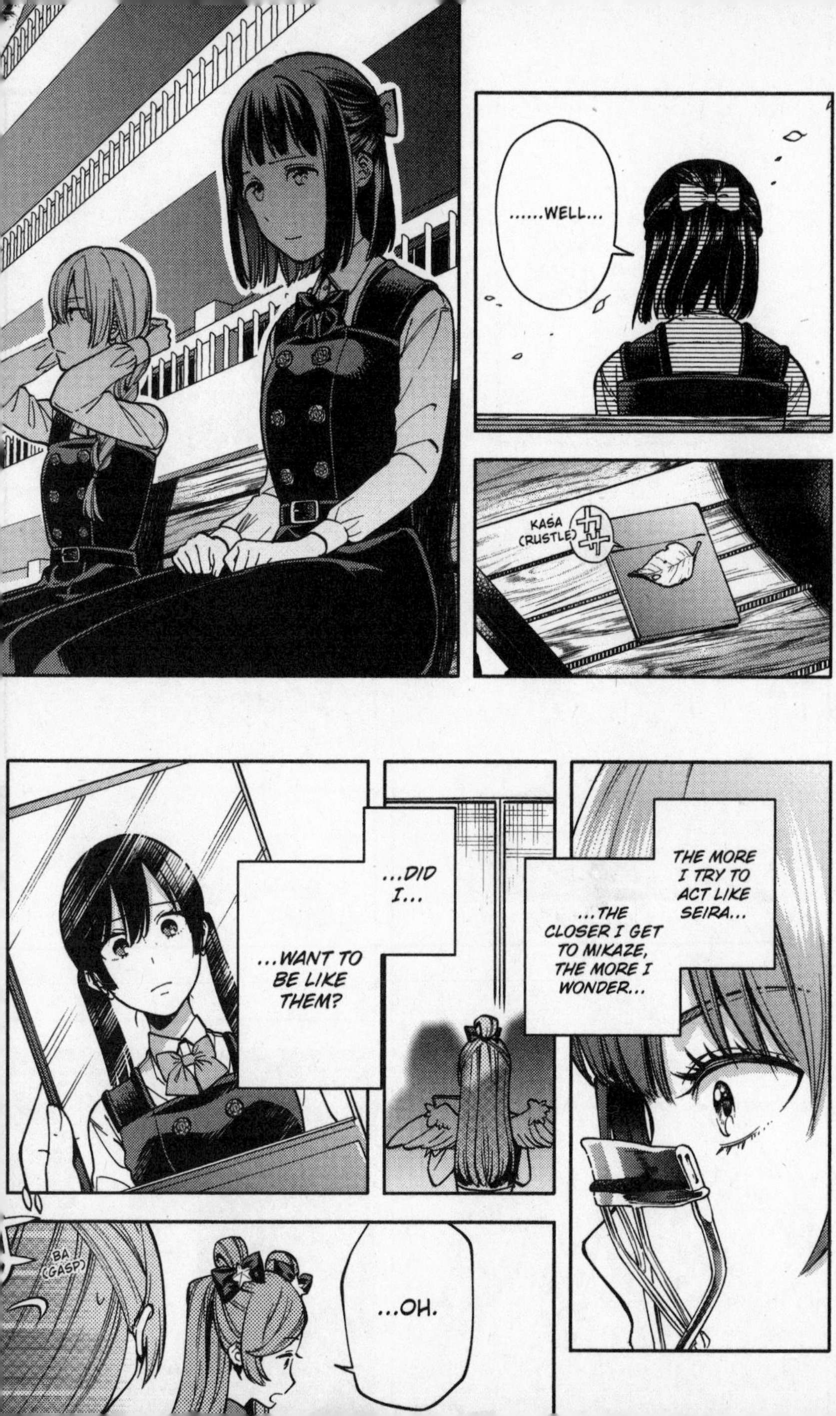
......WELL...
KASA (RUSTLE)
THE MORE I TRY TO ACT LIKE SEIRA...
...THE CLOSER I GET TO MIKAZE, THE MORE I WONDER...
...DID I...
...WANT TO BE LIKE THEM?
...OH.
BA (GASP)

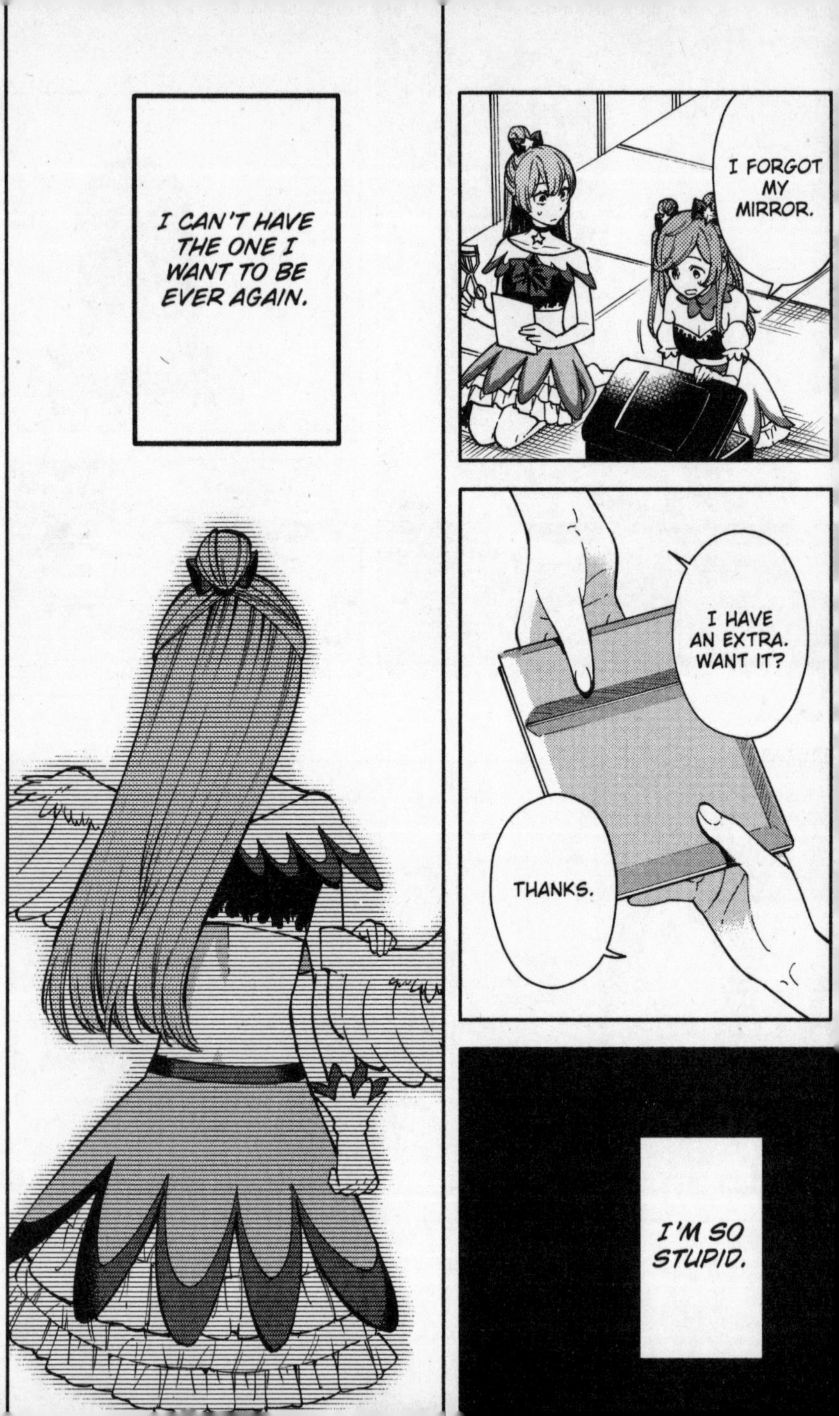
I FORGOT MY MIRROR.
I HAVE AN EXTRA. WANT IT?
THANKS.
I'M SO STUPID.
I CAN'T HAVE THE ONE I WANT TO BE EVER AGAIN.

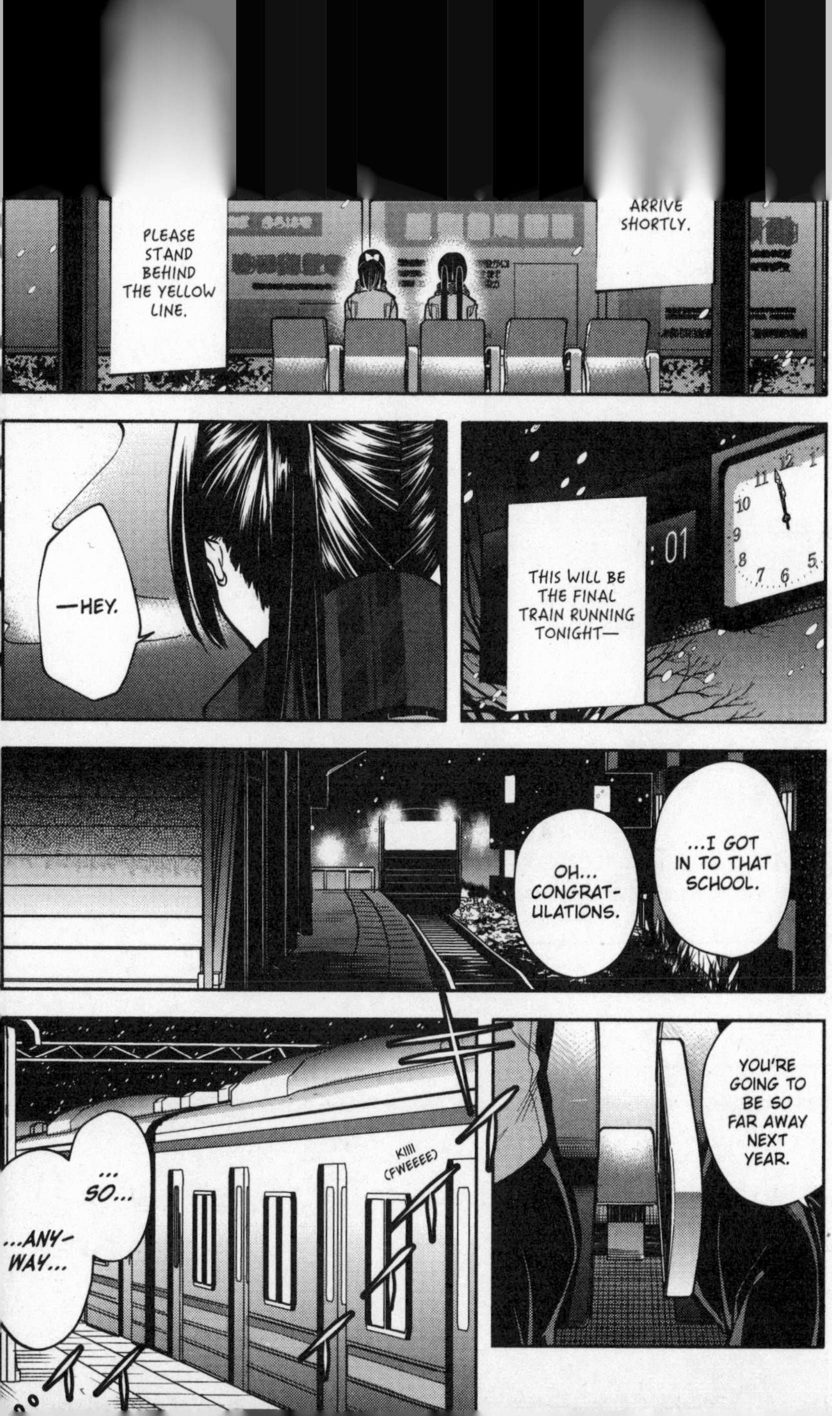
ARRIVE SHORTLY.
PLEASE STAND BEHIND THE YELLOW LINE.
THIS WILL BE THE FINAL TRAIN RUNNING TONIGHT—
—HEY.
...I GOT IN TO THAT SCHOOL.
OH... CONGRAT-ULATIONS.
YOU'RE GOING TO BE SO FAR AWAY NEXT YEAR.
KIIII (FWEEEE)
... SO...
...ANY-WAY...

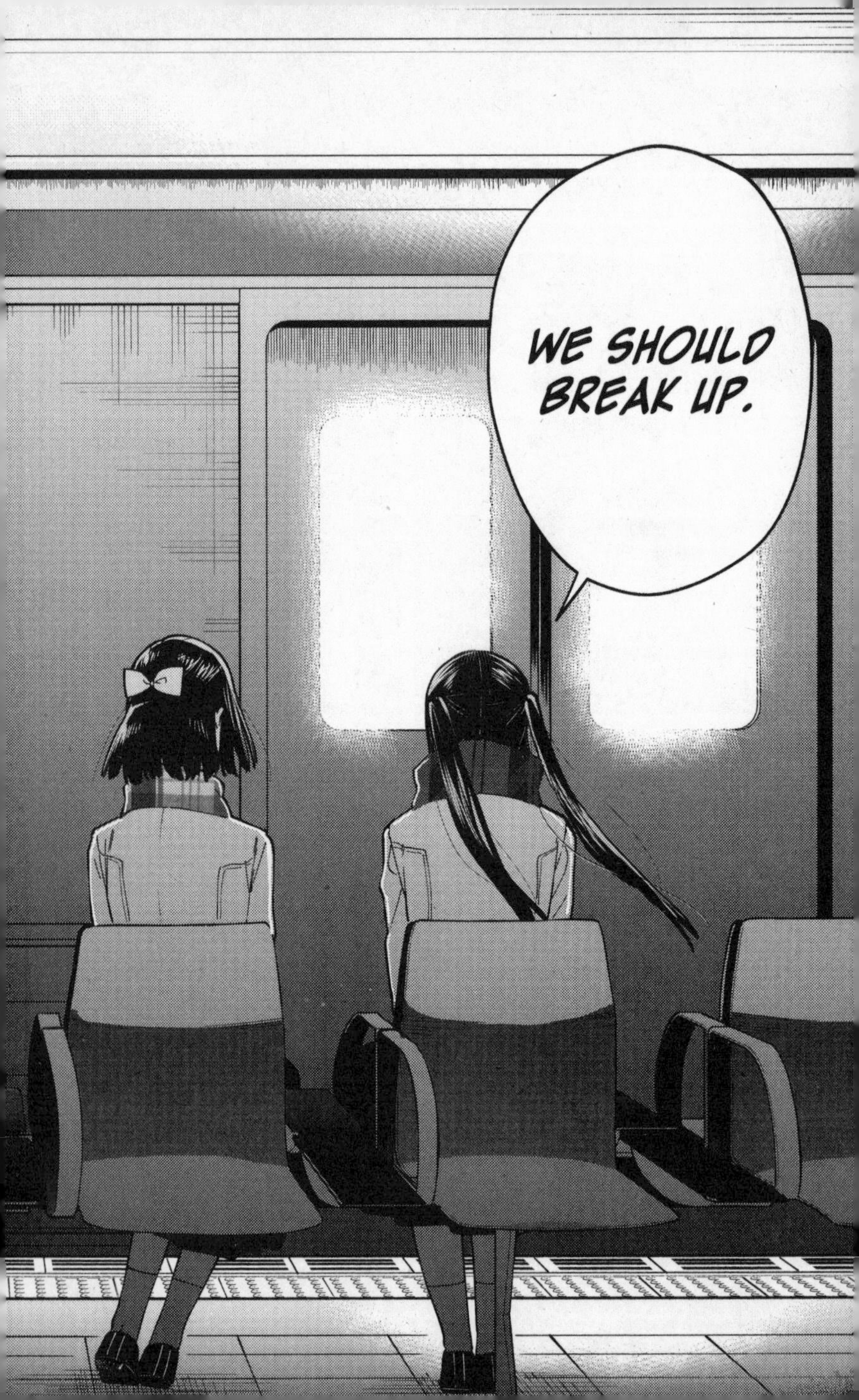
WE SHOULD BREAK UP.

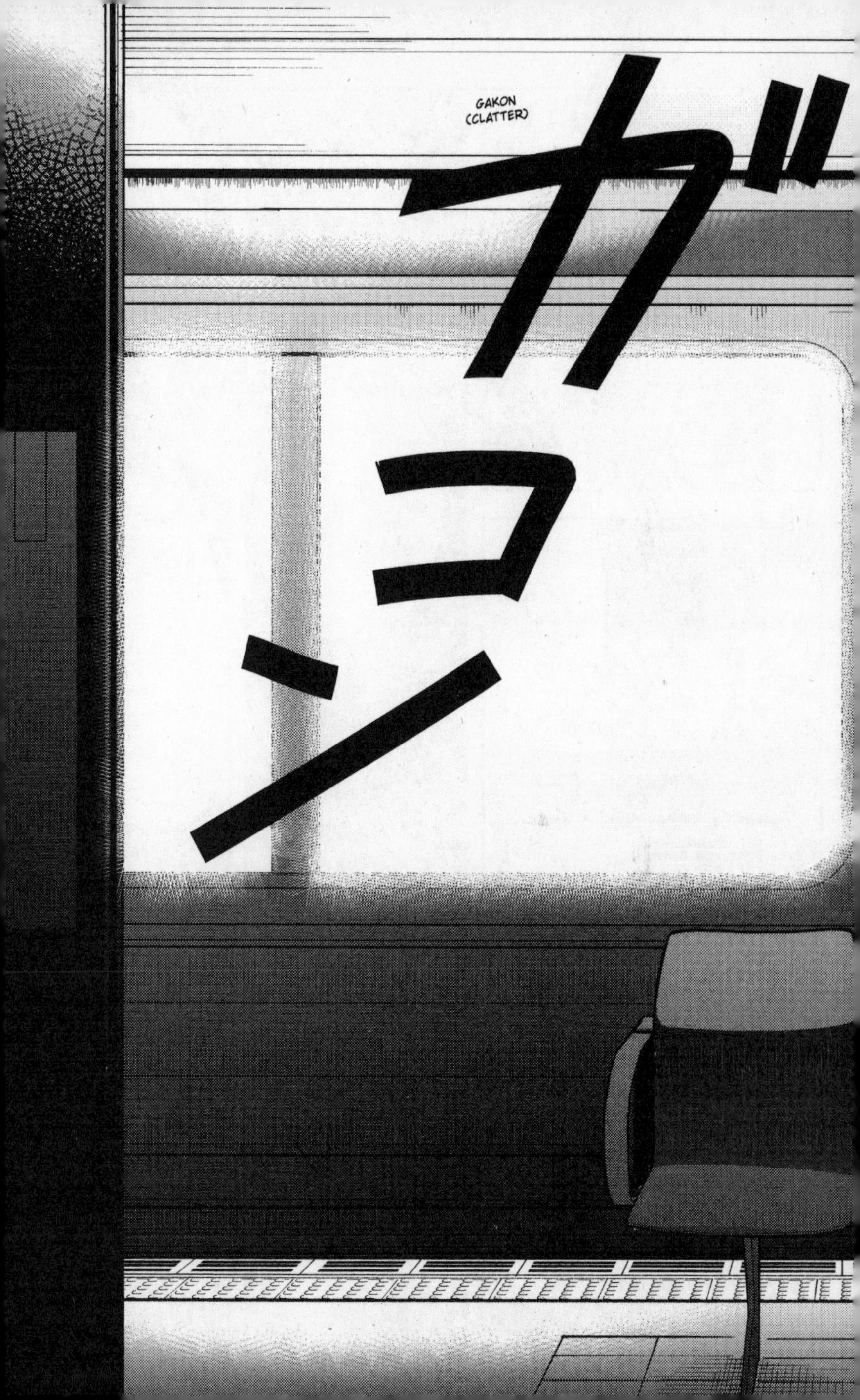
ガコン
GAKON (CLATTER)

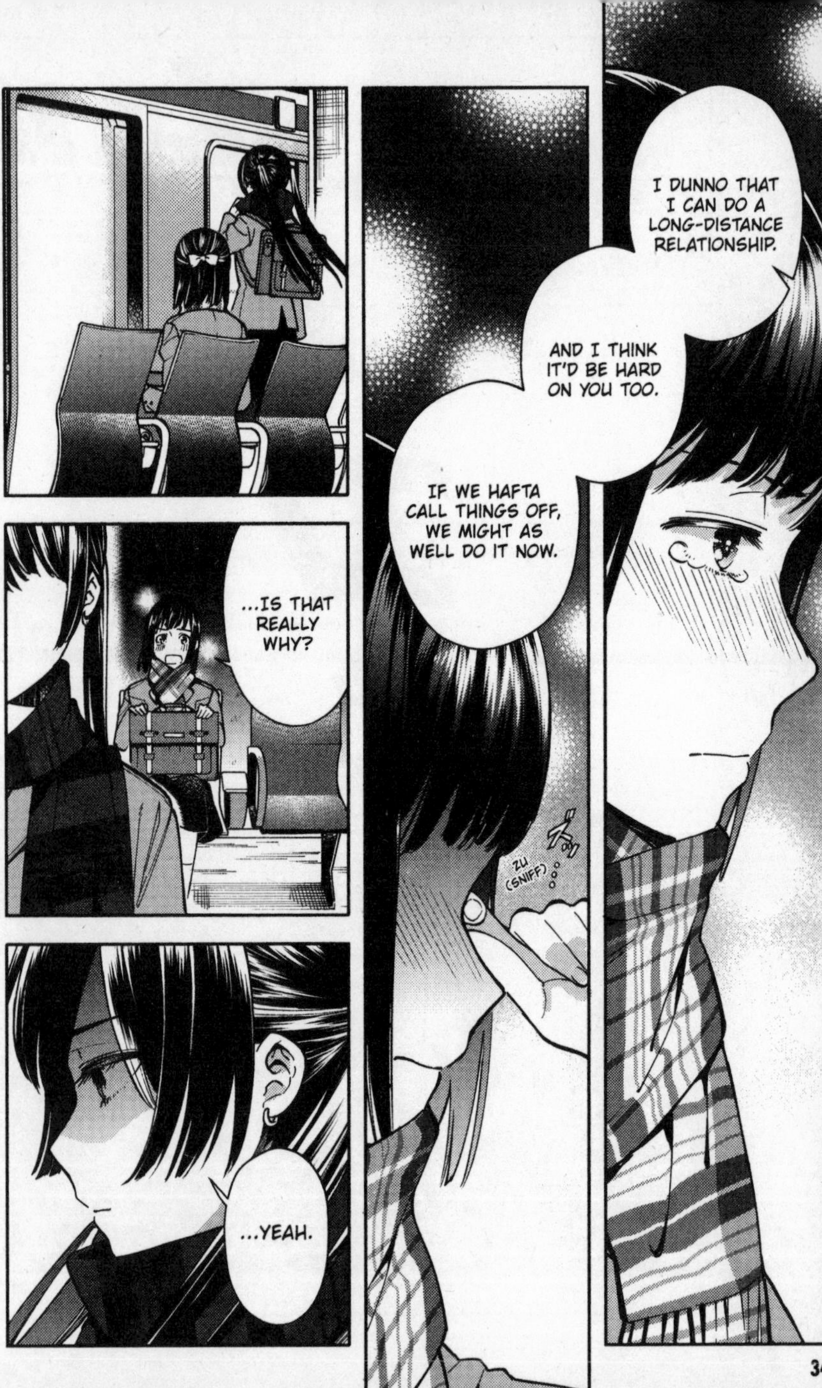
I DUNNO THAT I CAN DO A LONG-DISTANCE RELATIONSHIP.
AND I THINK IT'D BE HARD ON YOU TOO.
IF WE HAFTA CALL THINGS OFF, WE MIGHT AS WELL DO IT NOW.
ZU (SNIFF)
...IS THAT REALLY WHY?
...YEAH.

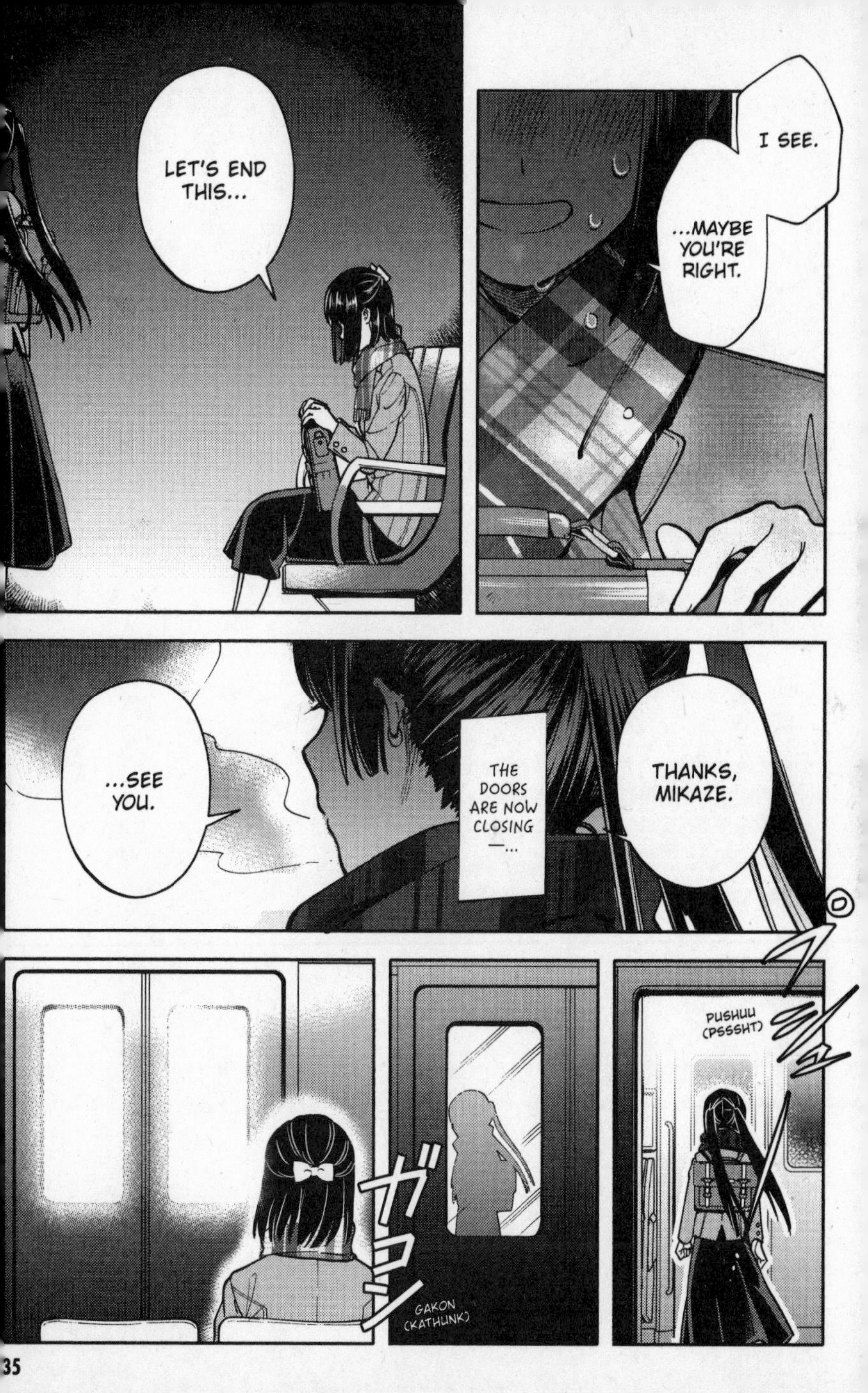
I SEE.
...MAYBE YOU'RE RIGHT.
LET'S END THIS...
THANKS, MIKAZE.
THE DOORS ARE NOW CLOSING —...
...SEE YOU.
PUSHUU (PSSSHT)
GAKON (KATHUNK)

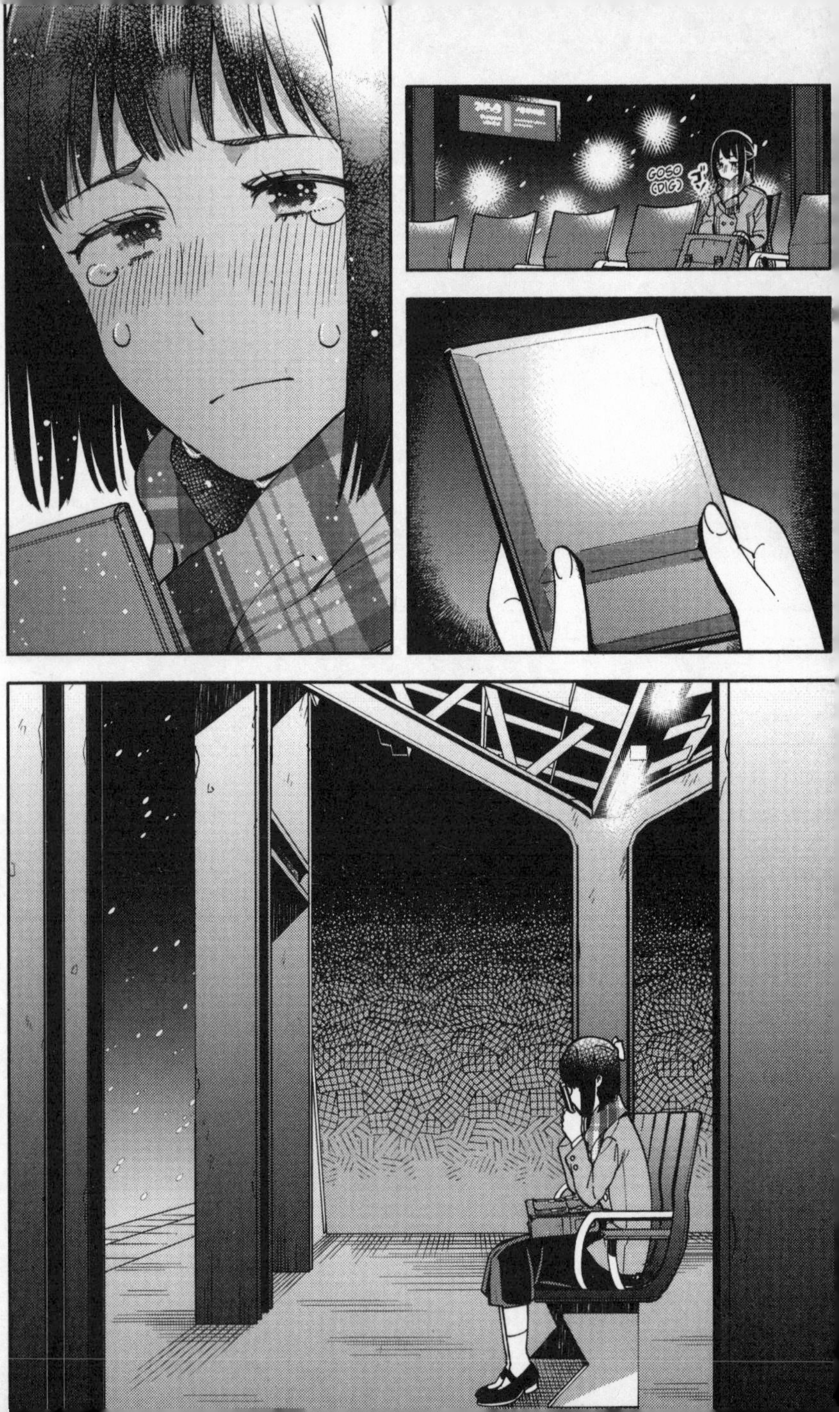
GOSO
(DIG)

The Yuri Business

HIMEKO
HANDLE.
A NORMAL OFFICE WORKER BY DAY.

HITOPPE
HANDLE.
A NORMAL COLLEGE STUDENT BY DAY.

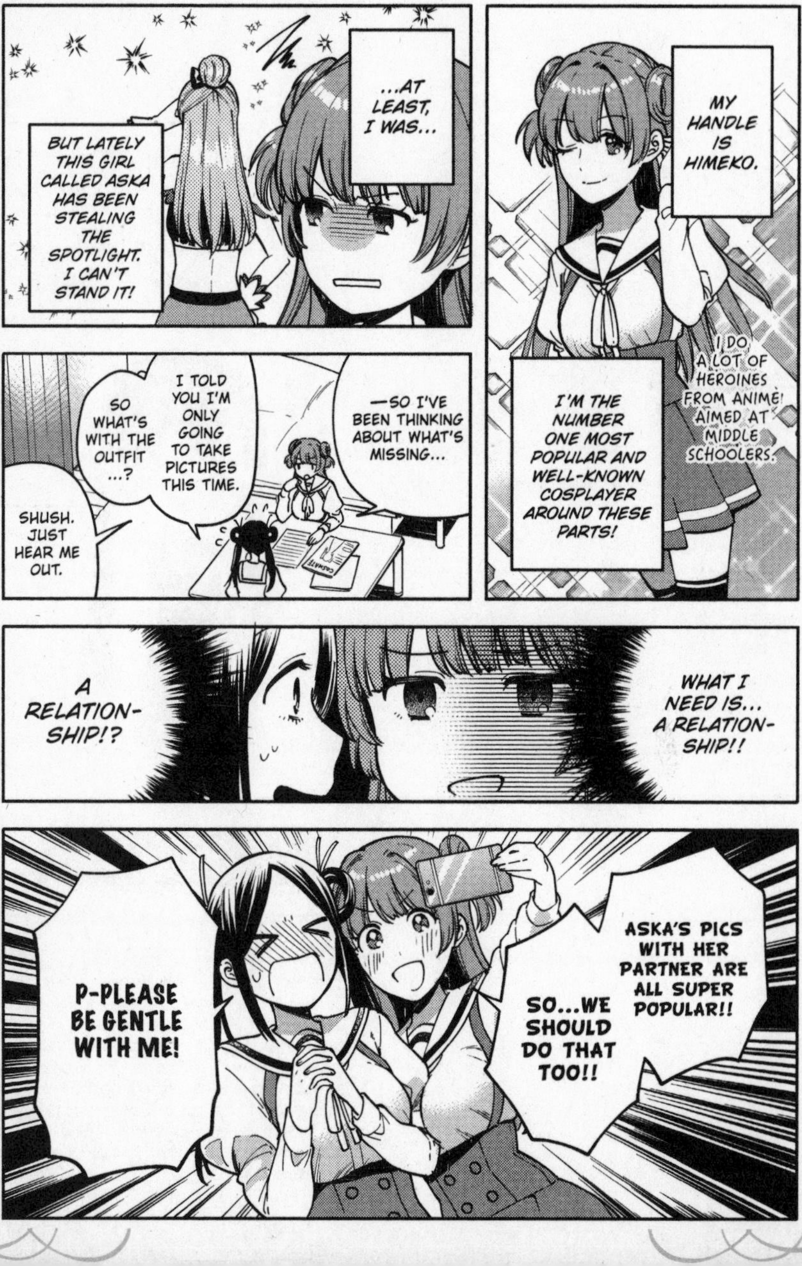

MY HANDLE IS HIMEKO.
I'M THE NUMBER ONE MOST POPULAR AND WELL-KNOWN COSPLAYER AROUND THESE PARTS!
I DO, A LOT OF HEROINES FROM ANIME! AIMED AT MIDDLE SCHOOLERS.
...AT LEAST, I WAS...
BUT LATELY THIS GIRL CALLED ASKA HAS BEEN STEALING THE SPOTLIGHT. I CAN'T STAND IT!
—SO I'VE BEEN THINKING ABOUT WHAT'S MISSING...
I TOLD YOU I'M ONLY GOING TO TAKE PICTURES THIS TIME.
SO WHAT'S WITH THE OUTFIT ...?
SHUSH. JUST HEAR ME OUT.
WHAT I NEED IS... A RELATIONSHIP!!
A RELATIONSHIP!?
ASKA'S PICS WITH HER PARTNER ARE ALL SUPER POPULAR!!
SO...WE SHOULD DO THAT TOO!!
P-PLEASE BE GENTLE WITH ME!

Asuka Sakurada

Asuka Sakurada

Third-year student at the Seiran Academy High School. Former basketball player. She had to repeat a year of school because of an injury she sustained playing basketball, so she's a year older than the others in her grade. She liked reading and didn't stand out much before being held back, but her jaded response to having to redo a year has caused her to draw attention. She's started cosplaying, and even her normal fashion has turned somewhat Lolita.

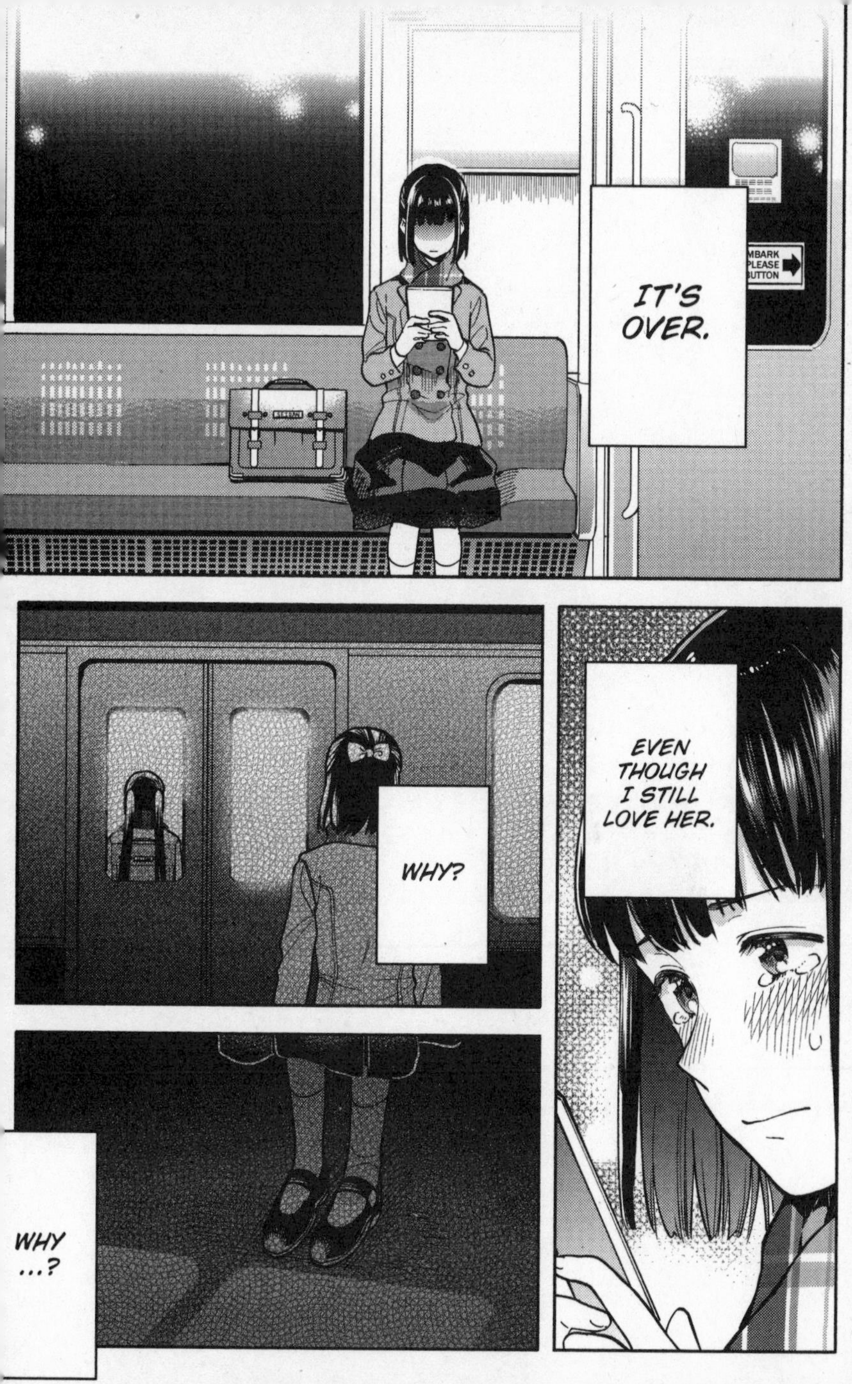
IT'S OVER.
EVEN THOUGH I STILL LOVE HER.
WHY?
WHY ...?

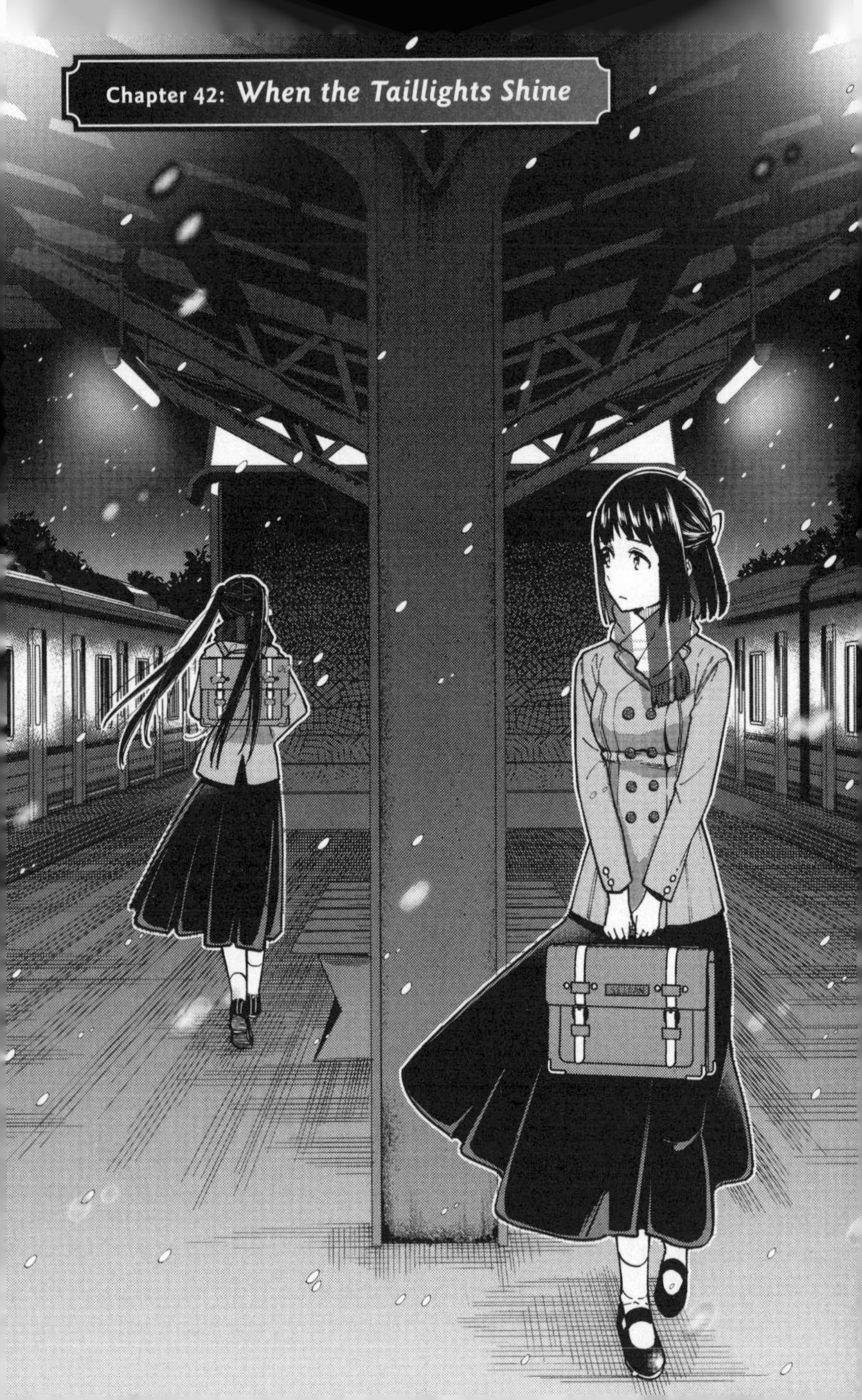
Chapter 42: When the Taillights Shine

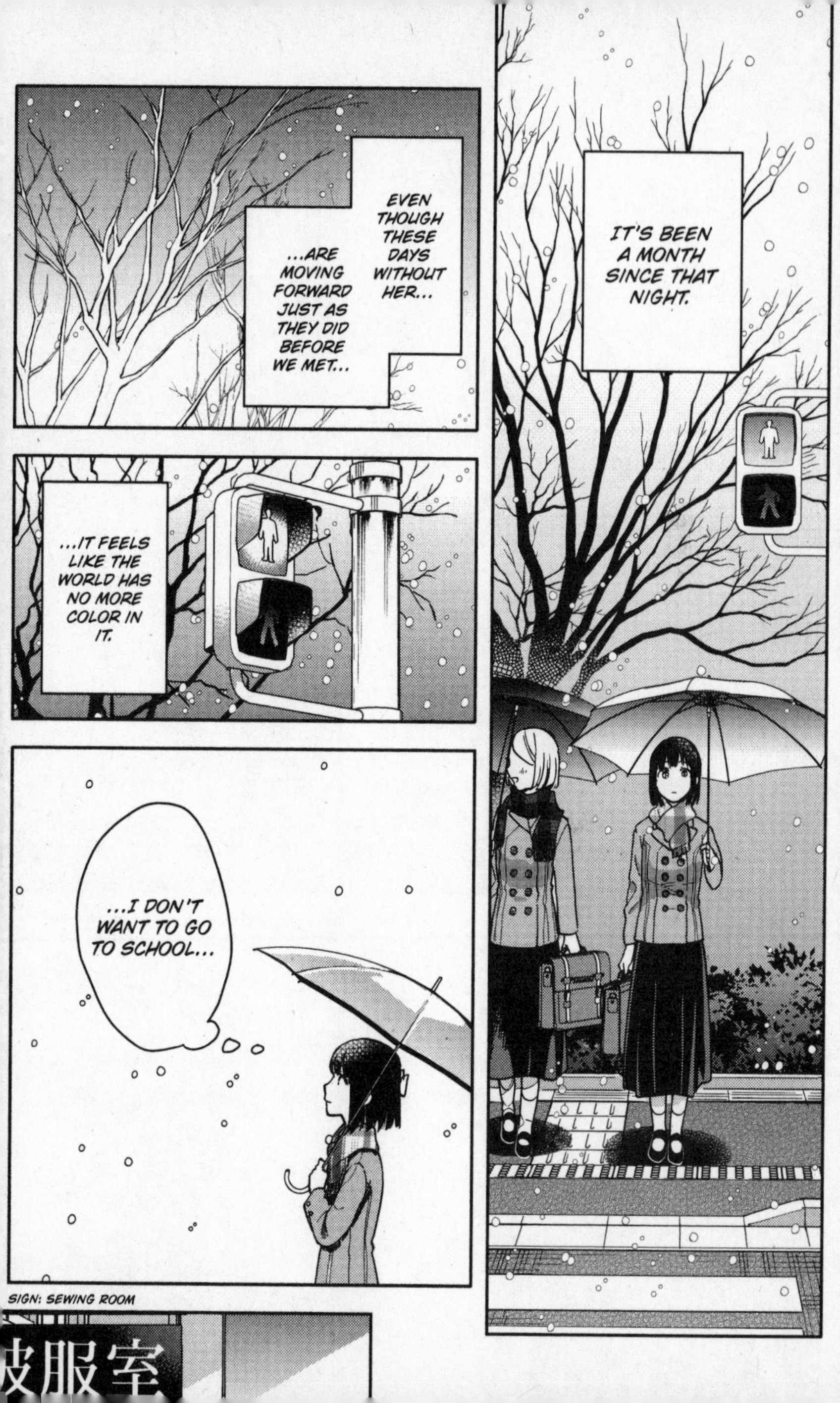
IT'S BEEN A MONTH SINCE THAT NIGHT.
EVEN THOUGH THESE DAYS WITHOUT HER...
...ARE MOVING FORWARD JUST AS THEY DID BEFORE WE MET...
...IT FEELS LIKE THE WORLD HAS NO MORE COLOR IN IT.
...I DON'T WANT TO GO TO SCHOOL...
SIGN: SEWING ROOM

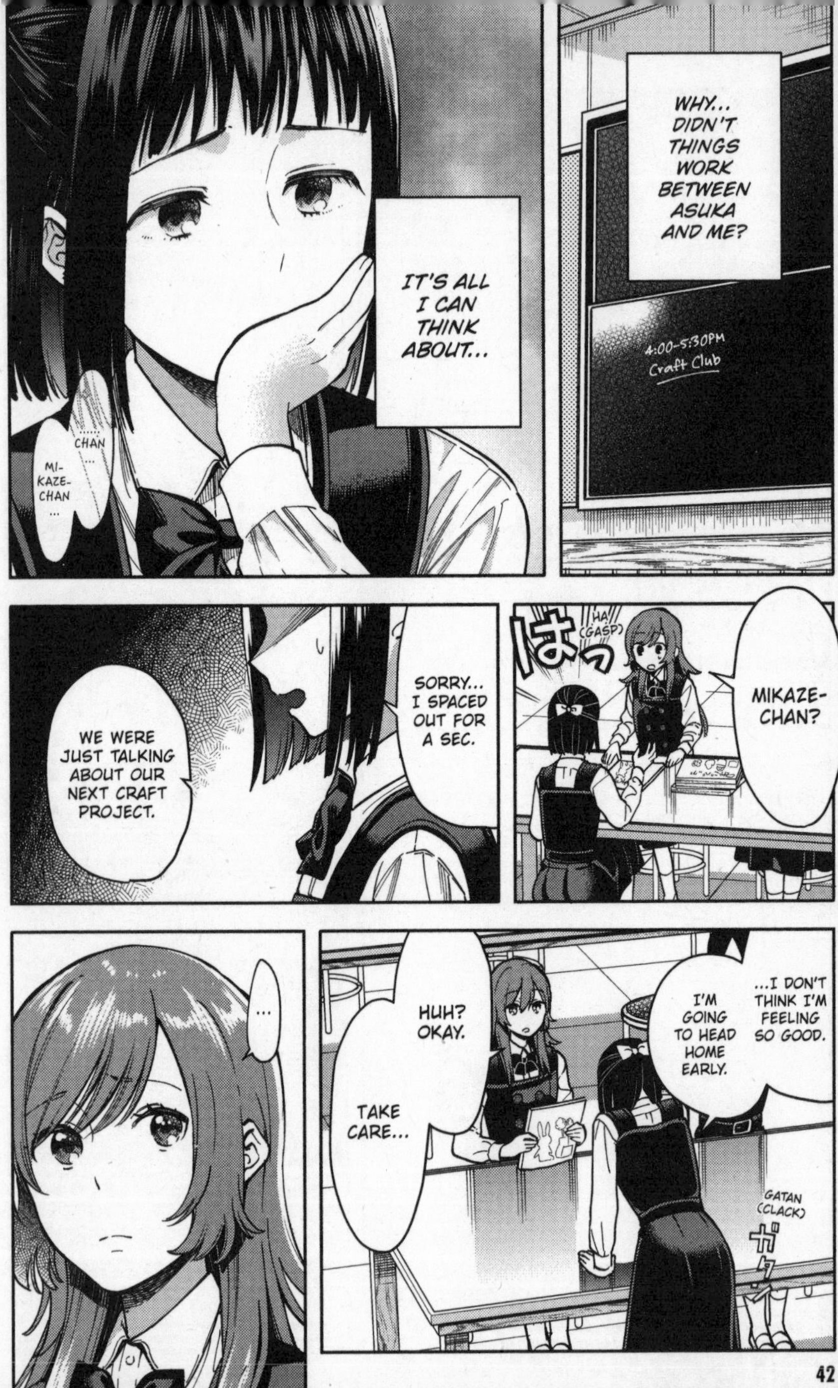
WHY... DIDN'T THINGS WORK BETWEEN ASUKA AND ME?
4:00-5:30PM Craft Club
IT'S ALL I CAN THINK ABOUT...
......CHAN ... MIKAZE-CHAN ...
HA (GASP)
はっ
MIKAZE-CHAN?
SORRY... I SPACED OUT FOR A SEC.
WE WERE JUST TALKING ABOUT OUR NEXT CRAFT PROJECT.
...I DON'T THINK I'M FEELING SO GOOD.
I'M GOING TO HEAD HOME EARLY.
HUH? OKAY.
TAKE CARE...
GATAN (CLACK)
ガタッ
...

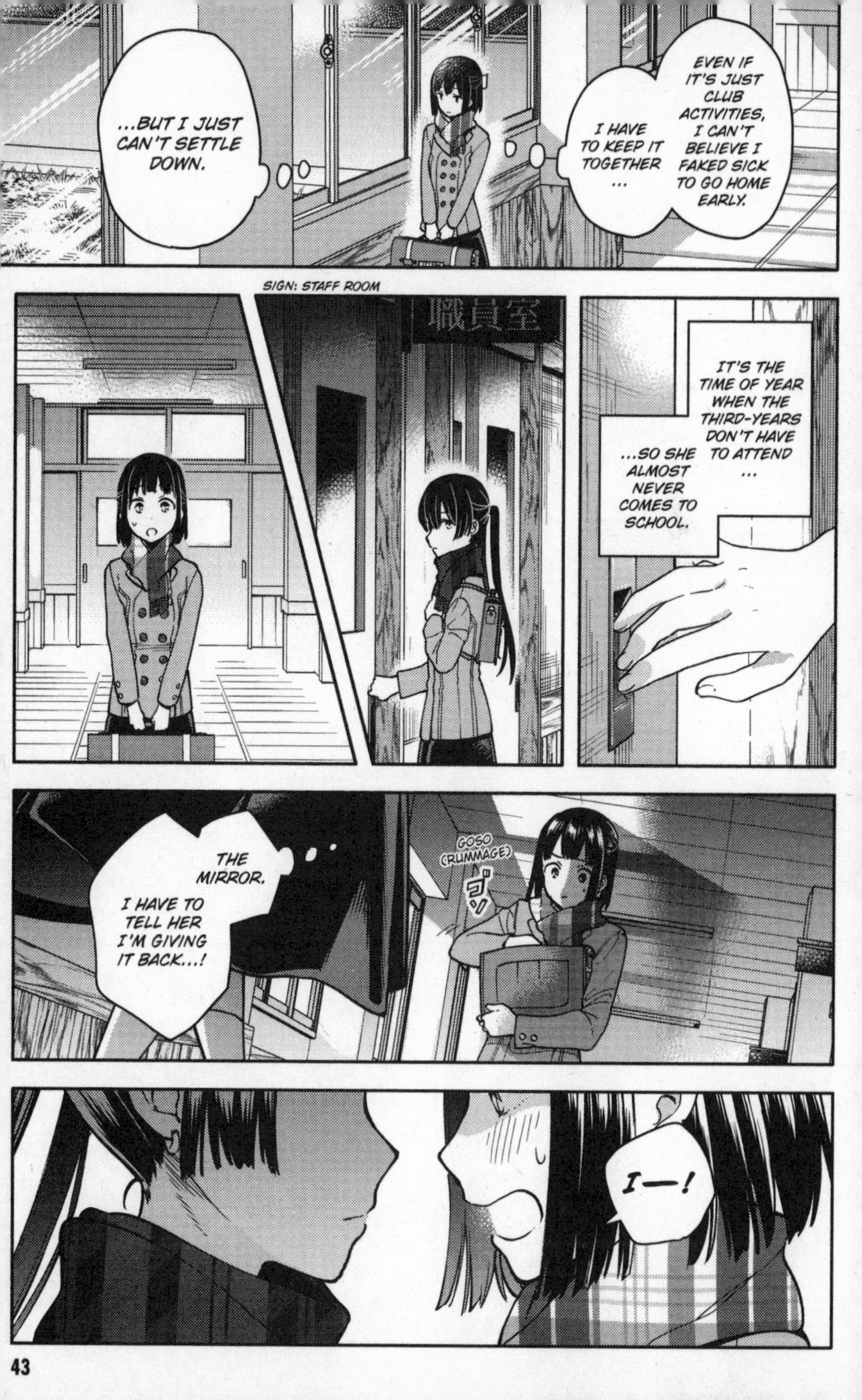
EVEN IF IT'S JUST CLUB ACTIVITIES, I CAN'T BELIEVE I FAKED SICK TO GO HOME EARLY.
I HAVE TO KEEP IT TOGETHER...
...BUT I JUST CAN'T SETTLE DOWN.
IT'S THE TIME OF YEAR WHEN THE THIRD-YEARS DON'T HAVE TO ATTEND...
...SO SHE ALMOST NEVER COMES TO SCHOOL.
SIGN: STAFF ROOM
GOSO (RUMMAGE)
THE MIRROR.
I HAVE TO TELL HER I'M GIVING IT BACK...!
I—!

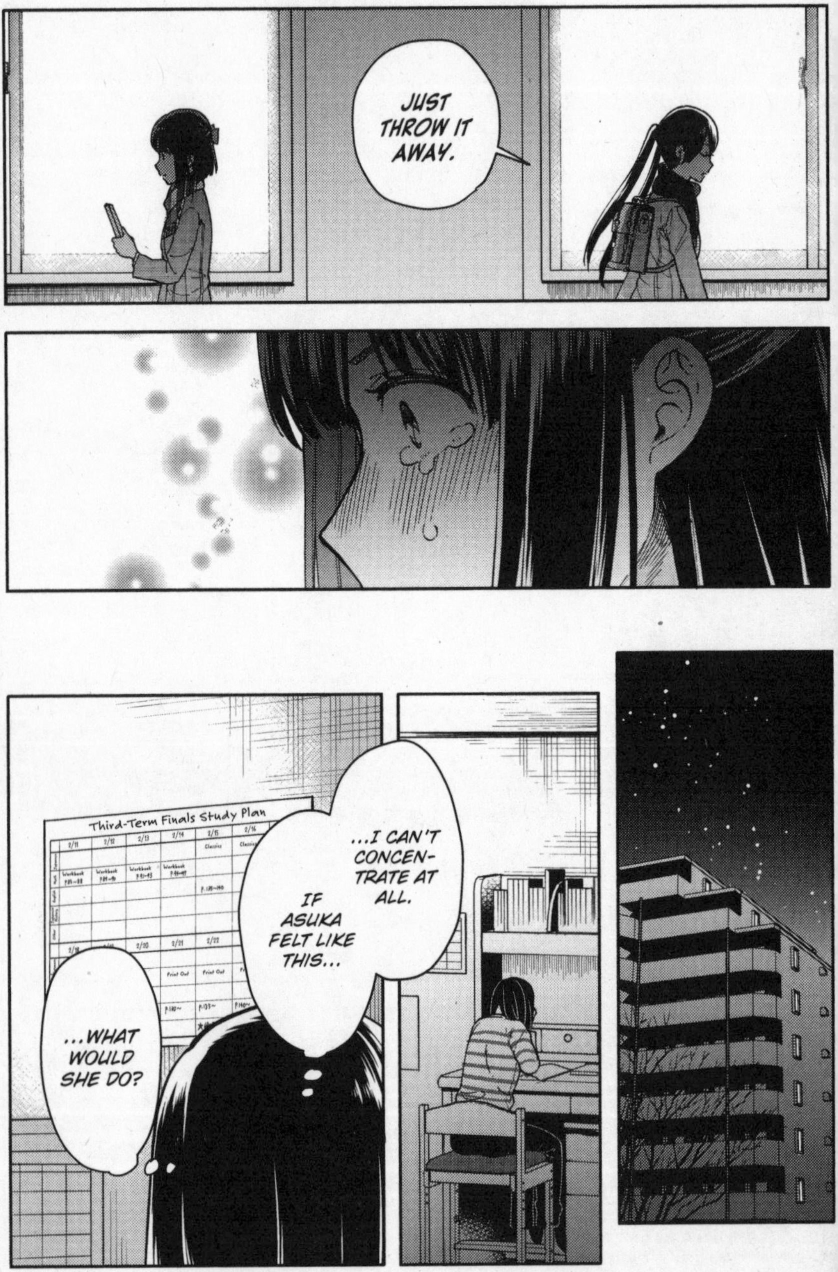
JUST THROW IT AWAY.
...I CAN'T CONCEN-TRATE AT ALL.
IF ASUKA FELT LIKE THIS...
Third-Term Finals Study Plan
...WHAT WOULD SHE DO?

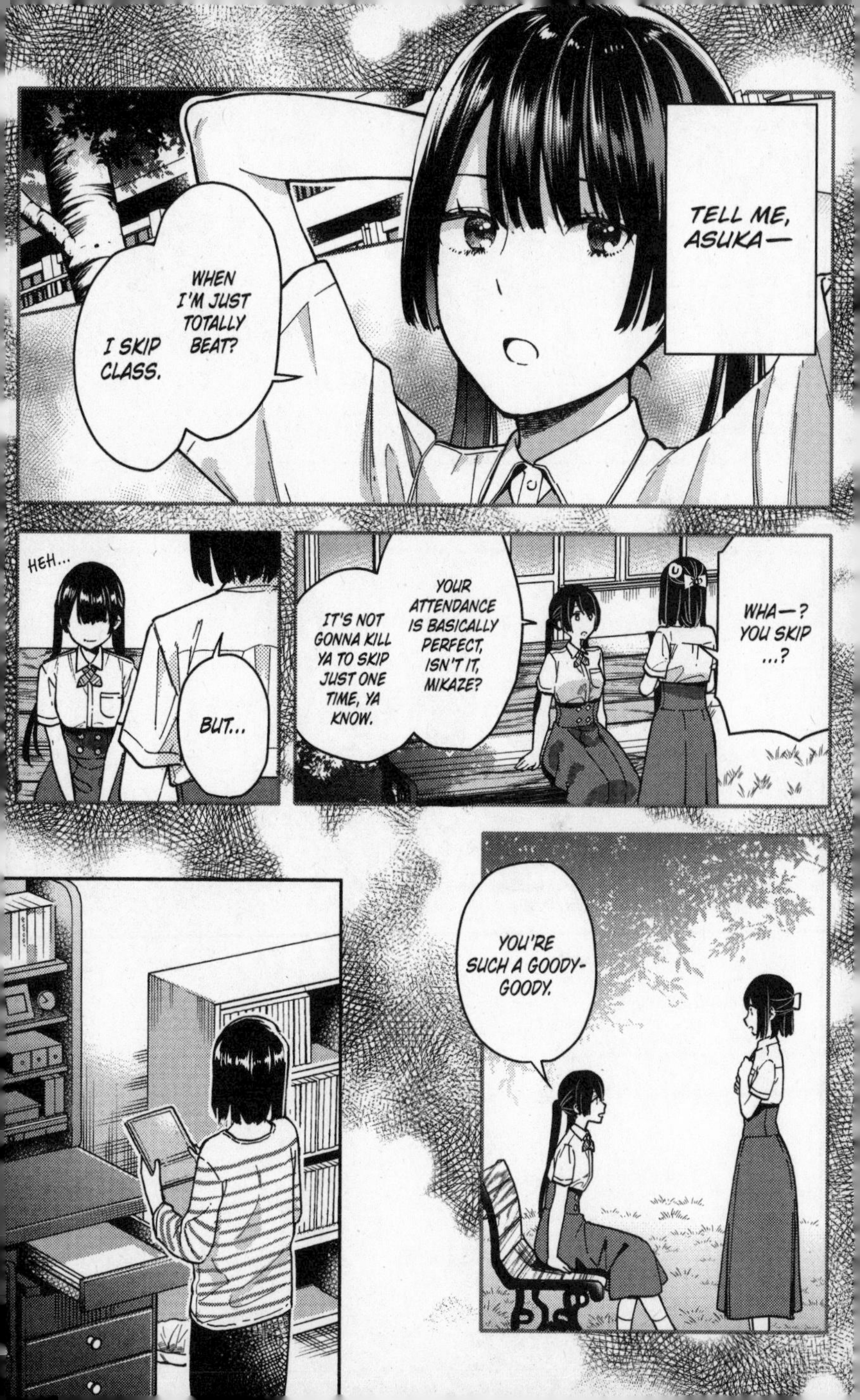
TELL ME, ASUKA—
WHEN I'M JUST TOTALLY BEAT? I SKIP CLASS.
WHA—? YOU SKIP ...?
YOUR ATTENDANCE IS BASICALLY PERFECT, ISN'T IT, MIKAZE? IT'S NOT GONNA KILL YA TO SKIP JUST ONE TIME, YA KNOW.
BUT...
HEH...
YOU'RE SUCH A GOODY-GOODY.

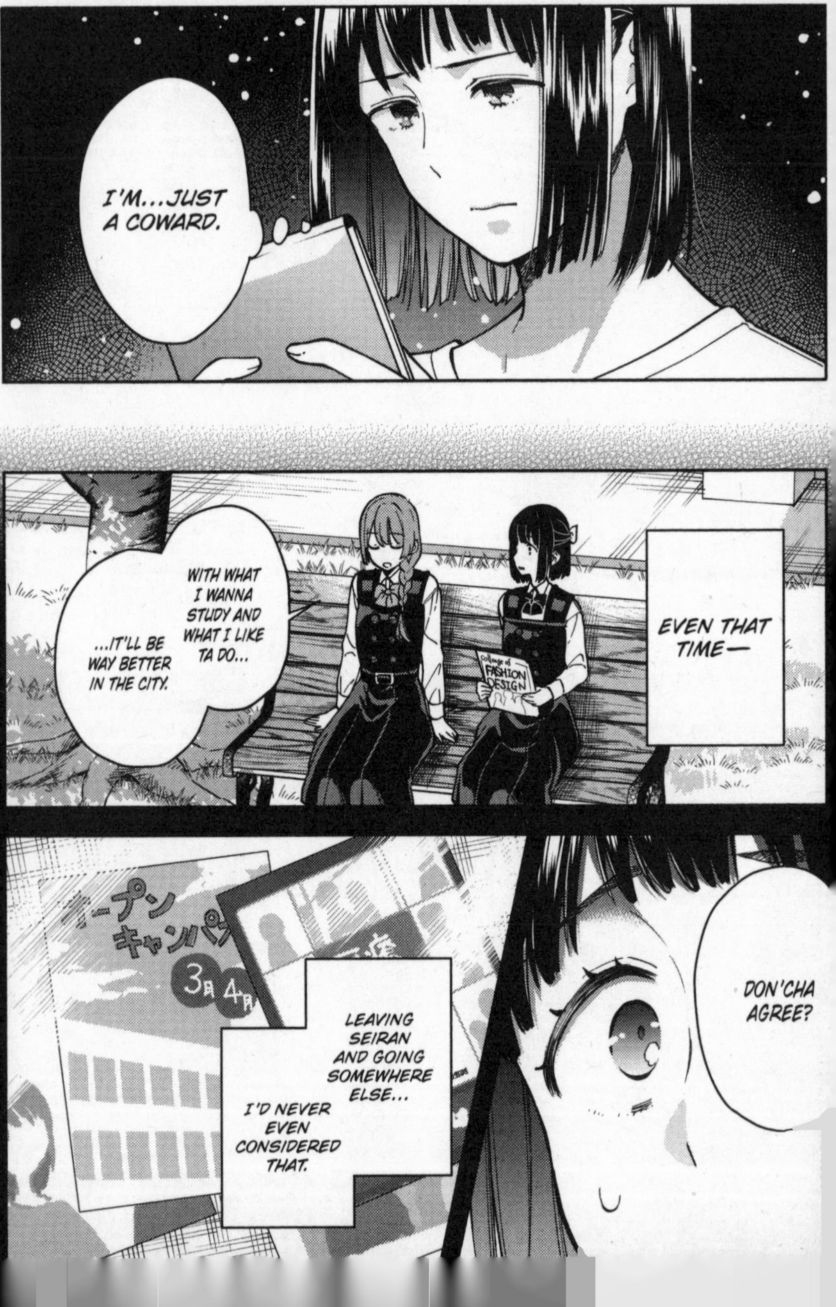
I'M...JUST A COWARD.
EVEN THAT TIME—
WITH WHAT I WANNA STUDY AND WHAT I LIKE TA DO...
...IT'LL BE WAY BETTER IN THE CITY.
College of FASHION DESIGN
DON'CHA AGREE?
LEAVING SEIRAN AND GOING SOMEWHERE ELSE...
I'D NEVER EVEN CONSIDERED THAT.

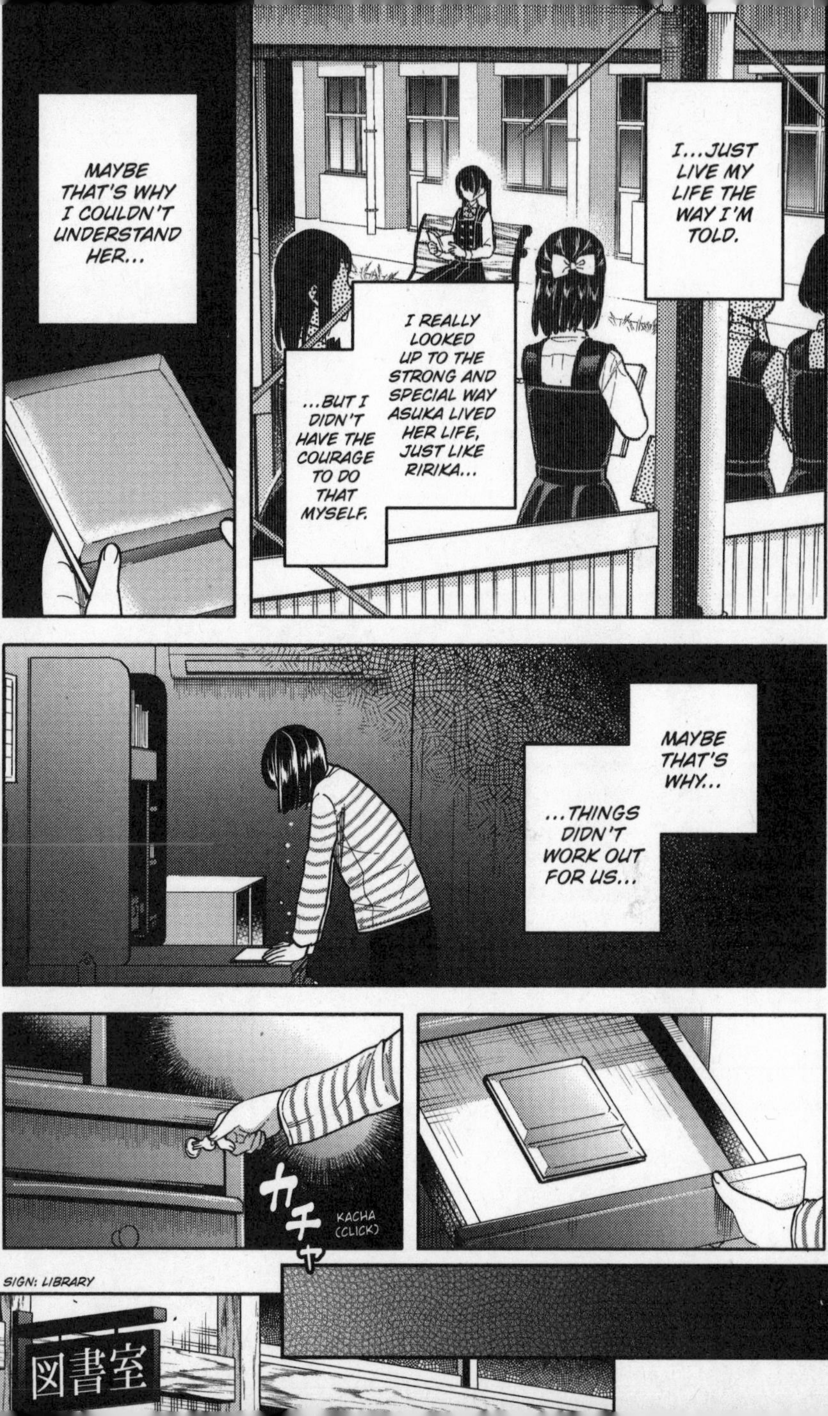
I...JUST LIVE MY LIFE THE WAY I'M TOLD.
I REALLY LOOKED UP TO THE STRONG AND SPECIAL WAY ASUKA LIVED HER LIFE, JUST LIKE RIRIKA...
...BUT I DIDN'T HAVE THE COURAGE TO DO THAT MYSELF.
MAYBE THAT'S WHY I COULDN'T UNDERSTAND HER...
MAYBE THAT'S WHY...
...THINGS DIDN'T WORK OUT FOR US...
カチャ
KACHA (CLICK)
SIGN: LIBRARY
図書室

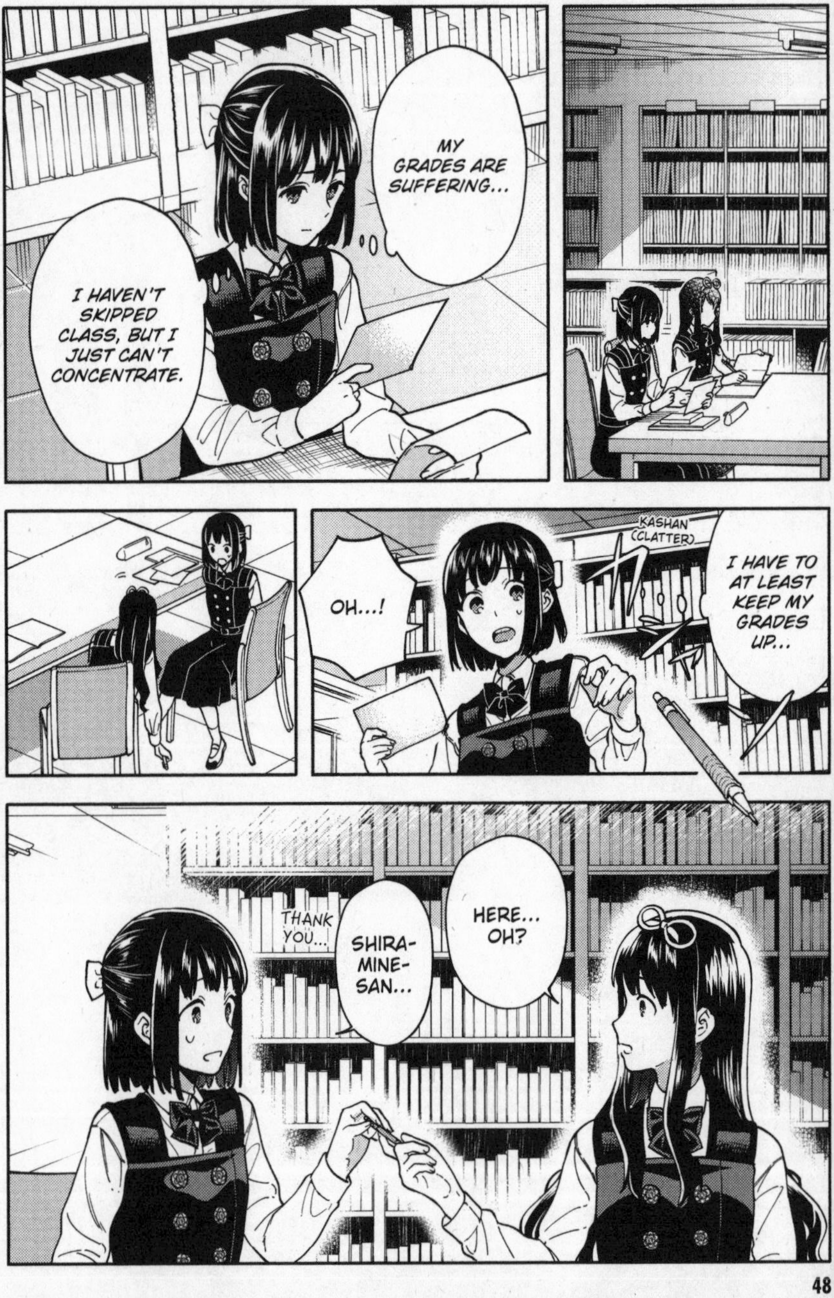
MY GRADES ARE SUFFERING...
I HAVEN'T SKIPPED CLASS, BUT I JUST CAN'T CONCENTRATE.
I HAVE TO AT LEAST KEEP MY GRADES UP...
KASHAN (CLATTER)
OH...!
HERE... OH?
SHIRA-MINE-SAN...
THANK YOU...

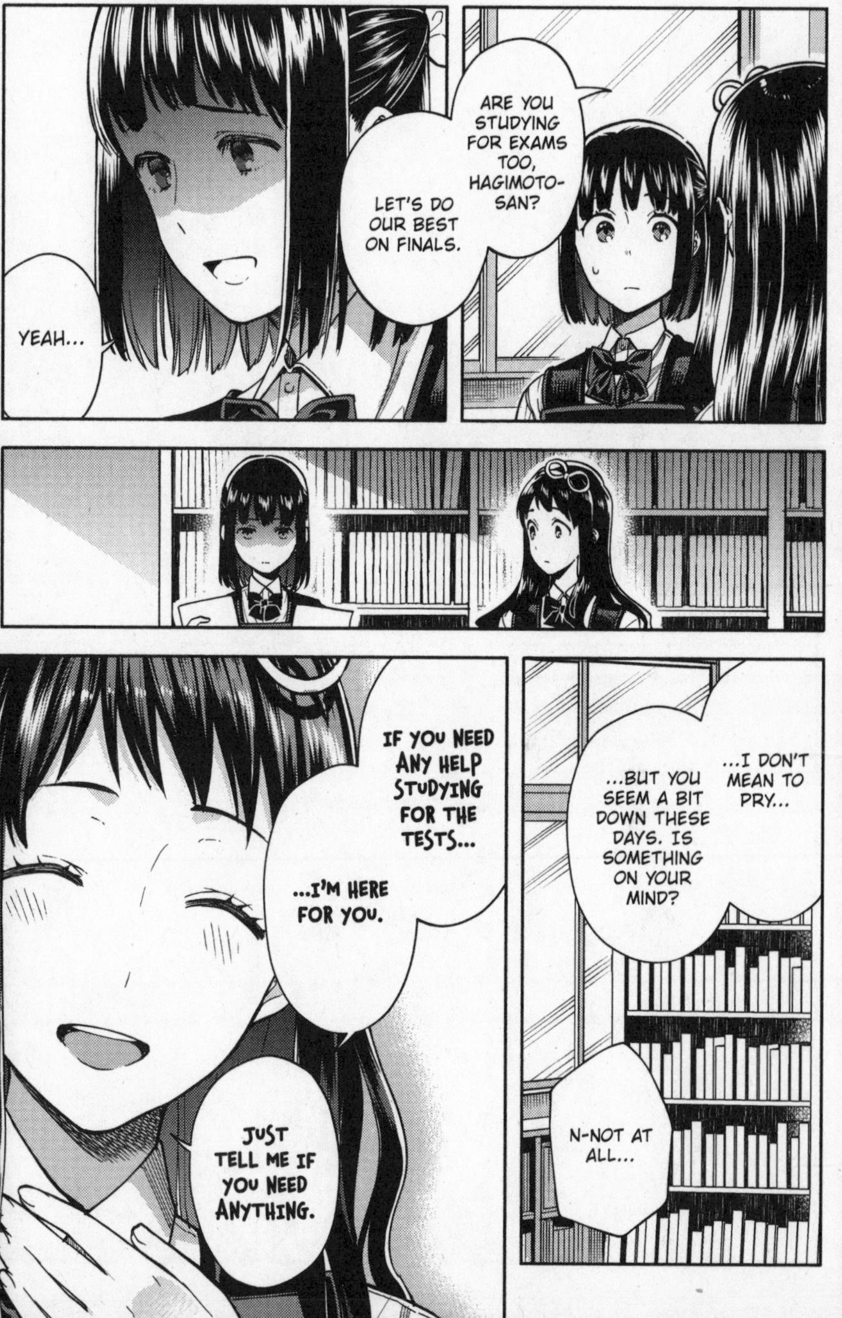
ARE YOU STUDYING FOR EXAMS TOO, HAGIMOTO-SAN?
LET'S DO OUR BEST ON FINALS.
YEAH...
...I DON'T MEAN TO PRY...
...BUT YOU SEEM A BIT DOWN THESE DAYS. IS SOMETHING ON YOUR MIND?
N-NOT AT ALL...
IF YOU NEED ANY HELP STUDYING FOR THE TESTS...
...I'M HERE FOR YOU.
JUST TELL ME IF YOU NEED ANYTHING.

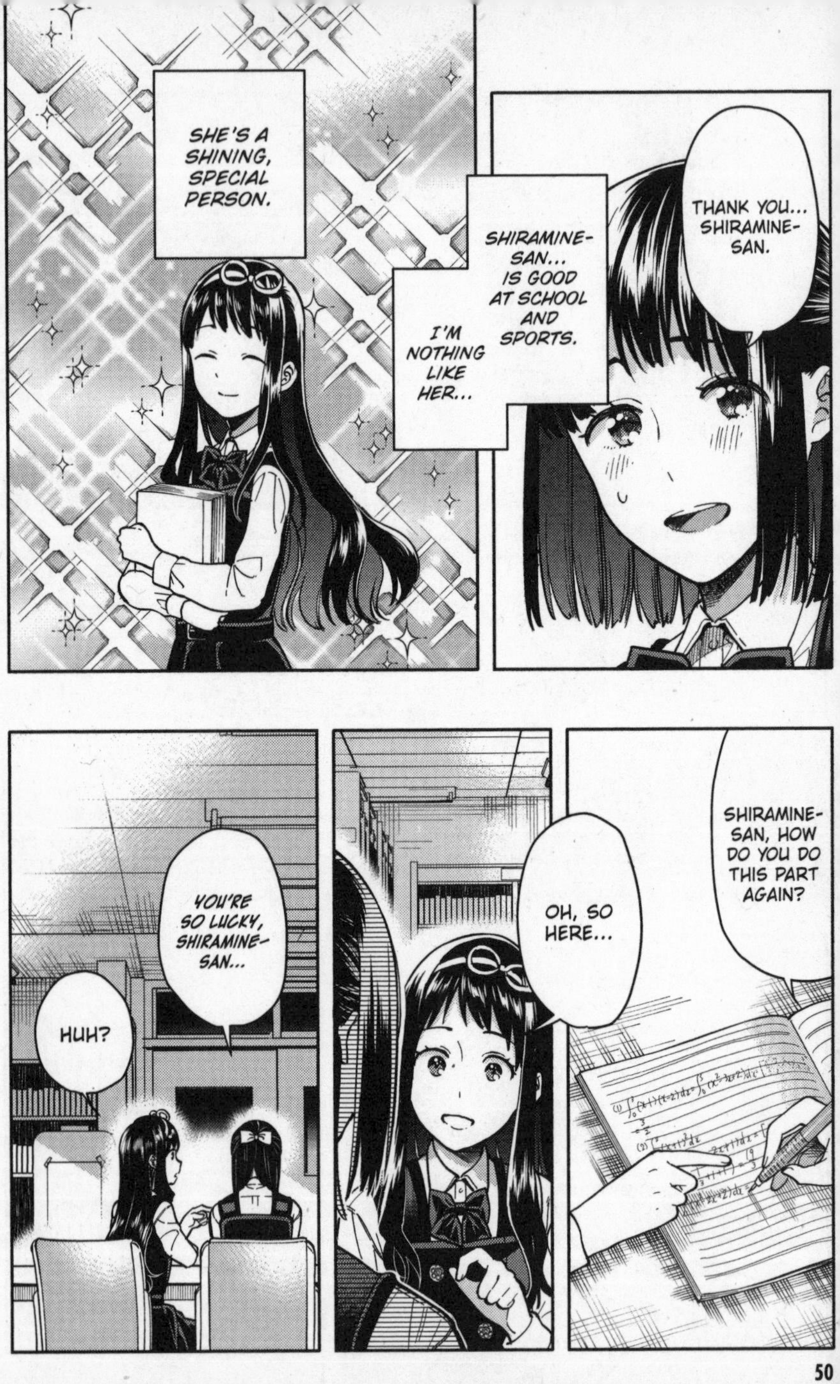
THANK YOU... SHIRAMINE-SAN.
SHIRAMINE-SAN... IS GOOD AT SCHOOL AND SPORTS.
I'M NOTHING LIKE HER...
SHE'S A SHINING, SPECIAL PERSON.
SHIRAMINE-SAN, HOW DO YOU DO THIS PART AGAIN?
OH, SO HERE...
YOU'RE SO LUCKY, SHIRAMINE-SAN...
HUH?

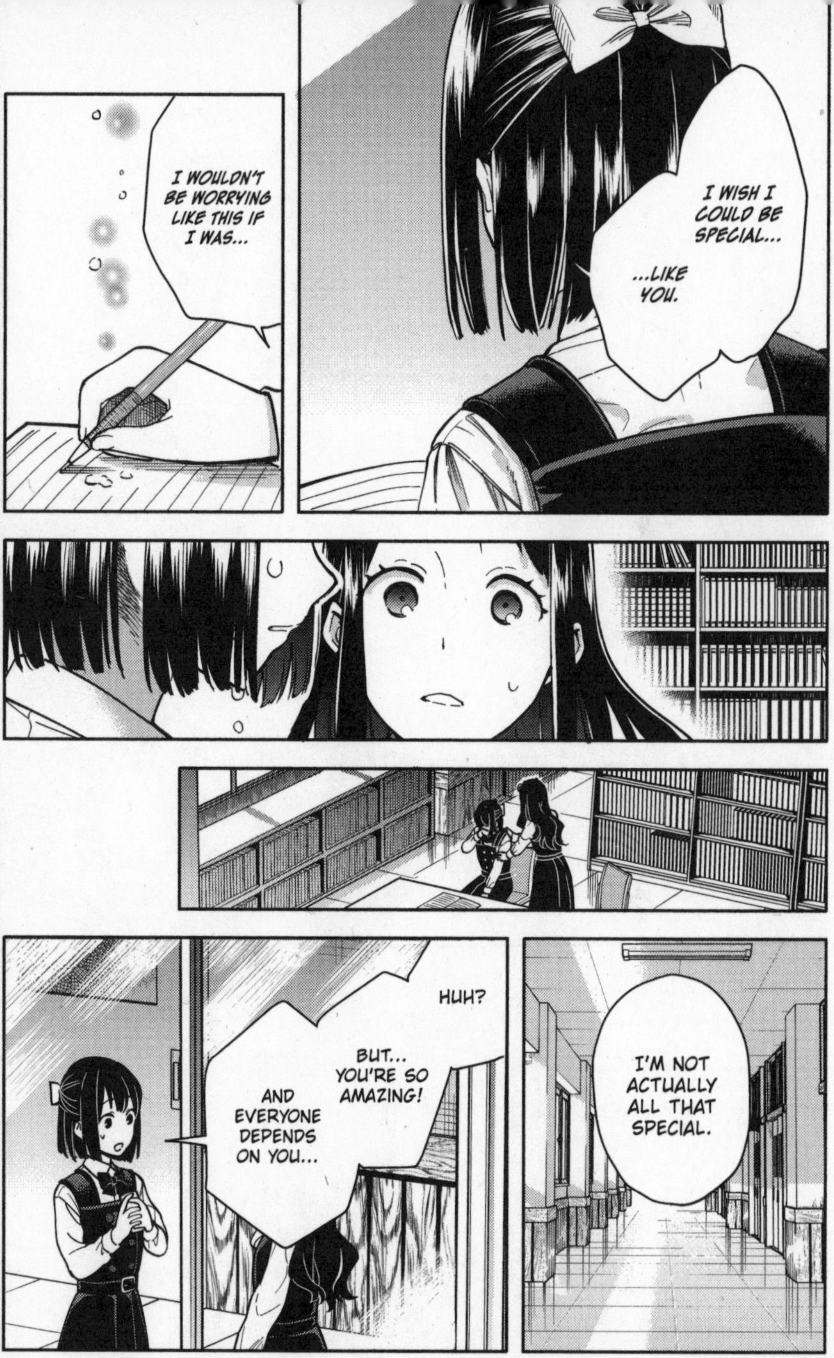
I WISH I COULD BE SPECIAL...
...LIKE YOU.
I WOULDN'T BE WORRYING LIKE THIS IF I WAS...
I'M NOT ACTUALLY ALL THAT SPECIAL.
HUH?
BUT... YOU'RE SO AMAZING!
AND EVERYONE DEPENDS ON YOU...

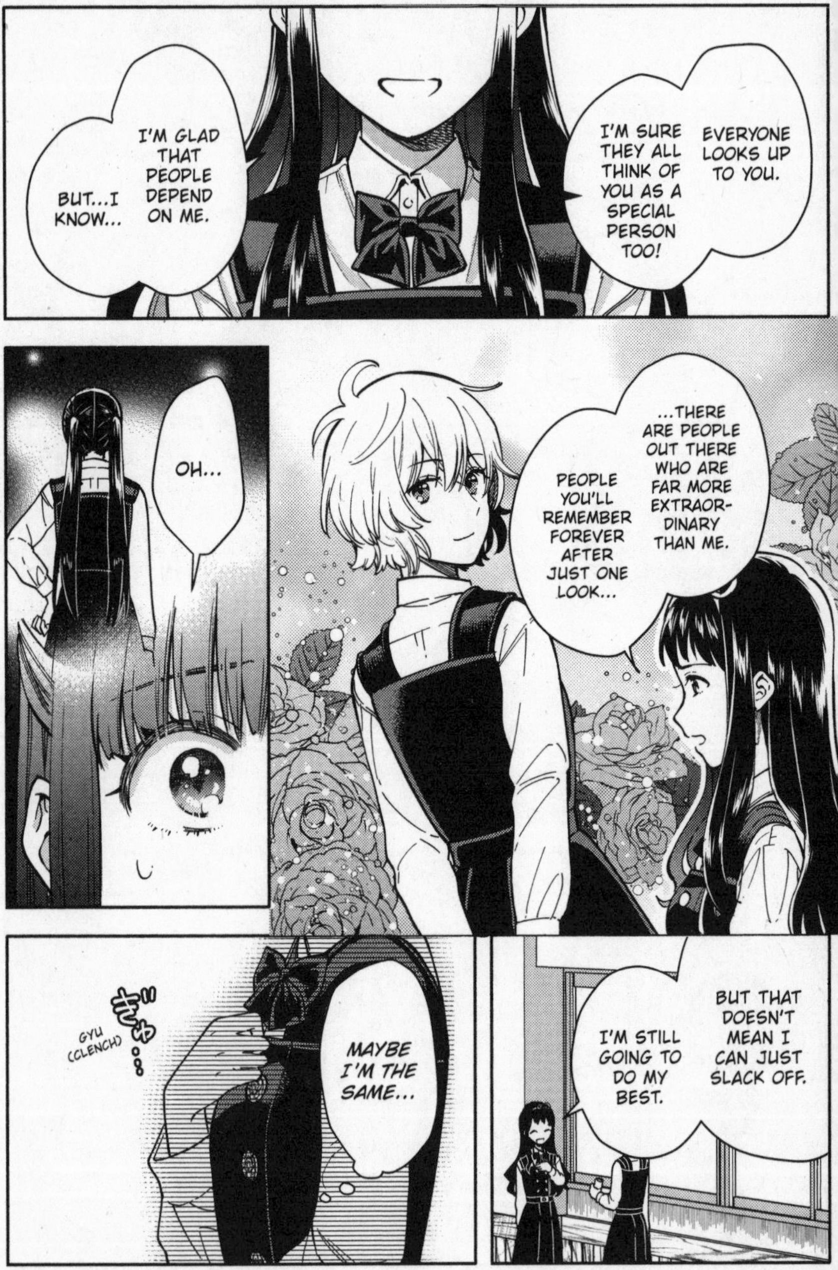
EVERYONE LOOKS UP TO YOU.
I'M SURE THEY ALL THINK OF YOU AS A SPECIAL PERSON TOO!
I'M GLAD THAT PEOPLE DEPEND ON ME.
BUT...I KNOW...
...THERE ARE PEOPLE OUT THERE WHO ARE FAR MORE EXTRAOR-DINARY THAN ME.
PEOPLE YOU'LL REMEMBER FOREVER AFTER JUST ONE LOOK...
OH...
BUT THAT DOESN'T MEAN I CAN JUST SLACK OFF.
I'M STILL GOING TO DO MY BEST.
MAYBE I'M THE SAME...
ぎゅ
GYU (CLENCH)

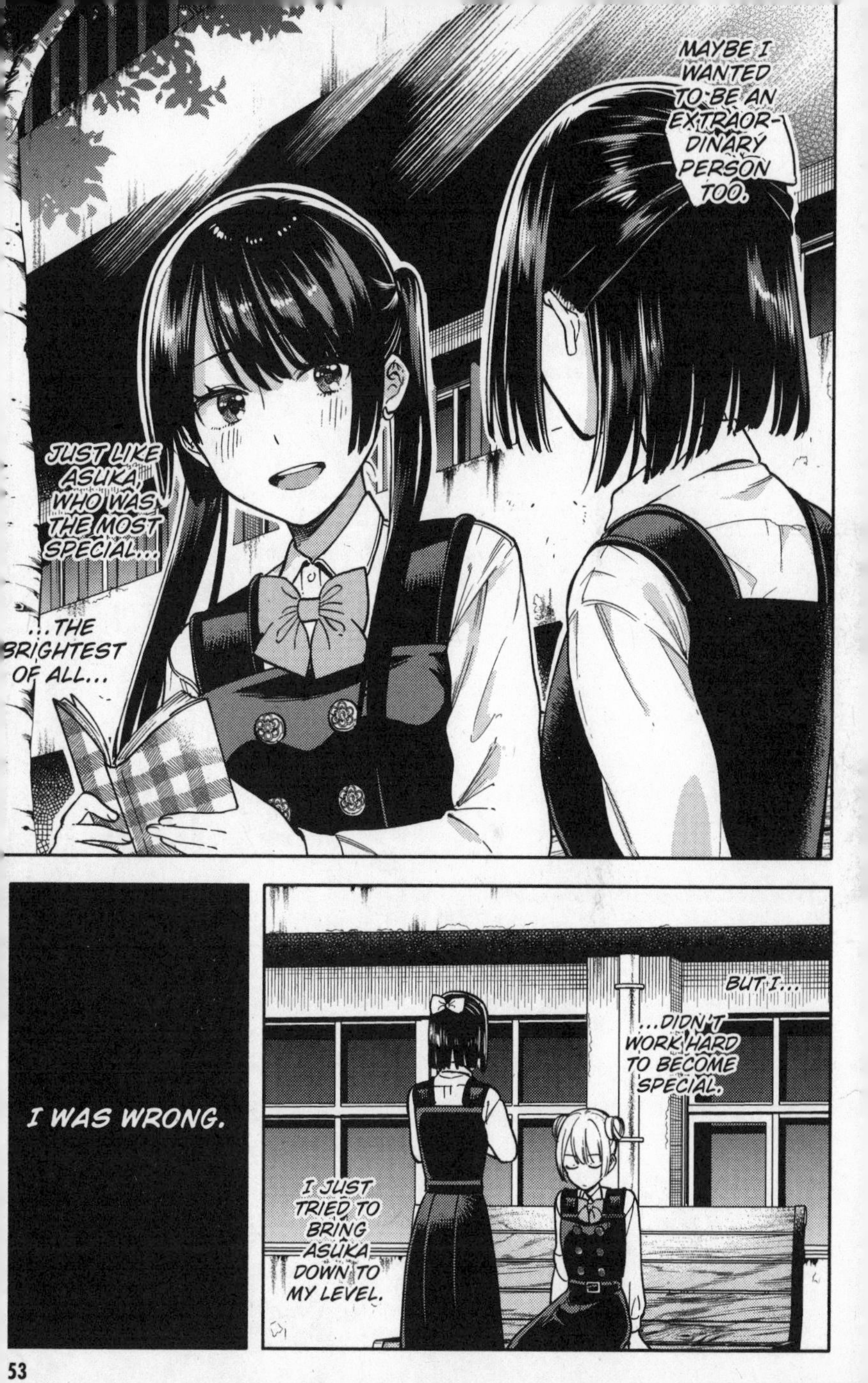
MAYBE I WANTED TO BE AN EXTRAOR-DINARY PERSON TOO.
JUST LIKE ASUKA, WHO WAS THE MOST SPECIAL...
...THE BRIGHTEST OF ALL...
BUT I...
...DIDN'T WORK HARD TO BECOME SPECIAL.
I JUST TRIED TO BRING ASUKA DOWN TO MY LEVEL.
I WAS WRONG.

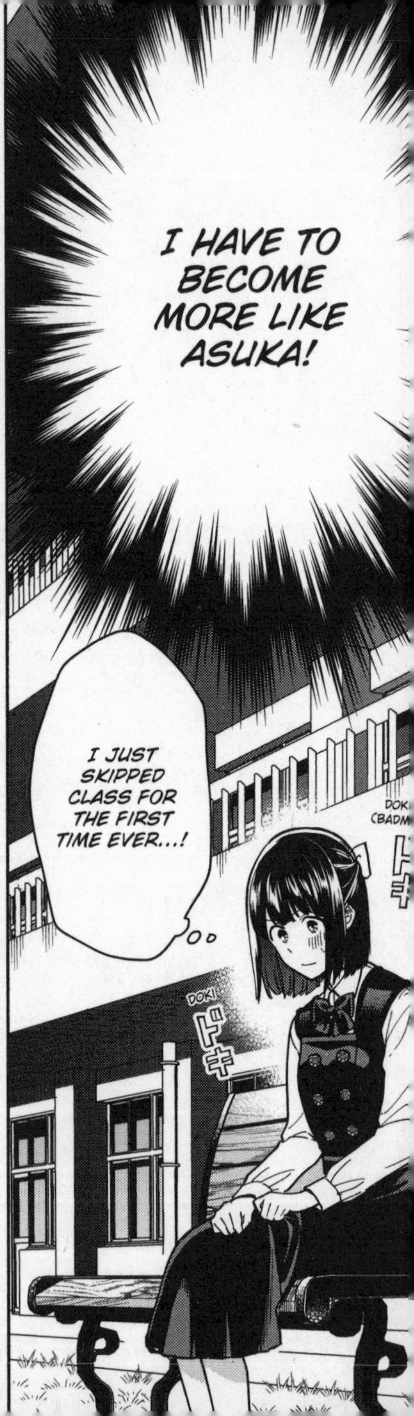
I HAVE TO BECOME MORE LIKE ASUKA!
I JUST SKIPPED CLASS FOR THE FIRST TIME EVER...!
DOKI
DOKI
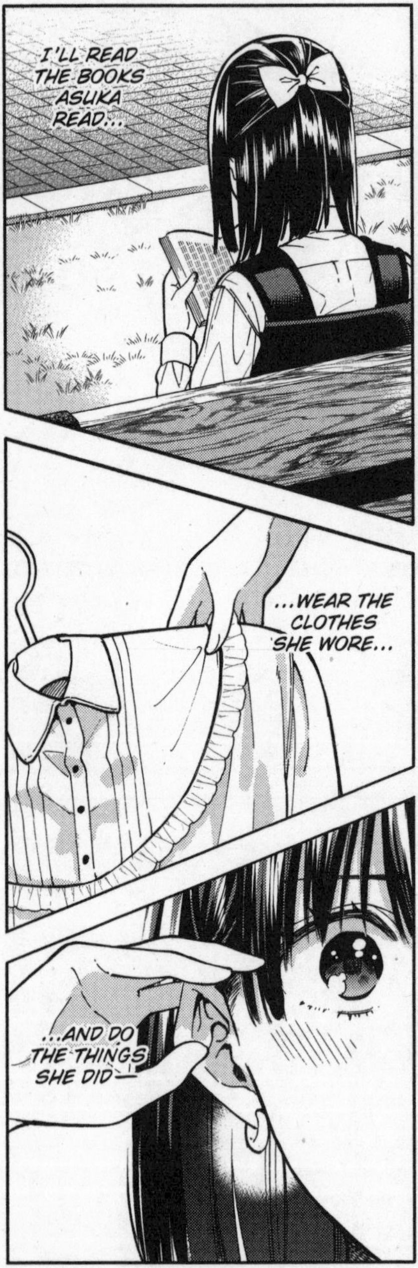
I'LL READ THE BOOKS ASUKA READ...
...WEAR THE CLOTHES SHE WORE...
...AND DO THE THINGS SHE DID—

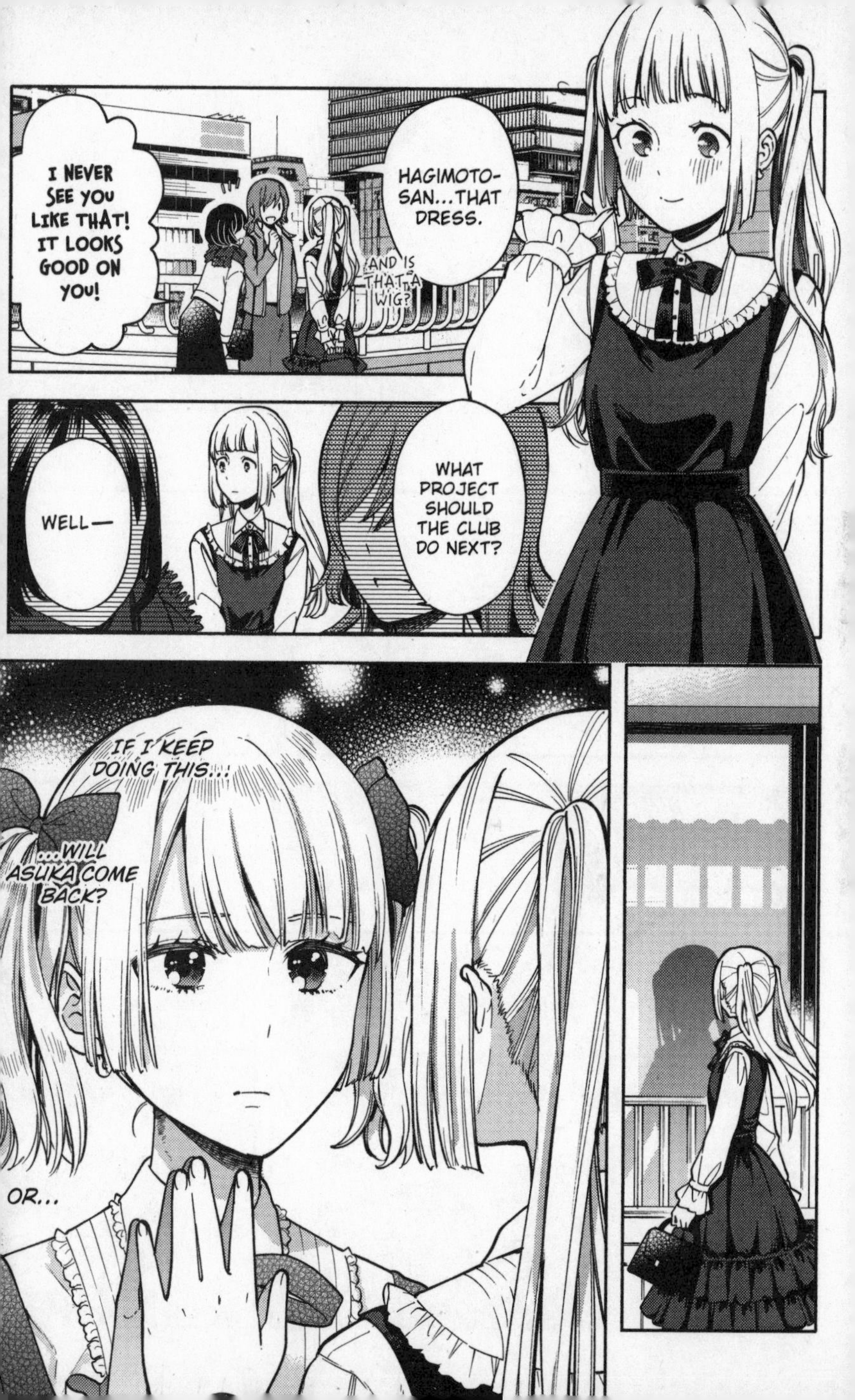
HAGIMOTO-SAN...THAT DRESS.
AND IS THAT A WIG?
I NEVER SEE YOU LIKE THAT! IT LOOKS GOOD ON YOU!
WHAT PROJECT SHOULD THE CLUB DO NEXT?
WELL—
IF I KEEP DOING THIS...
...WILL ASUKA COME BACK?
OR...

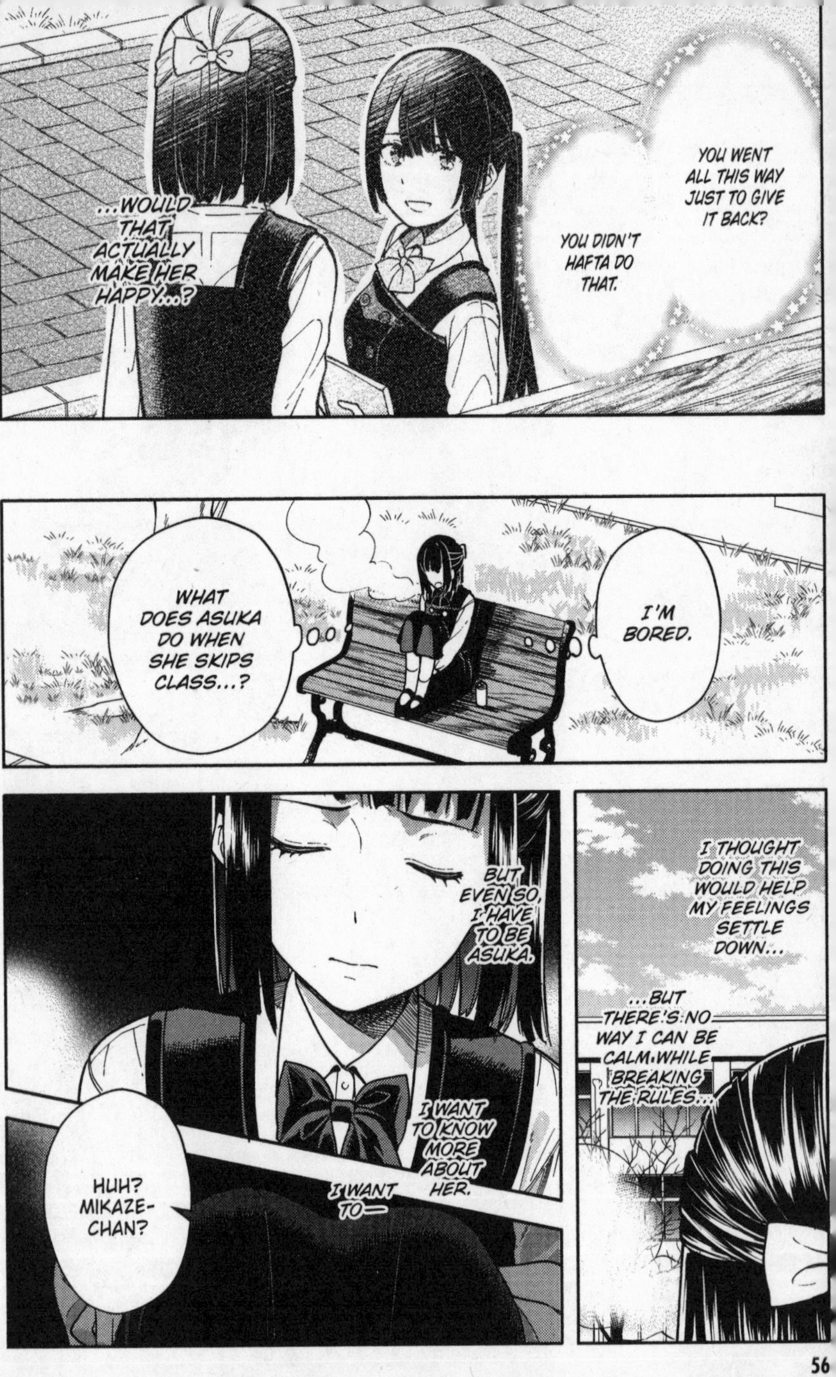
YOU WENT ALL THIS WAY JUST TO GIVE IT BACK?
YOU DIDN'T HAFTA DO THAT.
...WOULD THAT ACTUALLY MAKE HER HAPPY...?
I'M BORED.
WHAT DOES ASUKA DO WHEN SHE SKIPS CLASS...?
I THOUGHT DOING THIS WOULD HELP MY FEELINGS SETTLE DOWN...
...BUT THERE'S NO WAY I CAN BE CALM WHILE BREAKING THE RULES...
BUT EVEN SO, I HAVE TO BE ASUKA.
I WANT TO KNOW MORE ABOUT HER.
I WANT TO—
HUH? MIKAZE-CHAN?

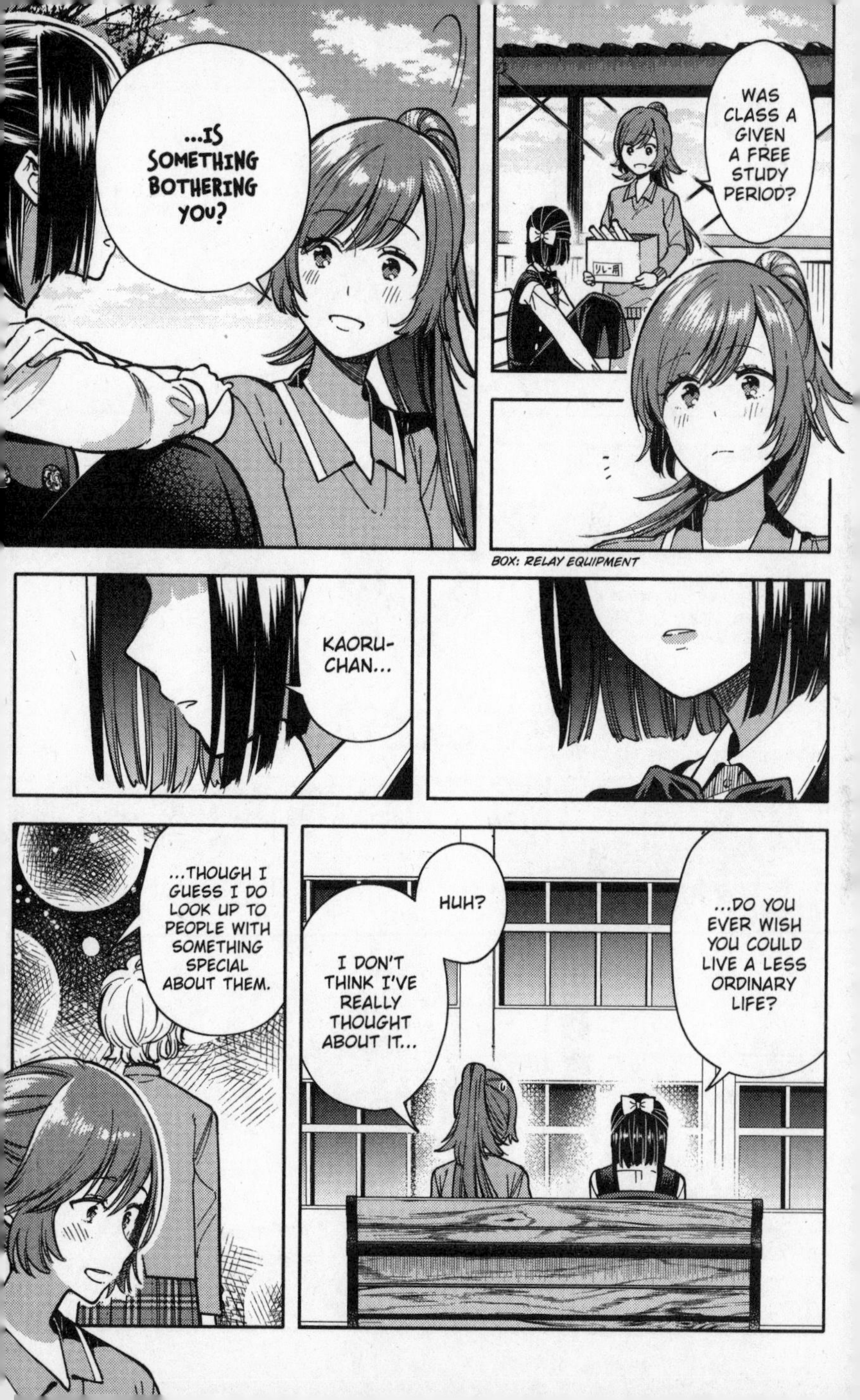
WAS CLASS A GIVEN A FREE STUDY PERIOD?
BOX: RELAY EQUIPMENT
...IS SOMETHING BOTHERING YOU?
KAORU-CHAN...
...DO YOU EVER WISH YOU COULD LIVE A LESS ORDINARY LIFE?
HUH?
I DON'T THINK I'VE REALLY THOUGHT ABOUT IT...
...THOUGH I GUESS I DO LOOK UP TO PEOPLE WITH SOMETHING SPECIAL ABOUT THEM.

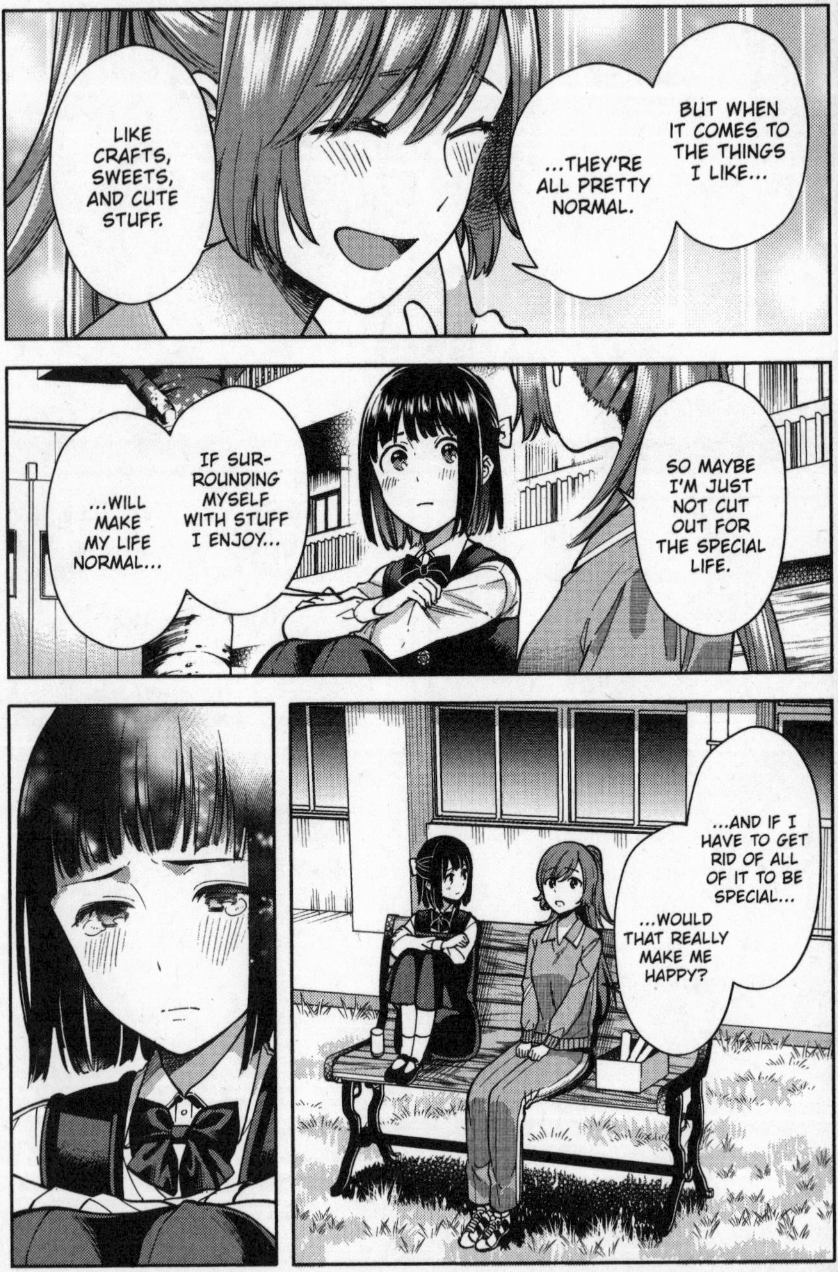
BUT WHEN IT COMES TO THE THINGS I LIKE...
...THEY'RE ALL PRETTY NORMAL.
LIKE CRAFTS, SWEETS, AND CUTE STUFF.
SO MAYBE I'M JUST NOT CUT OUT FOR THE SPECIAL LIFE.
IF SURROUNDING MYSELF WITH STUFF I ENJOY...
...WILL MAKE MY LIFE NORMAL...
...AND IF I HAVE TO GET RID OF ALL OF IT TO BE SPECIAL...
...WOULD THAT REALLY MAKE ME HAPPY?

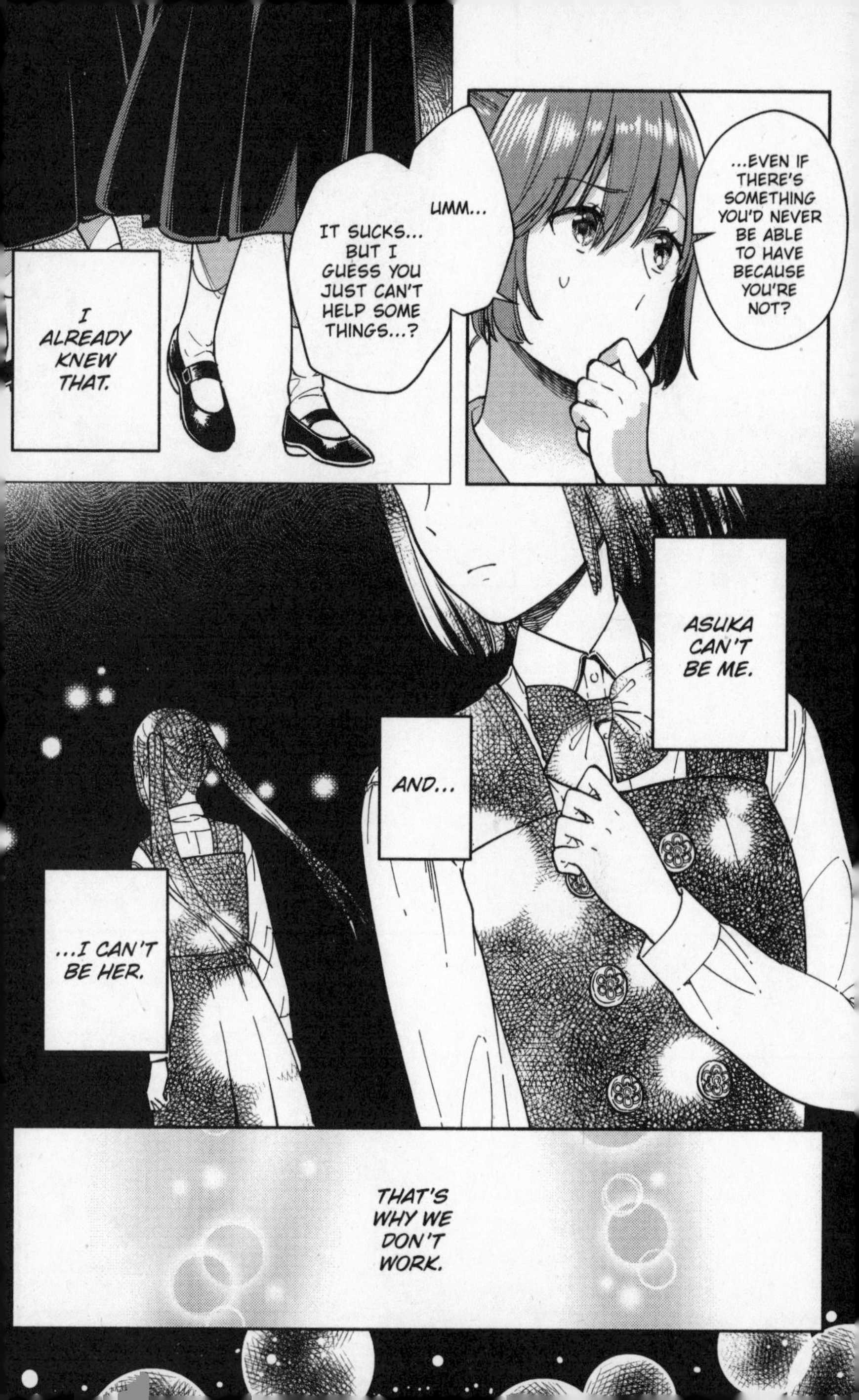
...EVEN IF THERE'S SOMETHING YOU'D NEVER BE ABLE TO HAVE BECAUSE YOU'RE NOT?
UMM...
IT SUCKS... BUT I GUESS YOU JUST CAN'T HELP SOME THINGS...?
I ALREADY KNEW THAT.
ASUKA CAN'T BE ME.
AND...
...I CAN'T BE HER.
THAT'S WHY WE DON'T WORK.

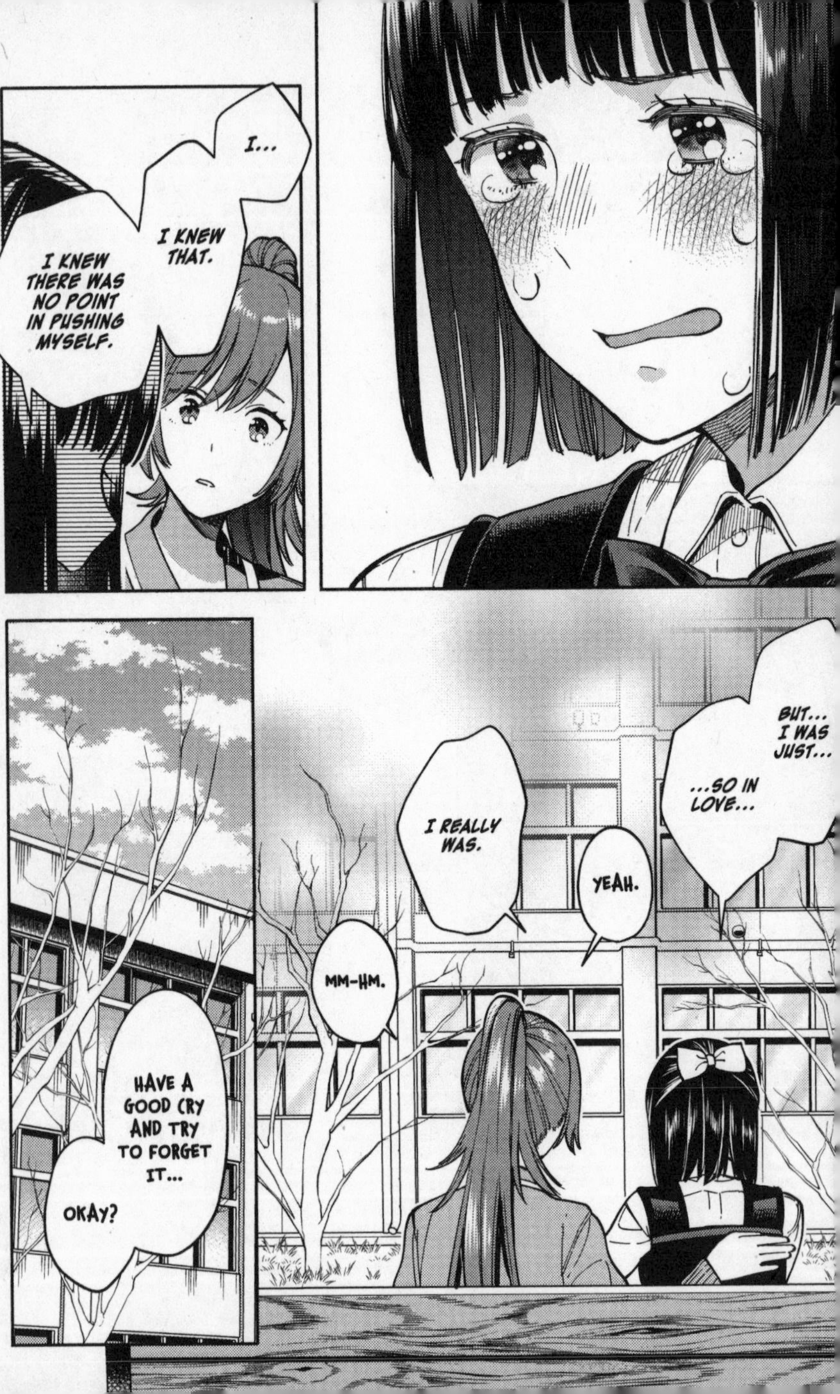
I...
I KNEW THAT.
I KNEW THERE WAS NO POINT IN PUSHING MYSELF.
BUT... I WAS JUST...
...SO IN LOVE...
I REALLY WAS.
YEAH.
MM-HM.
HAVE A GOOD CRY AND TRY TO FORGET IT...
OKAY?

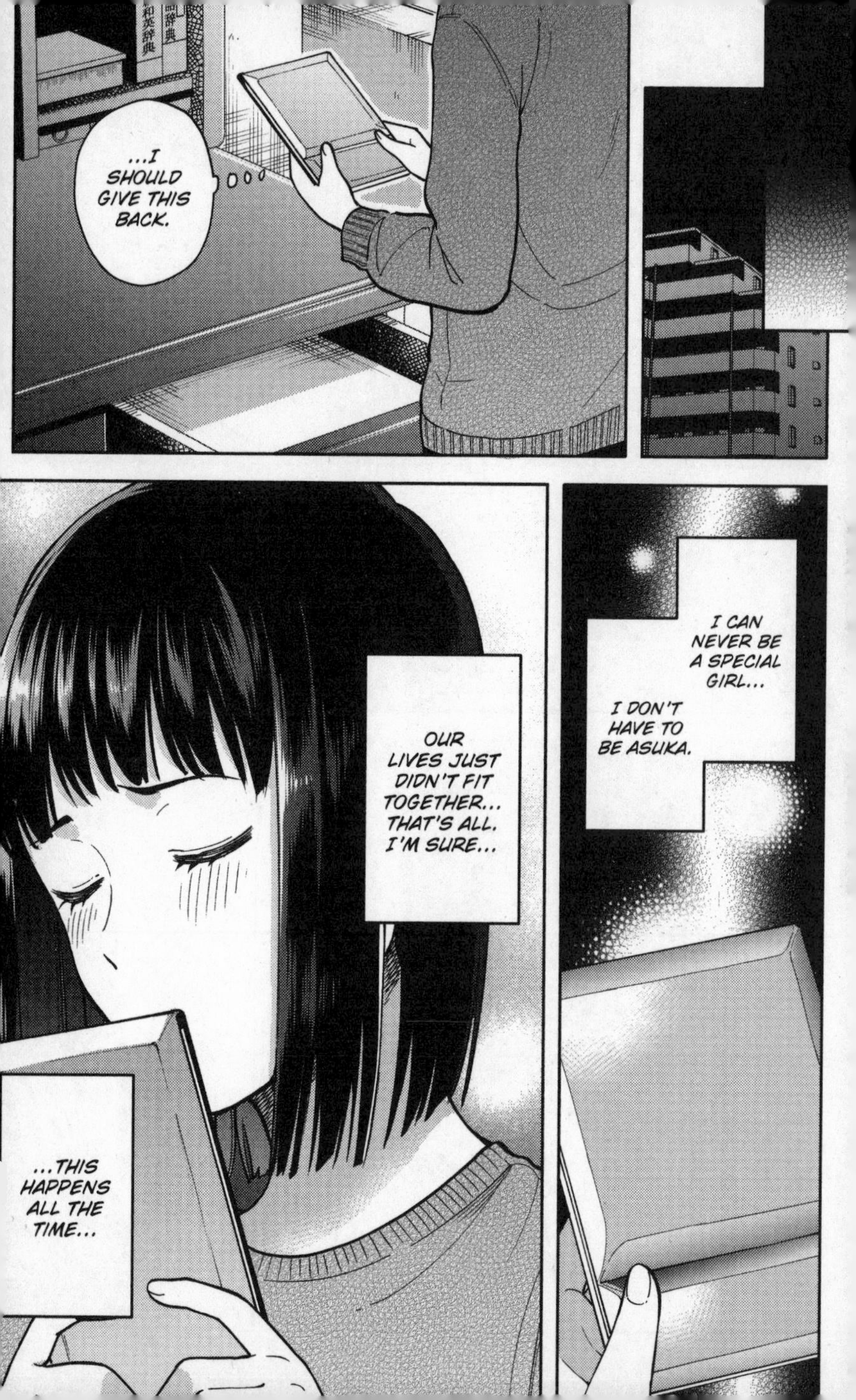

和英辞典
...I SHOULD GIVE THIS BACK.
I CAN NEVER BE A SPECIAL GIRL...
I DON'T HAVE TO BE ASUKA.
OUR LIVES JUST DIDN'T FIT TOGETHER... THAT'S ALL. I'M SURE...
...THIS HAPPENS ALL THE TIME...

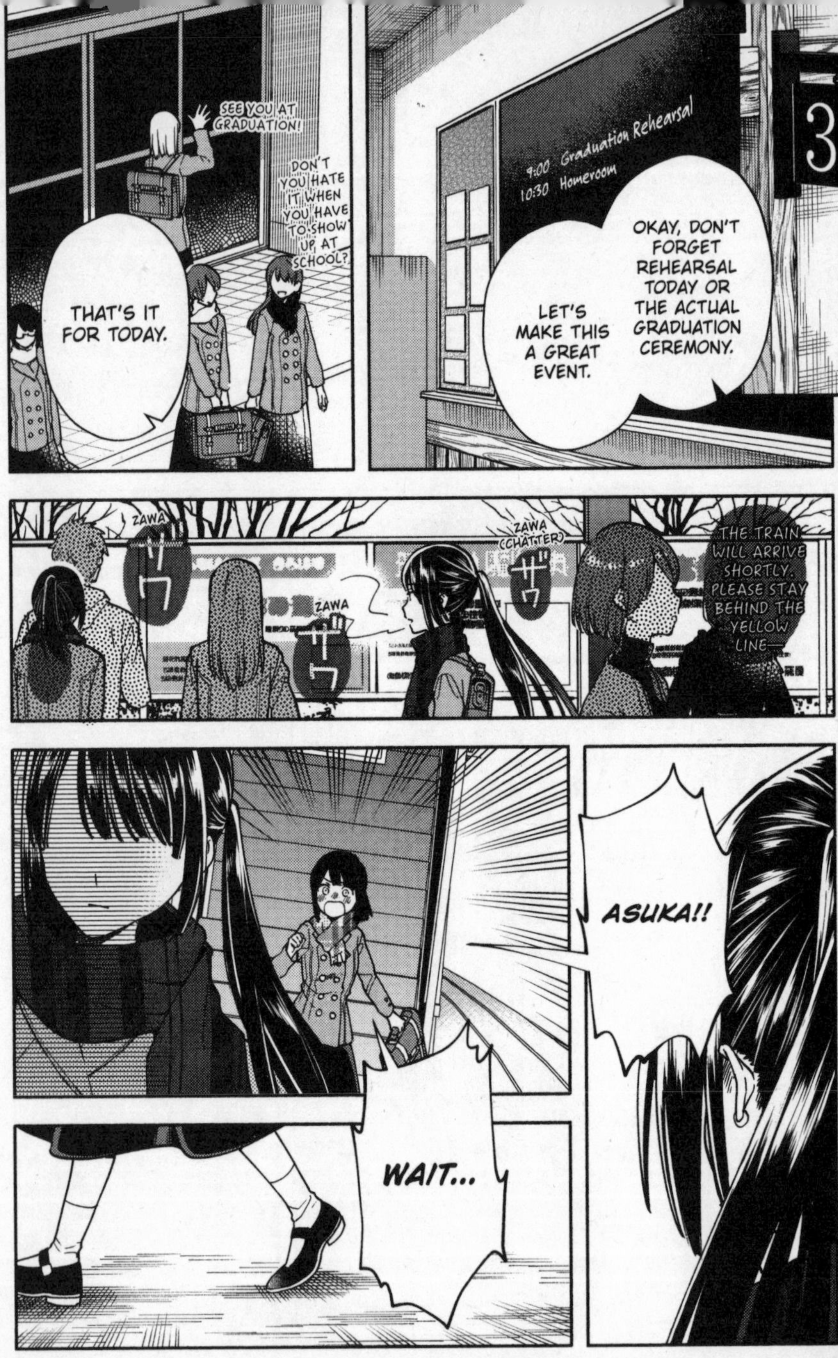
3
9:00 Graduation Rehearsal
10:30 Homeroom
OKAY, DON'T FORGET REHEARSAL TODAY OR THE ACTUAL GRADUATION CEREMONY.
LET'S MAKE THIS A GREAT EVENT.
SEE YOU AT GRADUATION!
DON'T YOU HATE IT WHEN YOU HAVE TO SHOW UP AT SCHOOL?
THAT'S IT FOR TODAY.
THE TRAIN WILL ARRIVE SHORTLY. PLEASE STAY BEHIND THE YELLOW LINE—
ZAWA (CHATTER)
ZAWA
ZAWA
ASUKA!!
WAIT...

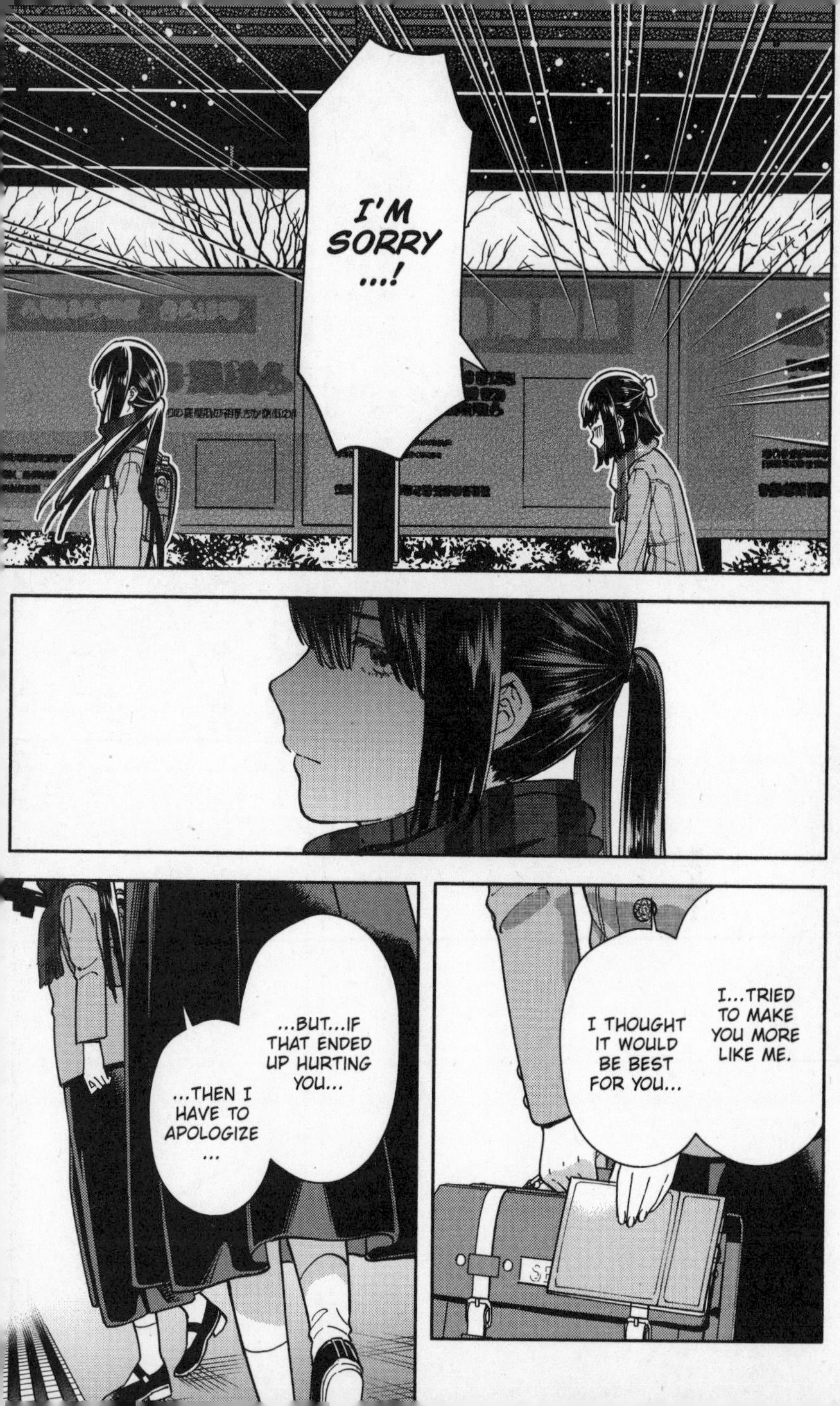
I'M SORRY ...!
I...TRIED TO MAKE YOU MORE LIKE ME.
I THOUGHT IT WOULD BE BEST FOR YOU...
...BUT...IF THAT ENDED UP HURTING YOU...
...THEN I HAVE TO APOLOGIZE ...

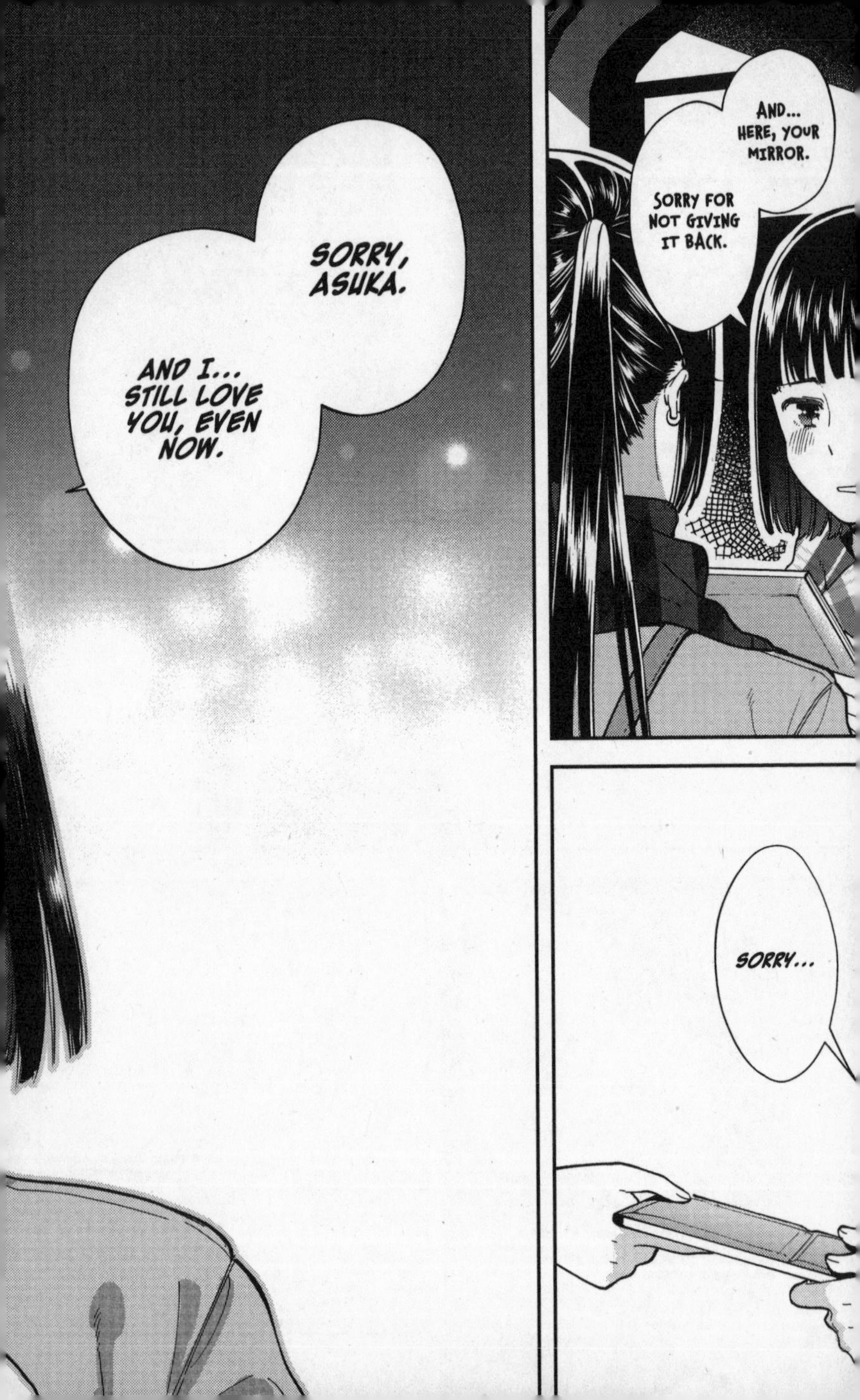
AND... HERE, YOUR MIRROR.
SORRY FOR NOT GIVING IT BACK.
SORRY...
SORRY, ASUKA.
AND I... STILL LOVE YOU, EVEN NOW.

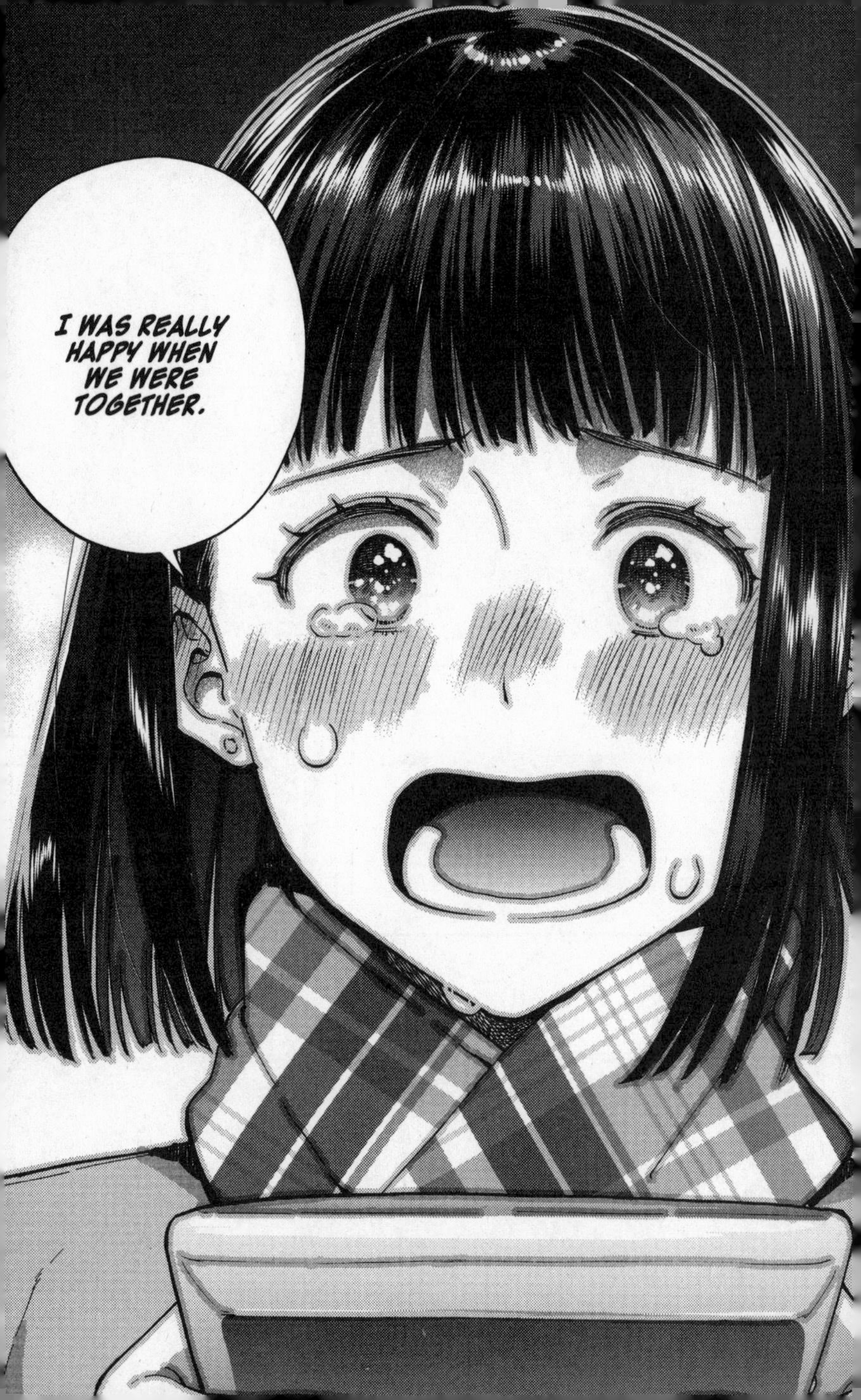
I WAS REALLY HAPPY WHEN WE WERE TOGETHER.

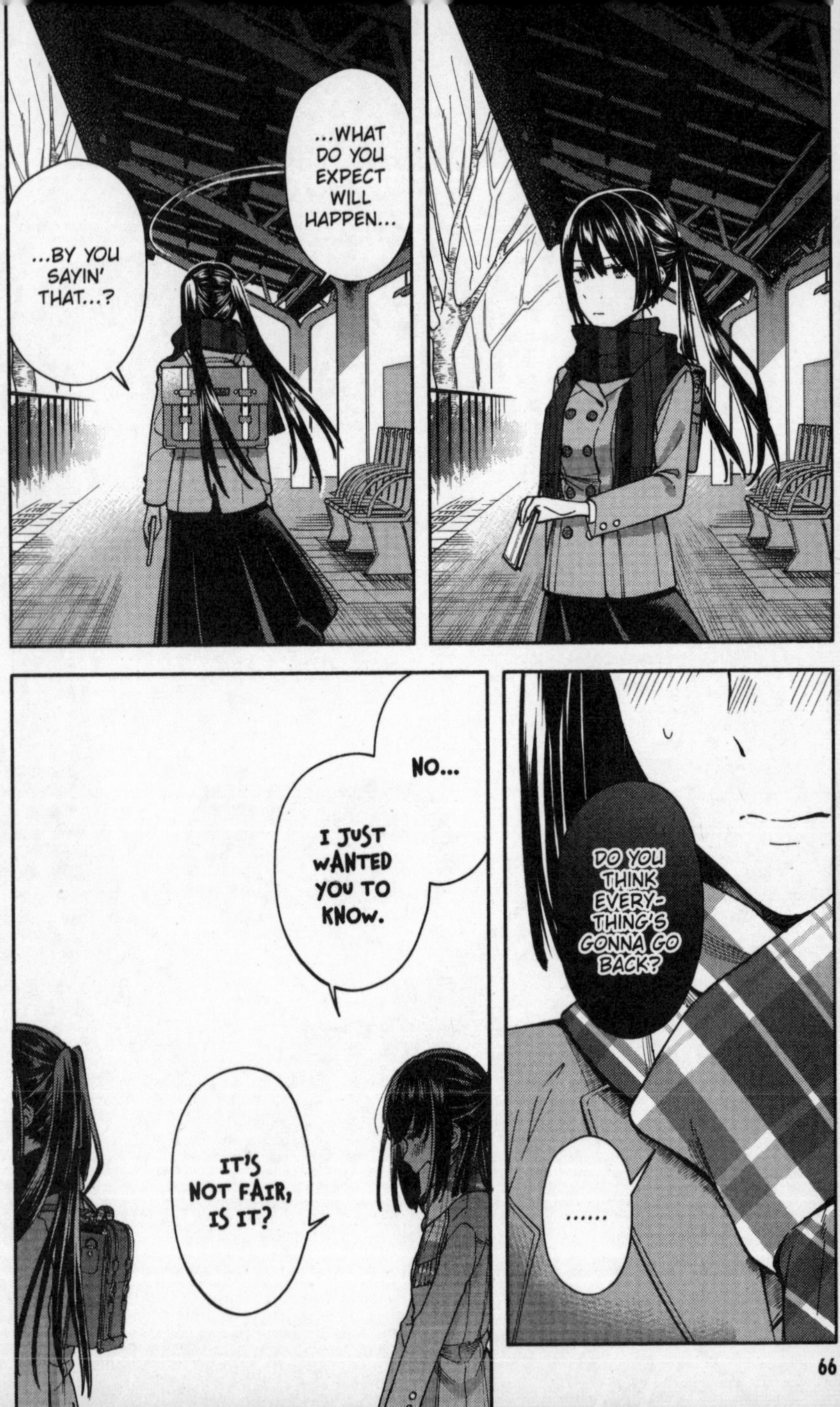
...WHAT DO YOU EXPECT WILL HAPPEN...
...BY YOU SAYIN' THAT...?
DO YOU THINK EVERY-THING'S GONNA GO BACK?
......
NO...
I JUST WANTED YOU TO KNOW.
IT'S NOT FAIR, IS IT?

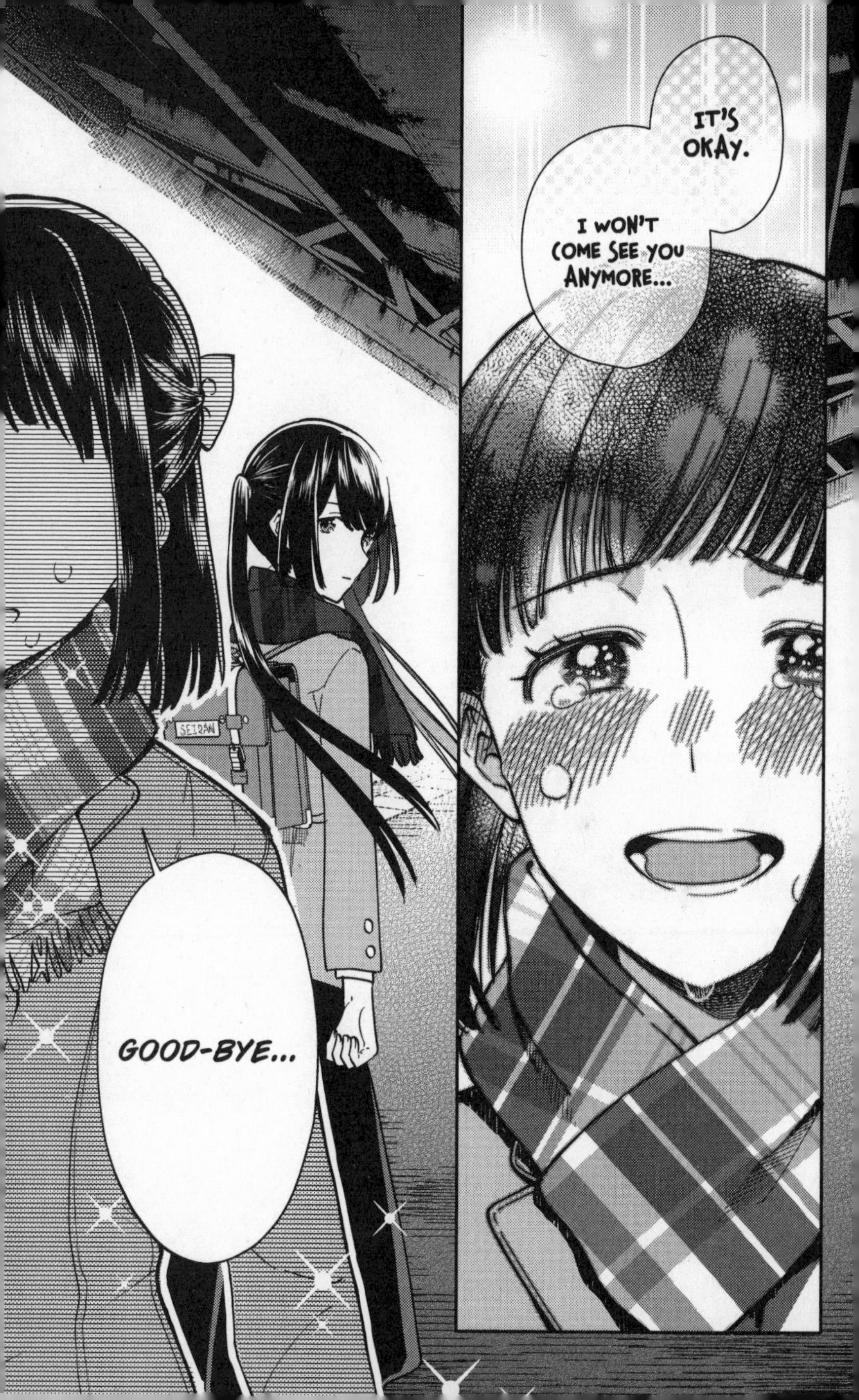
IT'S OKAY.
I WON'T COME SEE YOU ANYMORE...
GOOD-BYE...
SEIRAN

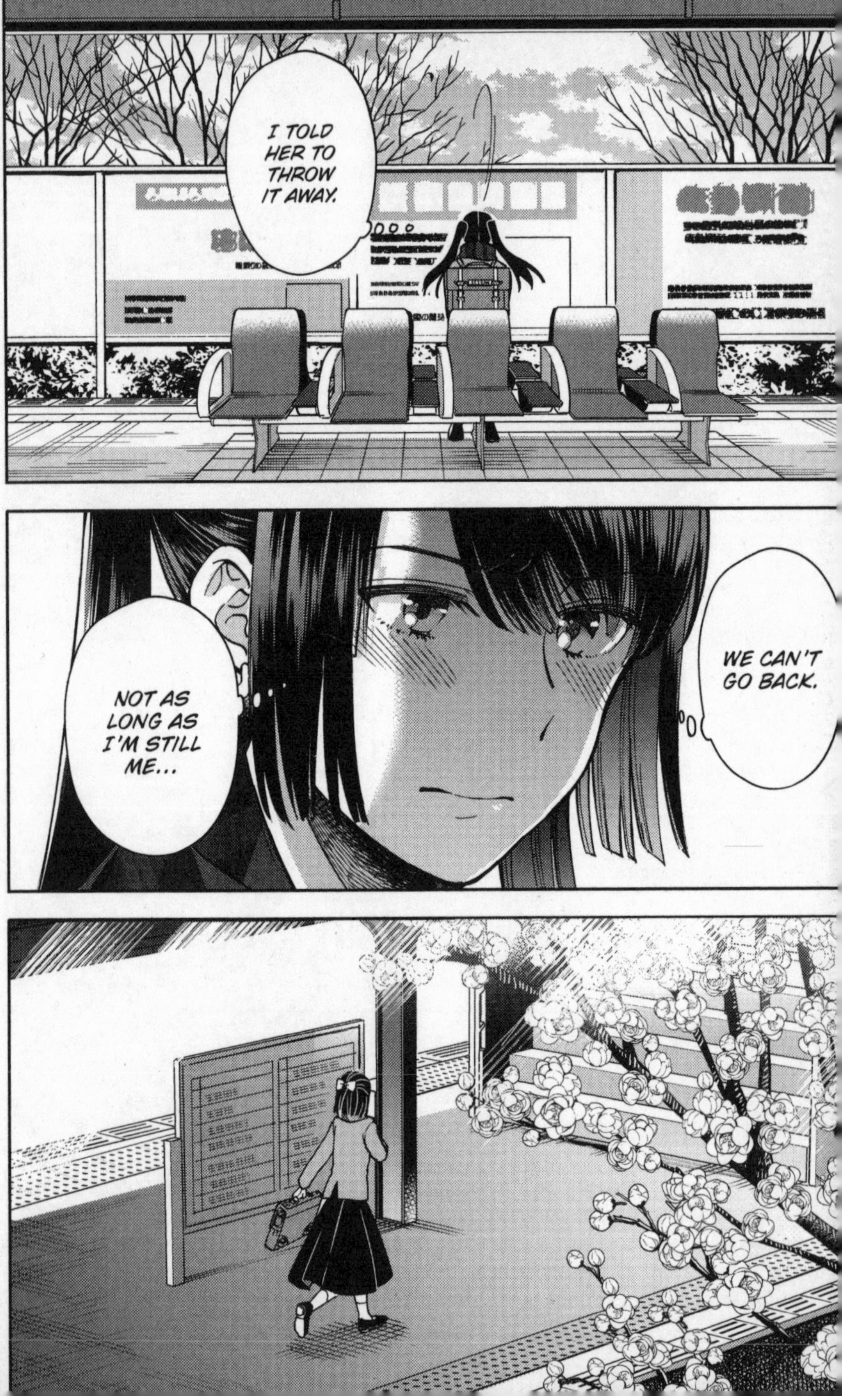
I TOLD HER TO THROW IT AWAY.
WE CAN'T GO BACK.
NOT AS LONG AS I'M STILL ME...

First Day of Finals

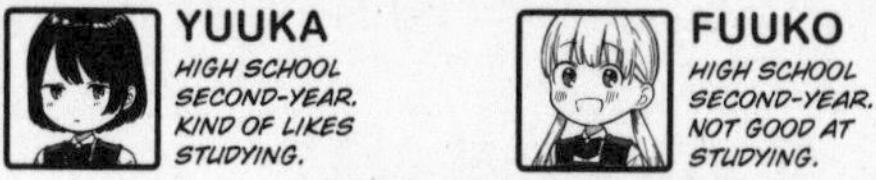
YUUKA
HIGH SCHOOL SECOND-YEAR. KIND OF LIKES STUDYING.
FUUKO
HIGH SCHOOL SECOND-YEAR. NOT GOOD AT STUDYING.

KISS THEATER: WHAT'S BEHIND THE STORY!? ✷ PEOPLE OTHER THAN THE MAIN CHARACTERS HAVE STORIES TOO. HERE,

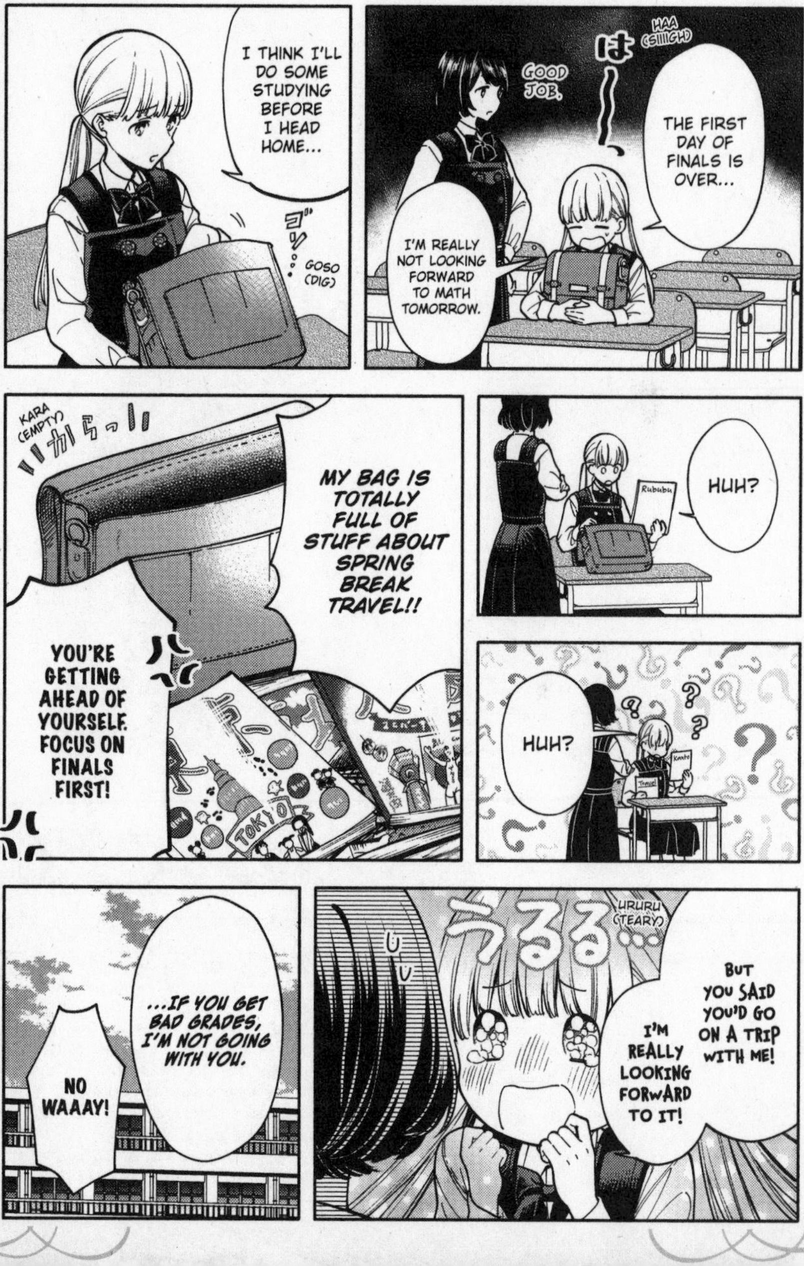
はー
HAA (SIIIIGH)
THE FIRST DAY OF FINALS IS OVER...
GOOD JOB.
I'M REALLY NOT LOOKING FORWARD TO MATH TOMORROW.
I THINK I'LL DO SOME STUDYING BEFORE I HEAD HOME...
ゴソ
GOSO (DIG)
HUH?
Rububu
HUH?
カらっ
KARA (EMPTY)
MY BAG IS TOTALLY FULL OF STUFF ABOUT SPRING BREAK TRAVEL!!
YOU'RE GETTING AHEAD OF YOURSELF. FOCUS ON FINALS FIRST!
TOKYO
うるる
URURU (TEARY)
じ
BUT YOU SAID YOU'D GO ON A TRIP WITH ME!
I'M REALLY LOOKING FORWARD TO IT!
...IF YOU GET BAD GRADES, I'M NOT GOING WITH YOU.
NO WAAAY!

Mikaze Hagimoto

Mikaze Hagimoto

Second-year student at Seiran Academy High School. In the craft club. She doesn't have any notable skills, and she leaves a somewhat ordinary first impression, but she's actually pretty strong-willed once you get to know her. She started cosplaying about a year ago because of a friend. She was making costumes of her favorite manga characters and doing things here and there, but after she met Asuka, she started getting into it much more passionately.

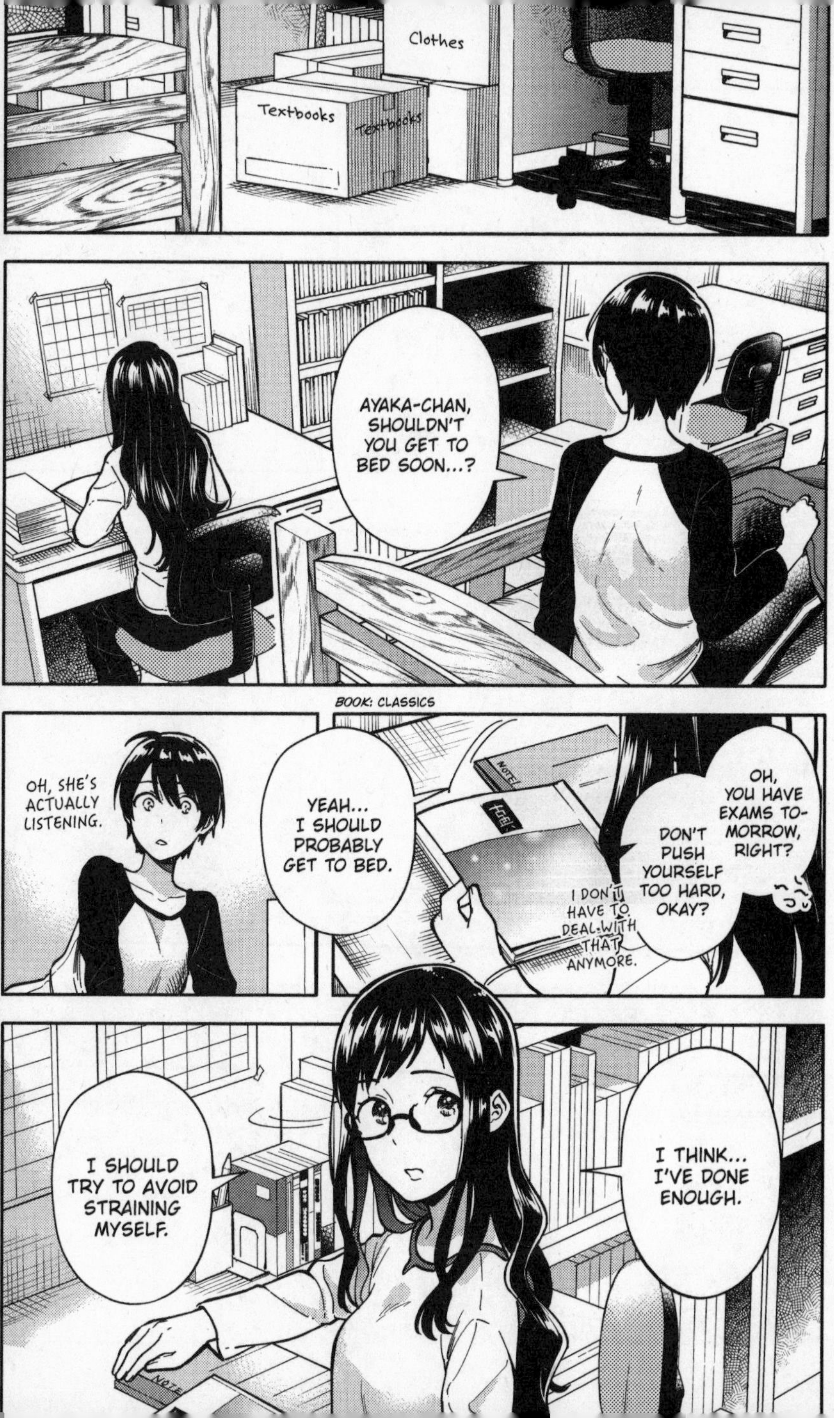
Clothes
Textbooks
Textbooks
AYAKA-CHAN, SHOULDN'T YOU GET TO BED SOON...?
BOOK: CLASSICS
OH, YOU HAVE EXAMS TO-MORROW, RIGHT?
DON'T PUSH YOURSELF TOO HARD, OKAY?
I DON'T HAVE TO DEAL WITH THAT ANYMORE.
YEAH... I SHOULD PROBABLY GET TO BED.
OH, SHE'S ACTUALLY LISTENING.
I THINK... I'VE DONE ENOUGH.
I SHOULD TRY TO AVOID STRAINING MYSELF.

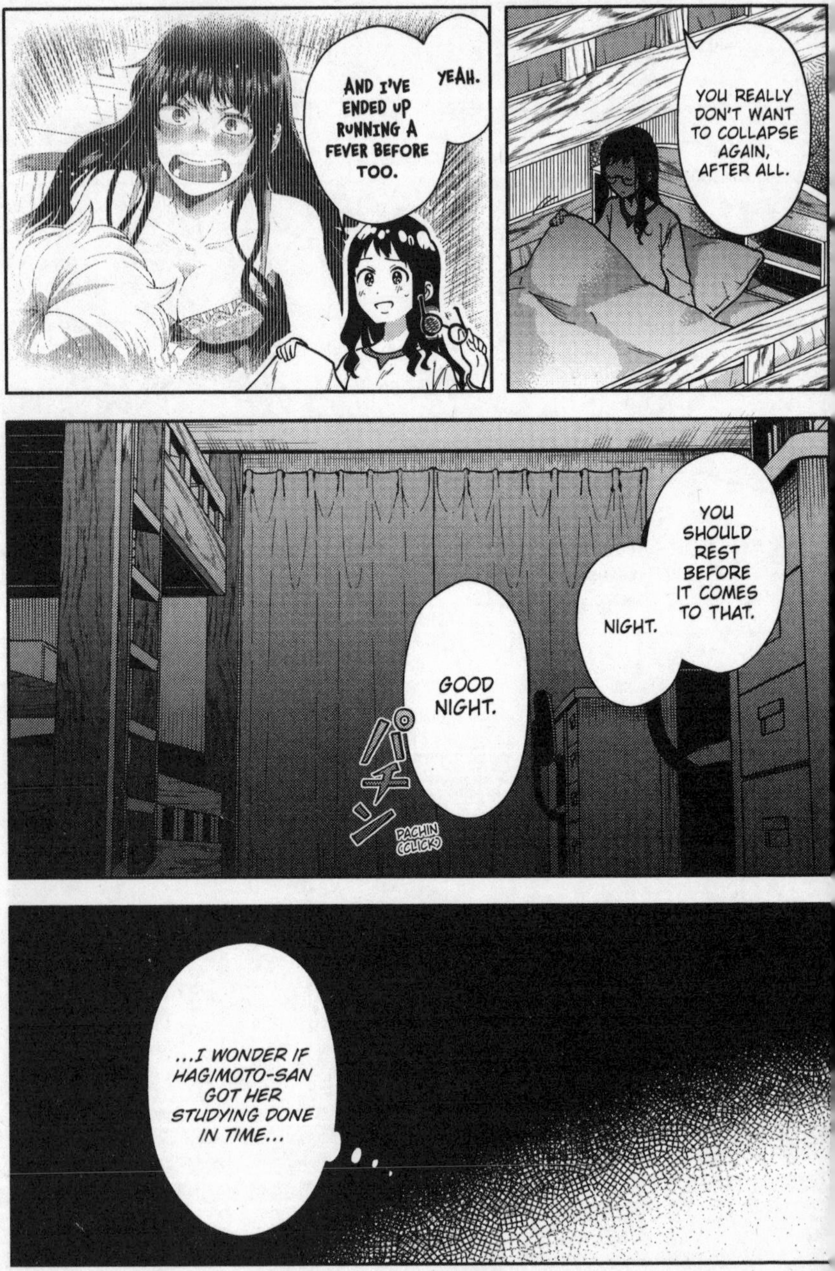
YOU REALLY DON'T WANT TO COLLAPSE AGAIN, AFTER ALL.
YEAH.
AND I'VE ENDED UP RUNNING A FEVER BEFORE TOO.
YOU SHOULD REST BEFORE IT COMES TO THAT.
NIGHT.
GOOD NIGHT.
パチン
PACHIN (CLICK)
...I WONDER IF HAGIMOTO-SAN GOT HER STUDYING DONE IN TIME...

Chapter 43: *A Fanfare for Her*

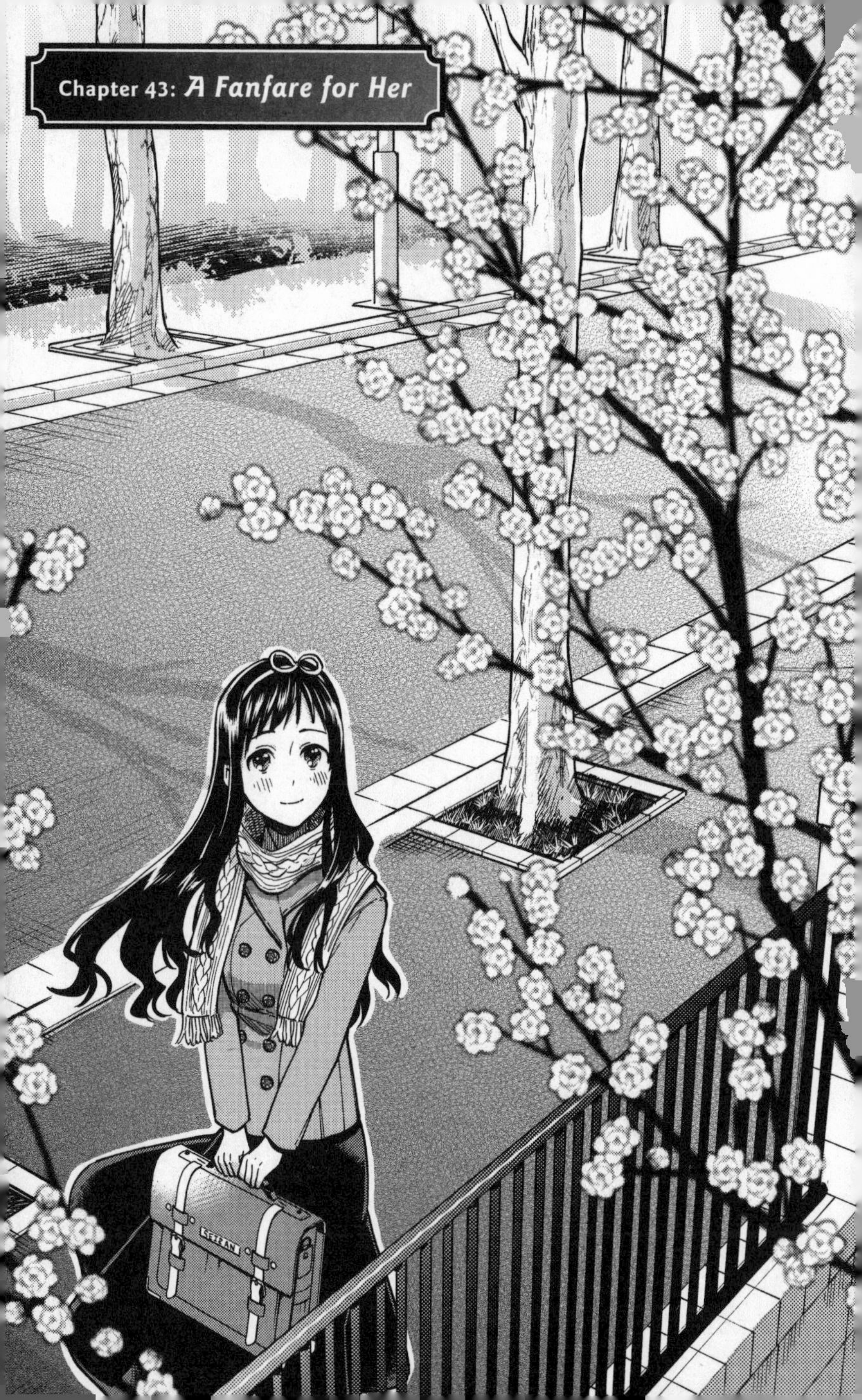

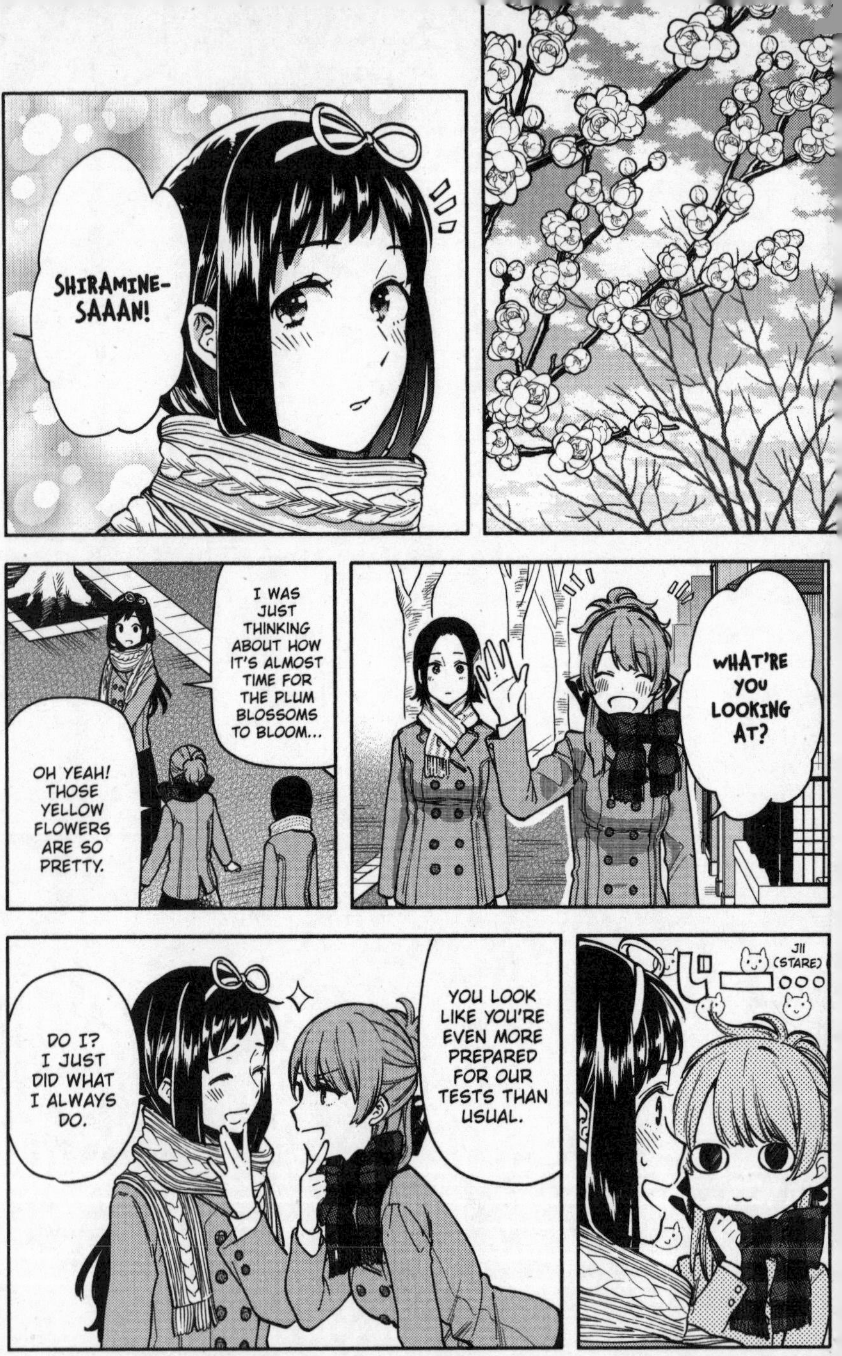
SHIRAMINE-SAAAN!
WHAT'RE YOU LOOKING AT?
I WAS JUST THINKING ABOUT HOW IT'S ALMOST TIME FOR THE PLUM BLOSSOMS TO BLOOM...
OH YEAH! THOSE YELLOW FLOWERS ARE SO PRETTY.
JII (STARE)
YOU LOOK LIKE YOU'RE EVEN MORE PREPARED FOR OUR TESTS THAN USUAL.
DO I? I JUST DID WHAT I ALWAYS DO.

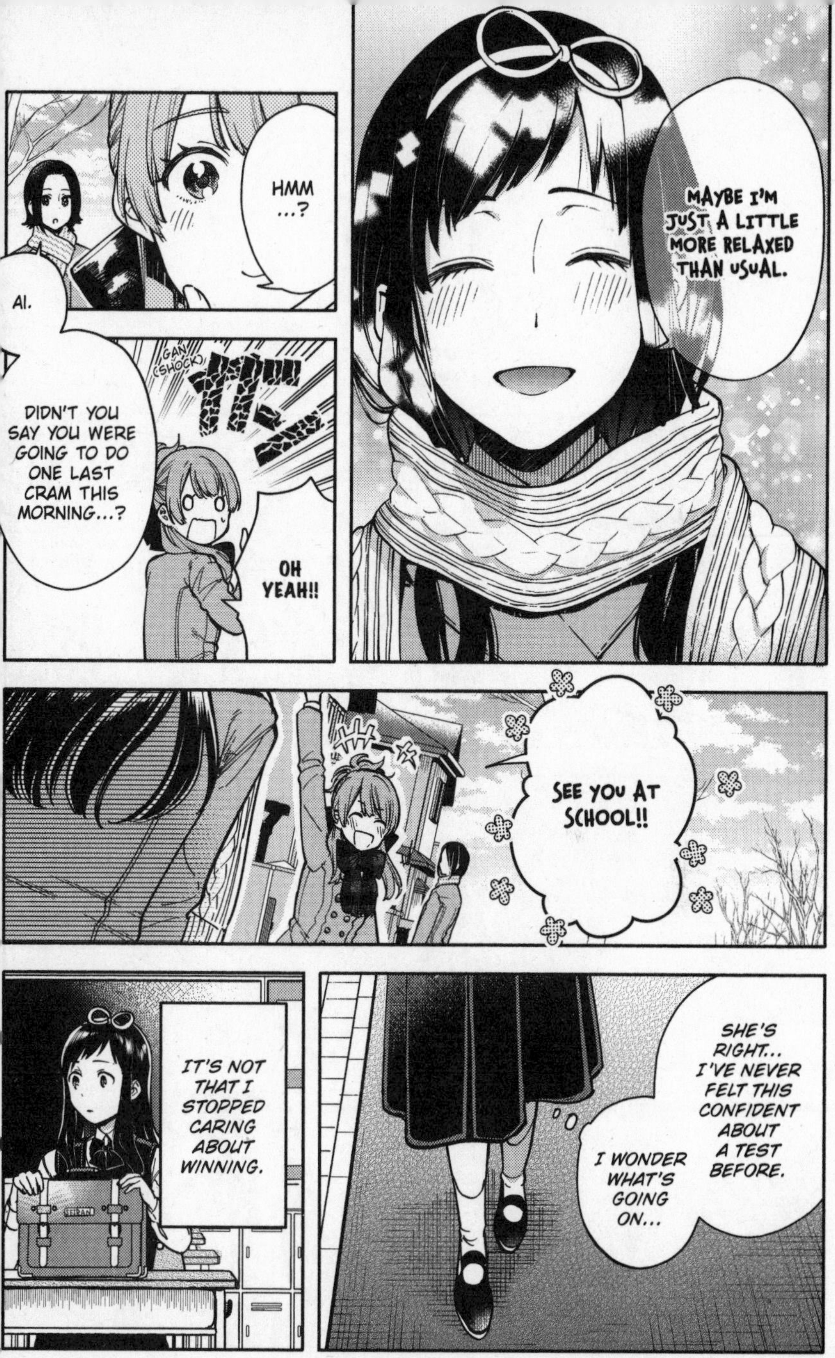
MAYBE I'M JUST A LITTLE MORE RELAXED THAN USUAL.
HMM ...?
AI.
DIDN'T YOU SAY YOU WERE GOING TO DO ONE LAST CRAM THIS MORNING...?
GAN (SHOCK)
OH YEAH!!
SEE YOU AT SCHOOL!!
SHE'S RIGHT... I'VE NEVER FELT THIS CONFIDENT ABOUT A TEST BEFORE.
I WONDER WHAT'S GOING ON...
IT'S NOT THAT I STOPPED CARING ABOUT WINNING.

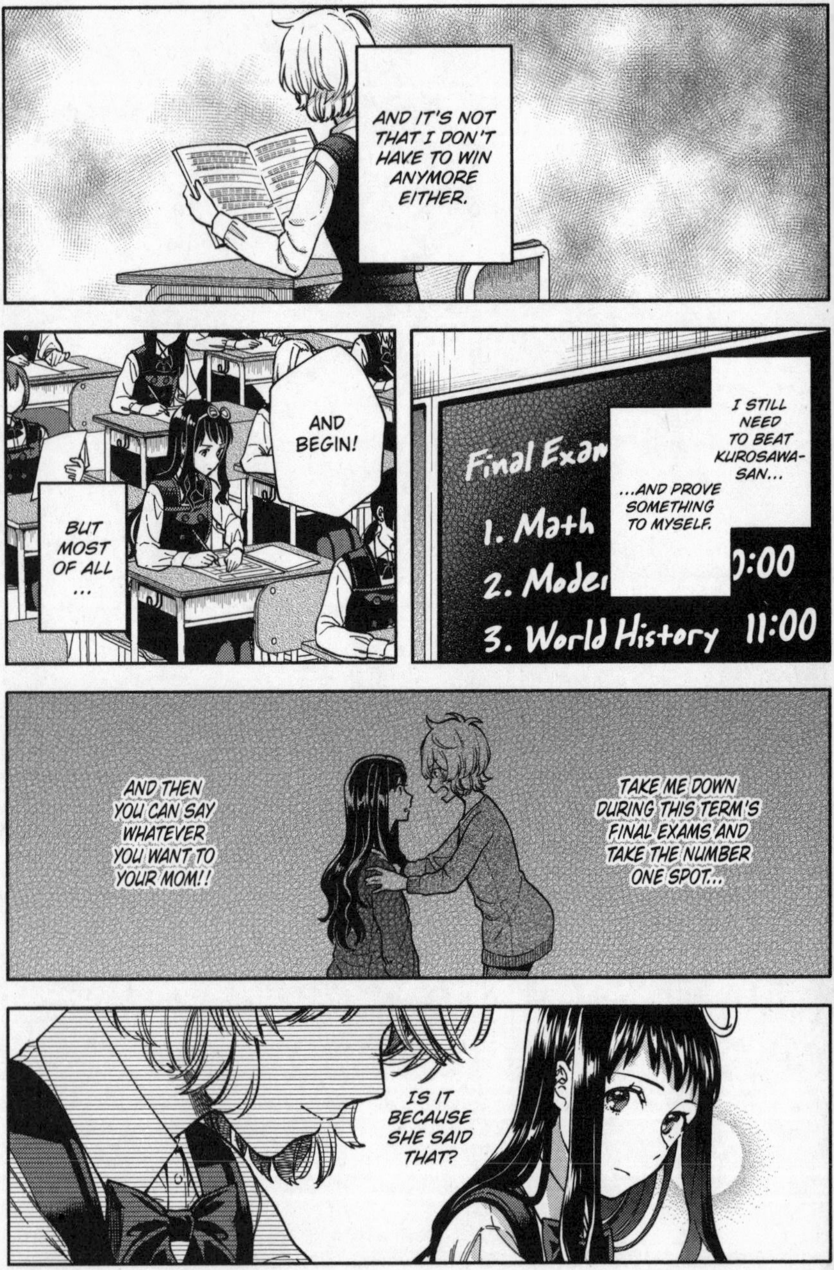
AND IT'S NOT THAT I DON'T HAVE TO WIN ANYMORE EITHER.
I STILL NEED TO BEAT KUROSAWA-SAN...
...AND PROVE SOMETHING TO MYSELF.
1. Math
3. World History 11:00
AND BEGIN!
BUT MOST OF ALL...
TAKE ME DOWN DURING THIS TERM'S FINAL EXAMS AND TAKE THE NUMBER ONE SPOT...
AND THEN YOU CAN SAY WHATEVER YOU WANT TO YOUR MOM!!
IS IT BECAUSE SHE SAID THAT?

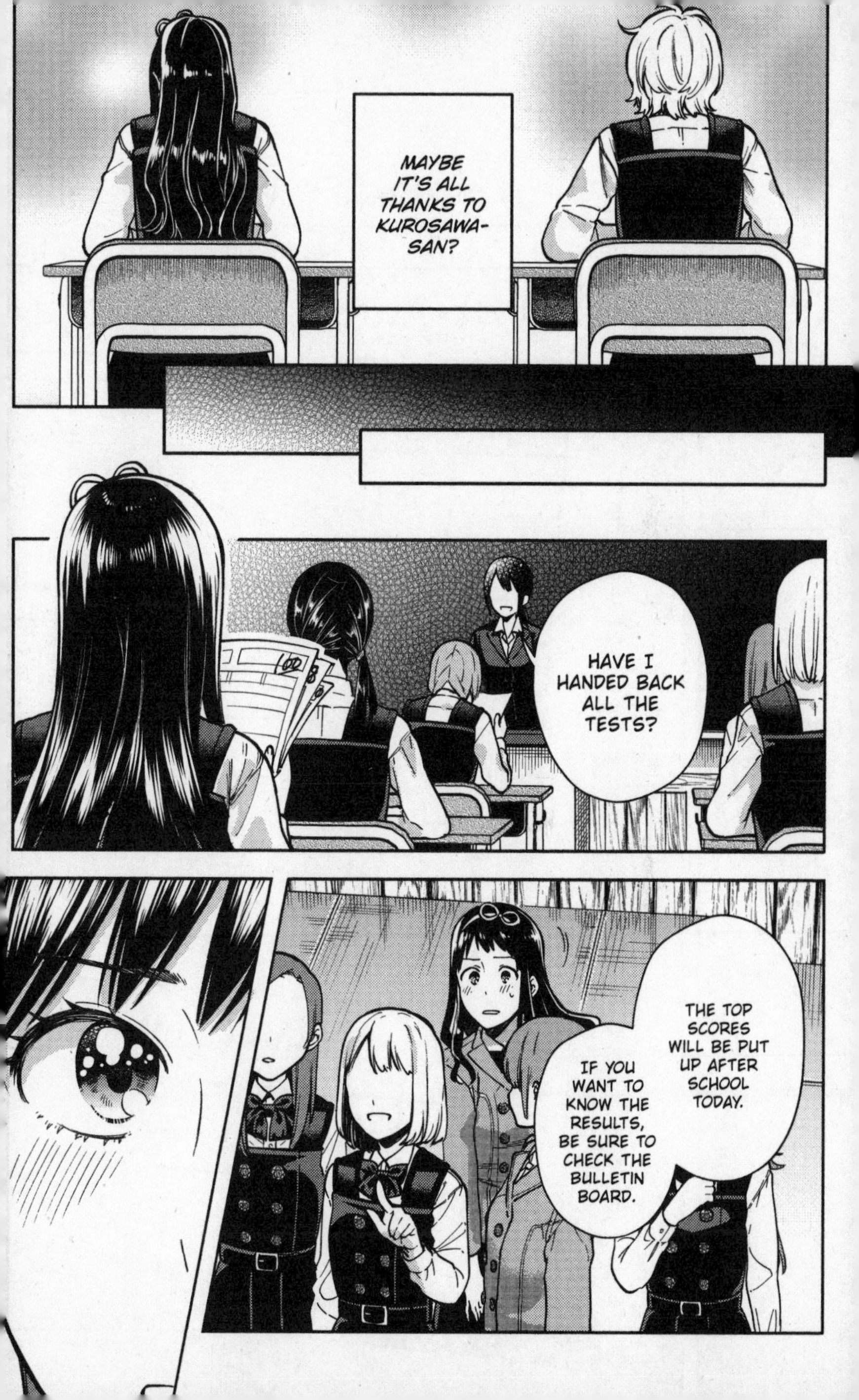
MAYBE IT'S ALL THANKS TO KUROSAWA-SAN?
HAVE I HANDED BACK ALL THE TESTS?
THE TOP SCORES WILL BE PUT UP AFTER SCHOOL TODAY.
IF YOU WANT TO KNOW THE RESULTS, BE SURE TO CHECK THE BULLETIN BOARD.

Year-End Final Exam Scores

	Name	Sco
1	Ayaka Shiramine	11
2	Yurine Kurosawa	11
3	Misato Fujiwara	11
4	Mifuyu Ohki	1
5	Kurumi Hisajima	1
6	Nagisa Tatsumi	
7	Akane Miyajima	
8	Suzuna Iba	
9	Ayano Uchibori	
10	Hikari Torayama	

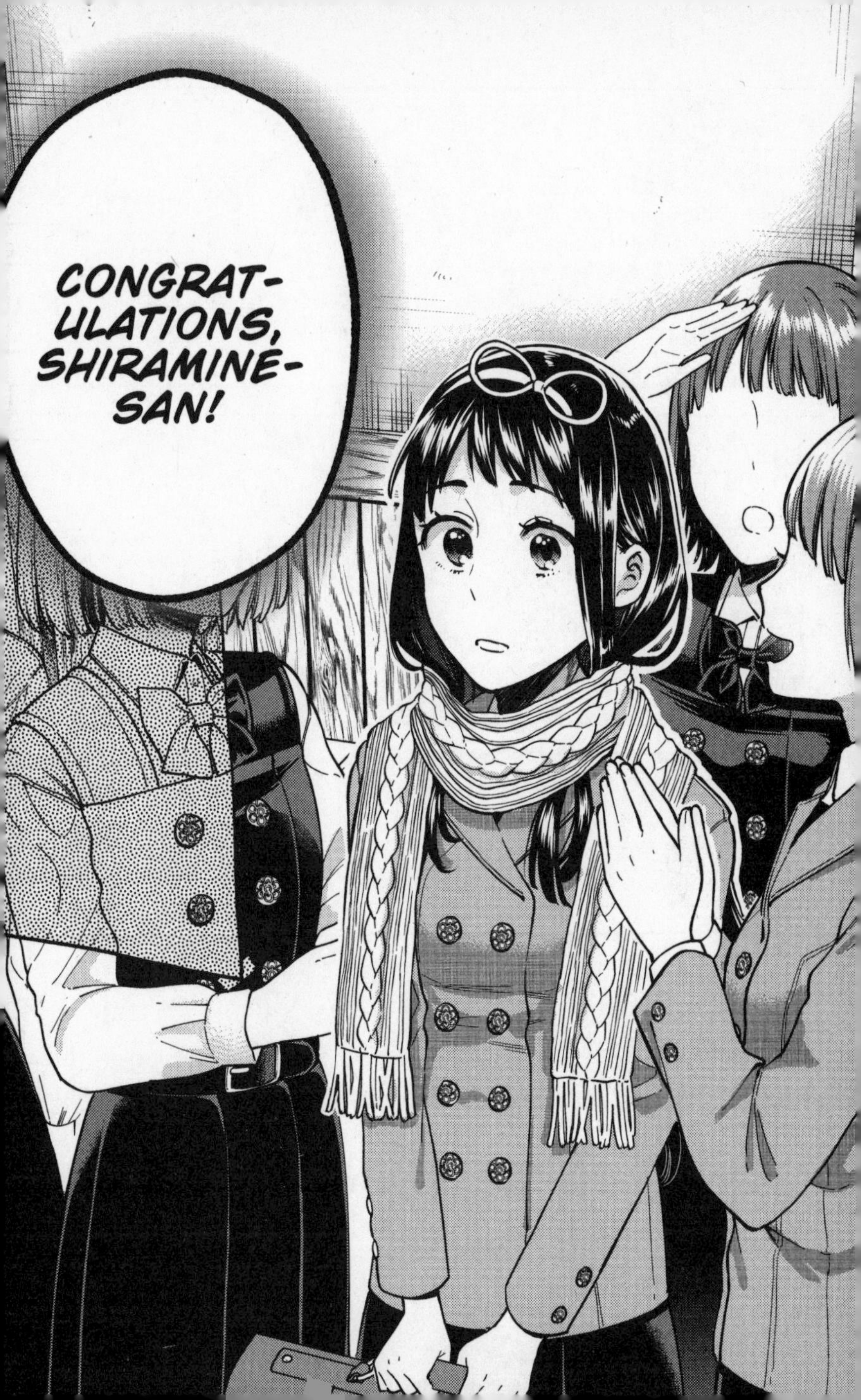
CONGRAT-ULATIONS, SHIRAMINE-SAN!

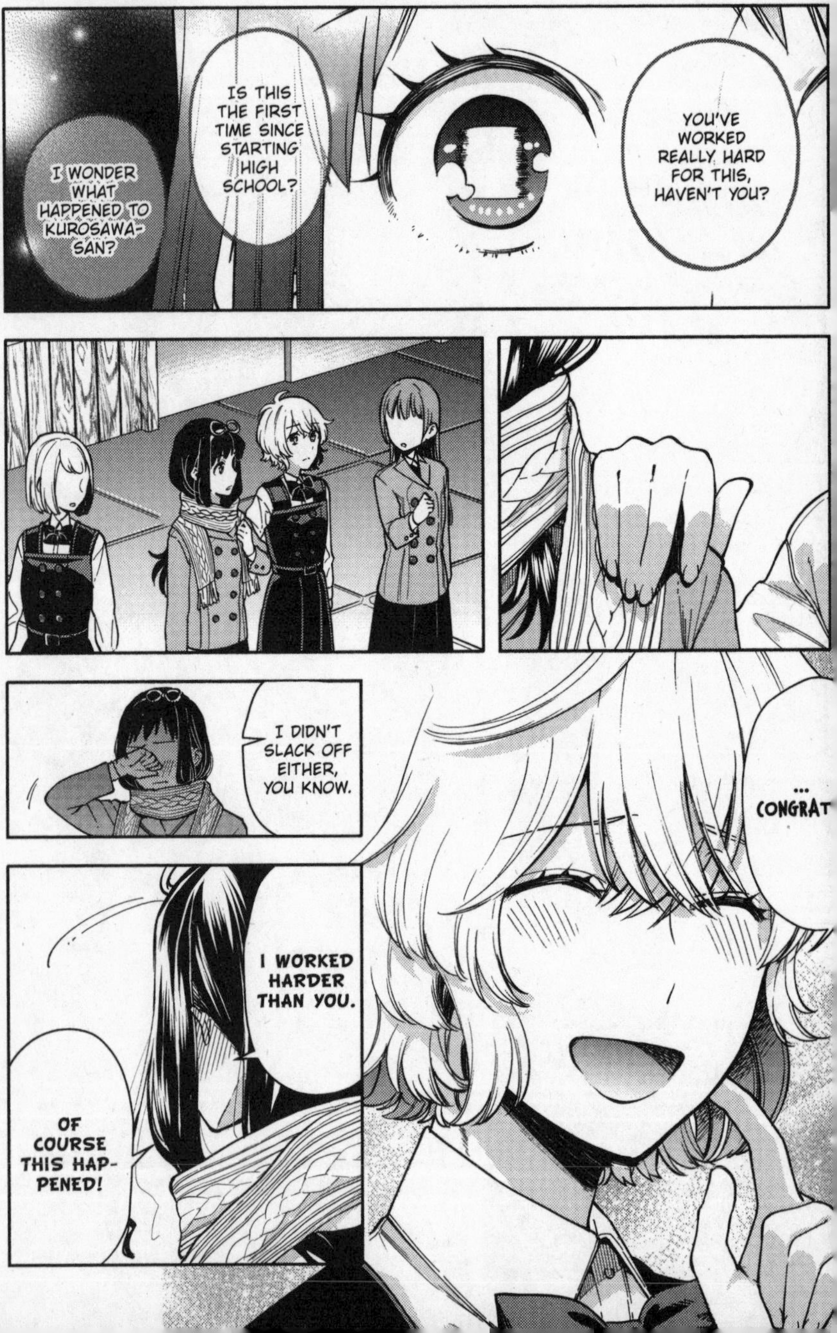
YOU'VE WORKED REALLY HARD FOR THIS, HAVEN'T YOU?
IS THIS THE FIRST TIME SINCE STARTING HIGH SCHOOL?
I WONDER WHAT HAPPENED TO KUROSAWA-SAN?
... CONGRAT
I DIDN'T SLACK OFF EITHER, YOU KNOW.
I WORKED HARDER THAN YOU.
OF COURSE THIS HAP-PENED!

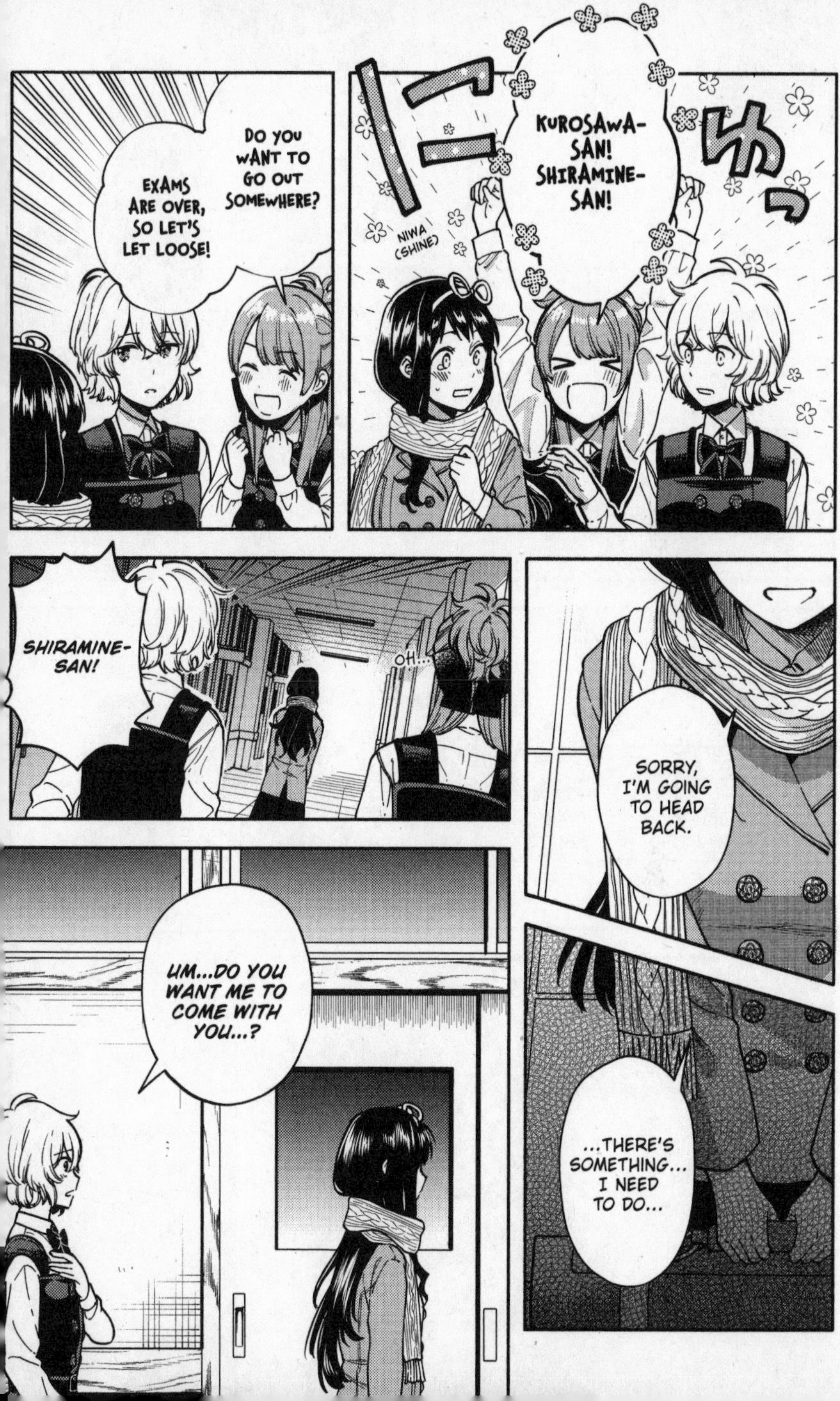
にゅっ
KUROSAWA-SAN! SHIRAMINE-SAN!
NIWA (SHINE)
DO YOU WANT TO GO OUT SOMEWHERE?
EXAMS ARE OVER, SO LET'S LET LOOSE!
SORRY, I'M GOING TO HEAD BACK.
...THERE'S SOMETHING... I NEED TO DO...
SHIRAMINE-SAN!
OH...
UM...DO YOU WANT ME TO COME WITH YOU...?
...

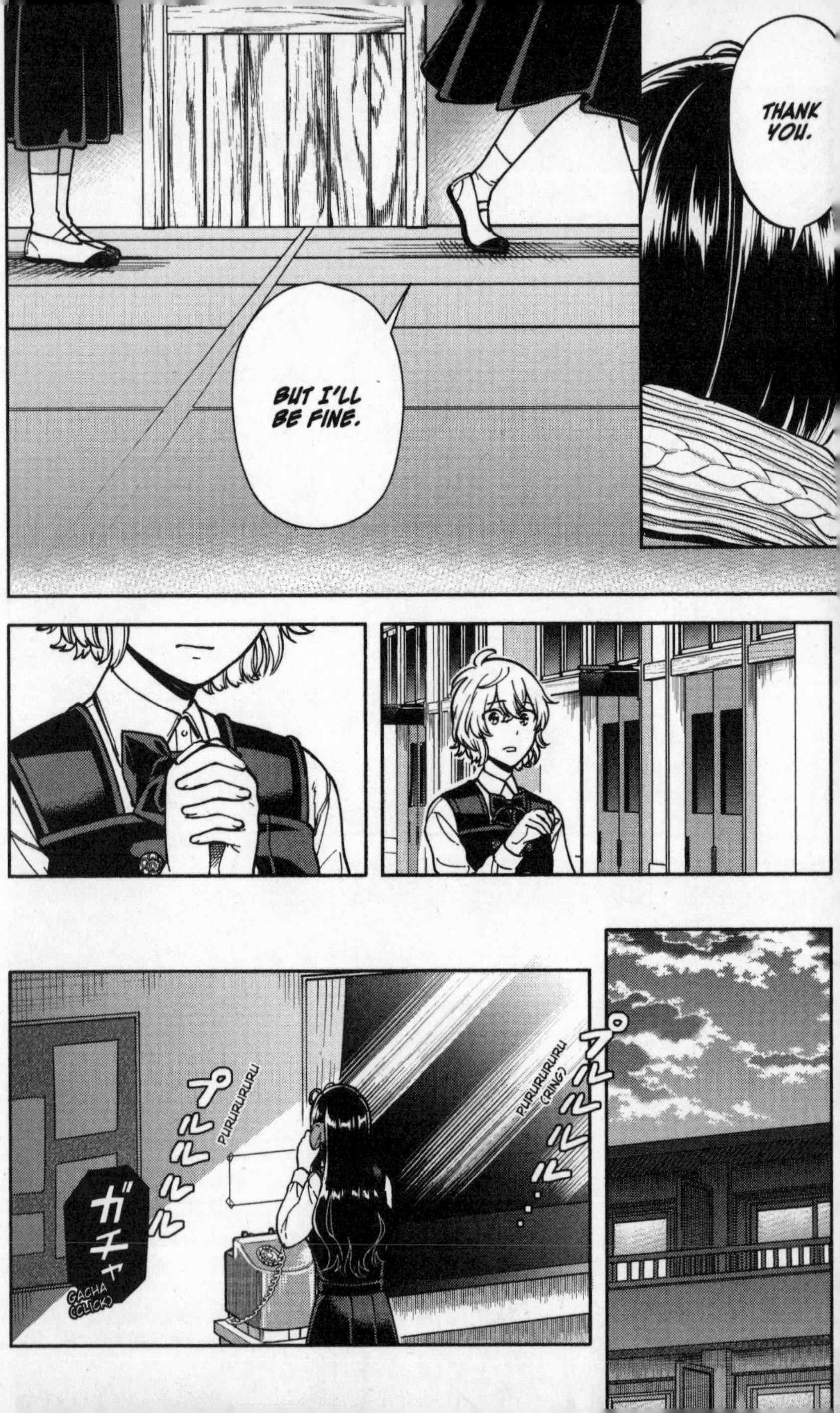
THANK YOU.
BUT I'LL BE FINE.
プルルル…
PURURURU (RING)
プルルル
PURURURU
ガチャ
GACHA (CLICK)

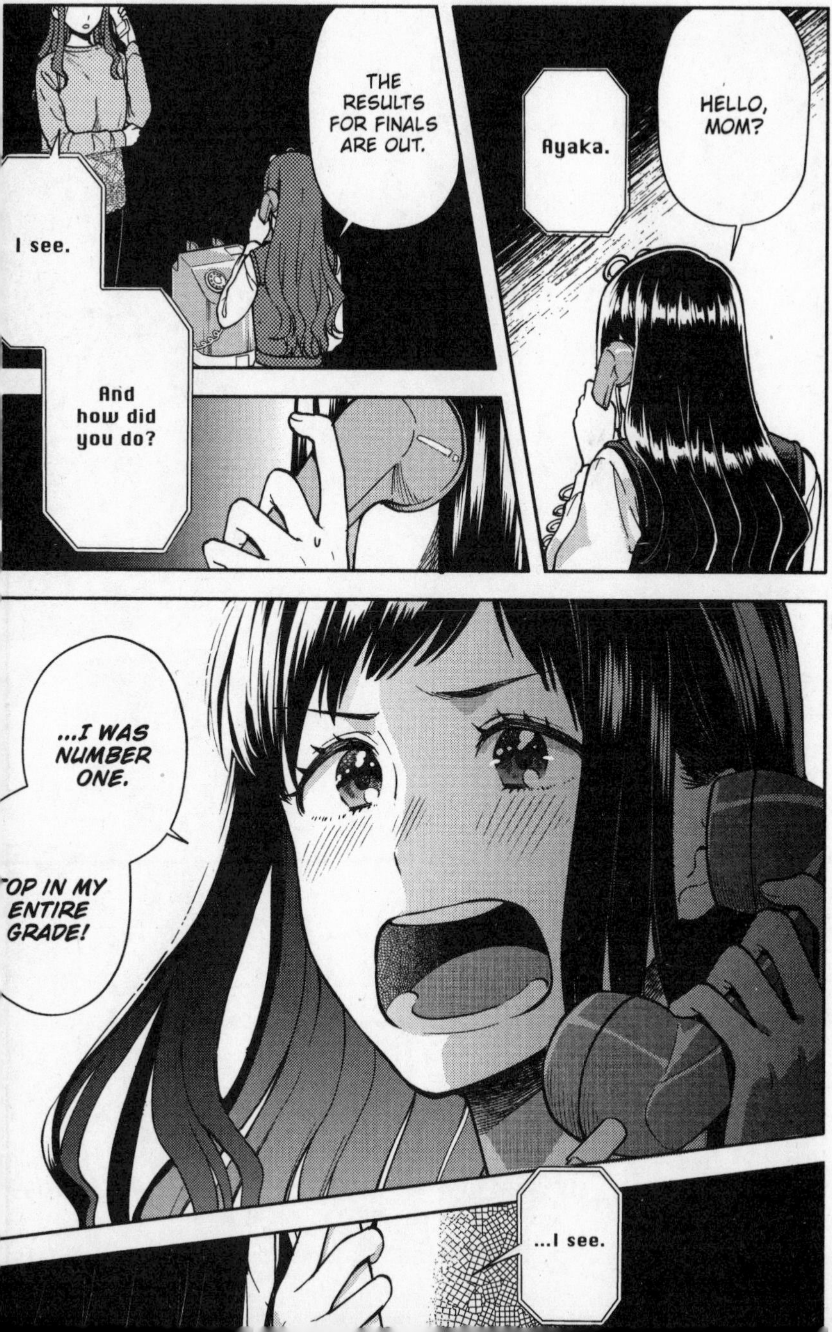
HELLO, MOM?
Ayaka.
THE RESULTS FOR FINALS ARE OUT.
I see.
And how did you do?
...I WAS NUMBER ONE.
OP IN MY ENTIRE GRADE!
...I see.

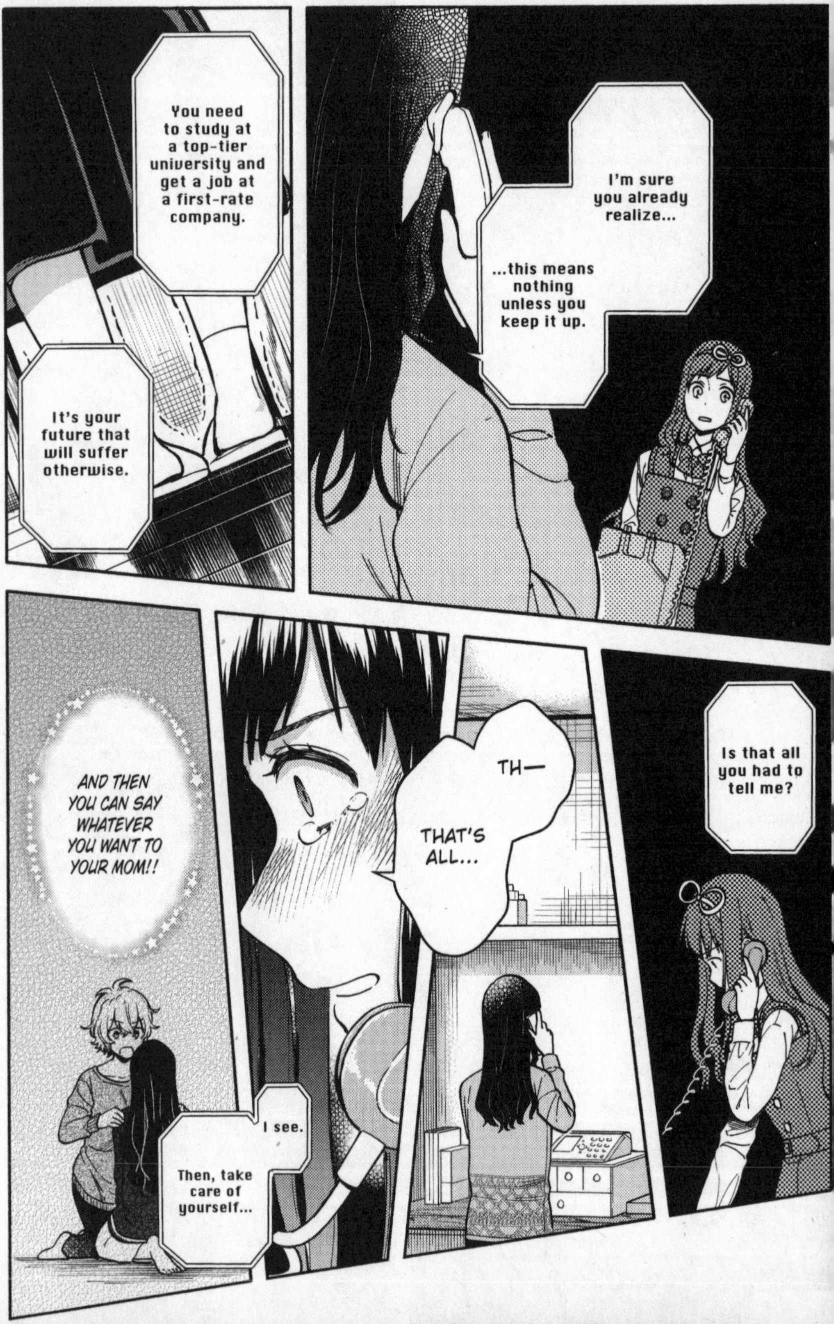
I'm sure you already realize...
...this means nothing unless you keep it up.
You need to study at a top-tier university and get a job at a first-rate company.
It's your future that will suffer otherwise.
Is that all you had to tell me?
TH—
THAT'S ALL...
I see.
Then, take care of yourself...
AND THEN YOU CAN SAY WHATEVER YOU WANT TO YOUR MOM!!

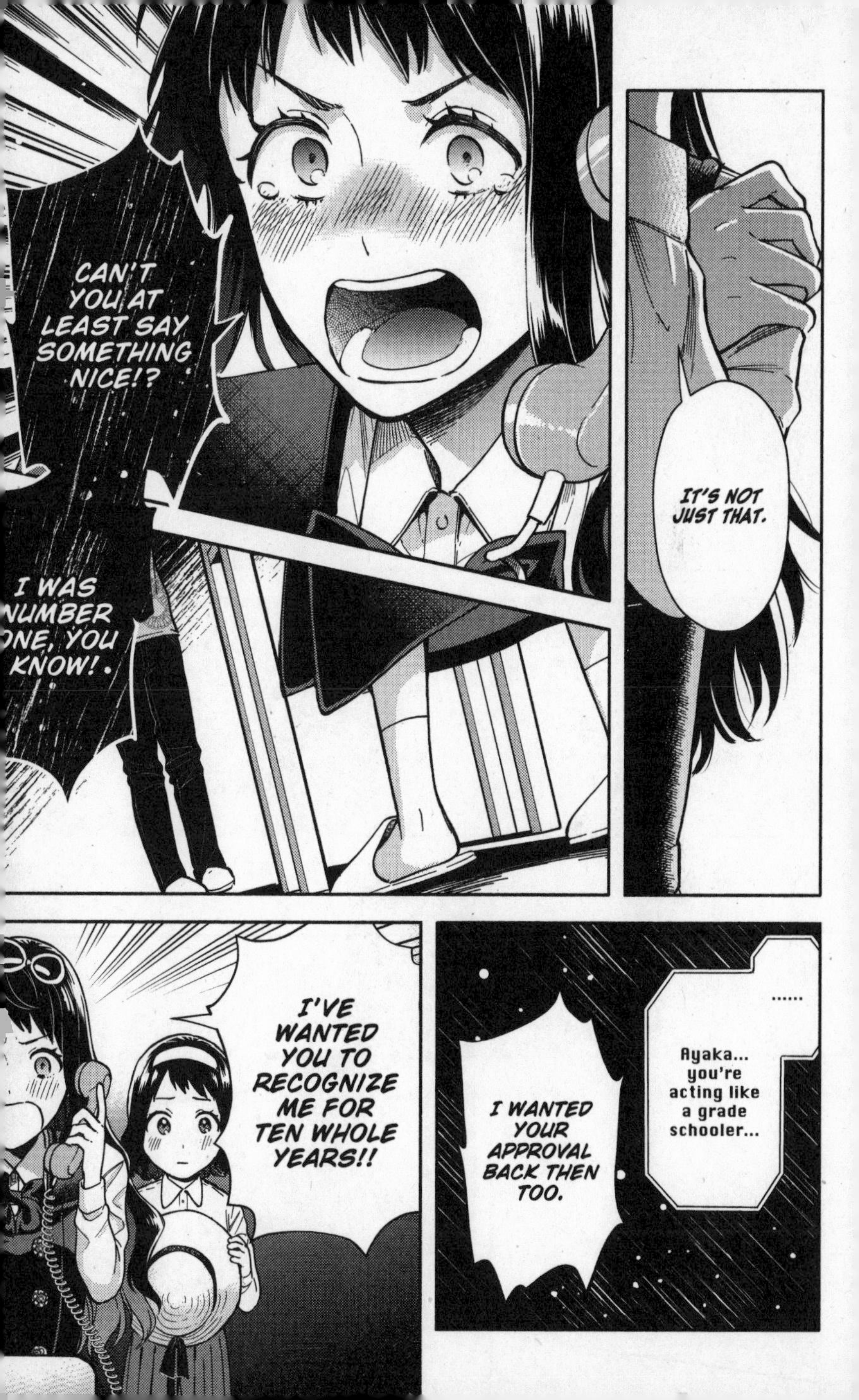
IT'S NOT JUST THAT.
CAN'T YOU AT LEAST SAY SOMETHING NICE!?
I WAS NUMBER ONE, YOU KNOW!
......
Ayaka... you're acting like a grade schooler...
I WANTED YOUR APPROVAL BACK THEN TOO.
I'VE WANTED YOU TO RECOGNIZE ME FOR TEN WHOLE YEARS!!

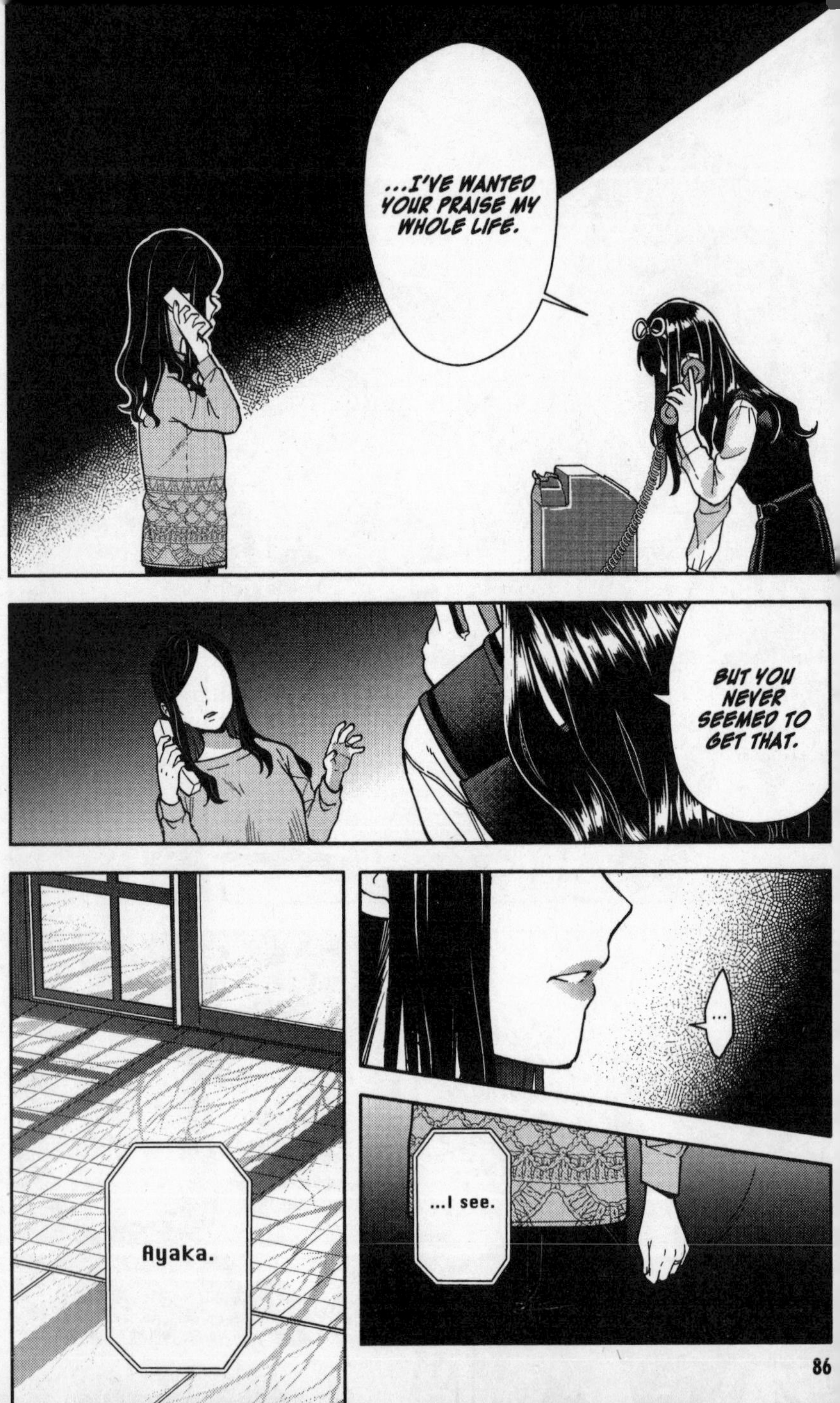
...I'VE WANTED YOUR PRAISE MY WHOLE LIFE.
BUT YOU NEVER SEEMED TO GET THAT.
...
...I see.
Ayaka.

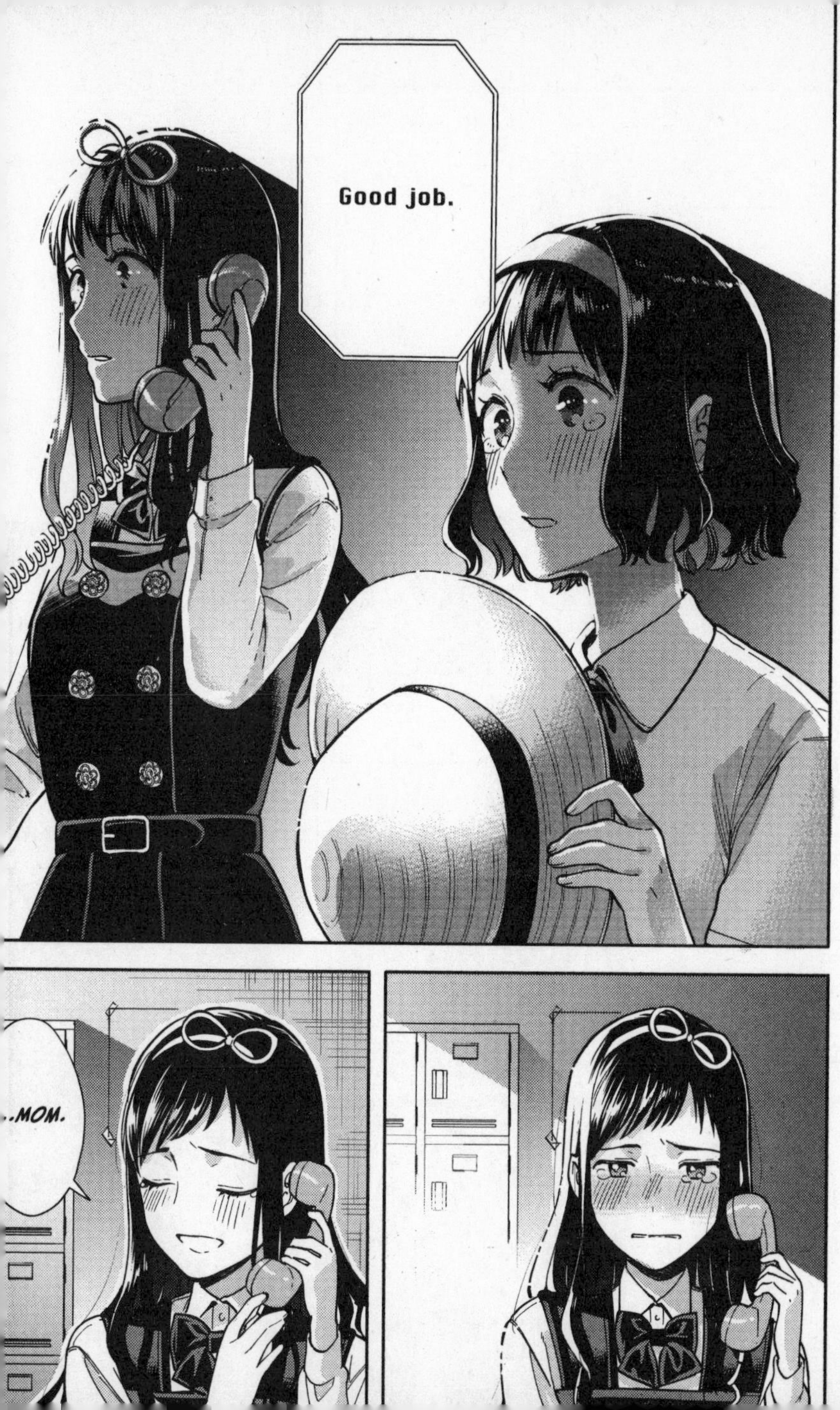
Good job.
..MOM.

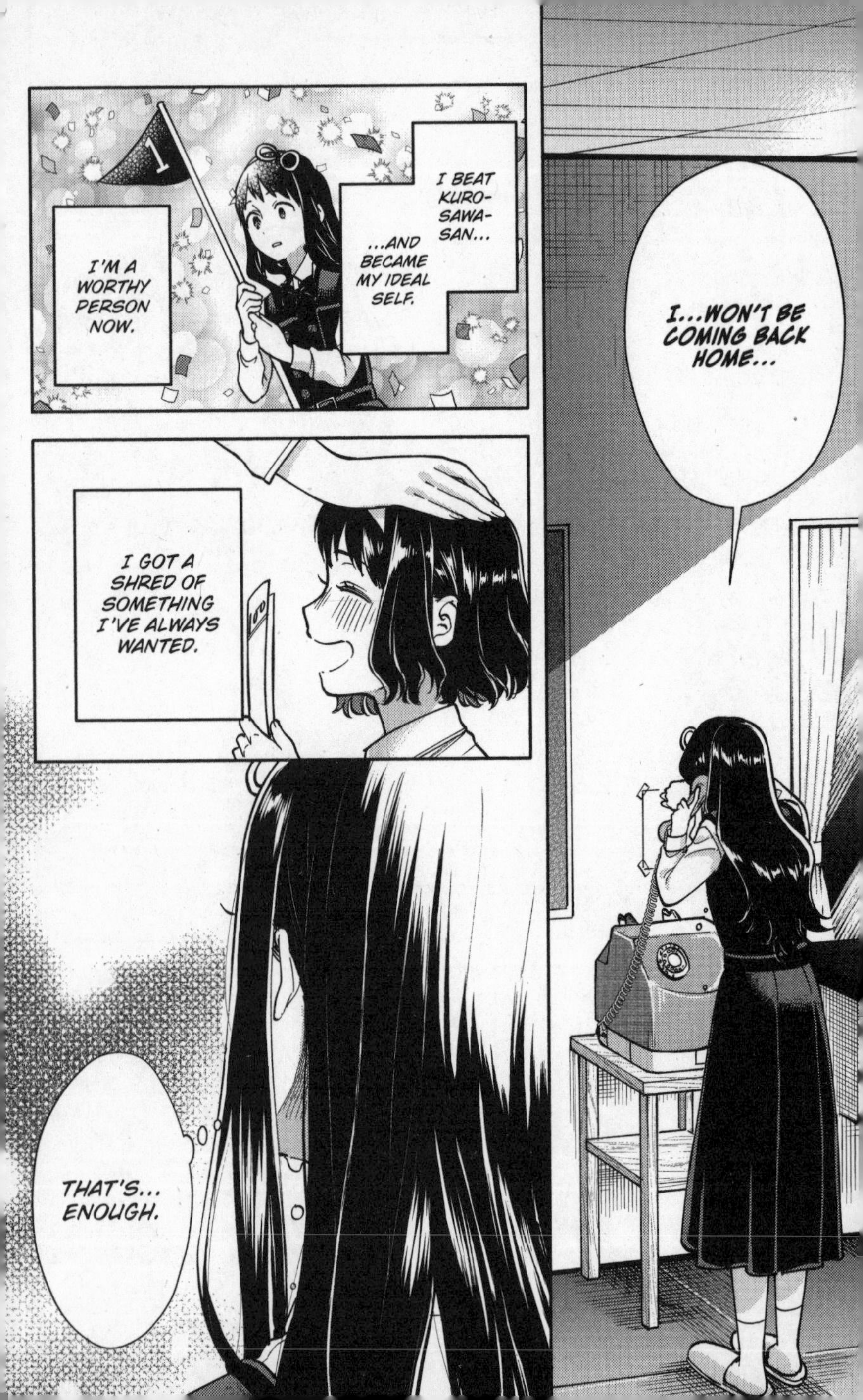
I...WON'T BE COMING BACK HOME...
I BEAT KURO-SAWA-SAN...
...AND BECAME MY IDEAL SELF.
I'M A WORTHY PERSON NOW.
I GOT A SHRED OF SOMETHING I'VE ALWAYS WANTED.
THAT'S... ENOUGH.

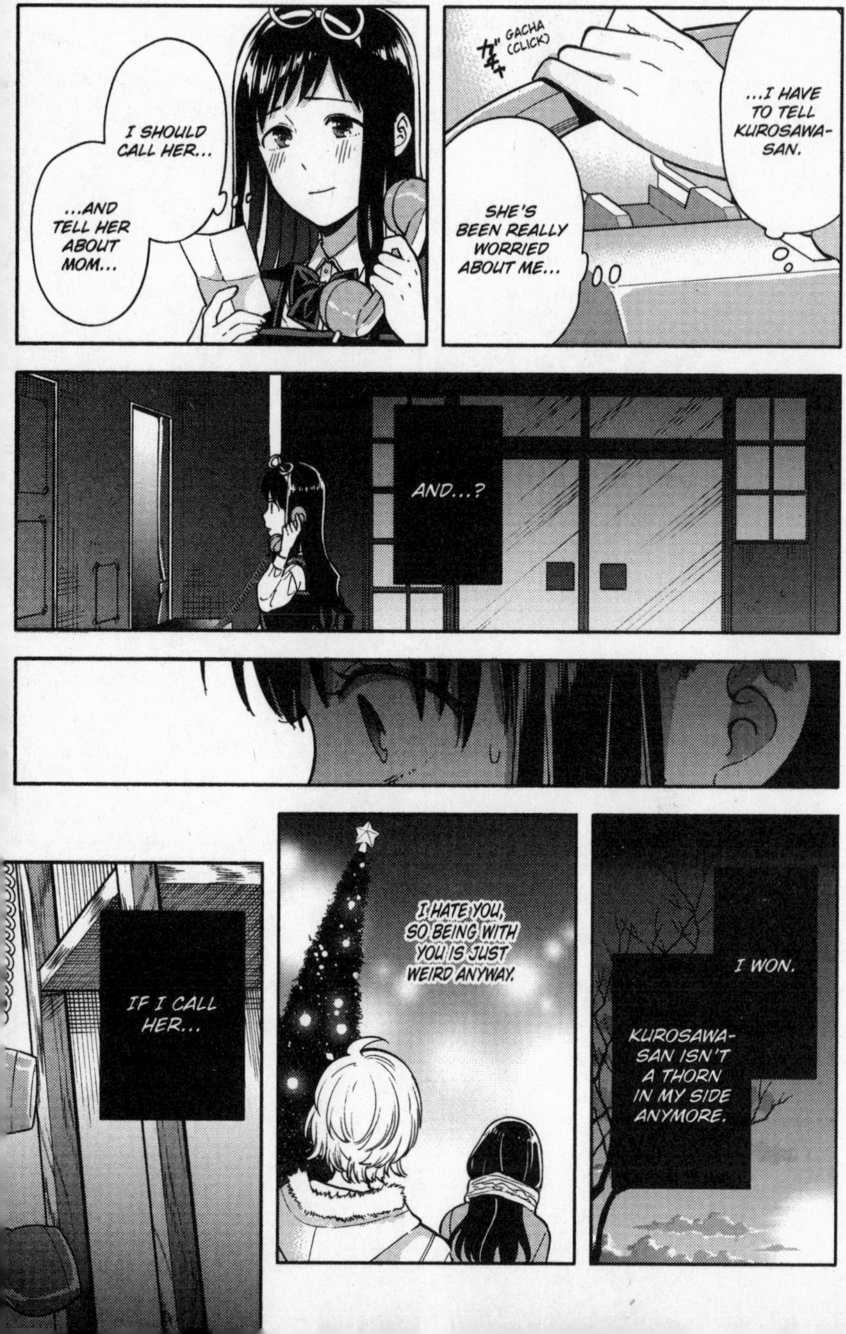
ガチャ
GACHA (CLICK)
...I HAVE TO TELL KUROSAWA-SAN.
SHE'S BEEN REALLY WORRIED ABOUT ME...
I SHOULD CALL HER...
...AND TELL HER ABOUT MOM...
AND...?
I WON.
KUROSAWA-SAN ISN'T A THORN IN MY SIDE ANYMORE.
I HATE YOU, SO BEING WITH YOU IS JUST WEIRD ANYWAY.
IF I CALL HER...

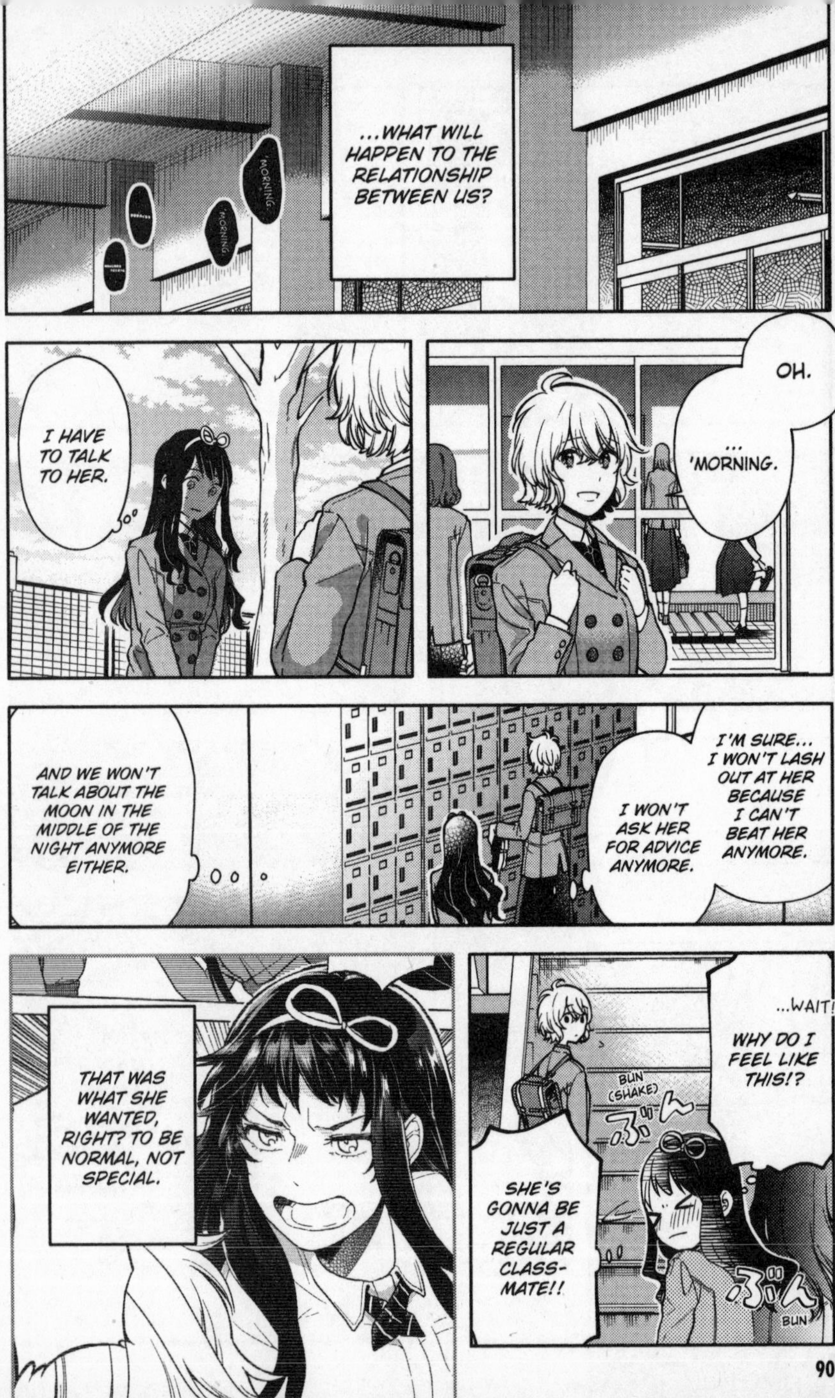
...WHAT WILL HAPPEN TO THE RELATIONSHIP BETWEEN US?
'MORNING
'MORNING
OH.
... 'MORNING.
I HAVE TO TALK TO HER.
I'M SURE... I WON'T LASH OUT AT HER BECAUSE I CAN'T BEAT HER ANYMORE.
I WON'T ASK HER FOR ADVICE ANYMORE.
AND WE WON'T TALK ABOUT THE MOON IN THE MIDDLE OF THE NIGHT ANYMORE EITHER.
...WAIT!
WHY DO I FEEL LIKE THIS!?
BUN (SHAKE)
SHE'S GONNA BE JUST A REGULAR CLASS-MATE!!
BUN
THAT WAS WHAT SHE WANTED, RIGHT? TO BE NORMAL, NOT SPECIAL.

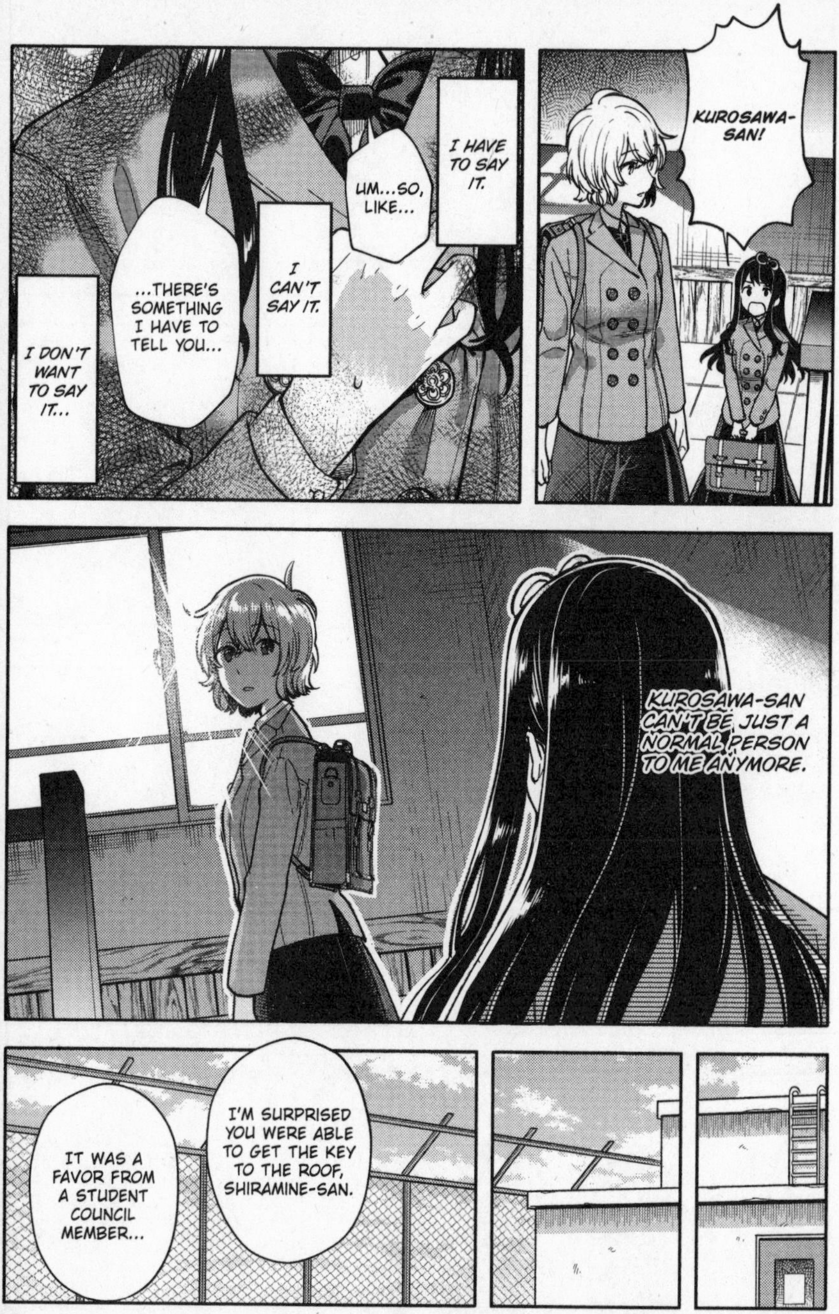
KUROSAWA-SAN!
I HAVE TO SAY IT.
UM...SO, LIKE...
I CAN'T SAY IT.
...THERE'S SOMETHING I HAVE TO TELL YOU...
I DON'T WANT TO SAY IT...
KUROSAWA-SAN CAN'T BE JUST A NORMAL PERSON TO ME ANYMORE.
I'M SURPRISED YOU WERE ABLE TO GET THE KEY TO THE ROOF, SHIRAMINE-SAN.
IT WAS A FAVOR FROM A STUDENT COUNCIL MEMBER...

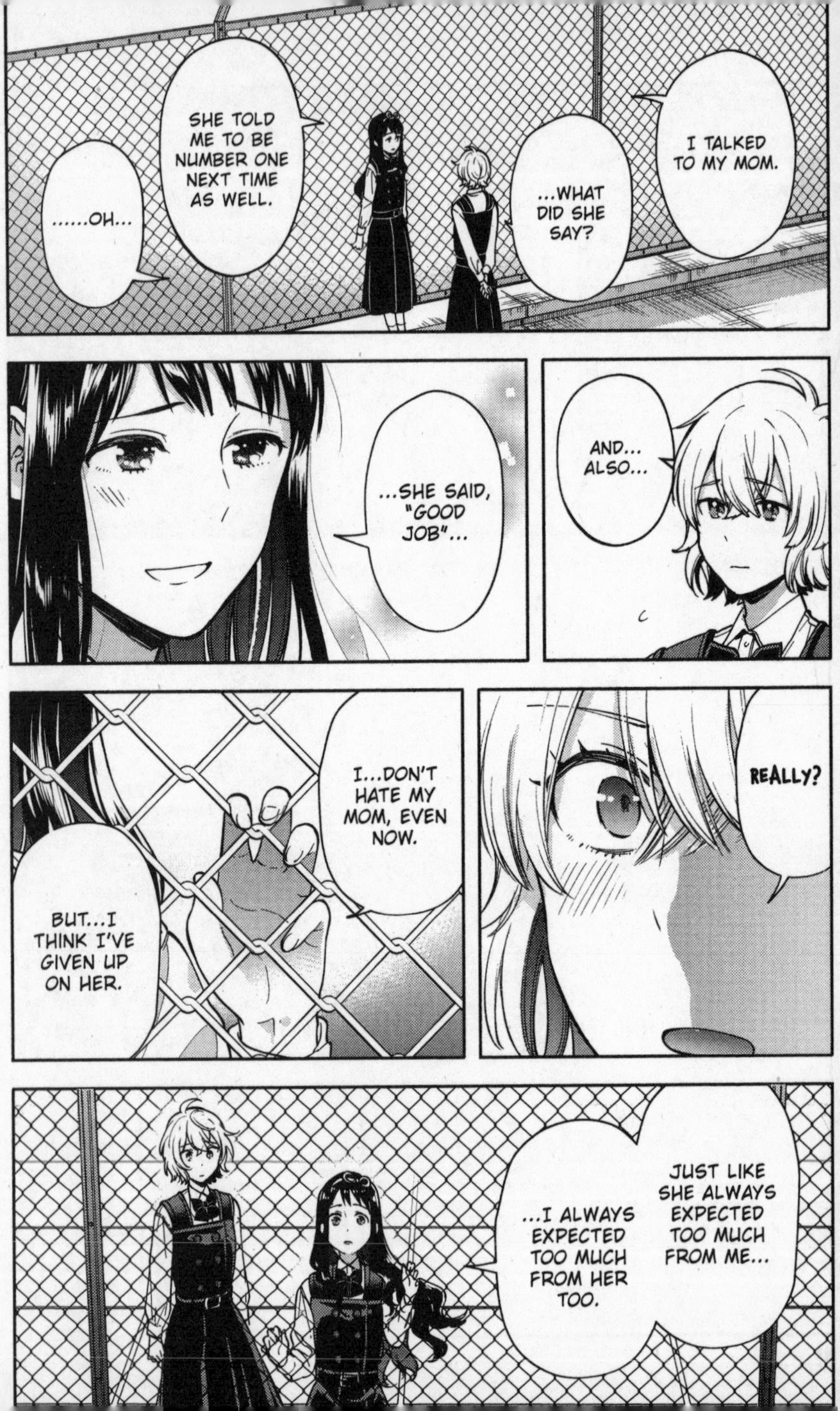
I TALKED TO MY MOM.
...WHAT DID SHE SAY?
SHE TOLD ME TO BE NUMBER ONE NEXT TIME AS WELL.
......OH...
AND... ALSO...
...SHE SAID, "GOOD JOB"...
REALLY?
I...DON'T HATE MY MOM, EVEN NOW.
BUT...I THINK I'VE GIVEN UP ON HER.
JUST LIKE SHE ALWAYS EXPECTED TOO MUCH FROM ME...
...I ALWAYS EXPECTED TOO MUCH FROM HER TOO.

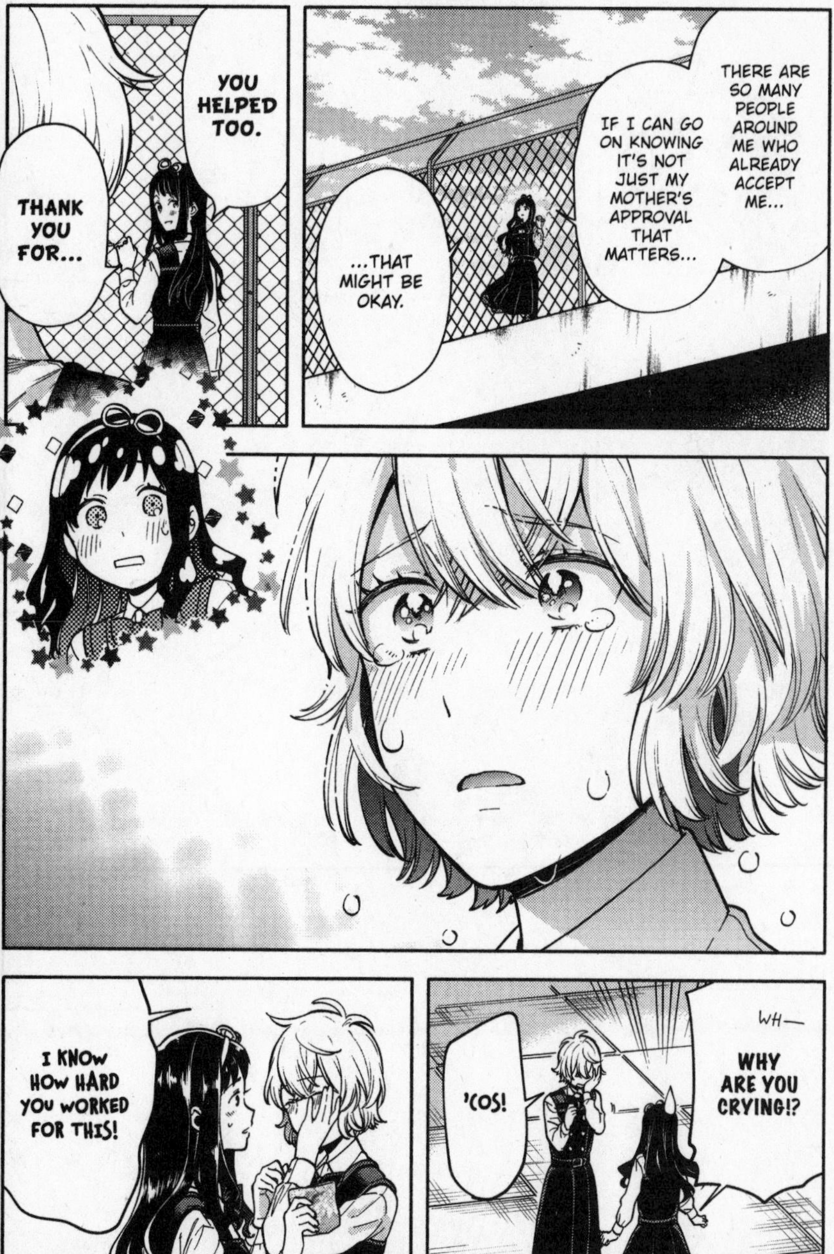
THERE ARE SO MANY PEOPLE AROUND ME WHO ALREADY ACCEPT ME...
IF I CAN GO ON KNOWING IT'S NOT JUST MY MOTHER'S APPROVAL THAT MATTERS...
...THAT MIGHT BE OKAY.
YOU HELPED TOO.
THANK YOU FOR...
WH—
WHY ARE YOU CRYING!?
'COS!
I KNOW HOW HARD YOU WORKED FOR THIS!

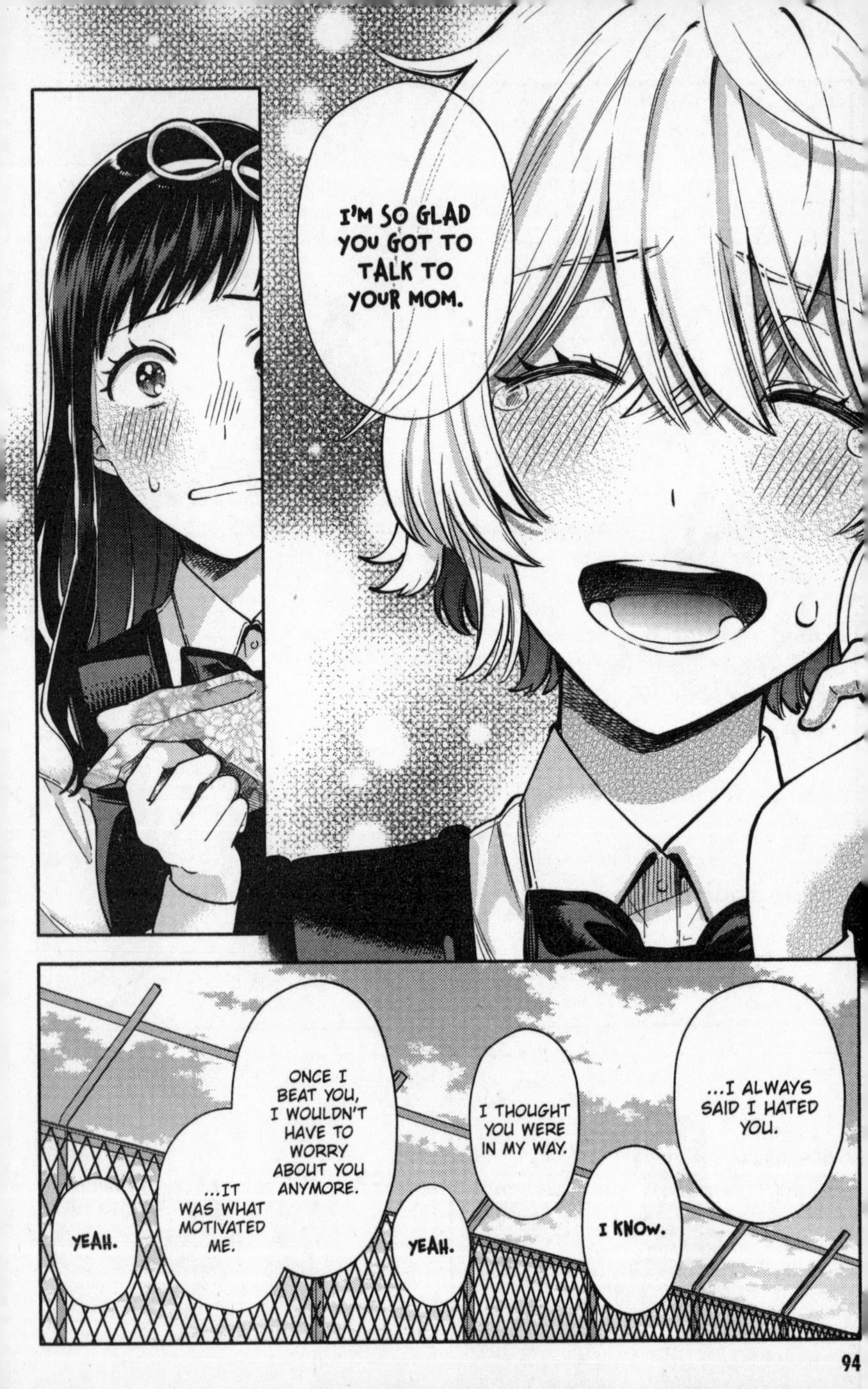
I'M SO GLAD YOU GOT TO TALK TO YOUR MOM.
...I ALWAYS SAID I HATED YOU.
I KNOW.
I THOUGHT YOU WERE IN MY WAY.
YEAH.
ONCE I BEAT YOU, I WOULDN'T HAVE TO WORRY ABOUT YOU ANYMORE.
...IT WAS WHAT MOTIVATED ME.
YEAH.

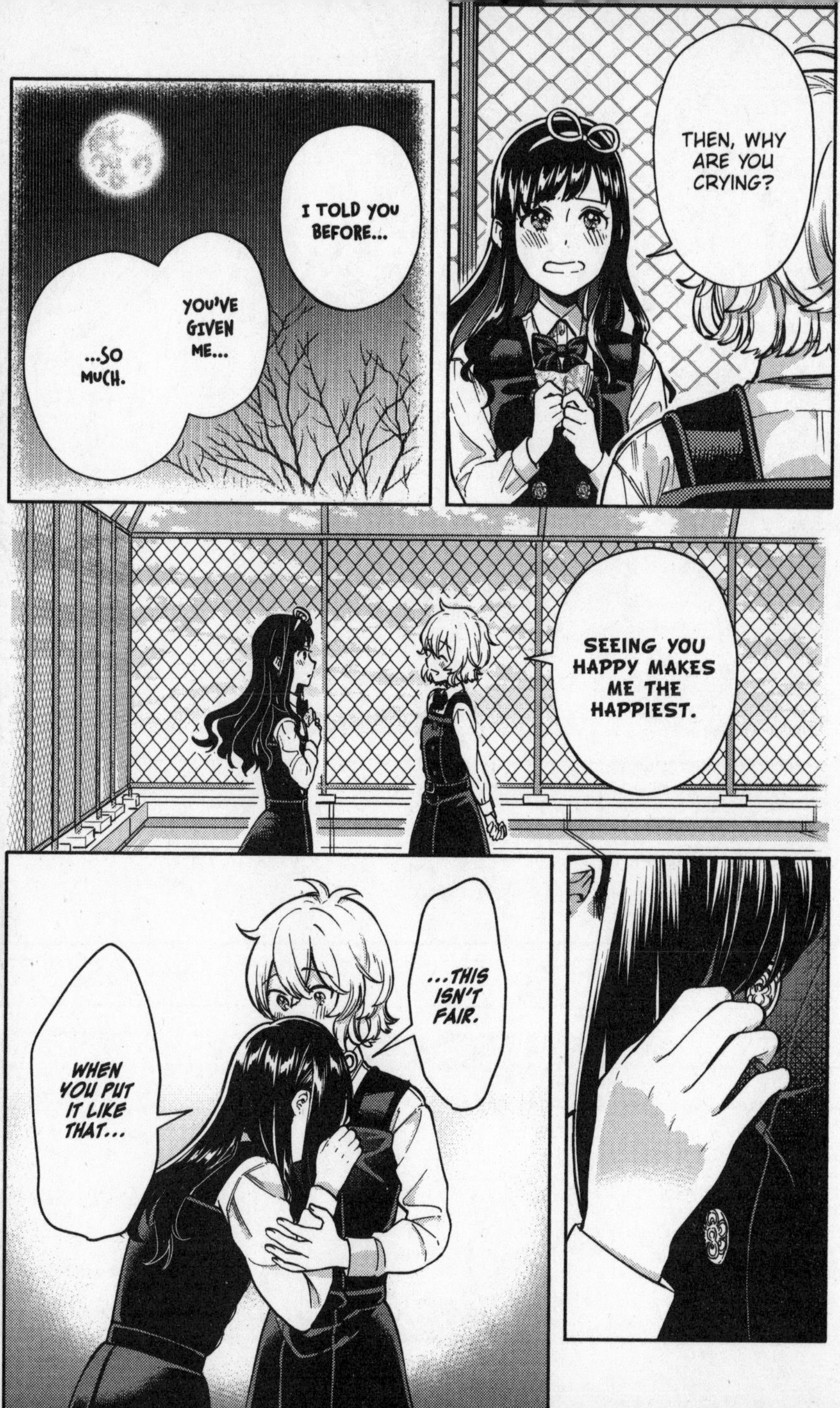
THEN, WHY ARE YOU CRYING?
I TOLD YOU BEFORE...
YOU'VE GIVEN ME...
...SO MUCH.
SEEING YOU HAPPY MAKES ME THE HAPPIEST.
...THIS ISN'T FAIR.
WHEN YOU PUT IT LIKE THAT...

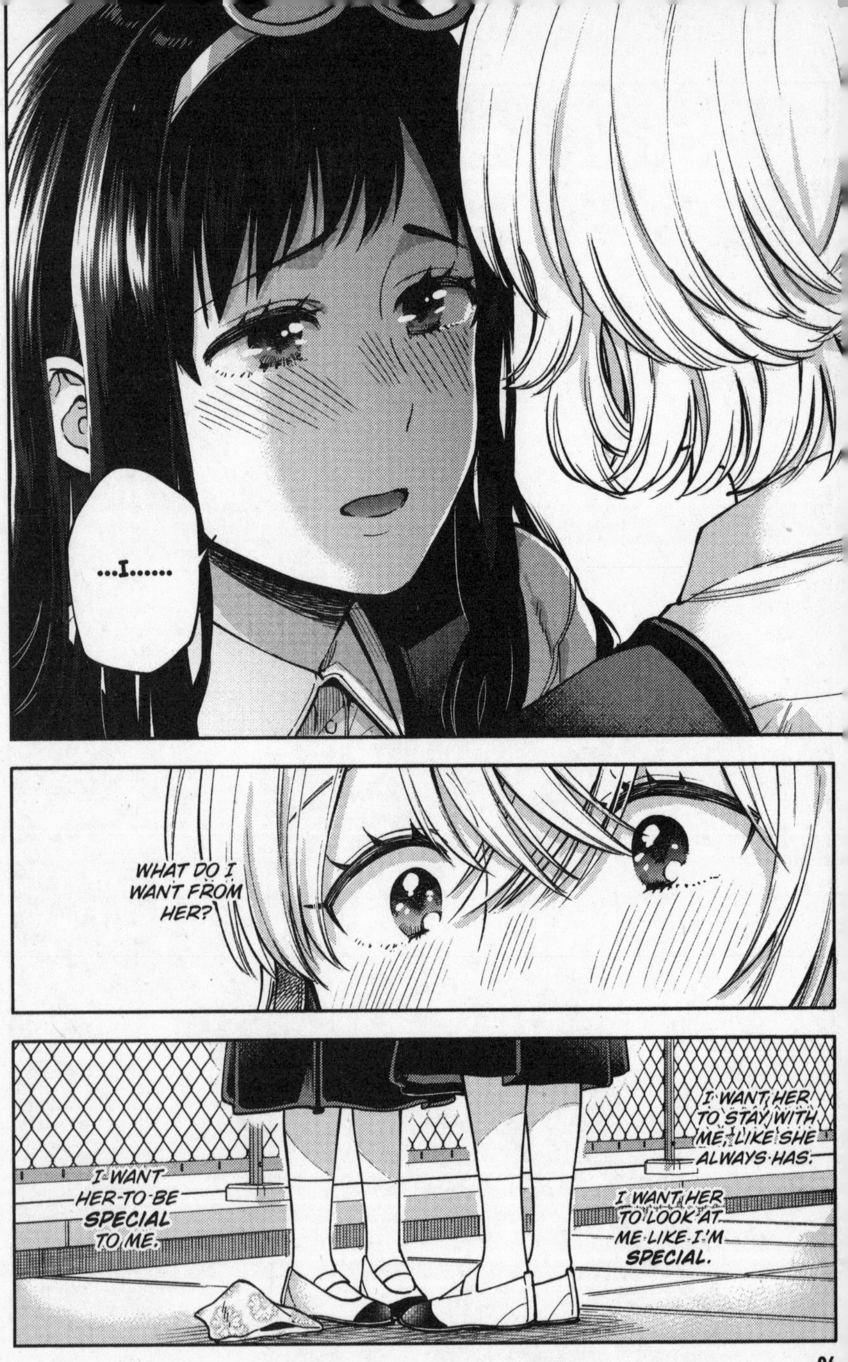
...I......
WHAT DO I WANT FROM HER?
I WANT HER TO STAY WITH ME, LIKE SHE ALWAYS HAS.
I WANT HER TO LOOK AT ME LIKE I'M SPECIAL.
I WANT HER TO BE SPECIAL TO ME.

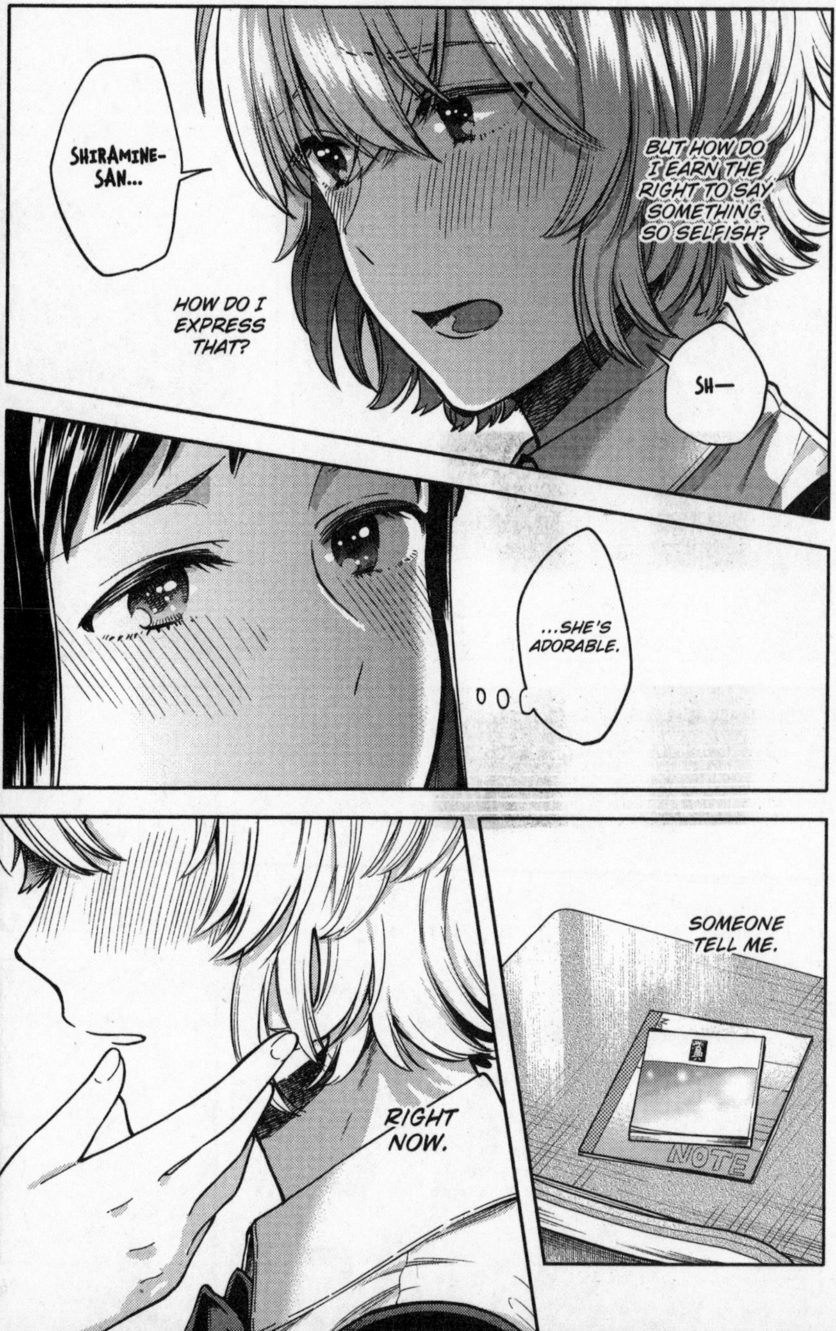
BUT HOW DO I EARN THE RIGHT TO SAY SOMETHING SO SELFISH?
SHIRAMINE-SAN...
HOW DO I EXPRESS THAT?
SH—
...SHE'S ADORABLE.
SOMEONE TELL ME.
NOTE
RIGHT NOW.

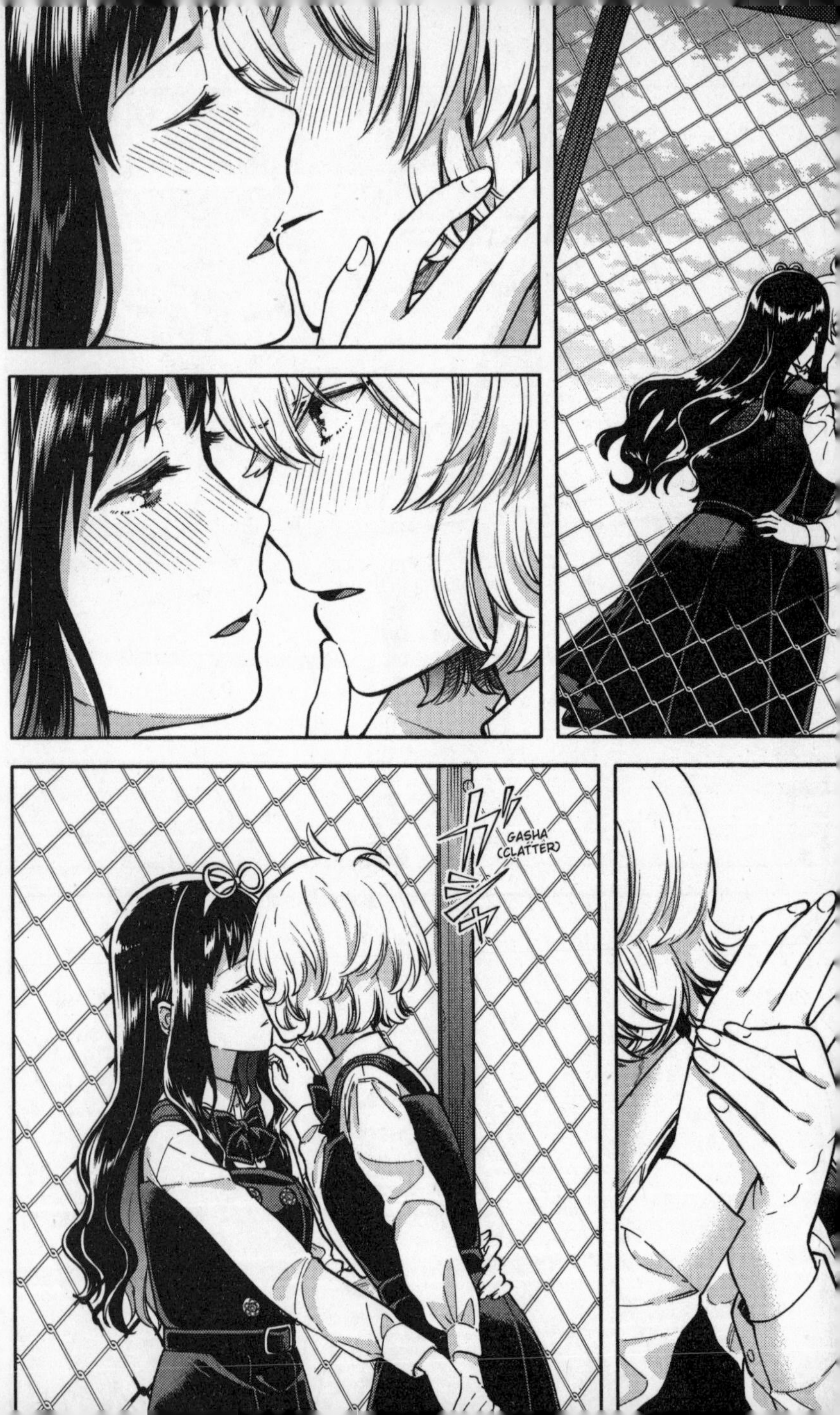
ガシャ
GASHA (CLATTER)

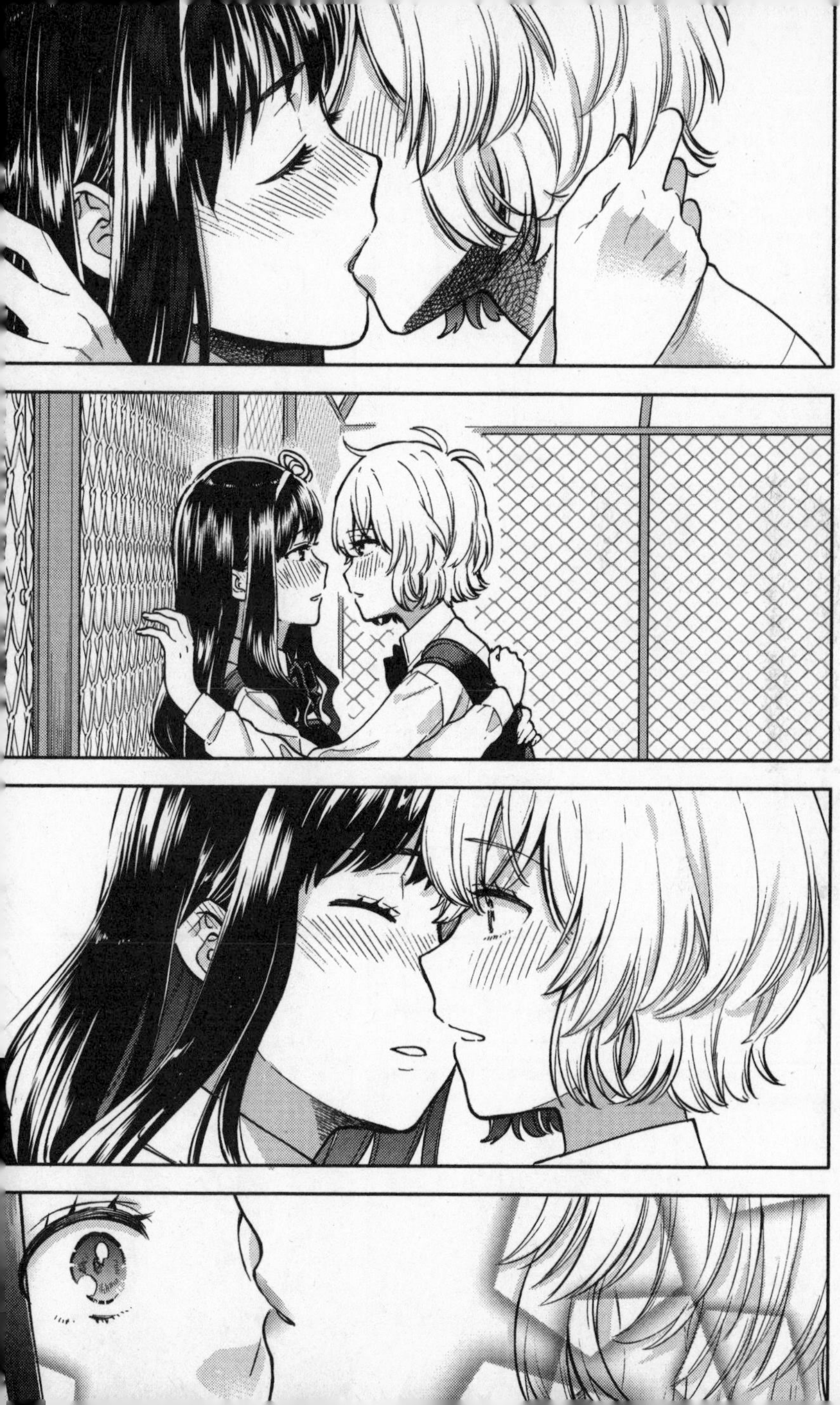

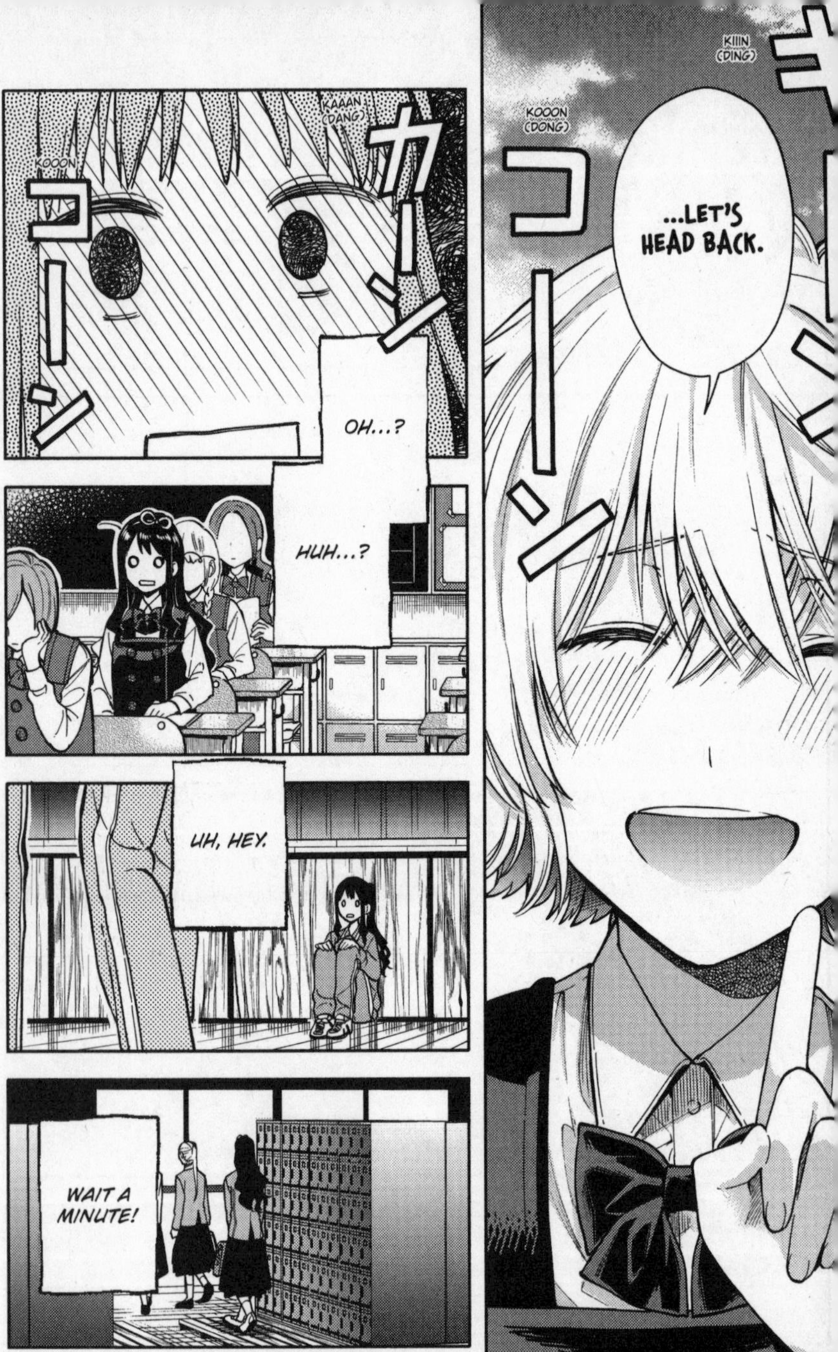
KIIIN (DING)
KOOON (DONG)
...LET'S HEAD BACK.
KAAAN (DANG)
KOOON
OH...?
HUH...?
UH, HEY.
WAIT A MINUTE!

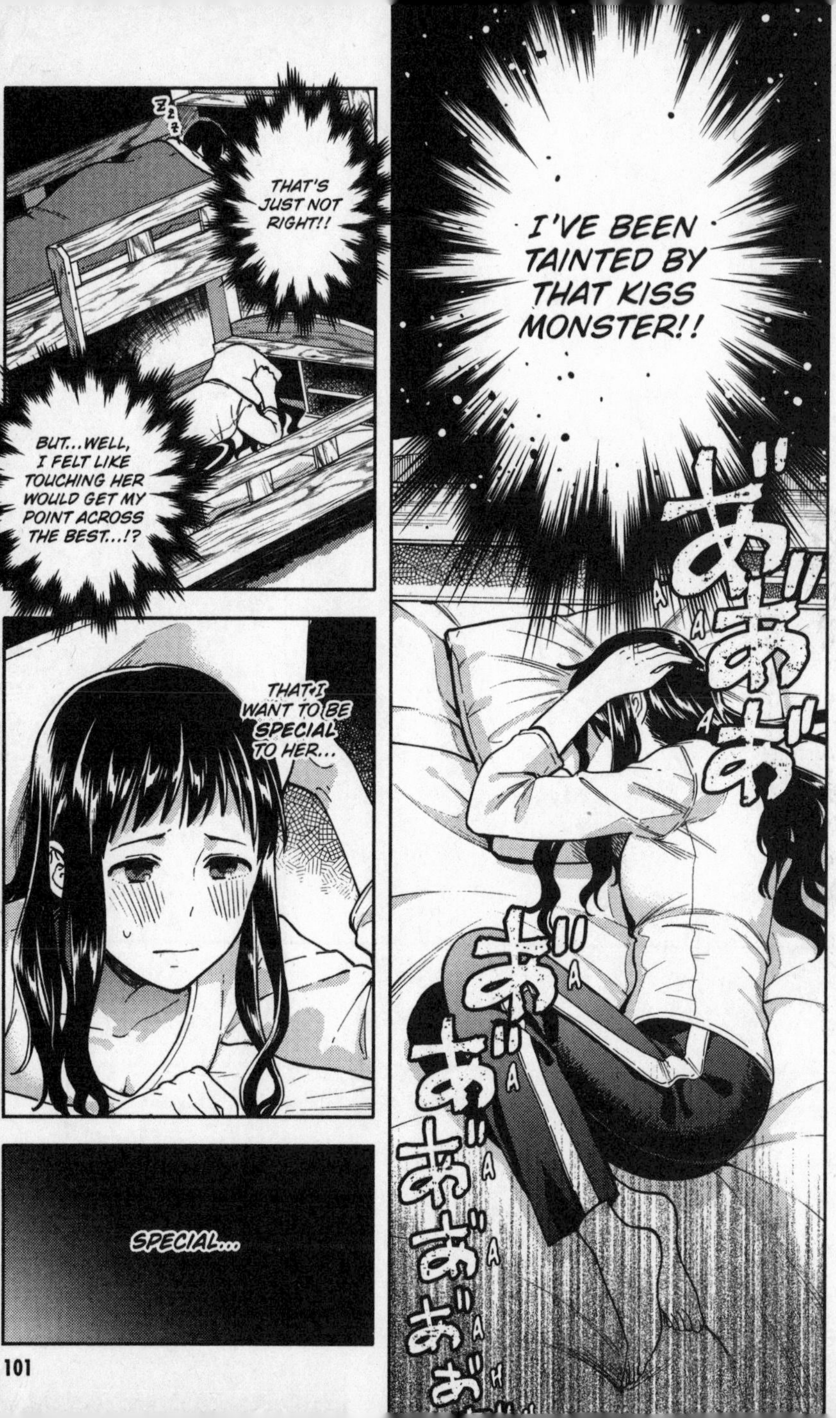
I'VE BEEN TAINTED BY THAT KISS MONSTER!!
ZZZ
THAT'S JUST NOT RIGHT!!
BUT...WELL, I FELT LIKE TOUCHING HER WOULD GET MY POINT ACROSS THE BEST...!?
THAT I WANT TO BE SPECIAL TO HER...
SPECIAL...

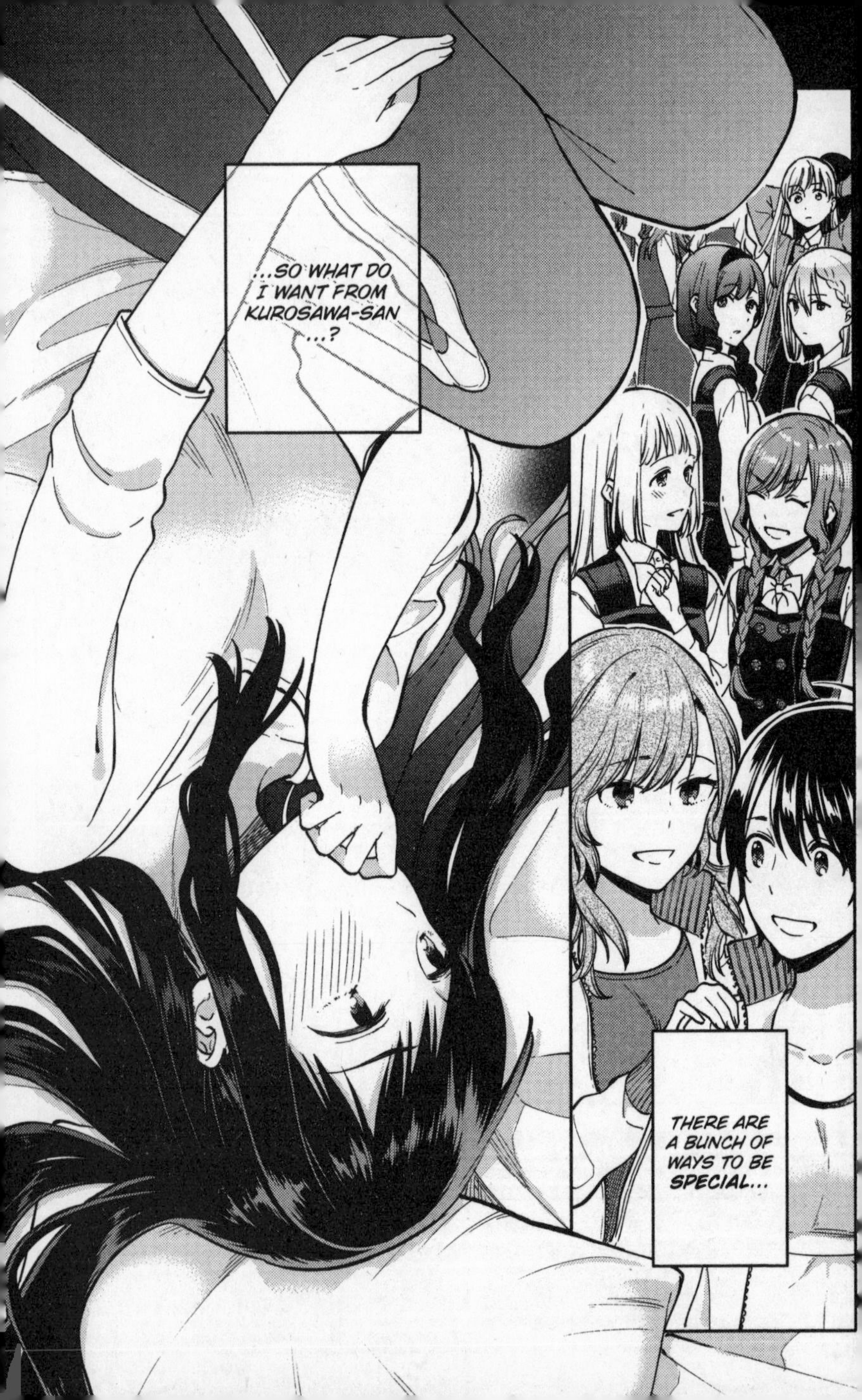
...SO WHAT DO I WANT FROM KUROSAWA-SAN ...?
THERE ARE A BUNCH OF WAYS TO BE SPECIAL...

The Final Exam Results

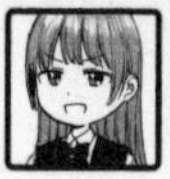

MAICHIYO

HIGH SCHOOL SECOND-YEAR. HAS MEDIOCRE GRADES.

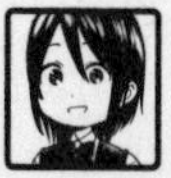

MAIMI

HIGH SCHOOL SECOND-YEAR. DOESN'T HAVE THE GREATEST GRADES.

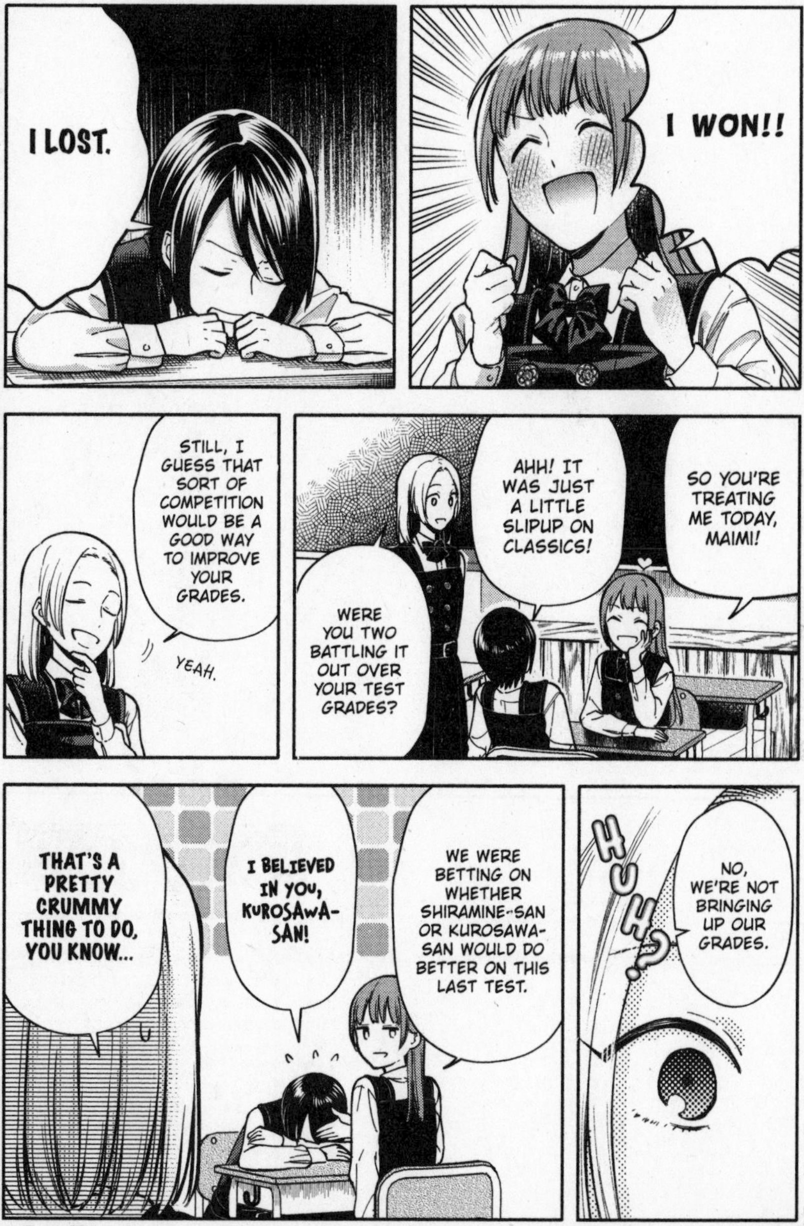

I WON!!
I LOST.
SO YOU'RE TREATING ME TODAY, MAIMI!
AHH! IT WAS JUST A LITTLE SLIPUP ON CLASSICS!
WERE YOU TWO BATTLING IT OUT OVER YOUR TEST GRADES?
STILL, I GUESS THAT SORT OF COMPETITION WOULD BE A GOOD WAY TO IMPROVE YOUR GRADES.
YEAH.
NO, WE'RE NOT BRINGING UP OUR GRADES.
HUH?
WE WERE BETTING ON WHETHER SHIRAMINE-SAN OR KUROSAWA-SAN WOULD DO BETTER ON THIS LAST TEST.
I BELIEVED IN YOU, KUROSAWA-SAN!
THAT'S A PRETTY CRUMMY THING TO DO, YOU KNOW...

KISS THEATER: WHAT'S BEHIND THE STORY!? ✳ PEOPLE OTHER THAN THE MAIN CHARACTERS HAVE STORIES TOO. HERE, WE PRESENT THE "LITTLE LOVE" STORIES HAPPENING BEHIND THE SCENES.

Ai Uehara

Ai Uehara

Second-year student at Seiran Academy High School. In the astronomy club. Has a simple and straightforward personality. She cares about her friends and knows a lot of people both at school and outside of it. She's not the greatest at studying, but she's working hard to attend the same school as her graduated senpai, Hoshino, and it looks like her grades are getting better little by little?

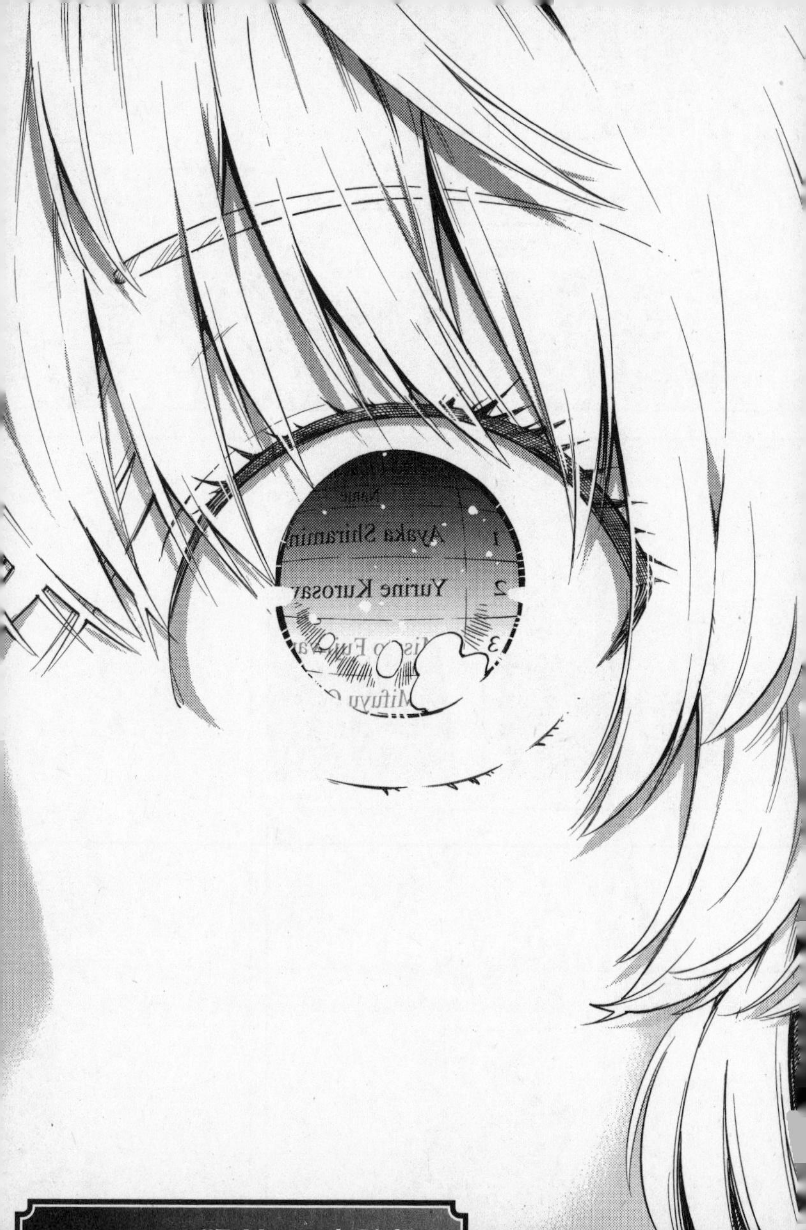

Chapter 44: "A Normal Girl"

Year-End Final Exam Scores

	Name	Score
1	Ayaka Shiramine	1175
2	Yurine Miyasawa	1162
3	Misuzu Kashiwara	1123
4		1115
5		112
		88
		74
		5
		7

...I LOST.

OH YEAH.

AH!

SHIRA-MINE-SAN...

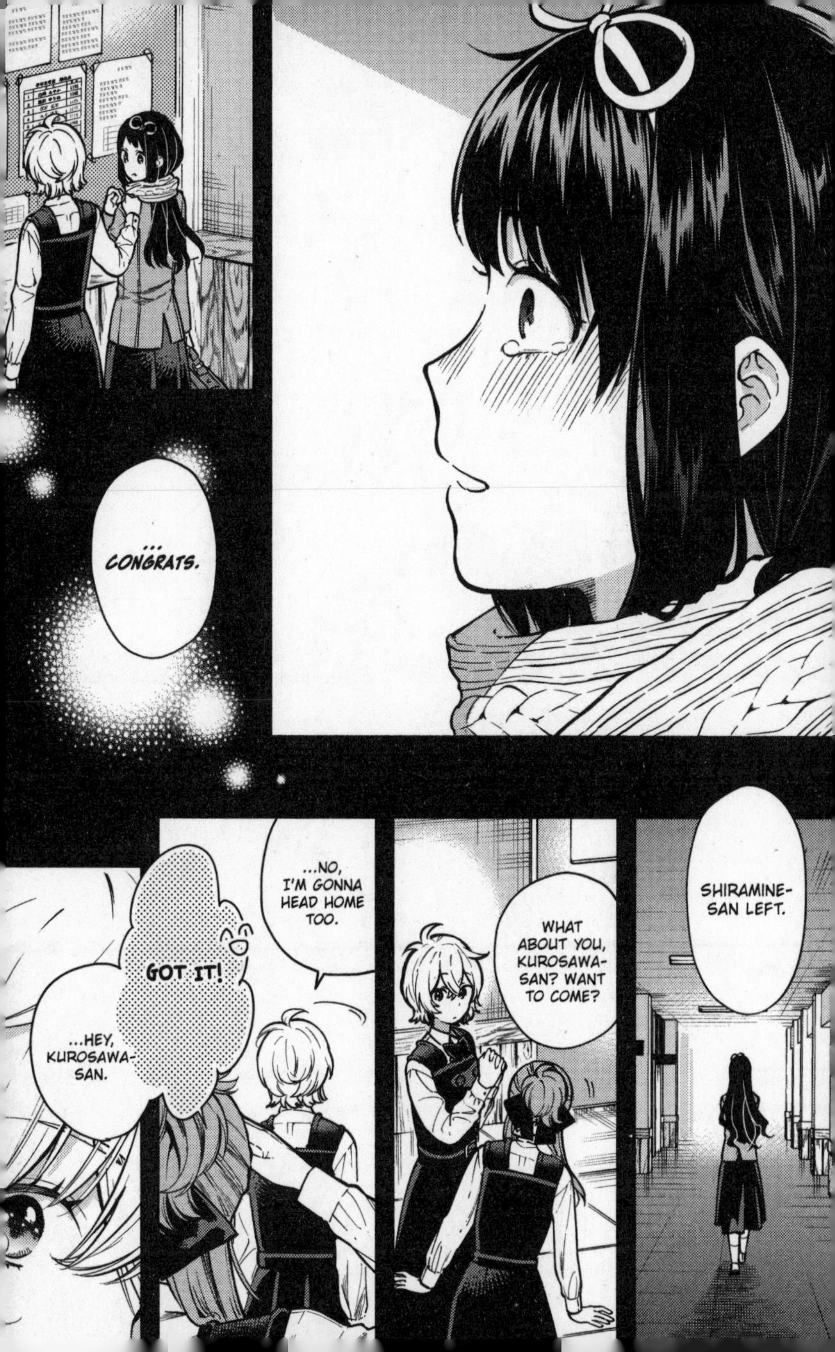
...CONGRATS.
SHIRAMINE-SAN LEFT.
WHAT ABOUT YOU, KUROSAWA-SAN? WANT TO COME?
...NO, I'M GONNA HEAD HOME TOO.
GOT IT!
...HEY, KUROSAWA-SAN.

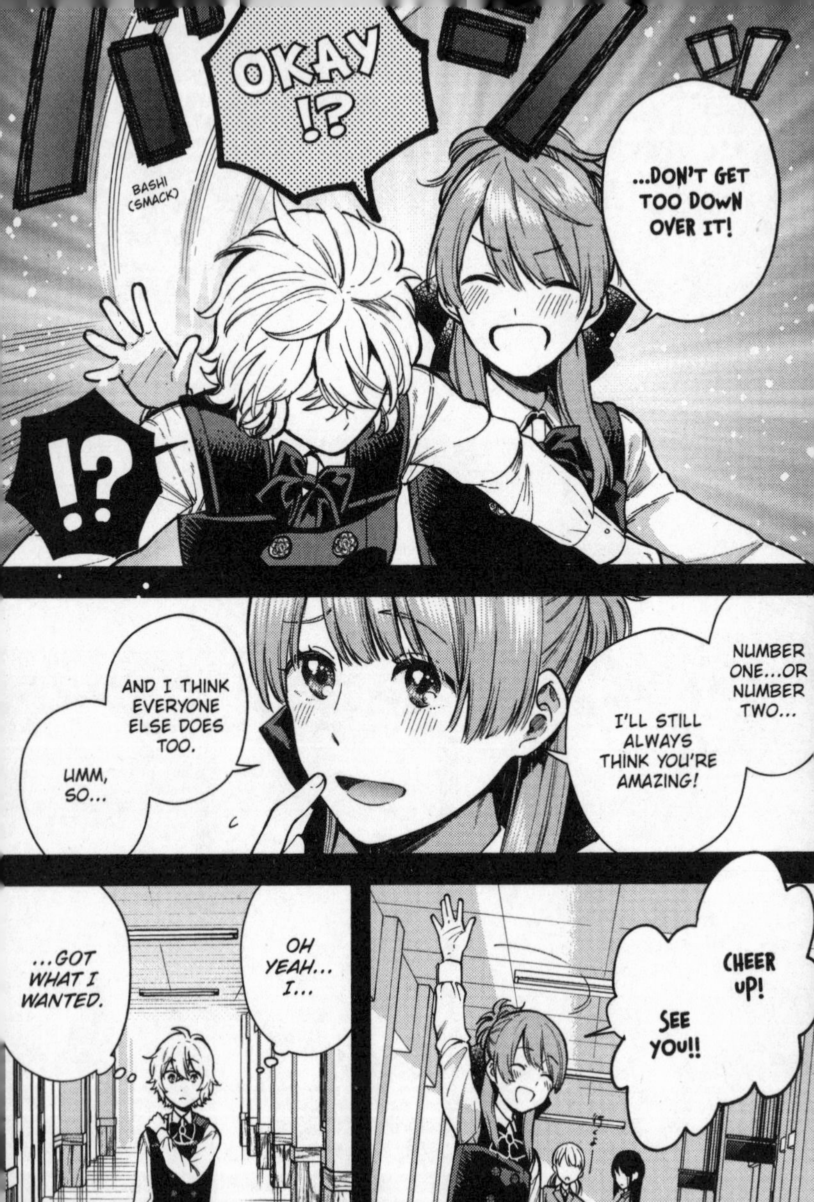
...DON'T GET TOO DOWN OVER IT!
OKAY !?
BASHI (SMACK)
!?
NUMBER ONE...OR NUMBER TWO...
I'LL STILL ALWAYS THINK YOU'RE AMAZING!
AND I THINK EVERYONE ELSE DOES TOO.
UMM, SO...
CHEER UP!
SEE YOU!!
OH YEAH... I...
...GOT WHAT I WANTED.

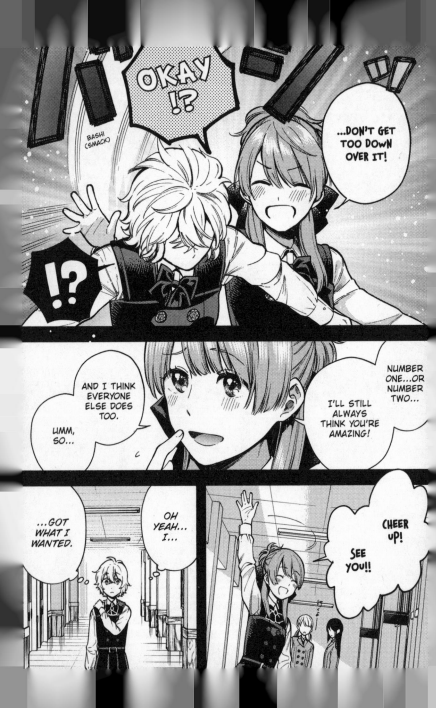

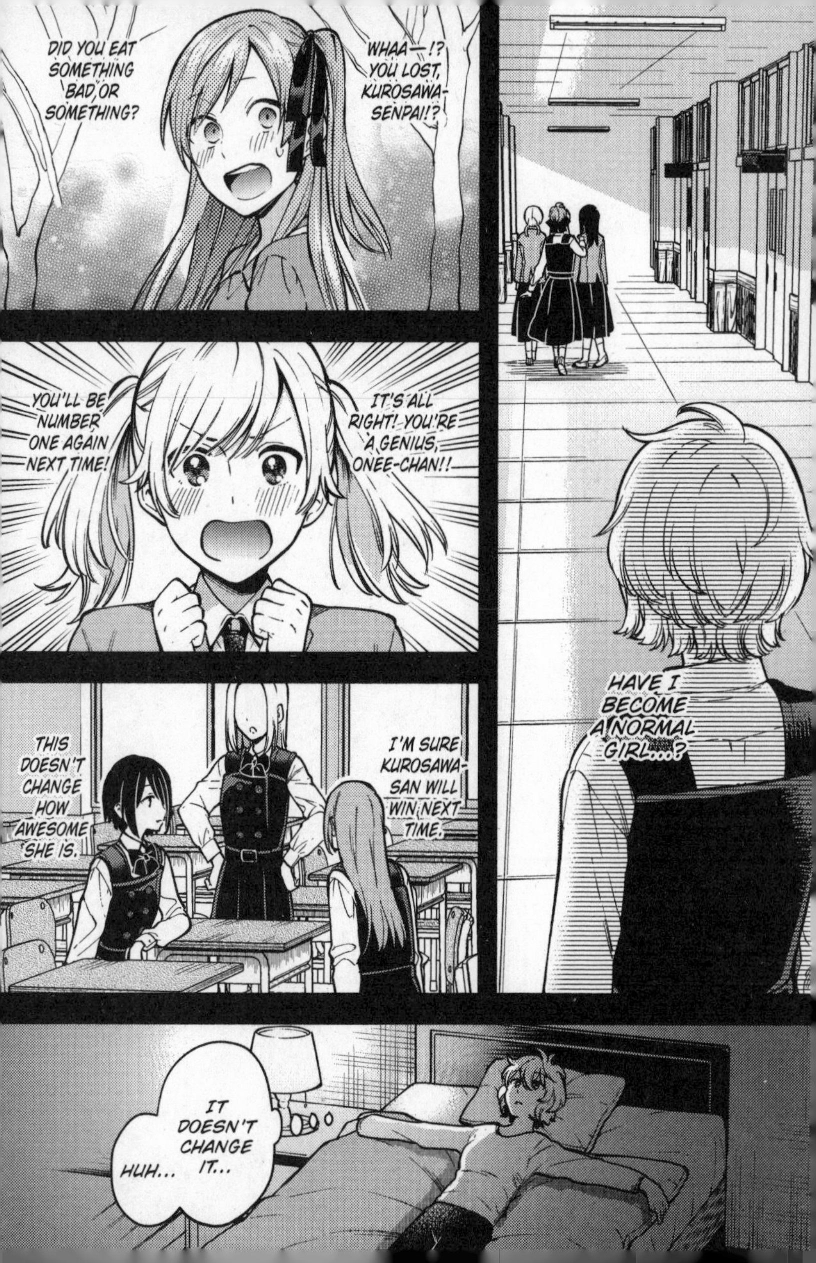
HAVE I BECOME A NORMAL GIRL...?
WHAA—!? YOU LOST, KUROSAWA-SENPAI!?
DID YOU EAT SOMETHING BAD OR SOMETHING?
IT'S ALL RIGHT! YOU'RE A GENIUS, ONEE-CHAN!!
YOU'LL BE NUMBER ONE AGAIN NEXT TIME!
I'M SURE KUROSAWA-SAN WILL WIN NEXT TIME.
THIS DOESN'T CHANGE HOW AWESOME SHE IS.
IT DOESN'T CHANGE IT...
HUH...

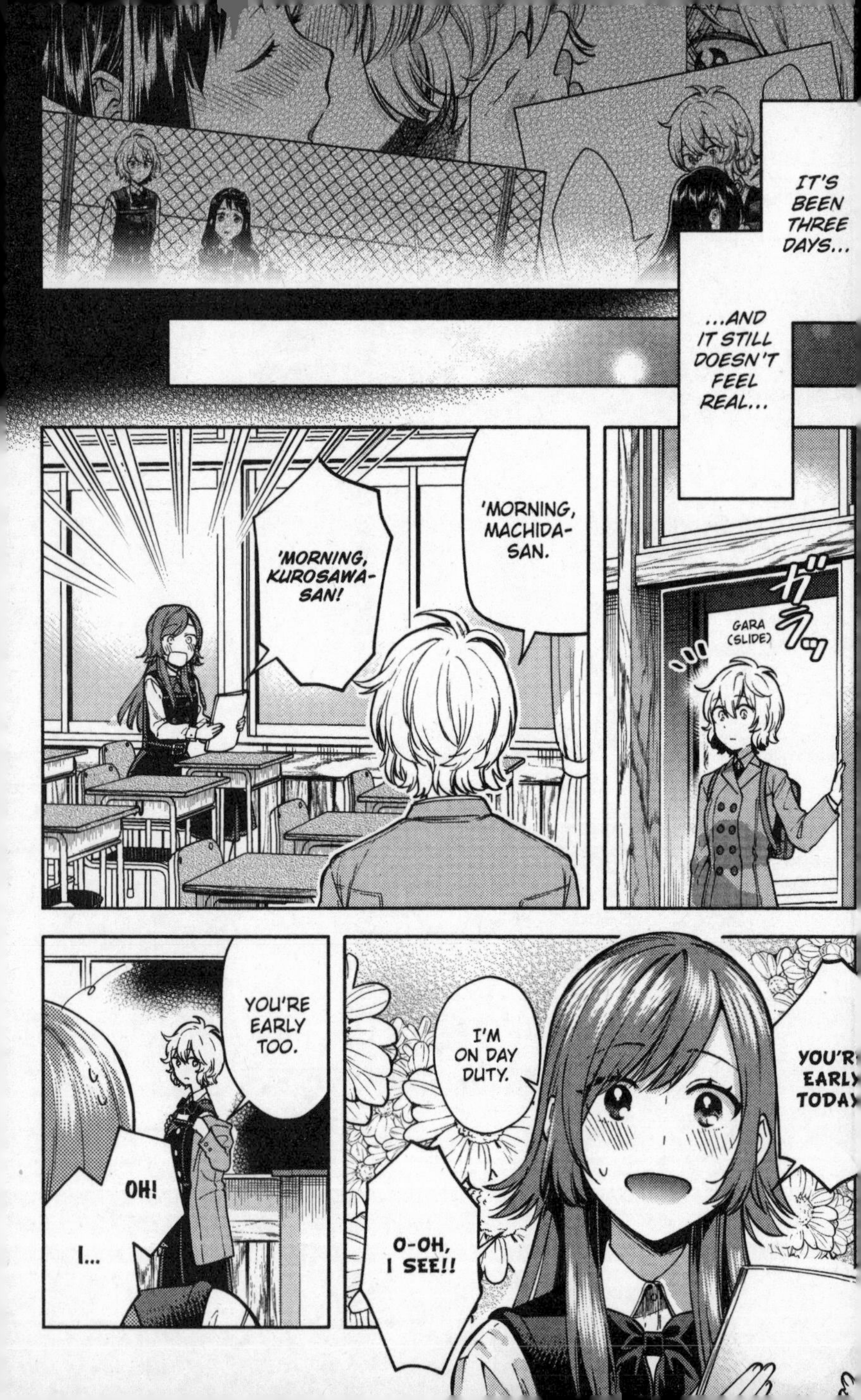

IT'S BEEN THREE DAYS...
...AND IT STILL DOESN'T FEEL REAL...
ガラッ
GARA (SLIDE)
...
'MORNING, MACHIDA-SAN.
'MORNING, KUROSAWA-SAN!
YOU'R EARLY TODAY
I'M ON DAY DUTY.
O-OH, I SEE!!
YOU'RE EARLY TOO.
OH!
I...

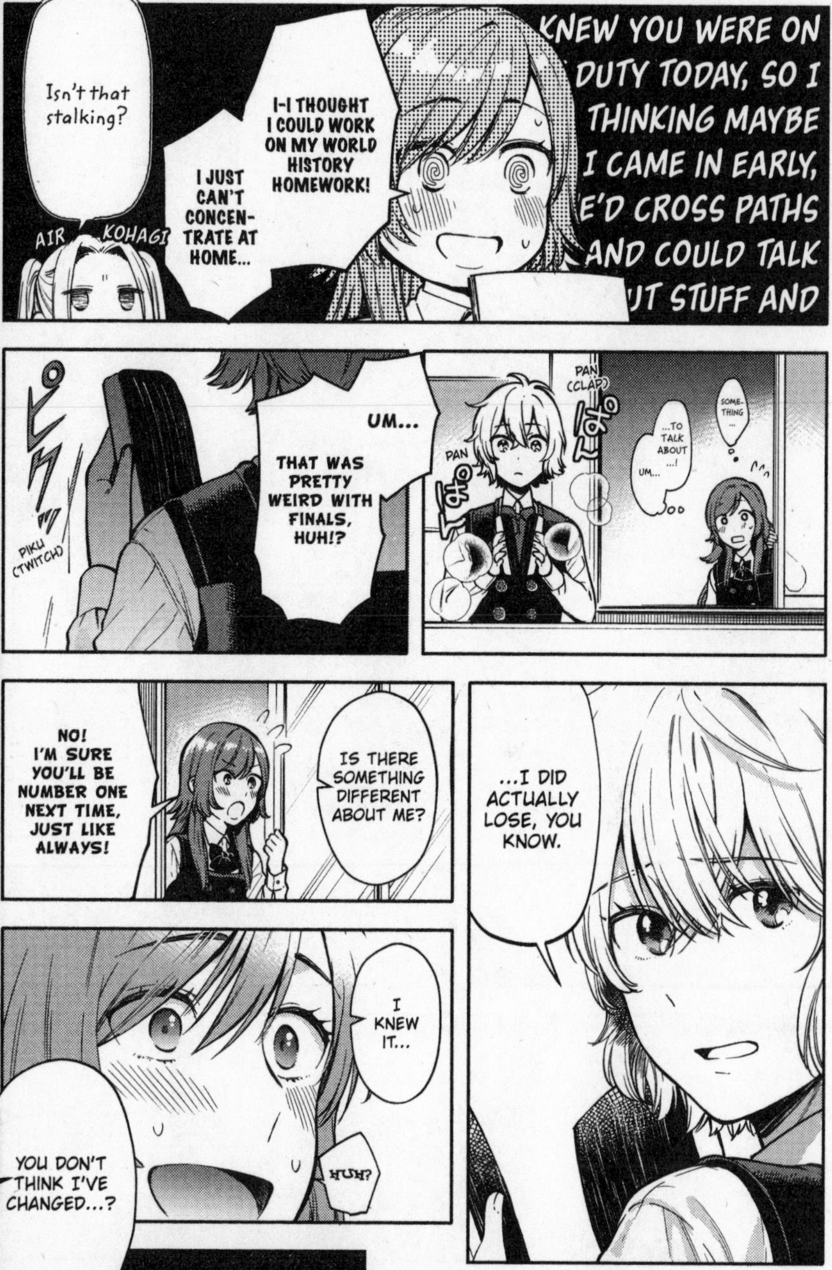
KNEW YOU WERE ON DUTY TODAY, SO I THINKING MAYBE I CAME IN EARLY, E'D CROSS PATHS AND COULD TALK UT STUFF AND
I-I THOUGHT I COULD WORK ON MY WORLD HISTORY HOMEWORK!
I JUST CAN'T CONCENTRATE AT HOME...
Isn't that stalking?
AIR KOHAGI
SOMETHING...
...TO TALK ABOUT...!
UM...
PAN (CLAP)
PAN
UM...
THAT WAS PRETTY WEIRD WITH FINALS, HUH!?
PIKU (TWITCH)
...I DID ACTUALLY LOSE, YOU KNOW.
IS THERE SOMETHING DIFFERENT ABOUT ME?
NO! I'M SURE YOU'LL BE NUMBER ONE NEXT TIME, JUST LIKE ALWAYS!
I KNEW IT...
HUH?
YOU DON'T THINK I'VE CHANGED...?

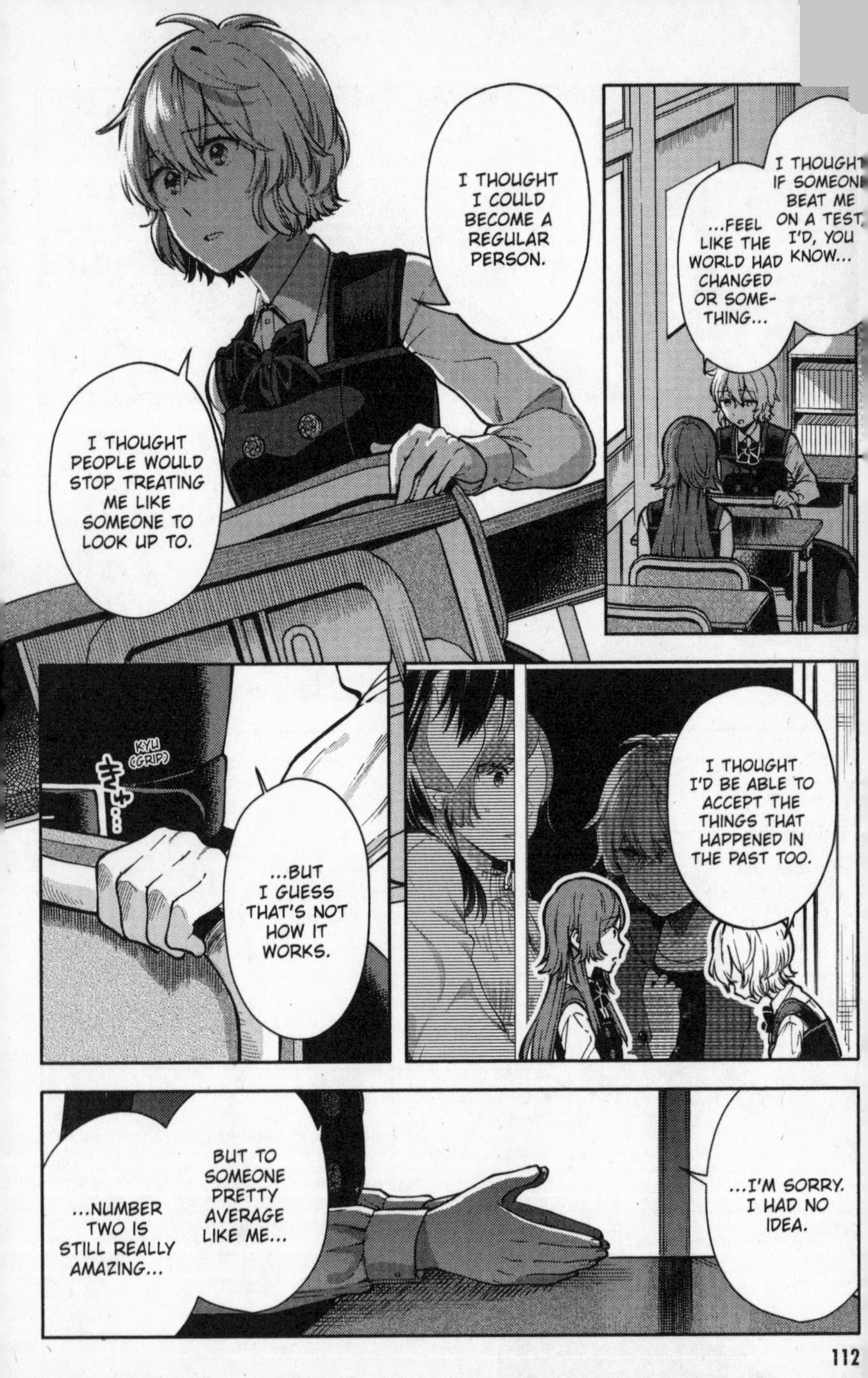
I THOUGHT IF SOMEONE BEAT ME ON A TEST, I'D, YOU KNOW...
...FEEL LIKE THE WORLD HAD CHANGED OR SOMETHING...
I THOUGHT I COULD BECOME A REGULAR PERSON.
I THOUGHT PEOPLE WOULD STOP TREATING ME LIKE SOMEONE TO LOOK UP TO.
I THOUGHT I'D BE ABLE TO ACCEPT THE THINGS THAT HAPPENED IN THE PAST TOO.
KYU (GRIP)
...BUT I GUESS THAT'S NOT HOW IT WORKS.
...I'M SORRY. I HAD NO IDEA.
BUT TO SOMEONE PRETTY AVERAGE LIKE ME...
...NUMBER TWO IS STILL REALLY AMAZING...

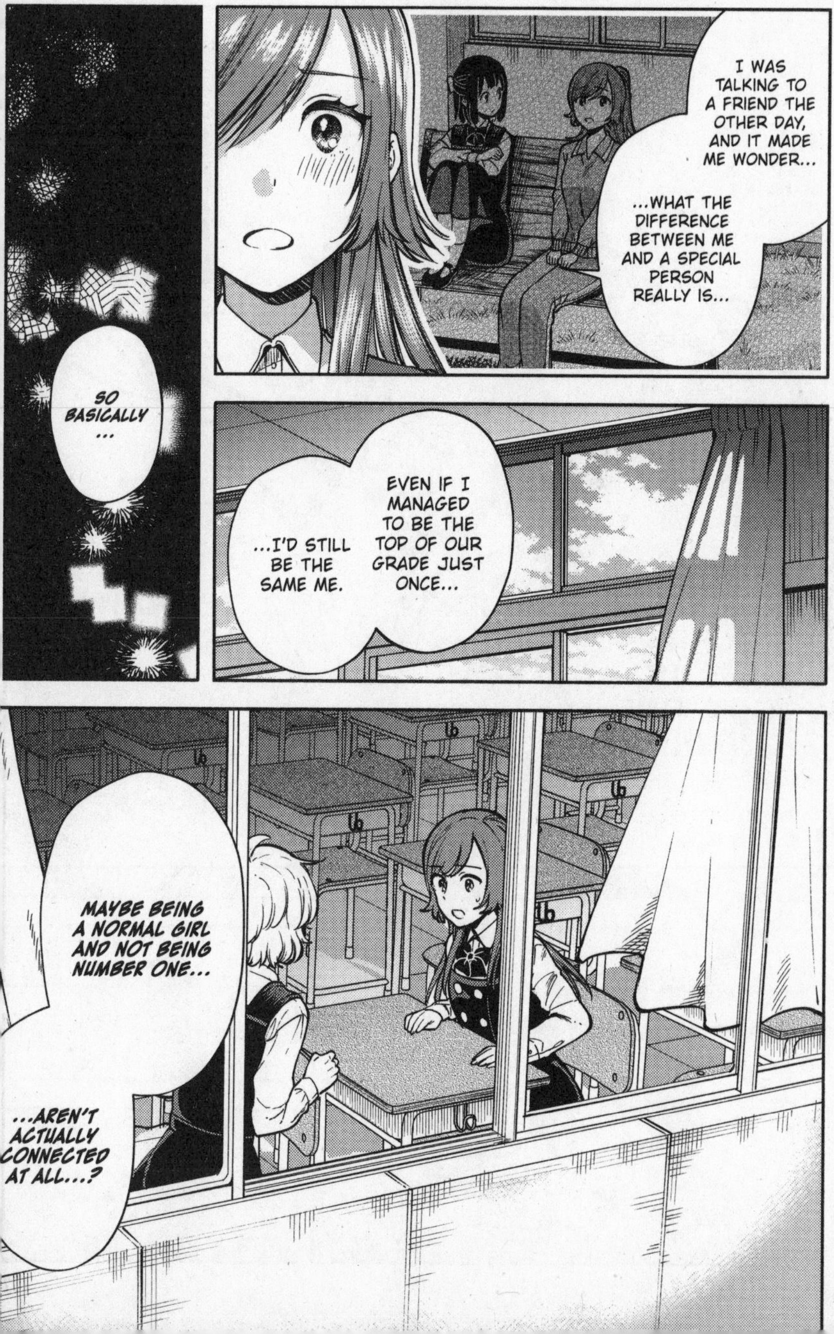
I WAS TALKING TO A FRIEND THE OTHER DAY, AND IT MADE ME WONDER...
...WHAT THE DIFFERENCE BETWEEN ME AND A SPECIAL PERSON REALLY IS...
EVEN IF I MANAGED TO BE THE TOP OF OUR GRADE JUST ONCE...
...I'D STILL BE THE SAME ME.
SO BASICALLY...
MAYBE BEING A NORMAL GIRL AND NOT BEING NUMBER ONE...
...AREN'T ACTUALLY CONNECTED AT ALL...?

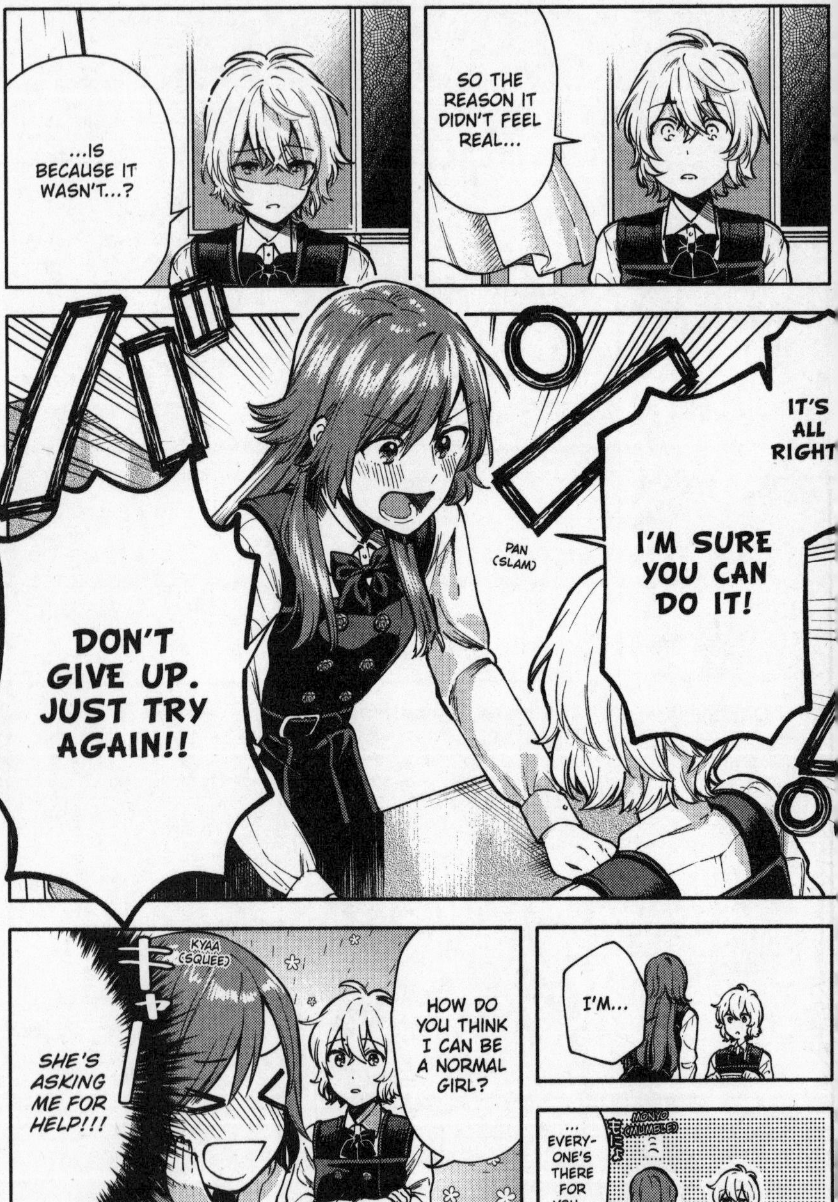
SO THE REASON IT DIDN'T FEEL REAL...
...IS BECAUSE IT WASN'T...?
IT'S ALL RIGHT
I'M SURE YOU CAN DO IT!
PAN (SLAM)
DON'T GIVE UP. JUST TRY AGAIN!!
I'M...
... EVERY-ONE'S THERE FOR YOU...
MONYO (MUMBLE)
MONYO
HOW DO YOU THINK I CAN BE A NORMAL GIRL?
KYAA (SQUEE)
SHE'S ASKING ME FOR HELP!!!

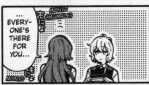

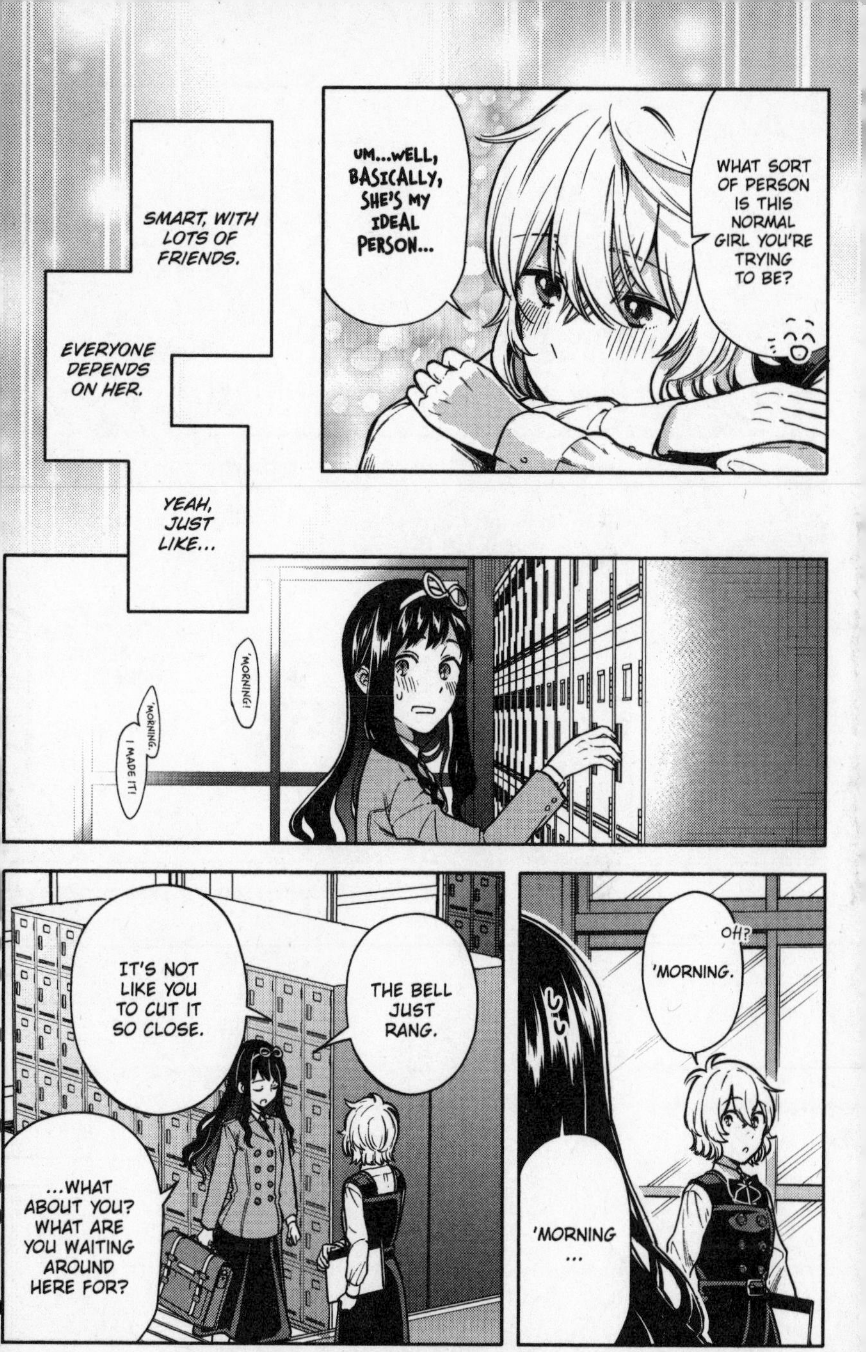
WHAT SORT OF PERSON IS THIS NORMAL GIRL YOU'RE TRYING TO BE?
UM...WELL, BASICALLY, SHE'S MY IDEAL PERSON...
SMART, WITH LOTS OF FRIENDS.
EVERYONE DEPENDS ON HER.
YEAH, JUST LIKE...
'MORNING!
'MORNING. I MADE IT!
OH?
'MORNING.
'MORNING ...
THE BELL JUST RANG.
IT'S NOT LIKE YOU TO CUT IT SO CLOSE.
...WHAT ABOUT YOU? WHAT ARE YOU WAITING AROUND HERE FOR?

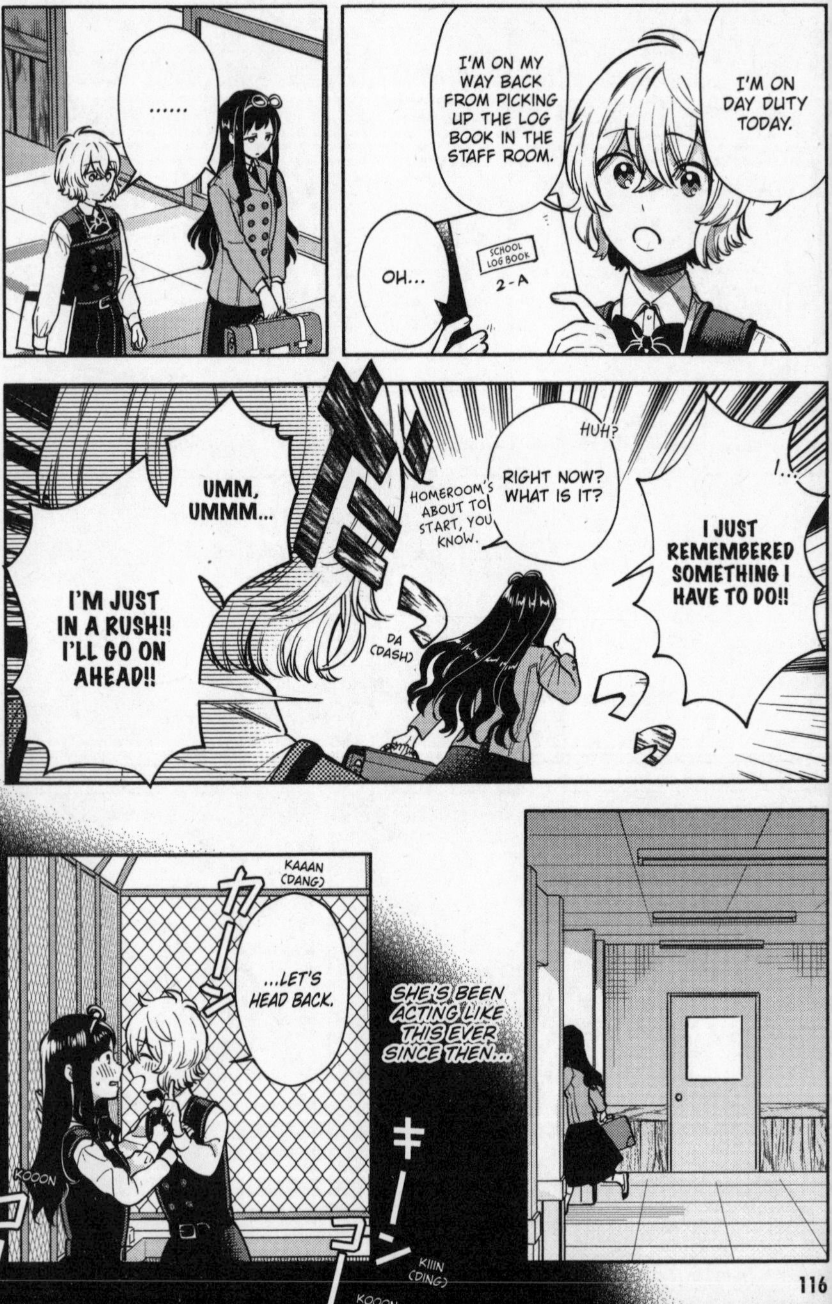
I'M ON DAY DUTY TODAY.
I'M ON MY WAY BACK FROM PICKING UP THE LOG BOOK IN THE STAFF ROOM.
SCHOOL LOG BOOK
2-A
OH...
......
I...
I JUST REMEMBERED SOMETHING I HAVE TO DO!!
HUH?
RIGHT NOW? WHAT IS IT?
HOMEROOM'S ABOUT TO START, YOU KNOW.
DA (DASH)
UMM, UMMM...
I'M JUST IN A RUSH!! I'LL GO ON AHEAD!!
SHE'S BEEN ACTING LIKE THIS EVER SINCE THEN...
KAAAN (DANG)
...LET'S HEAD BACK.
KIIIN (DING)
KOOON
KOOON

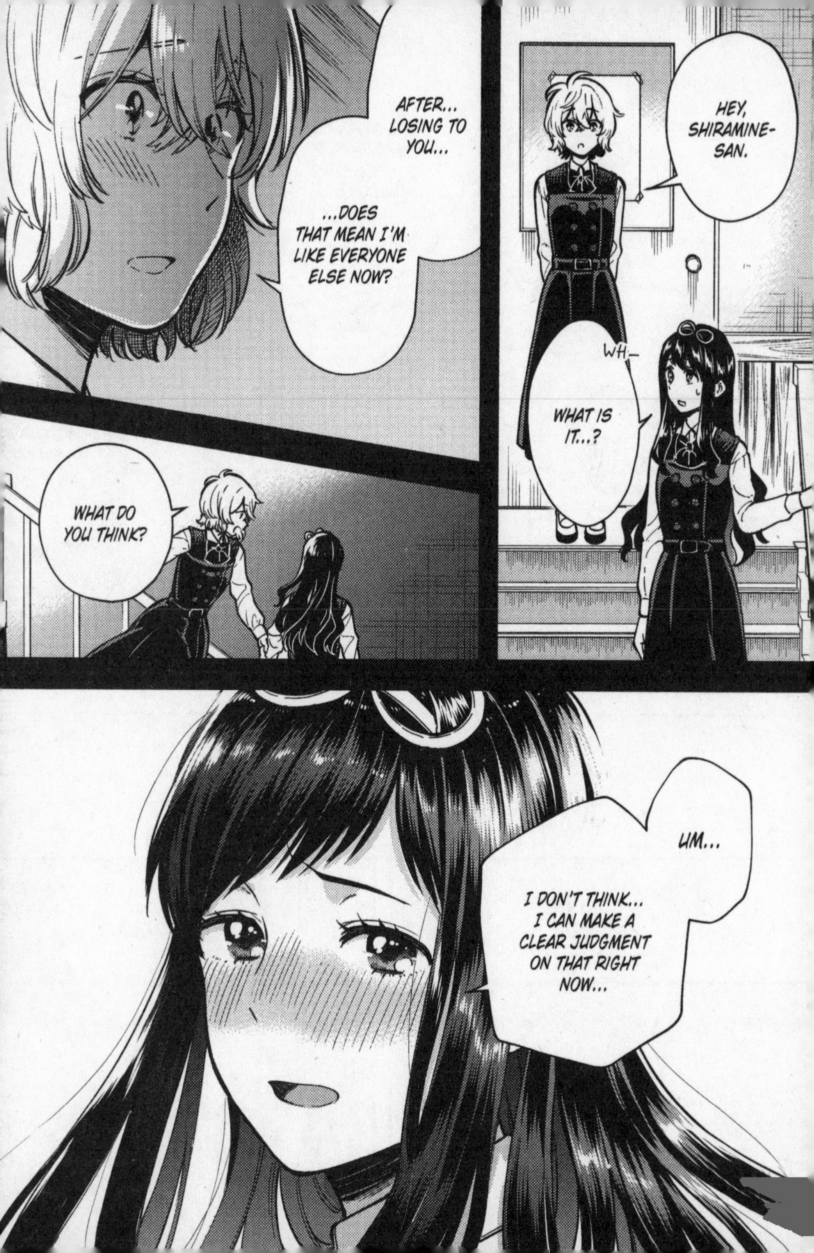
HEY, SHIRAMINE-SAN.
WH—
WHAT IS IT...?
AFTER... LOSING TO YOU...
...DOES THAT MEAN I'M LIKE EVERYONE ELSE NOW?
WHAT DO YOU THINK?
UM...
I DON'T THINK... I CAN MAKE A CLEAR JUDGMENT ON THAT RIGHT NOW...

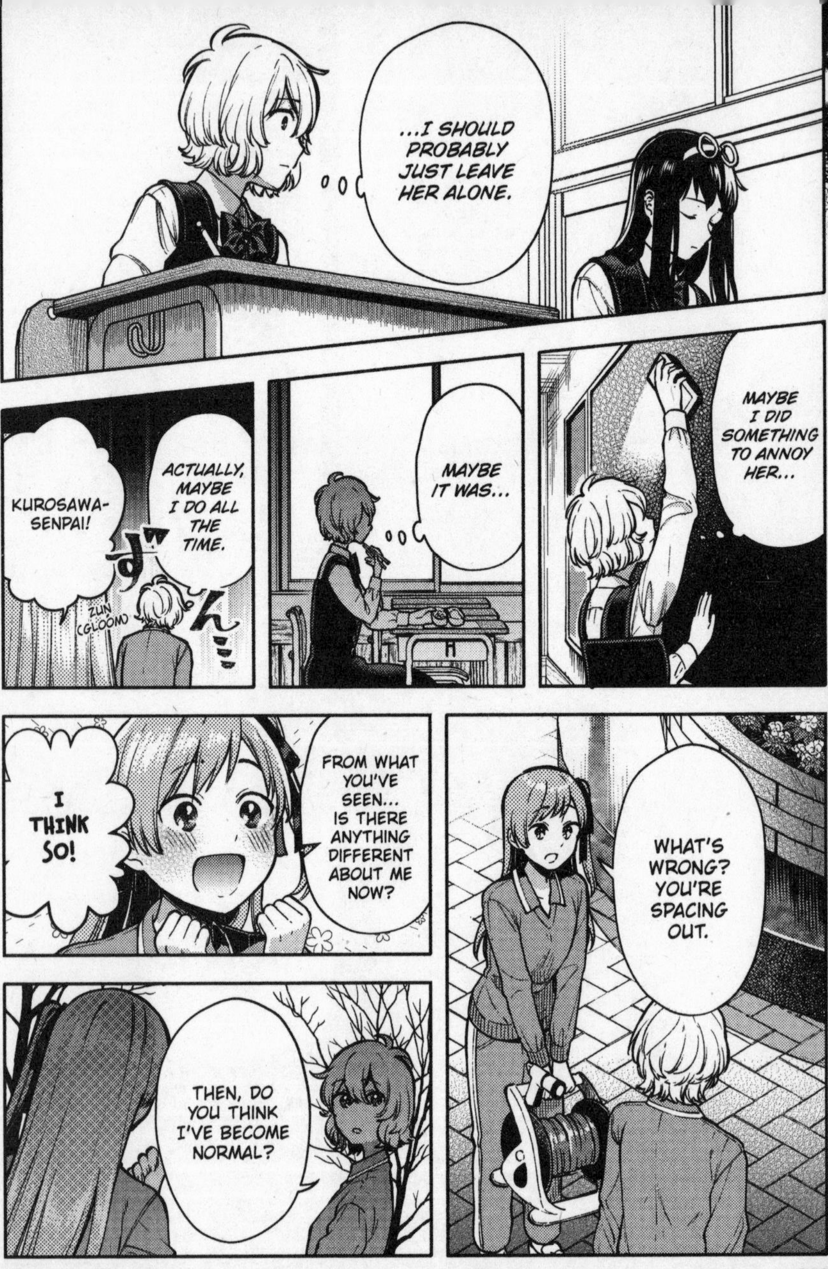
...I SHOULD PROBABLY JUST LEAVE HER ALONE.
MAYBE I DID SOMETHING TO ANNOY HER...
MAYBE IT WAS...
ACTUALLY, MAYBE I DO ALL THE TIME.
KUROSAWA-SENPAI!
ZUN (GLOOM)
WHAT'S WRONG? YOU'RE SPACING OUT.
FROM WHAT YOU'VE SEEN... IS THERE ANYTHING DIFFERENT ABOUT ME NOW?
I THINK SO!
THEN, DO YOU THINK I'VE BECOME NORMAL?

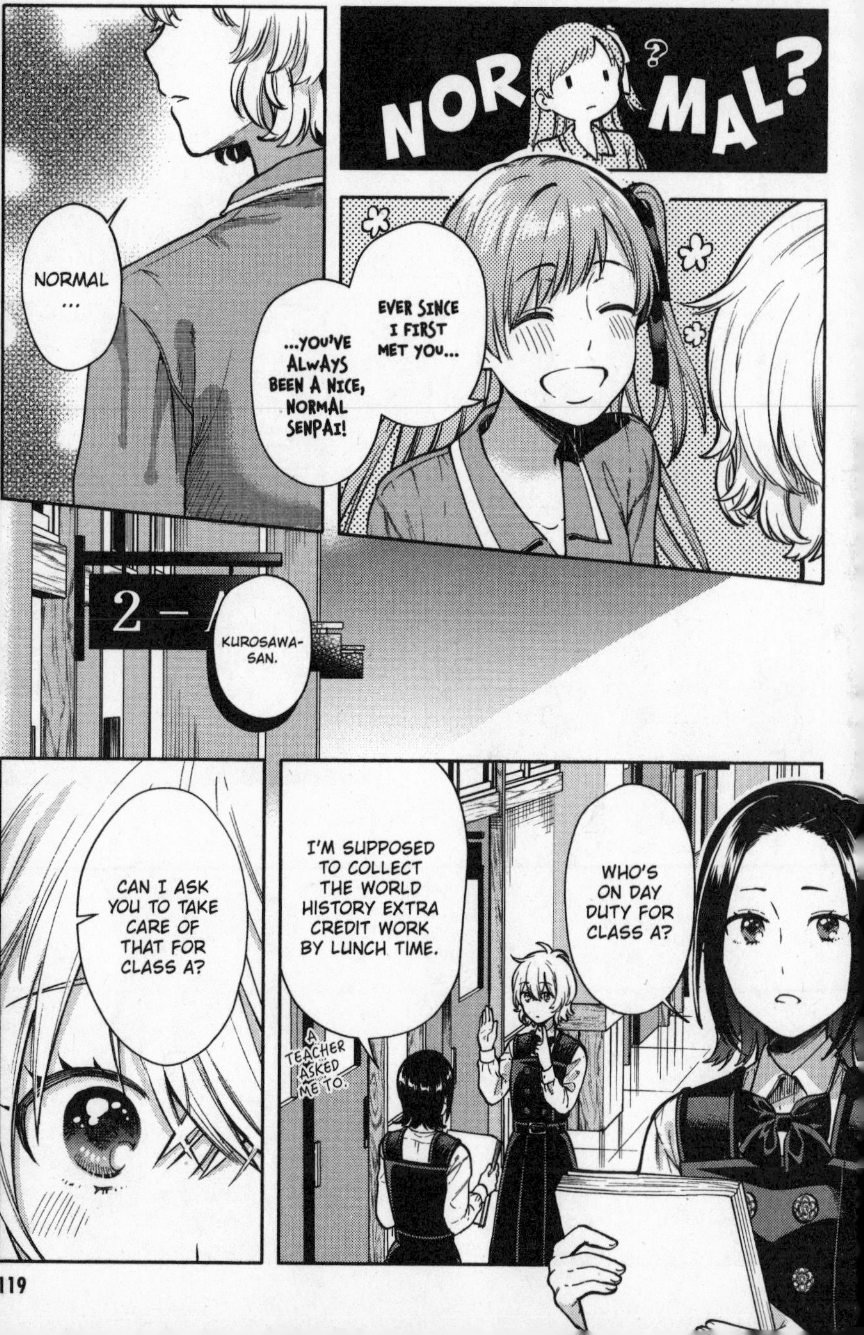
NORMAL?
EVER SINCE I FIRST MET YOU...
...YOU'VE ALWAYS BEEN A NICE, NORMAL SENPAI!
NORMAL ...
KUROSAWA-SAN.
WHO'S ON DAY DUTY FOR CLASS A?
I'M SUPPOSED TO COLLECT THE WORLD HISTORY EXTRA CREDIT WORK BY LUNCH TIME.
A TEACHER ASKED ME TO.
CAN I ASK YOU TO TAKE CARE OF THAT FOR CLASS A?

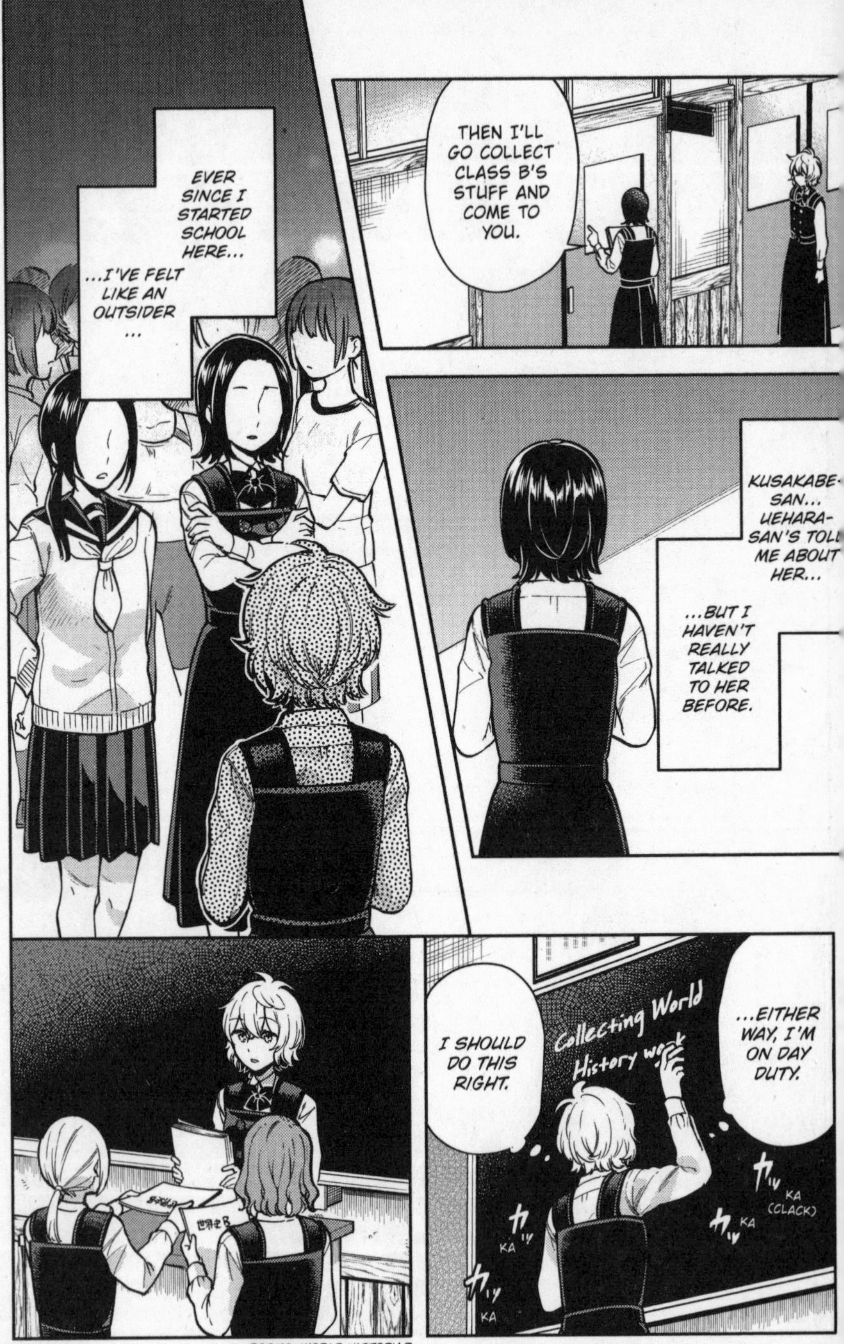
THEN I'LL GO COLLECT CLASS B'S STUFF AND COME TO YOU.
KUSAKABE-SAN... UEHARA-SAN'S TOLD ME ABOUT HER...
...BUT I HAVEN'T REALLY TALKED TO HER BEFORE.
EVER SINCE I STARTED SCHOOL HERE...
...I'VE FELT LIKE AN OUTSIDER...
...EITHER WAY, I'M ON DAY DUTY.
I SHOULD DO THIS RIGHT.
Collecting World History work
カッ KA (CLACK)
カッ KA
カッ KA
カッ KA
世界史B
BOOKS: WORLD HISTORY B

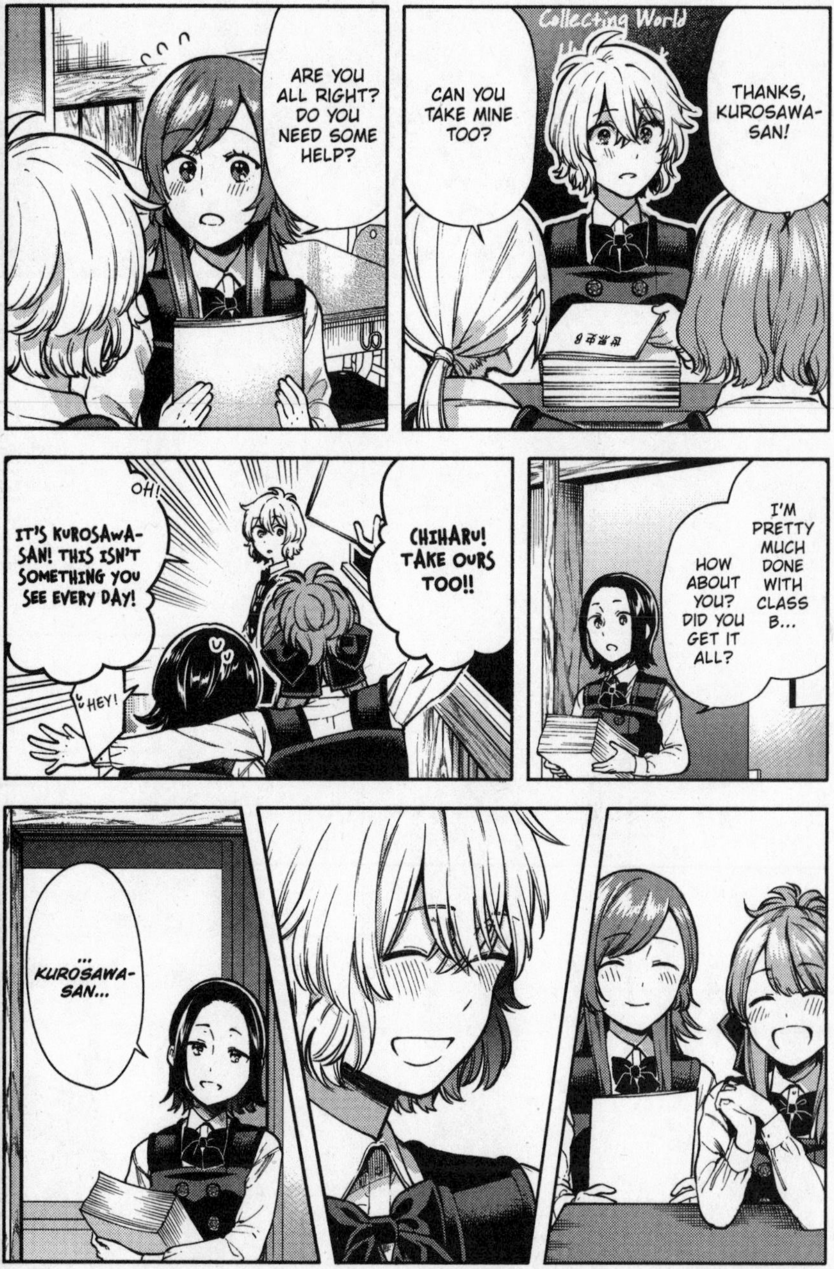
Collecting World
THANKS, KUROSAWA-SAN!
CAN YOU TAKE MINE TOO?
ARE YOU ALL RIGHT? DO YOU NEED SOME HELP?
I'M PRETTY MUCH DONE WITH CLASS B...
HOW ABOUT YOU? DID YOU GET IT ALL?
CHIHARU! TAKE OURS TOO!!
OH!
IT'S KUROSAWA-SAN! THIS ISN'T SOMETHING YOU SEE EVERY DAY!
HEY!
... KUROSAWA-SAN...

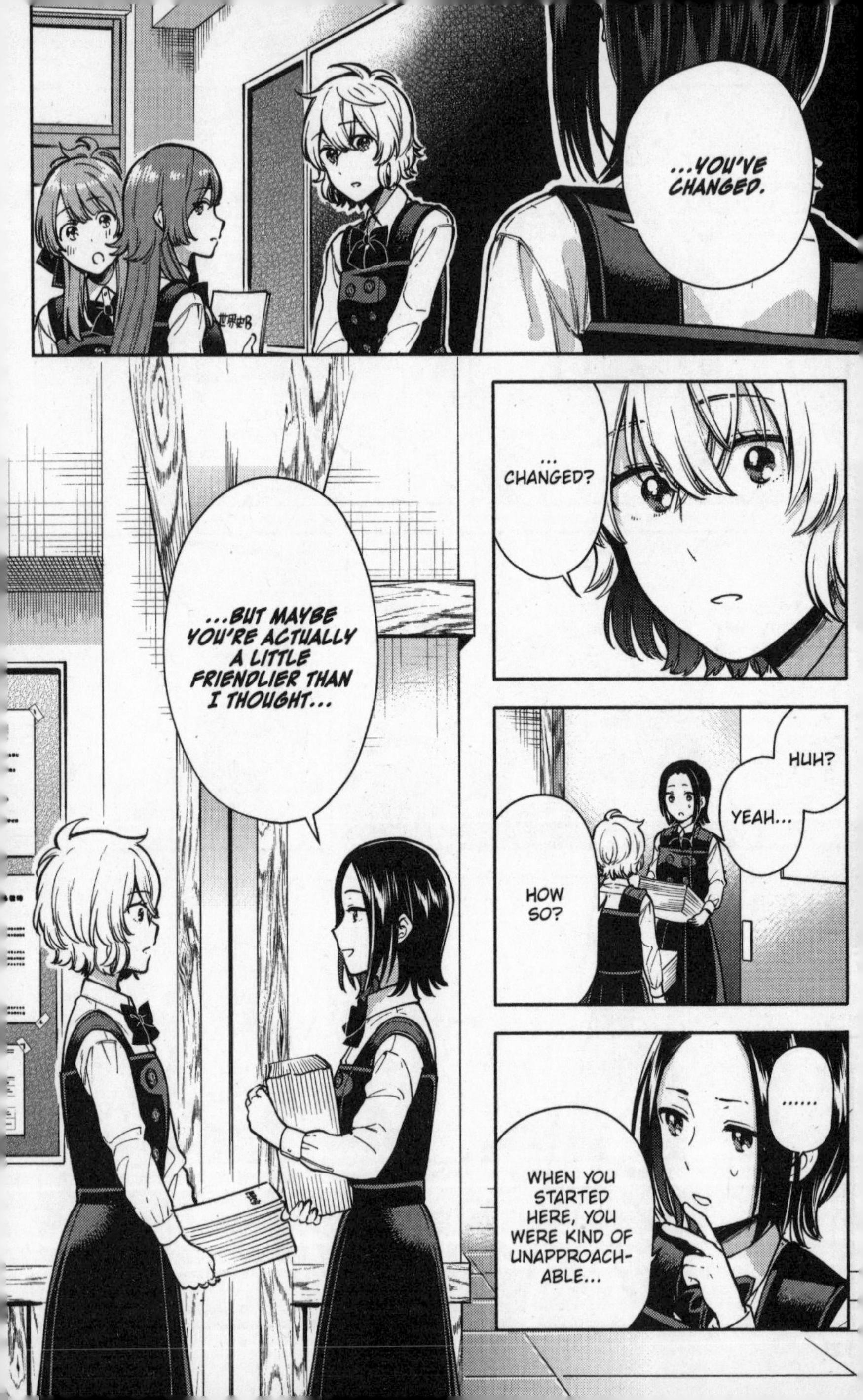
...YOU'VE CHANGED.
世界史B
... CHANGED?
HUH? YEAH...
HOW SO?
......
WHEN YOU STARTED HERE, YOU WERE KIND OF UNAPPROACH-ABLE...
...BUT MAYBE YOU'RE ACTUALLY A LITTLE FRIENDLIER THAN I THOUGHT...

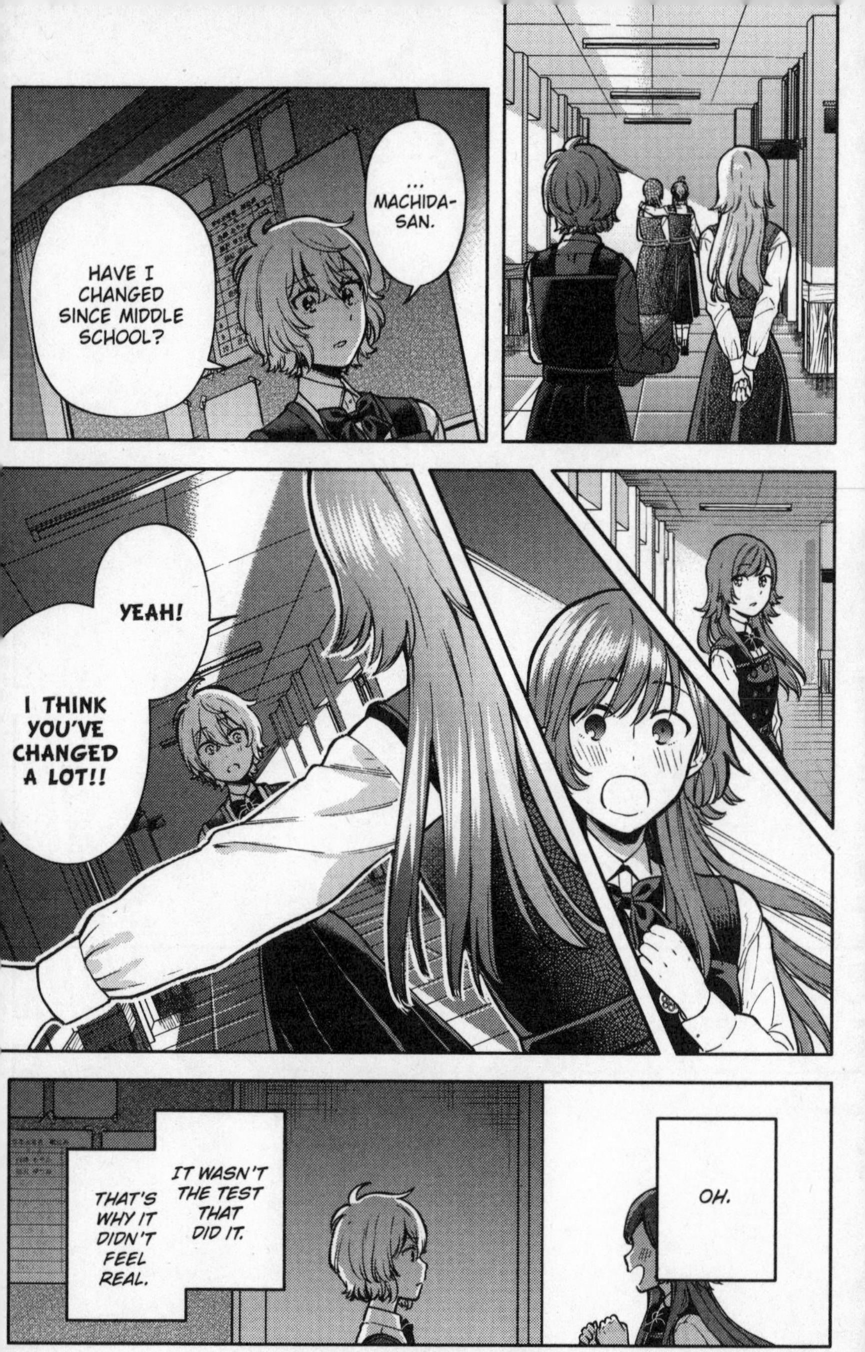

...MACHIDA-SAN.
HAVE I CHANGED SINCE MIDDLE SCHOOL?
YEAH!
I THINK YOU'VE CHANGED A LOT!!
OH.
IT WASN'T THE TEST THAT DID IT.
THAT'S WHY IT DIDN'T FEEL REAL.

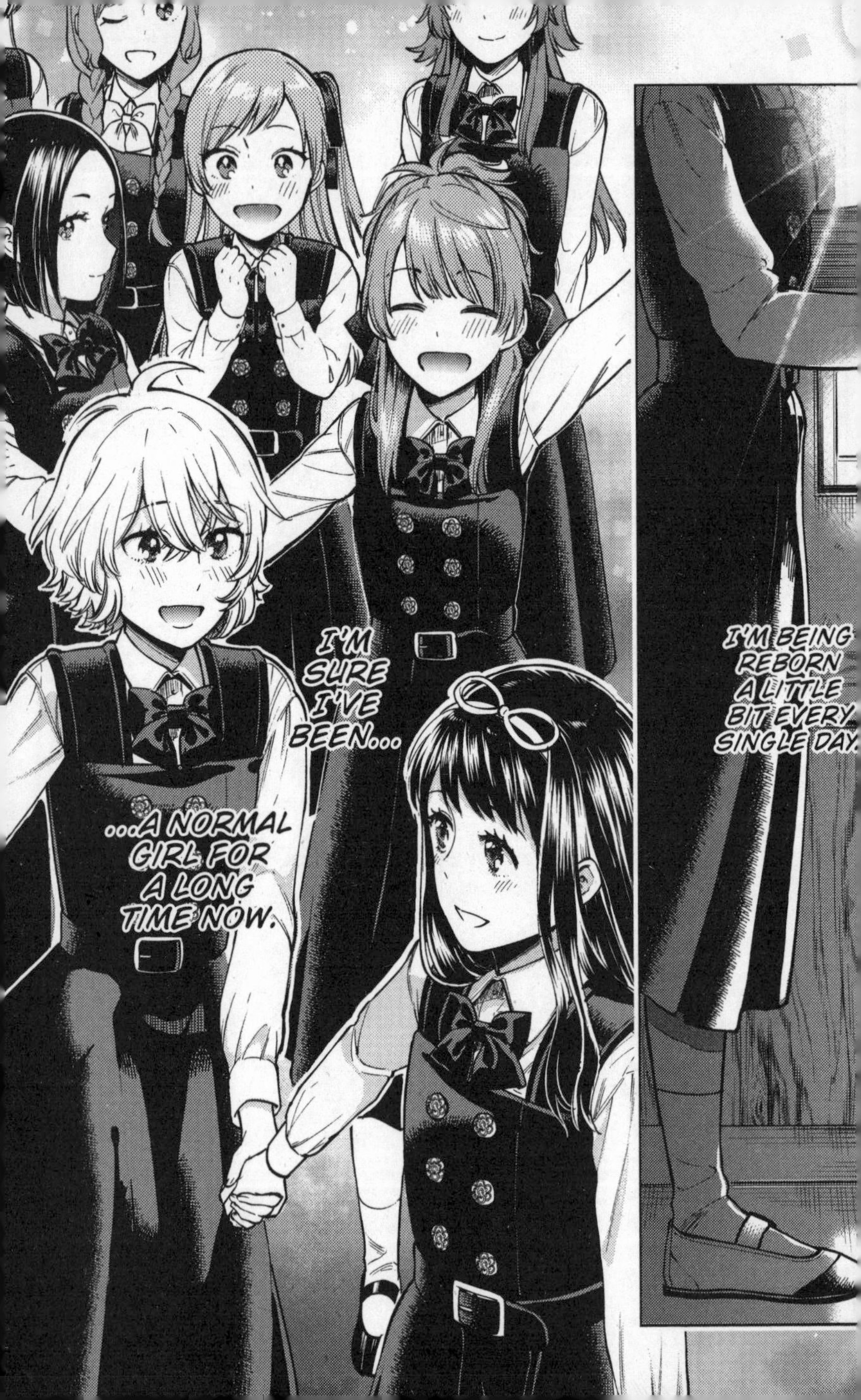
I'M BEING REBORN A LITTLE BIT EVERY SINGLE DAY.
I'M SURE I'VE BEEN...
...A NORMAL GIRL FOR A LONG TIME NOW.

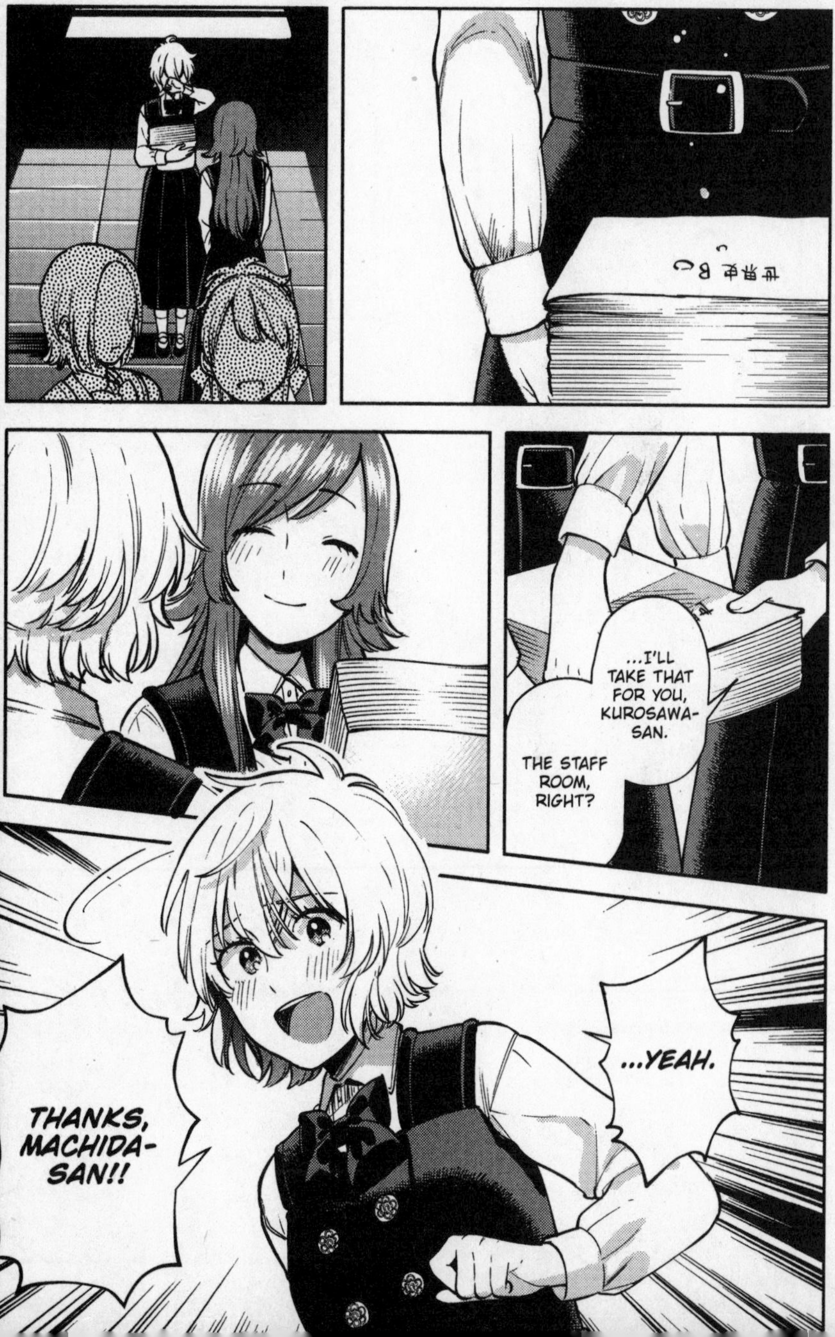
...I'LL TAKE THAT FOR YOU, KUROSAWA-SAN.
THE STAFF ROOM, RIGHT?
...YEAH.
THANKS, MACHIDA-SAN!!

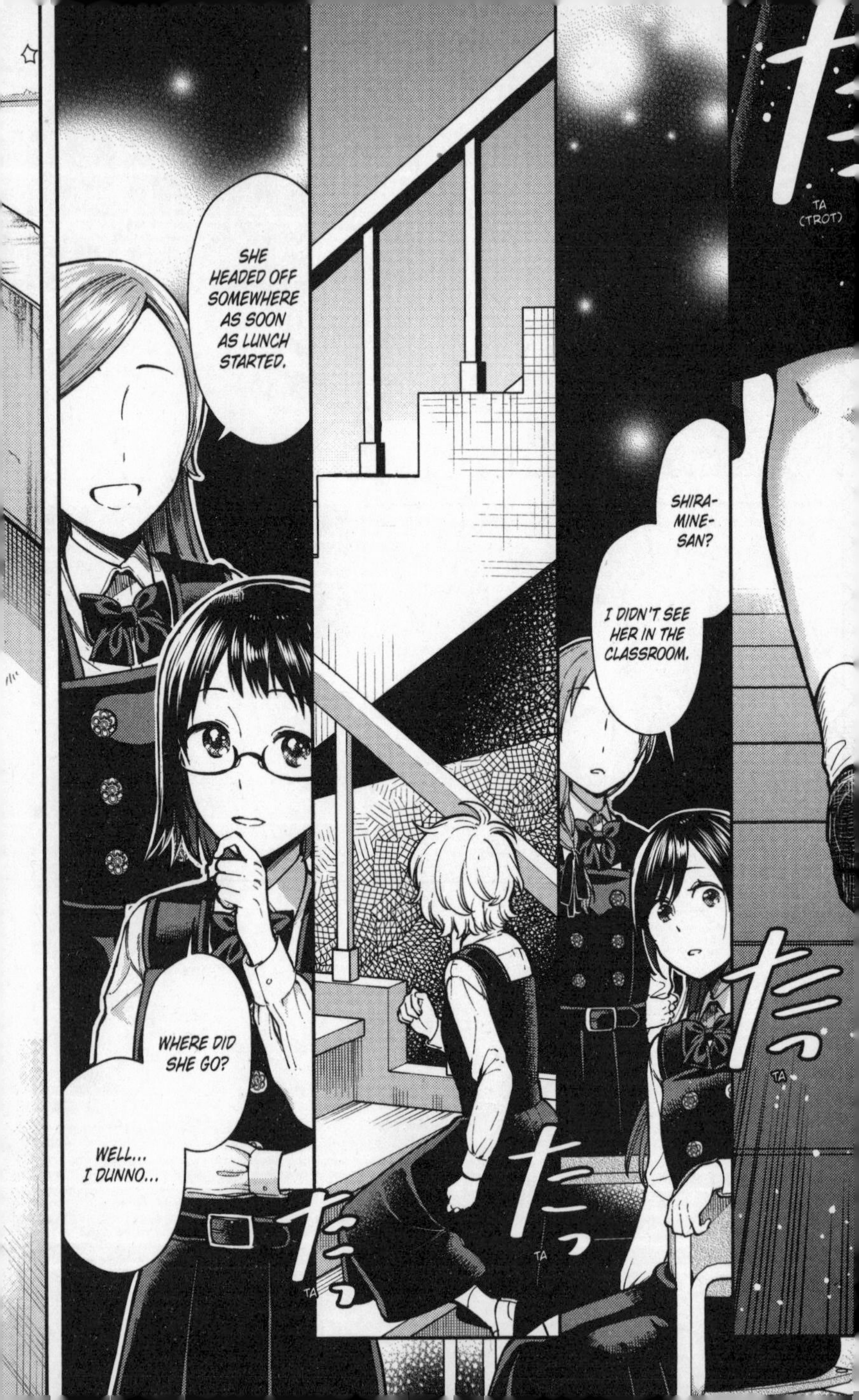
TA (TROT)
SHIRA-MINE-SAN?
I DIDN'T SEE HER IN THE CLASSROOM.
TA
TA
TA
SHE HEADED OFF SOMEWHERE AS SOON AS LUNCH STARTED.
WHERE DID SHE GO?
WELL... I DUNNO...

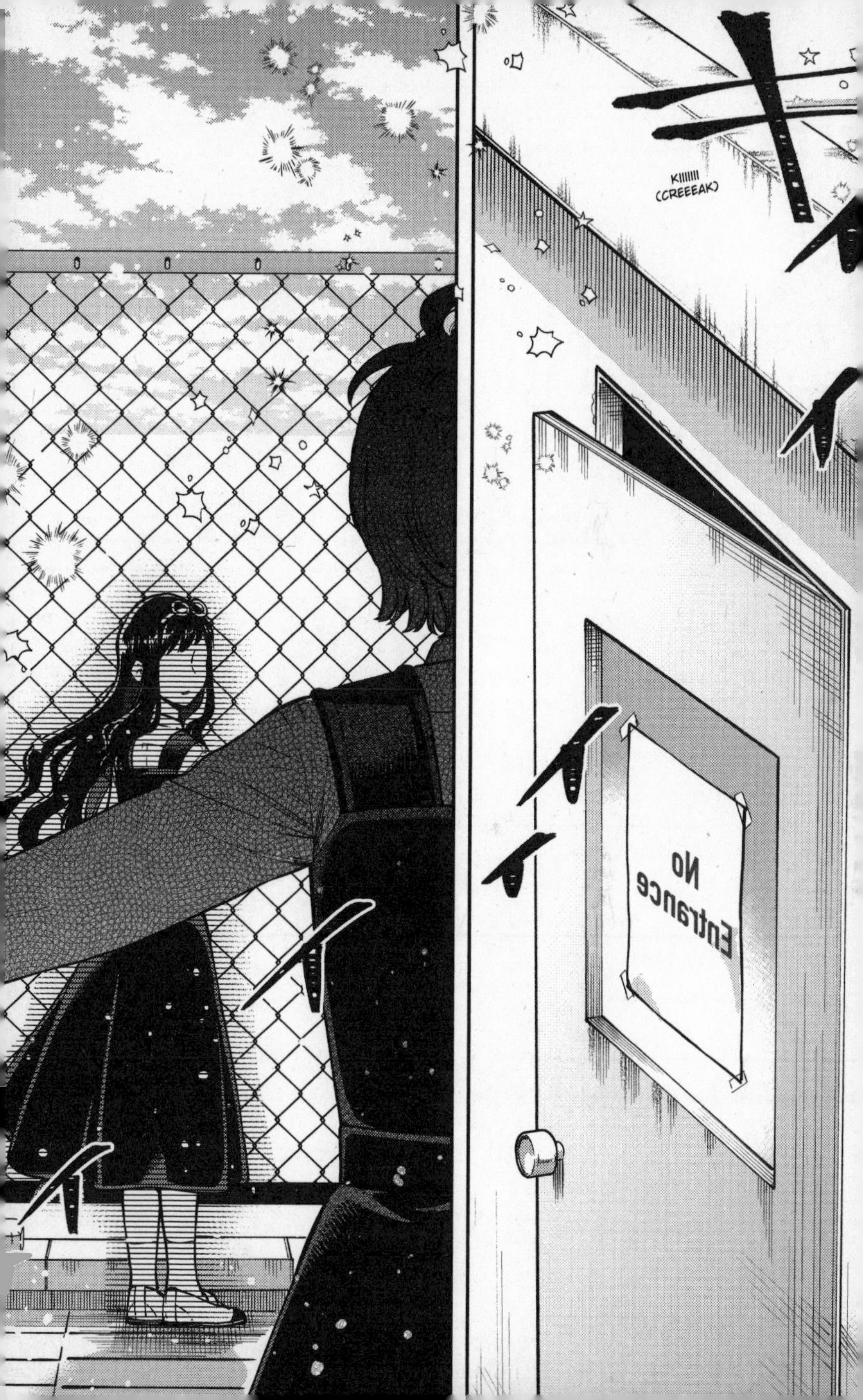
KIIIIII
(CREEEAK)
No Entrance

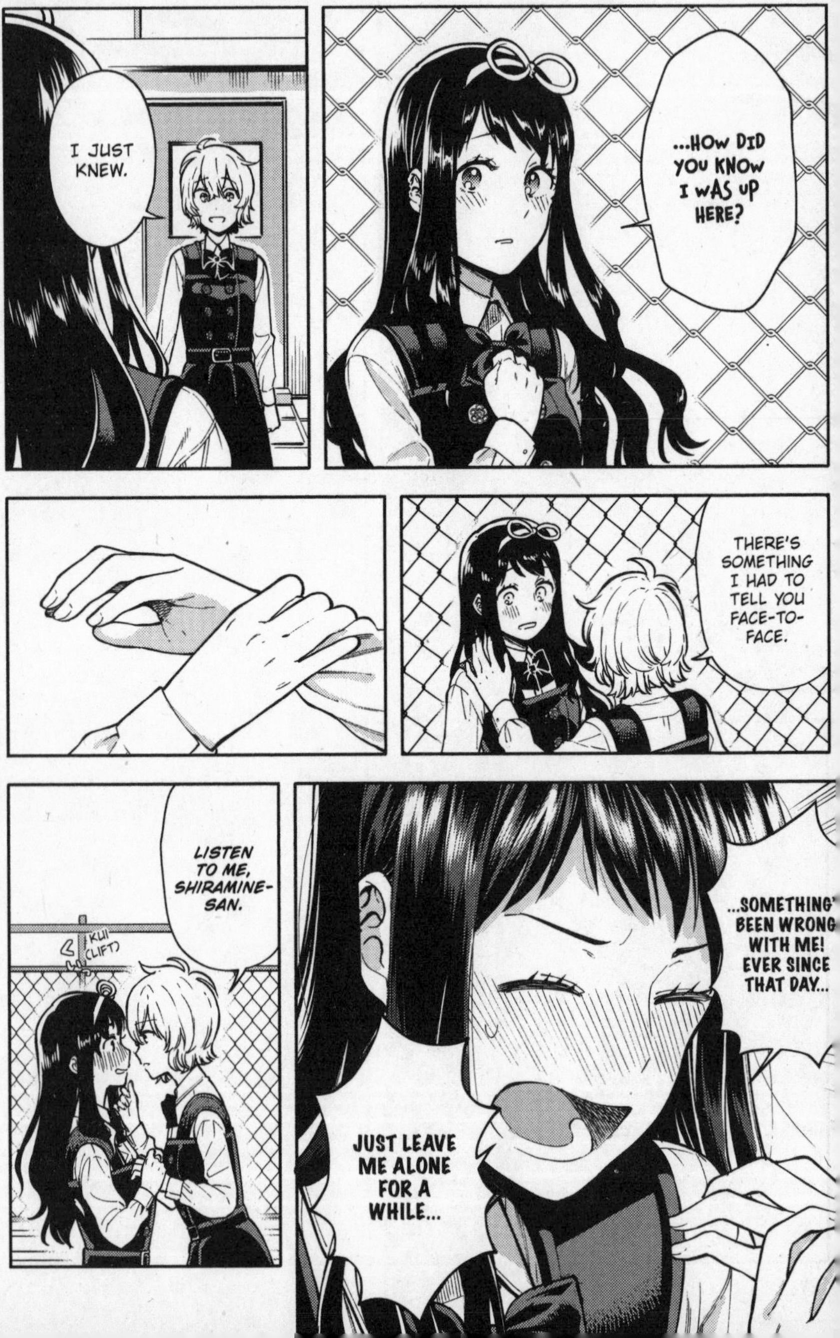
...HOW DID YOU KNOW I WAS UP HERE?
I JUST KNEW.
THERE'S SOMETHING I HAD TO TELL YOU FACE-TO-FACE.
...SOMETHING' BEEN WRONG WITH ME! EVER SINCE THAT DAY...
JUST LEAVE ME ALONE FOR A WHILE...
LISTEN TO ME, SHIRAMINE-SAN.
KUI (LIFT)

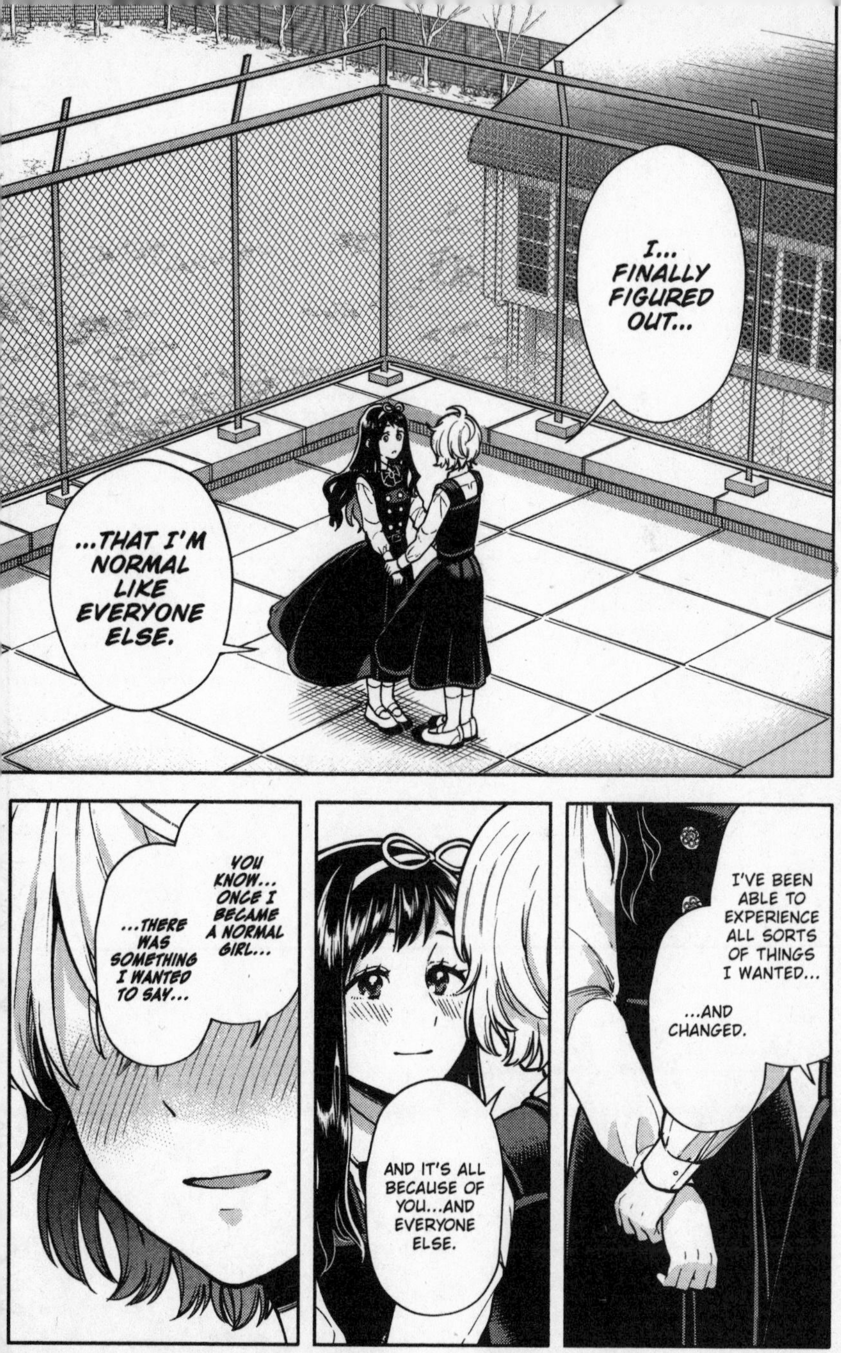
I... FINALLY FIGURED OUT...
...THAT I'M NORMAL LIKE EVERYONE ELSE.
I'VE BEEN ABLE TO EXPERIENCE ALL SORTS OF THINGS I WANTED...
...AND CHANGED.
AND IT'S ALL BECAUSE OF YOU...AND EVERYONE ELSE.
YOU KNOW... ONCE I BECAME A NORMAL GIRL...
...THERE WAS SOMETHING I WANTED TO SAY...

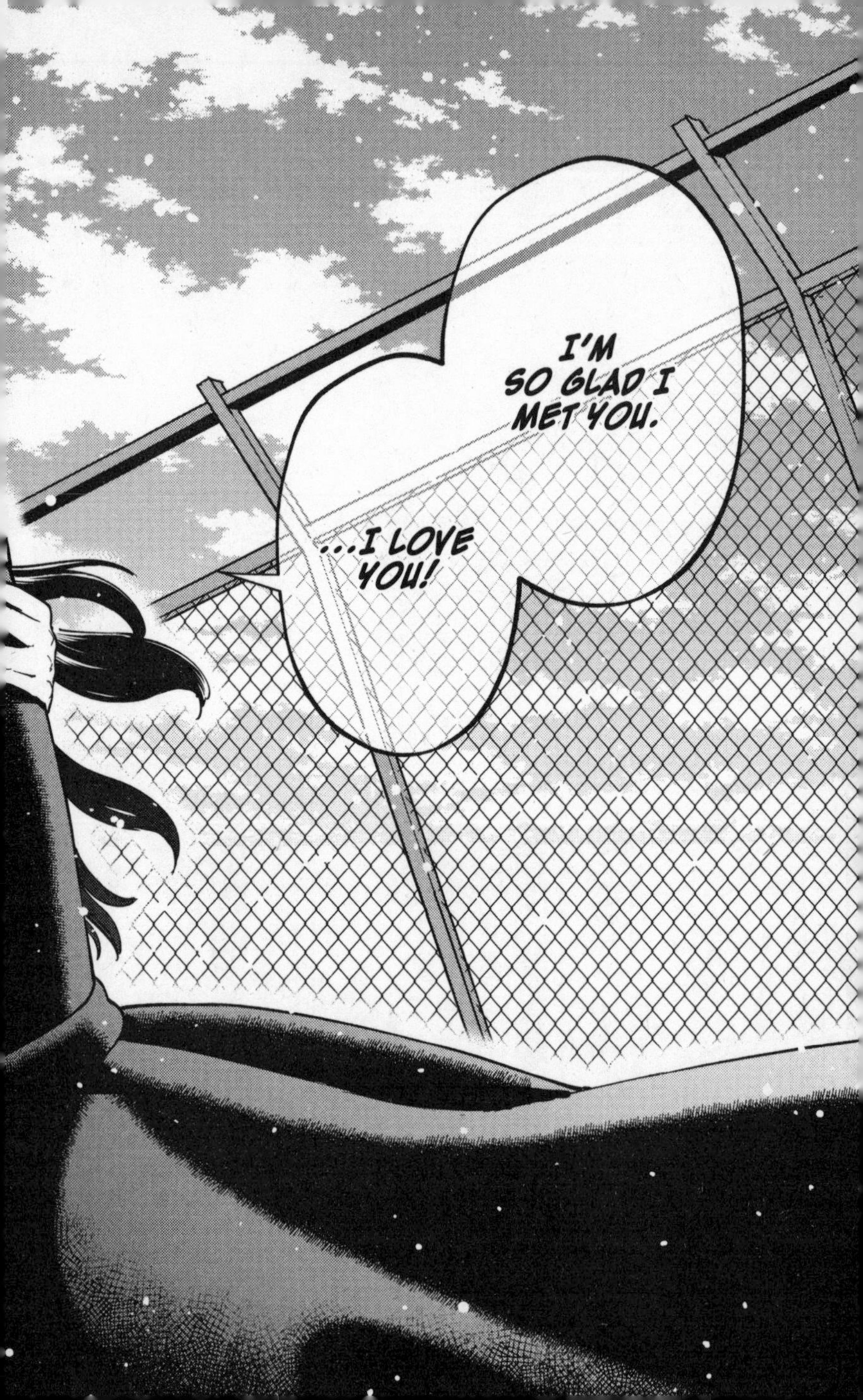
I'M SO GLAD I MET YOU.
...I LOVE YOU!

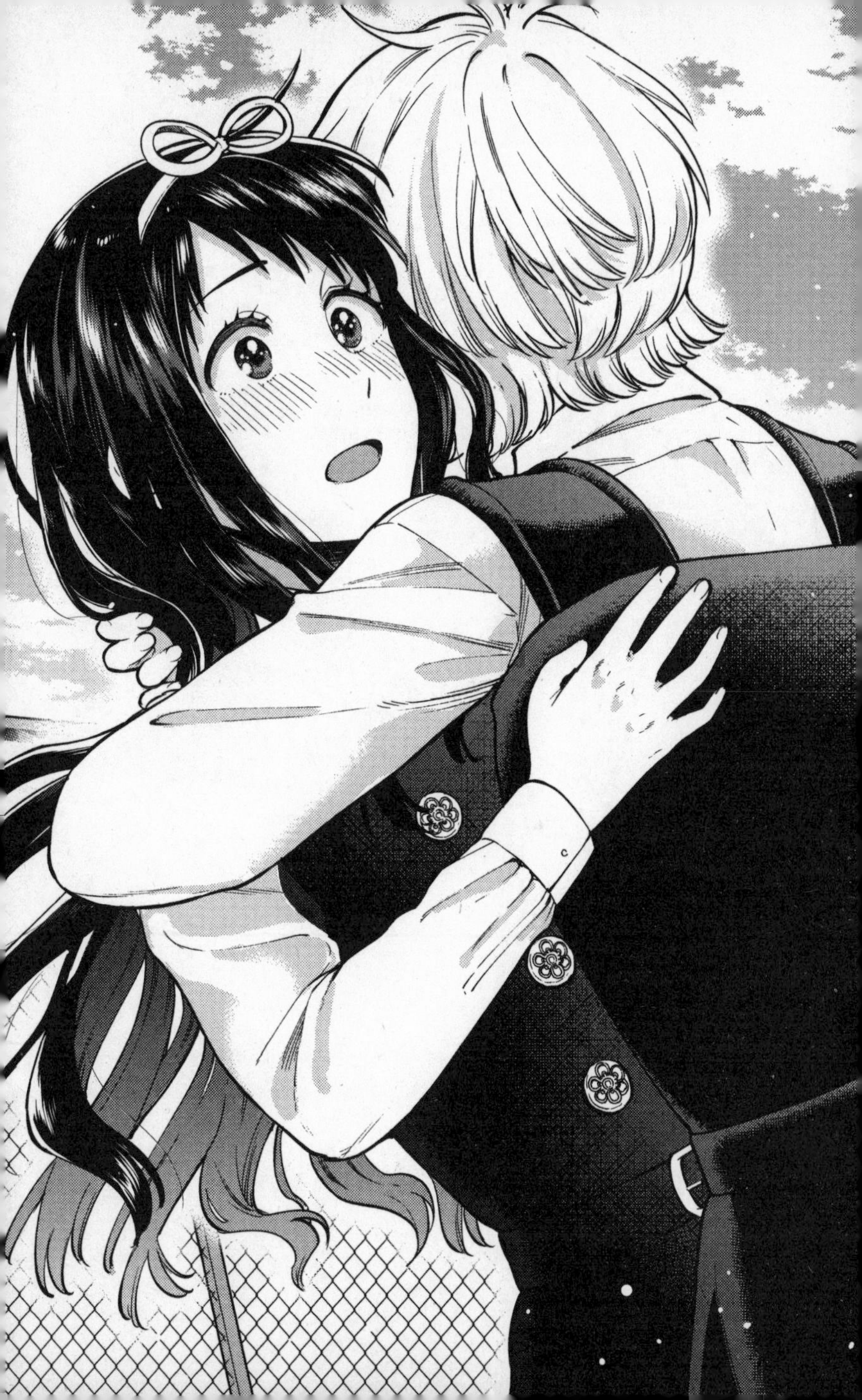

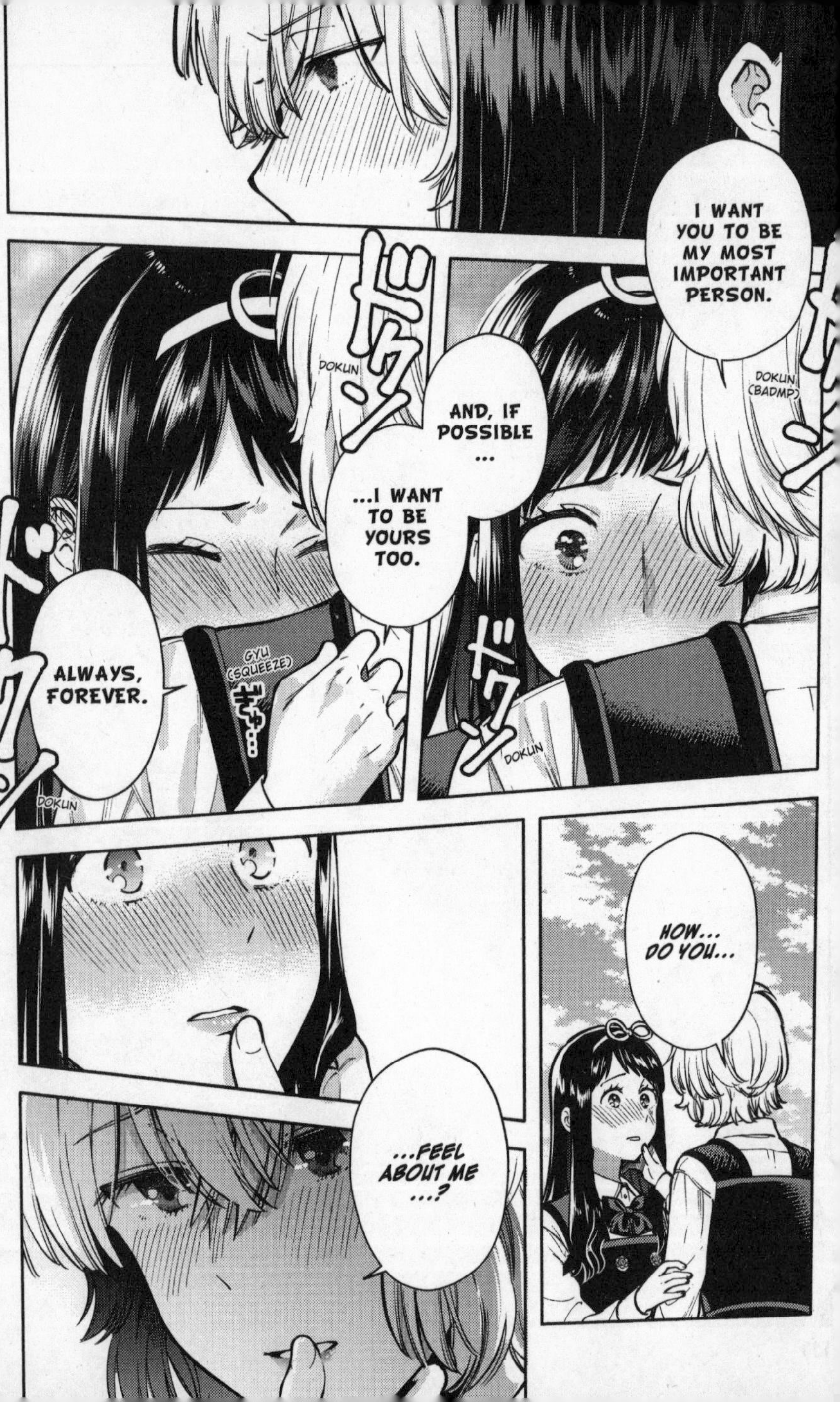

I WANT YOU TO BE MY MOST IMPORTANT PERSON.
ドクン
DOKUN (BADMP)
AND, IF POSSIBLE ...
ドクン
DOKUN
ドクン
DOKUN
...I WANT TO BE YOURS TOO.
ぎゅ…
GYU (SQUEEZE)
ALWAYS, FOREVER.
ドクン
DOKUN
HOW... DO YOU...
...FEEL ABOUT ME ...?

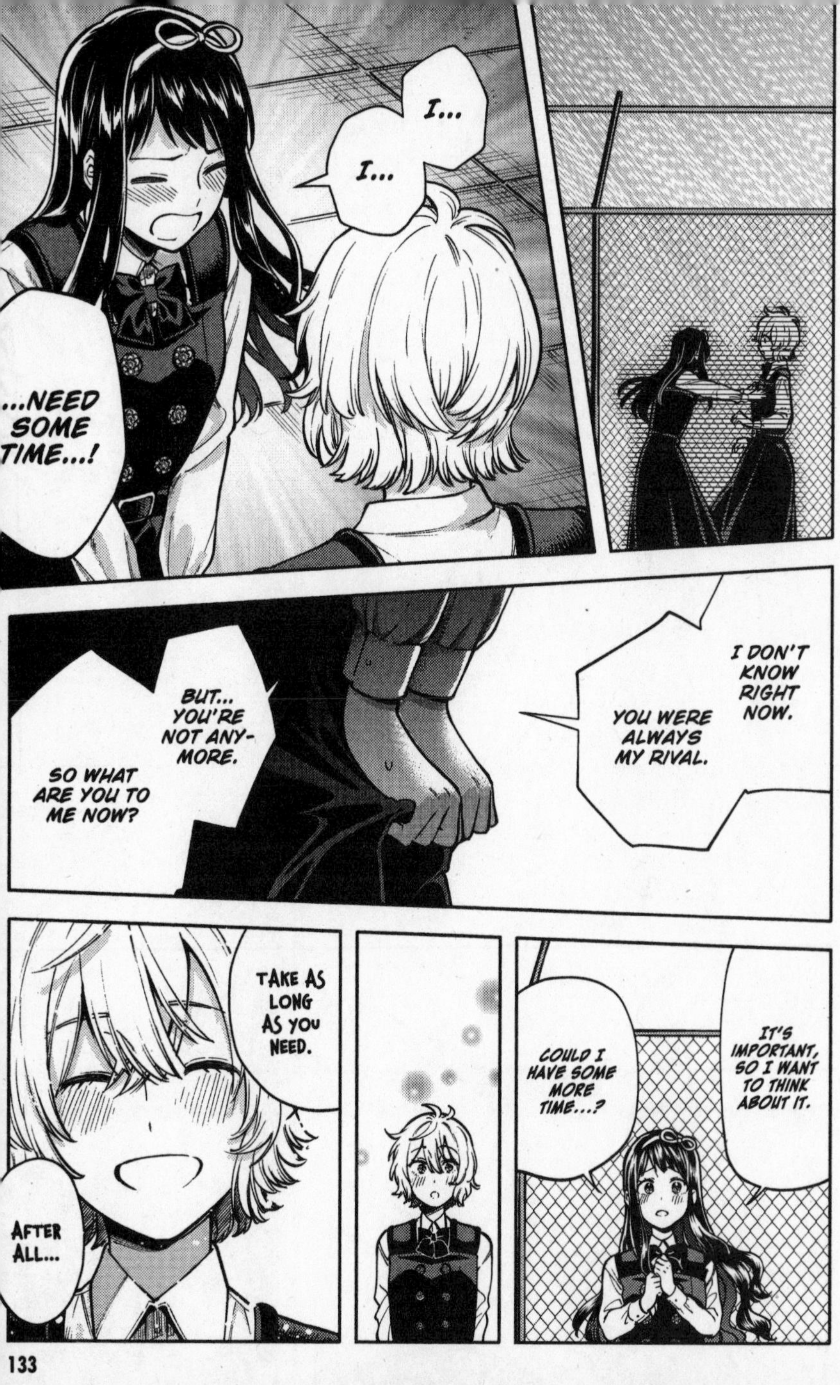
I... I...
...NEED SOME TIME...!
I DON'T KNOW RIGHT NOW.
YOU WERE ALWAYS MY RIVAL.
BUT... YOU'RE NOT ANY-MORE.
SO WHAT ARE YOU TO ME NOW?
IT'S IMPORTANT, SO I WANT TO THINK ABOUT IT.
COULD I HAVE SOME MORE TIME...?
TAKE AS LONG AS YOU NEED.
AFTER ALL...

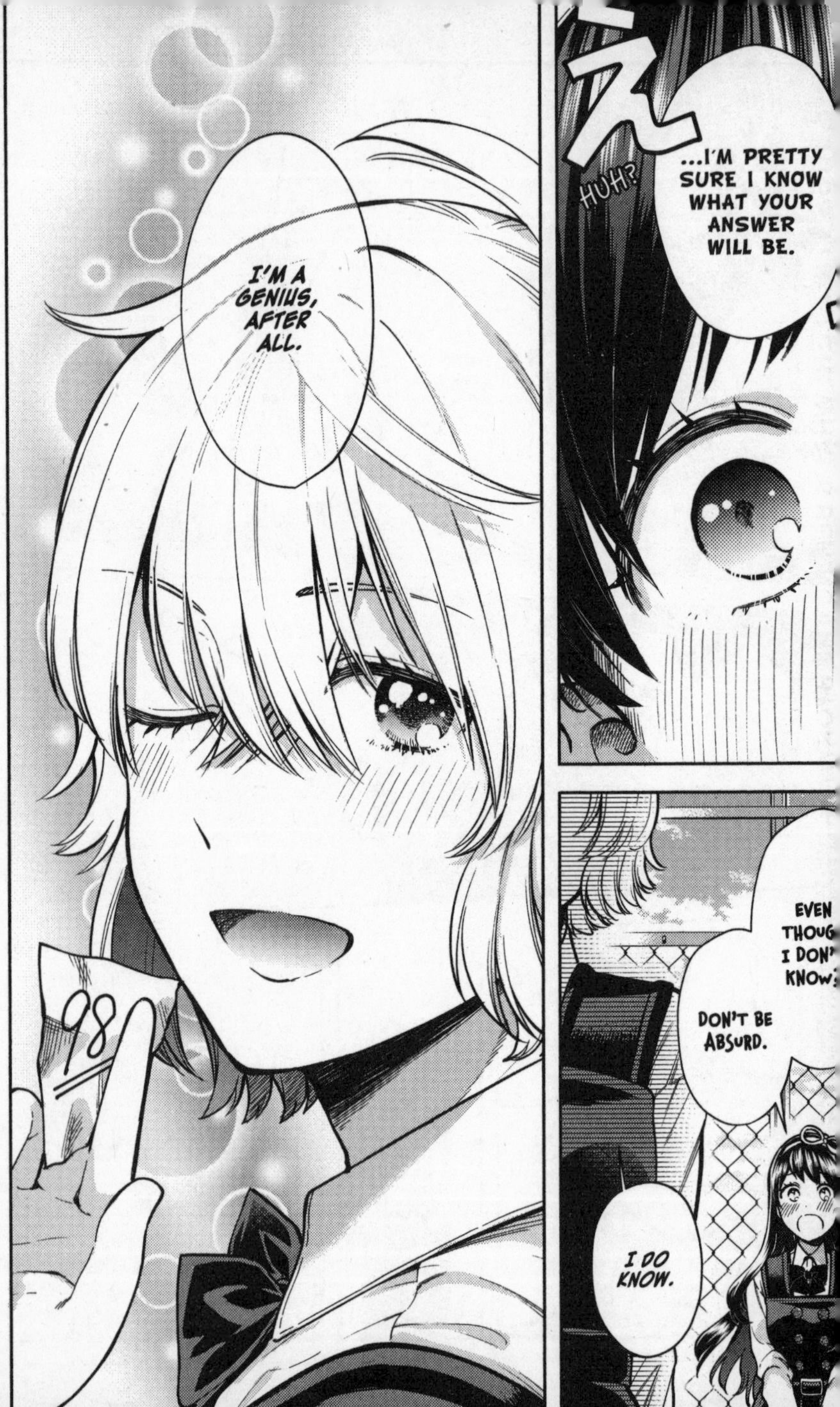
HUH?
...I'M PRETTY SURE I KNOW WHAT YOUR ANSWER WILL BE.
EVEN THOUG I DON' KNOW?
DON'T BE ABSURD.
I DO KNOW.
I'M A GENIUS, AFTER ALL.
98

KISS THEATER: WHAT'S BEHIND THE STORY!?

PEOPLE OTHER THAN THE MAIN CHARACTERS HAVE STORIES TOO. HERE, WE PRESENT THE "LITTLE LOVE" STORIES HAPPENING BEHIND THE SCENES

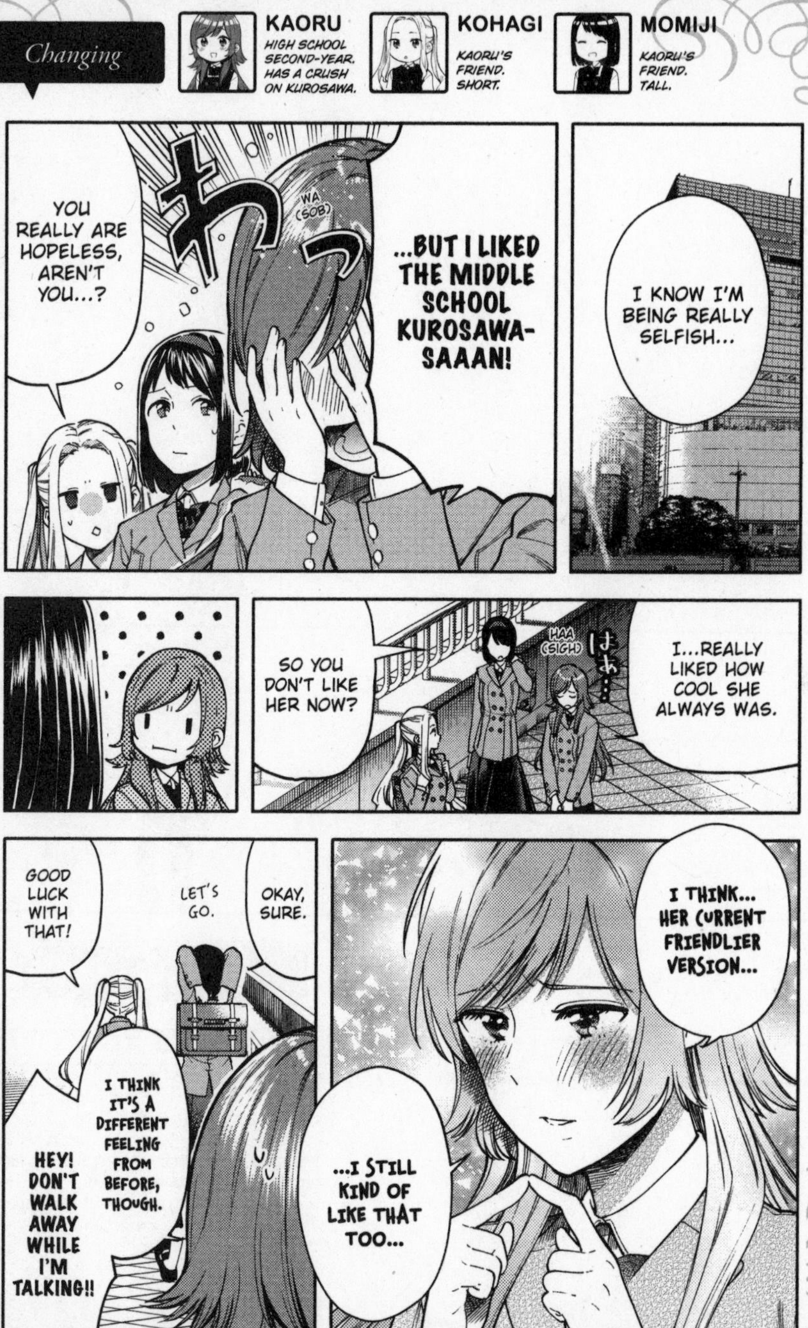

Changing
KAORU
HIGH SCHOOL SECOND-YEAR. HAS A CRUSH ON KUROSAWA.
KOHAGI
KAORU'S FRIEND. SHORT.
MOMIJI
KAORU'S FRIEND. TALL.
I KNOW I'M BEING REALLY SELFISH...
...BUT I LIKED THE MIDDLE SCHOOL KUROSAWA-SAAAN!
WA (SOB)
YOU REALLY ARE HOPELESS, AREN'T YOU...?
I...REALLY LIKED HOW COOL SHE ALWAYS WAS.
HAA (SIGH)
SO YOU DON'T LIKE HER NOW?
I THINK... HER CURRENT FRIENDLIER VERSION...
...I STILL KIND OF LIKE THAT TOO...
OKAY, SURE.
LET'S GO.
GOOD LUCK WITH THAT!
I THINK IT'S A DIFFERENT FEELING FROM BEFORE, THOUGH.
HEY! DON'T WALK AWAY WHILE I'M TALKING!!

Kaoru Machida

Kaoru Machida

Second-year student at Seiran Academy High School. In the craft club. She's had a crush on Kurosawa since middle school. She was never able to find a way to get to know her, but after becoming a second-year, she finally managed to have some conversations with her. Because of her reserved and gentle nature, she's always had a fair number of friends both then and now.

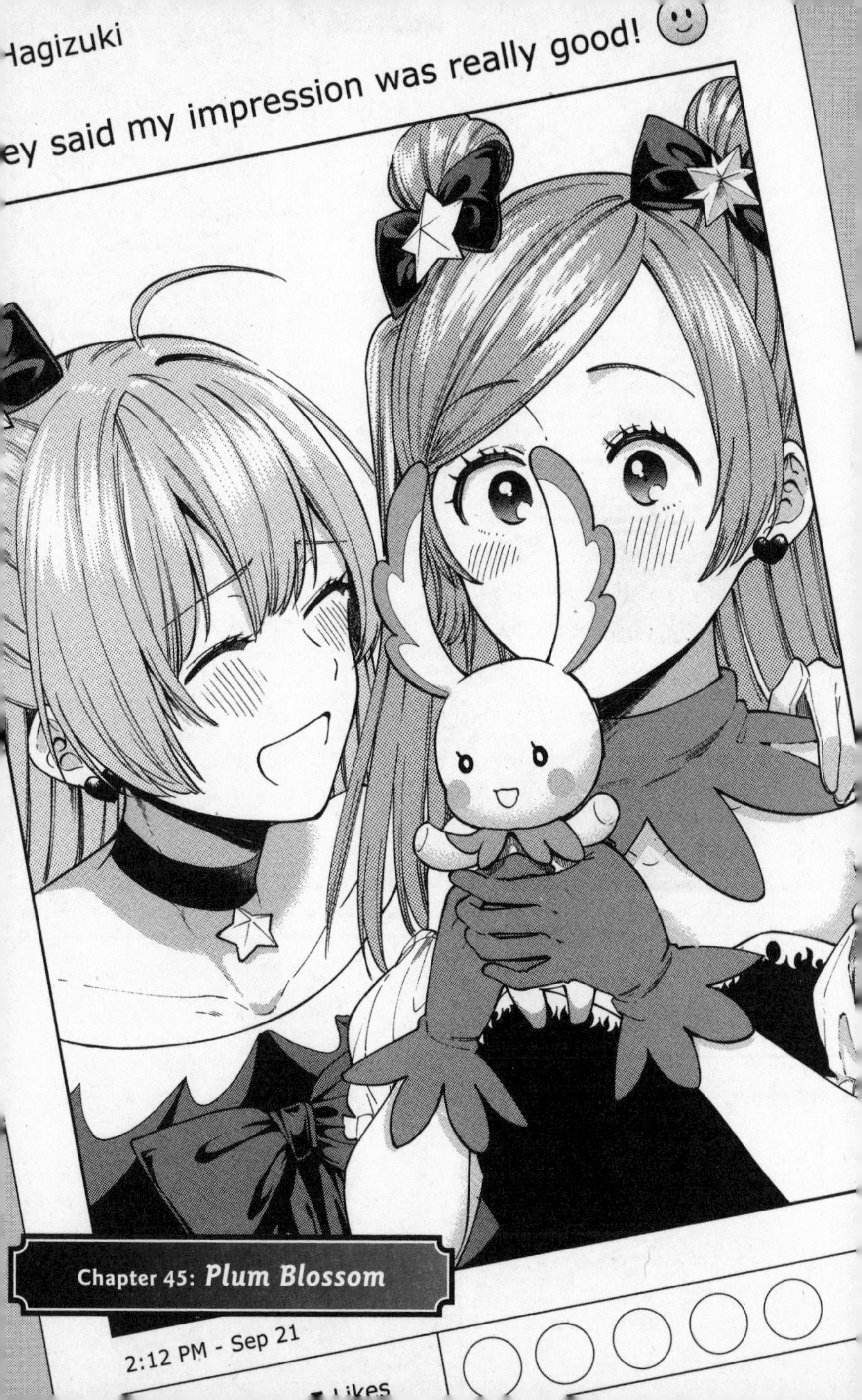
Hagizuki
ey said my impression was really good!
2:12 PM - Sep 21
Likes

Chapter 45: *Plum Blossom*

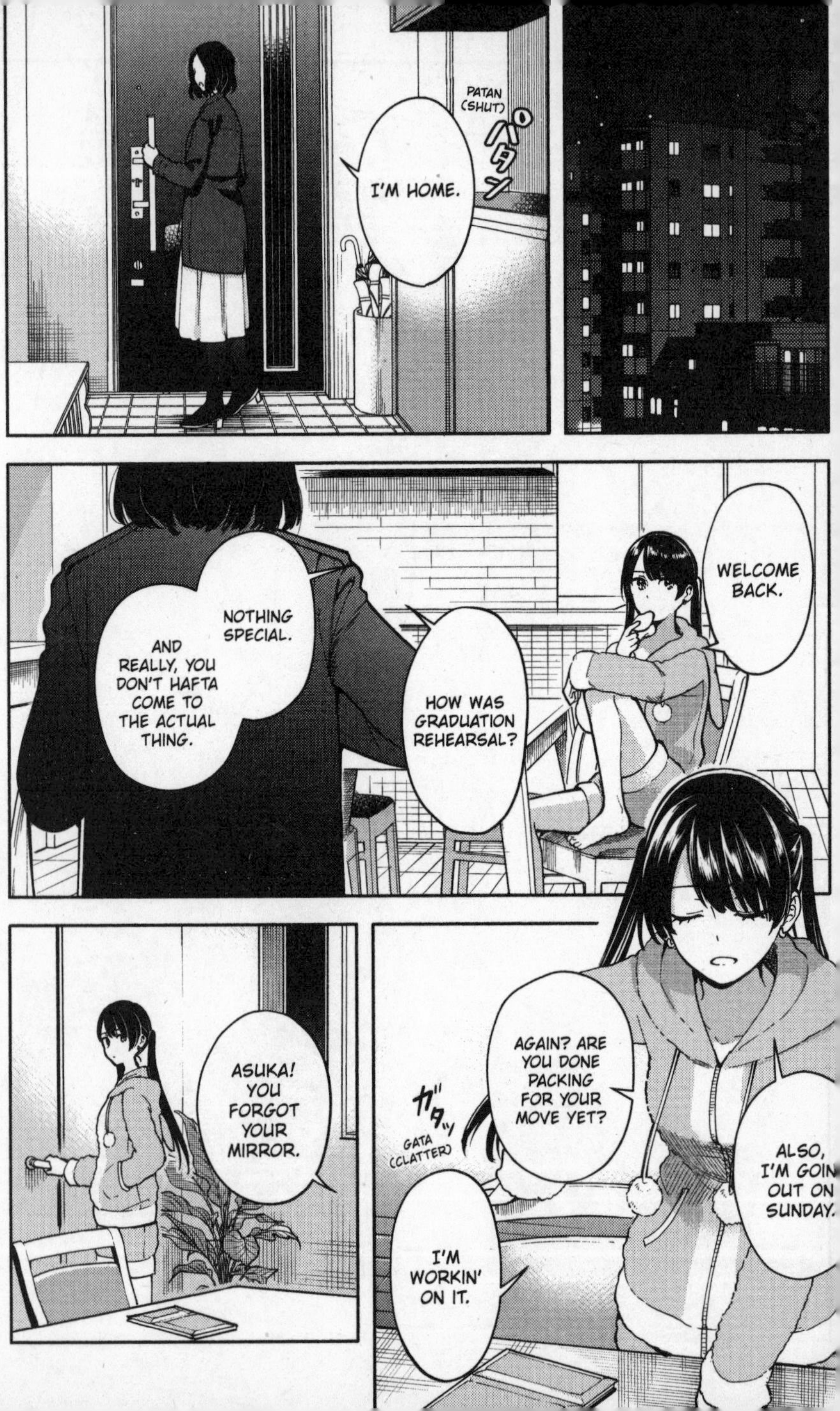
PATAN (SHUT)
I'M HOME.
WELCOME BACK.
HOW WAS GRADUATION REHEARSAL?
NOTHING SPECIAL.
AND REALLY, YOU DON'T HAFTA COME TO THE ACTUAL THING.
ALSO, I'M GOIN OUT ON SUNDAY.
AGAIN? ARE YOU DONE PACKING FOR YOUR MOVE YET?
GATA (CLATTER)
I'M WORKIN' ON IT.
ASUKA! YOU FORGOT YOUR MIRROR.

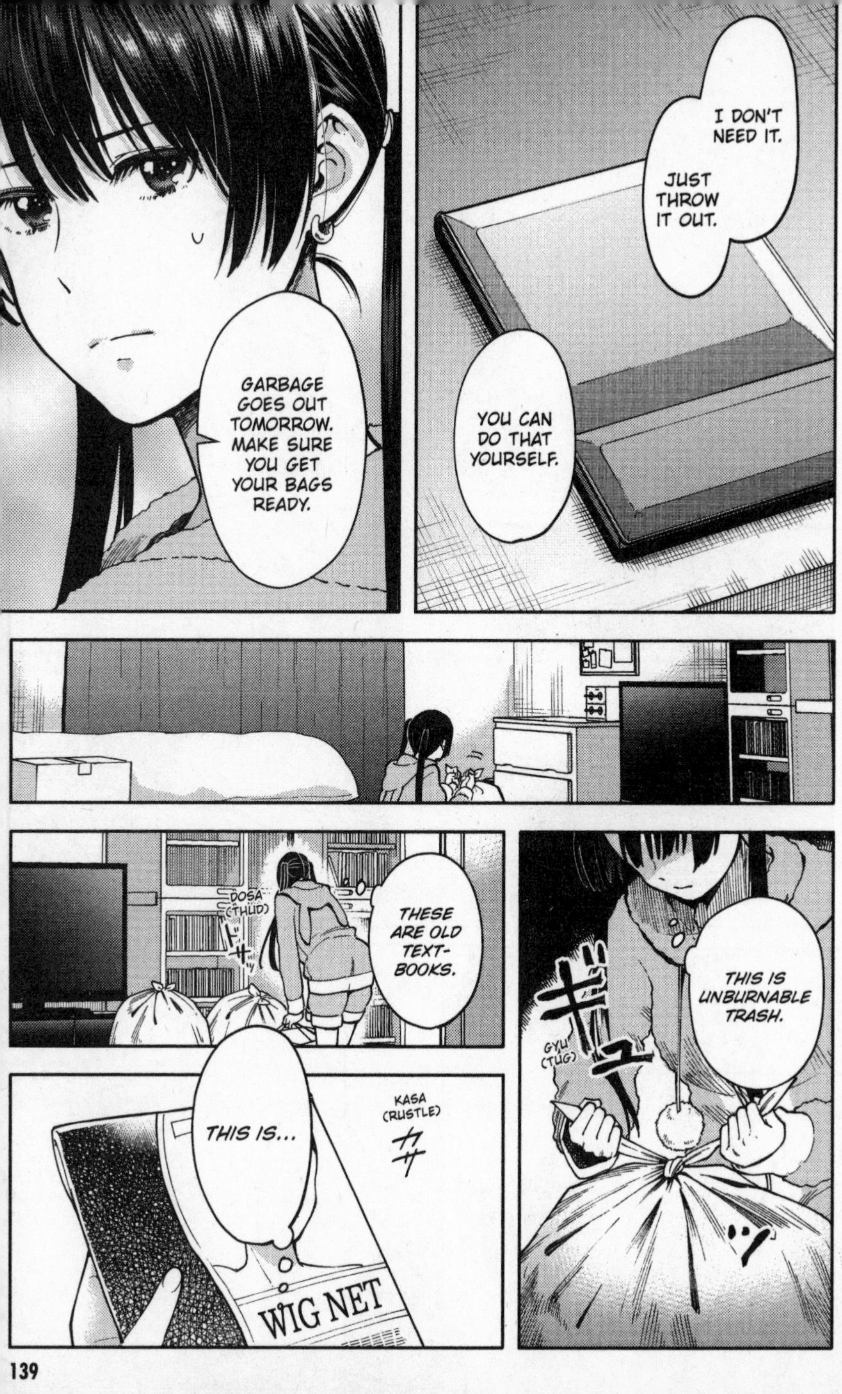
I DON'T NEED IT.
JUST THROW IT OUT.
YOU CAN DO THAT YOURSELF.
GARBAGE GOES OUT TOMORROW. MAKE SURE YOU GET YOUR BAGS READY.
ギュ
GYU (TUG)
THIS IS UNBURNABLE TRASH.
ドサ
DOSA (THUD)
THESE ARE OLD TEXT-BOOKS.
THIS IS...
KASA (RUSTLE)
カサ
WIG NET

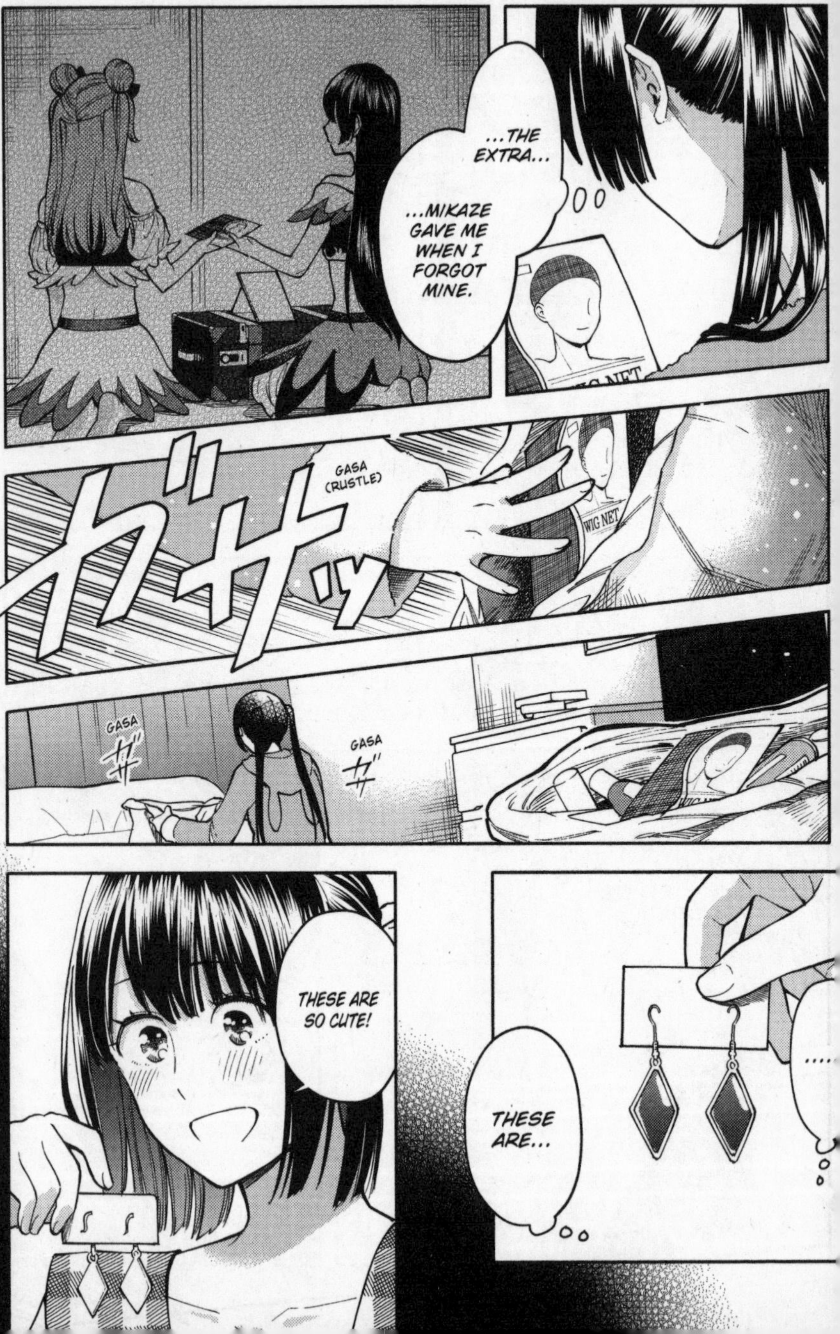
...THE EXTRA...
...MIKAZE GAVE ME WHEN I FORGOT MINE.
WIG NET
GASA (RUSTLE)
ガサッ
WIG NET
GASA
ガ
GASA
ガ
....
THESE ARE...
THESE ARE SO CUTE!

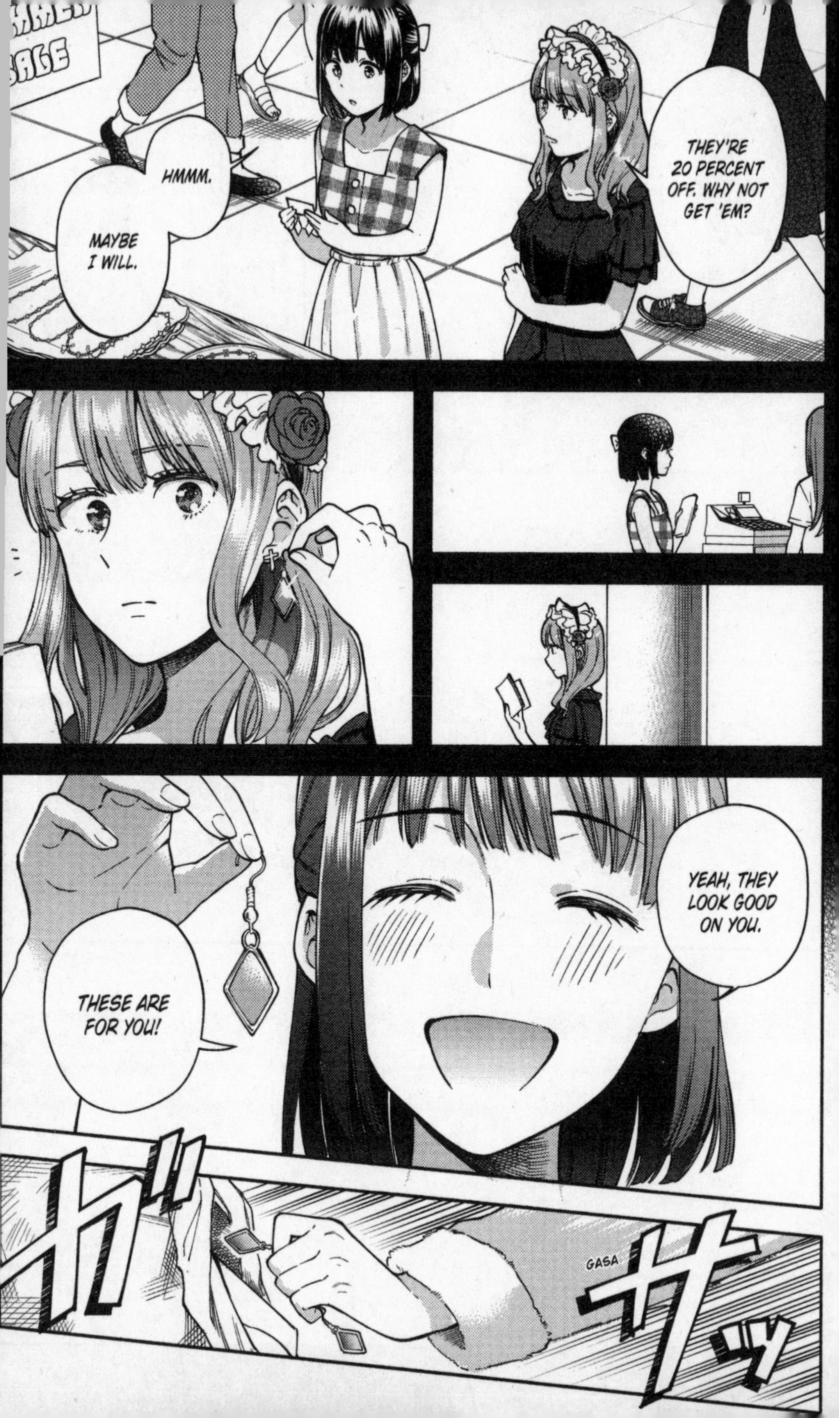
THEY'RE 20 PERCENT OFF. WHY NOT GET 'EM?
HMMM.
MAYBE I WILL.
YEAH, THEY LOOK GOOD ON YOU.
THESE ARE FOR YOU!
GASA

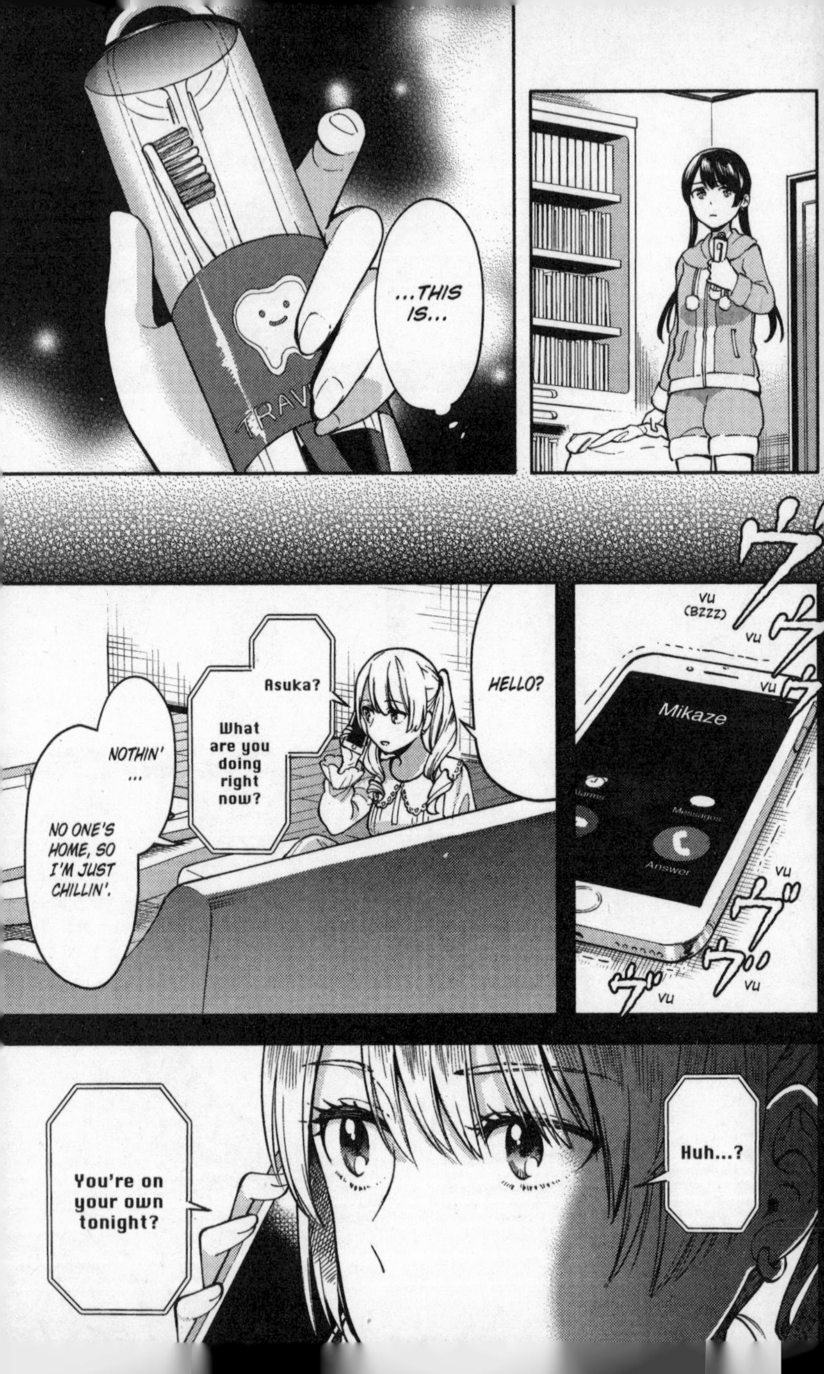
...THIS IS...
VU (BZZZ)
VU
VU
Mikaze
Alarms
Messages
Answer
VU
VU
VU
HELLO?
Asuka?
What are you doing right now?
NOTHIN'...
NO ONE'S HOME, SO I'M JUST CHILLIN'.
Huh...?
You're on your own tonight?

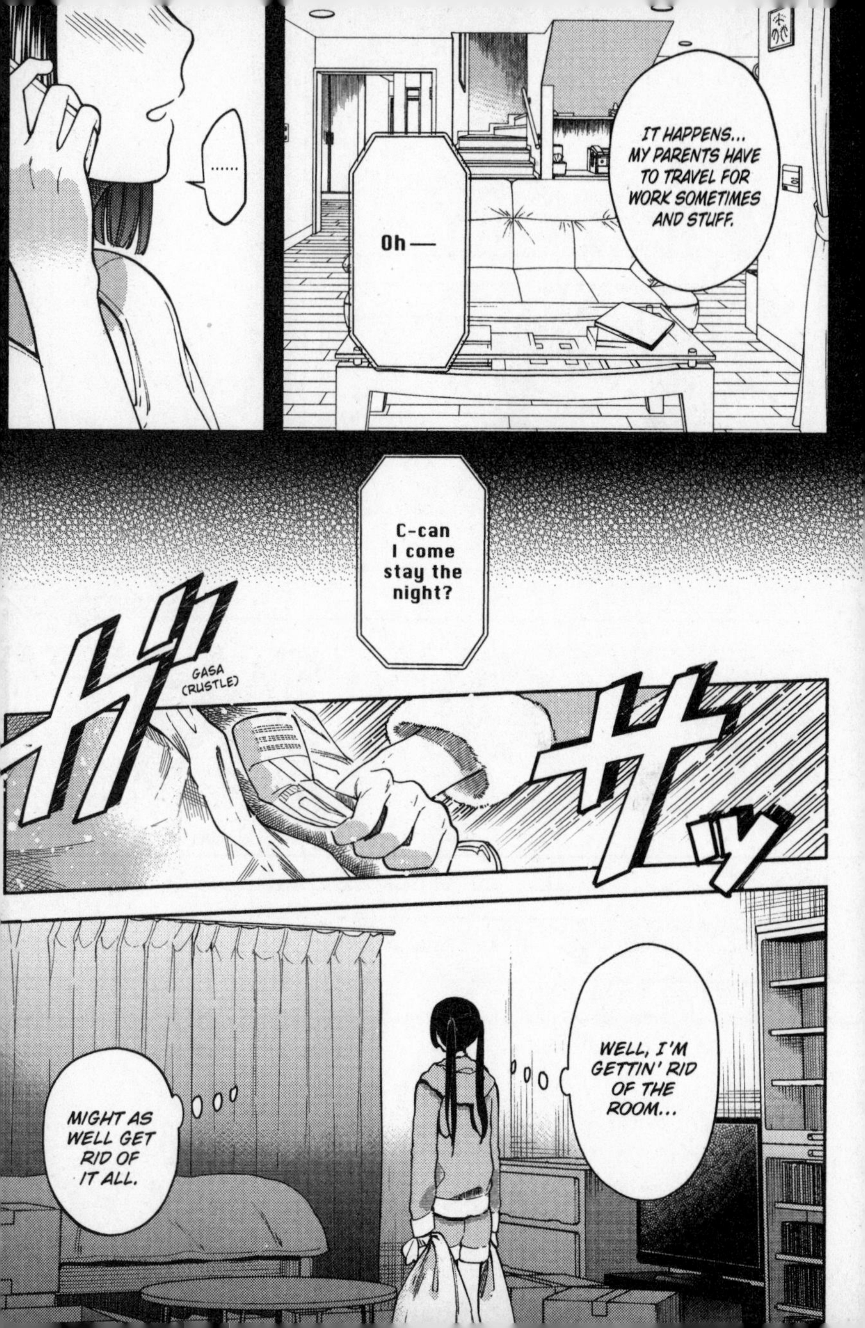
IT HAPPENS... MY PARENTS HAVE TO TRAVEL FOR WORK SOMETIMES AND STUFF.
Oh—
......
C-can I come stay the night?
ガサッ
GASA (RUSTLE)
WELL, I'M GETTIN' RID OF THE ROOM...
MIGHT AS WELL GET RID OF IT ALL.

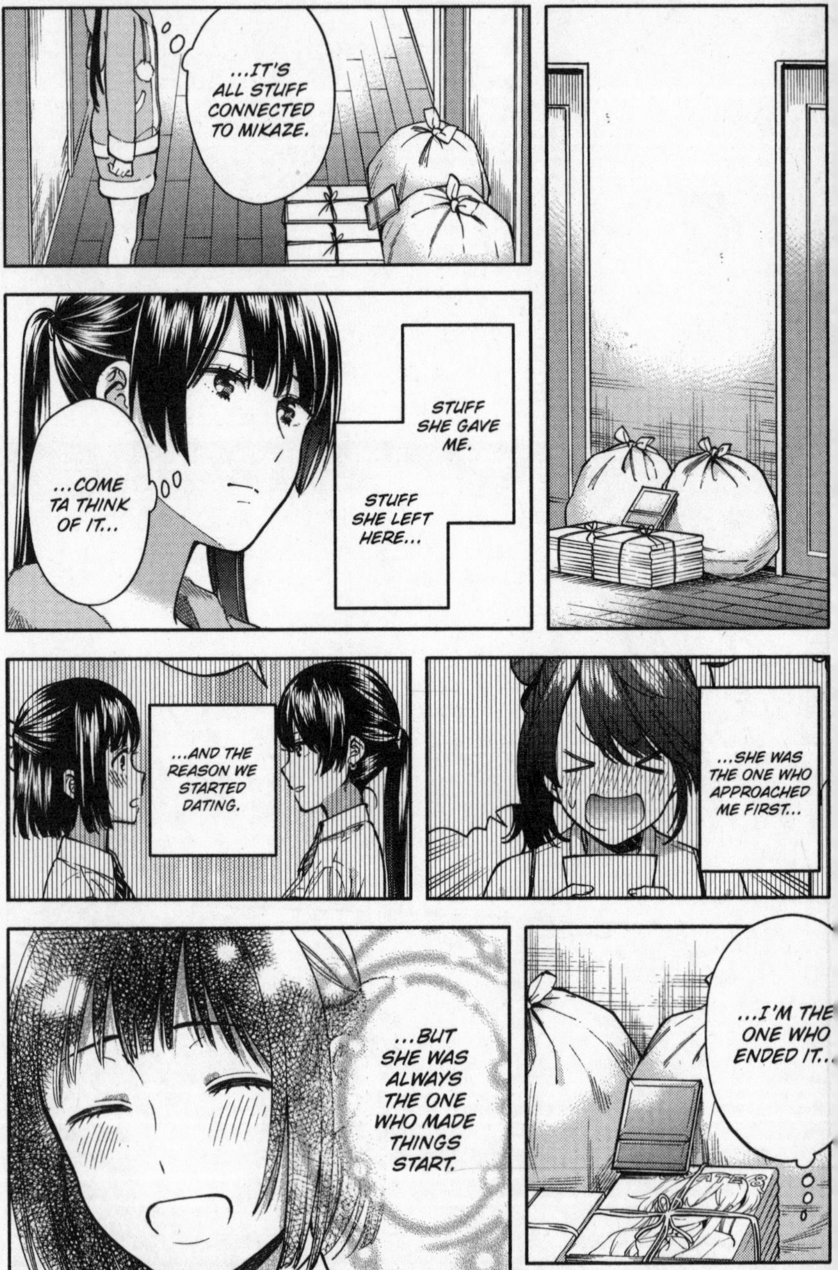
...IT'S ALL STUFF CONNECTED TO MIKAZE.
STUFF SHE GAVE ME.
STUFF SHE LEFT HERE...
...COME TA THINK OF IT...
...SHE WAS THE ONE WHO APPROACHED ME FIRST...
...AND THE REASON WE STARTED DATING.
...I'M THE ONE WHO ENDED IT...
...BUT SHE WAS ALWAYS THE ONE WHO MADE THINGS START.

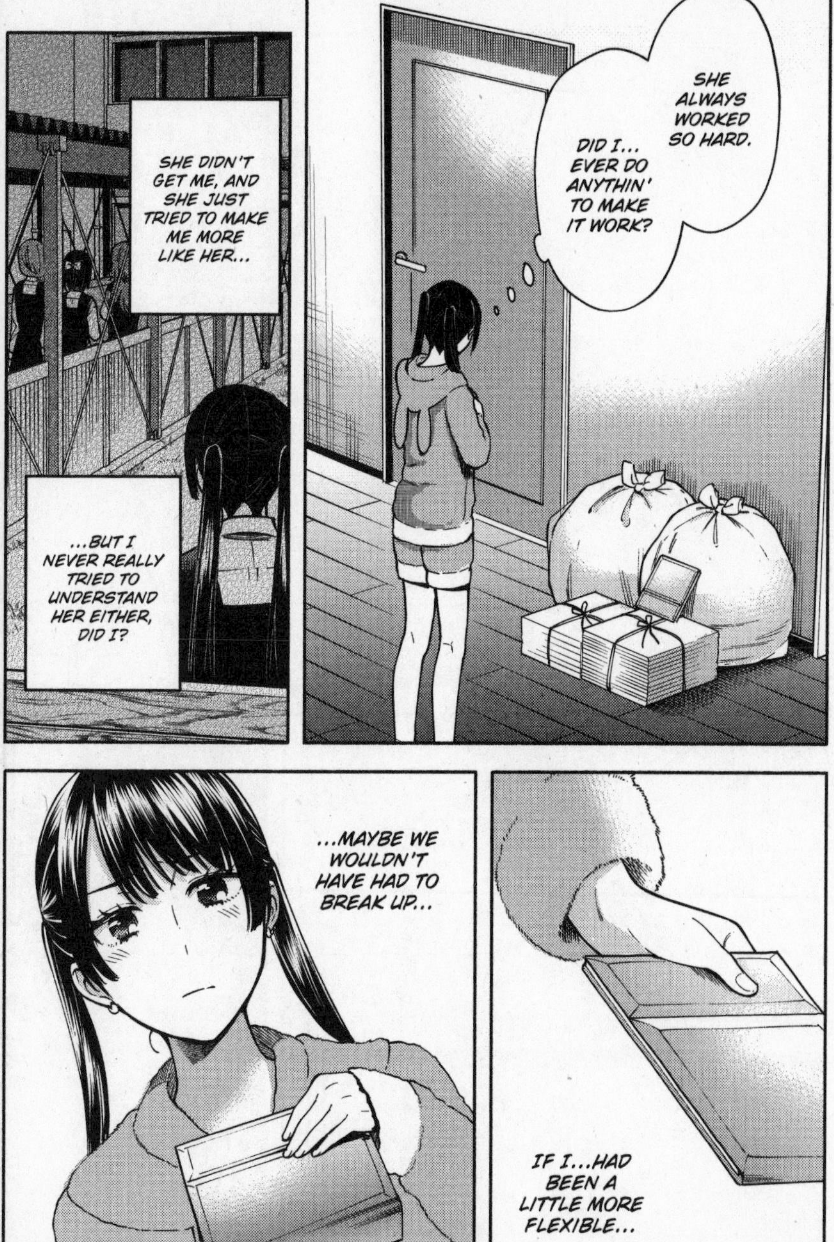
SHE ALWAYS WORKED SO HARD.
DID I... EVER DO ANYTHIN' TO MAKE IT WORK?
SHE DIDN'T GET ME, AND SHE JUST TRIED TO MAKE ME MORE LIKE HER...
...BUT I NEVER REALLY TRIED TO UNDERSTAND HER EITHER, DID I?
IF I...HAD BEEN A LITTLE MORE FLEXIBLE...
...MAYBE WE WOULDN'T HAVE HAD TO BREAK UP...

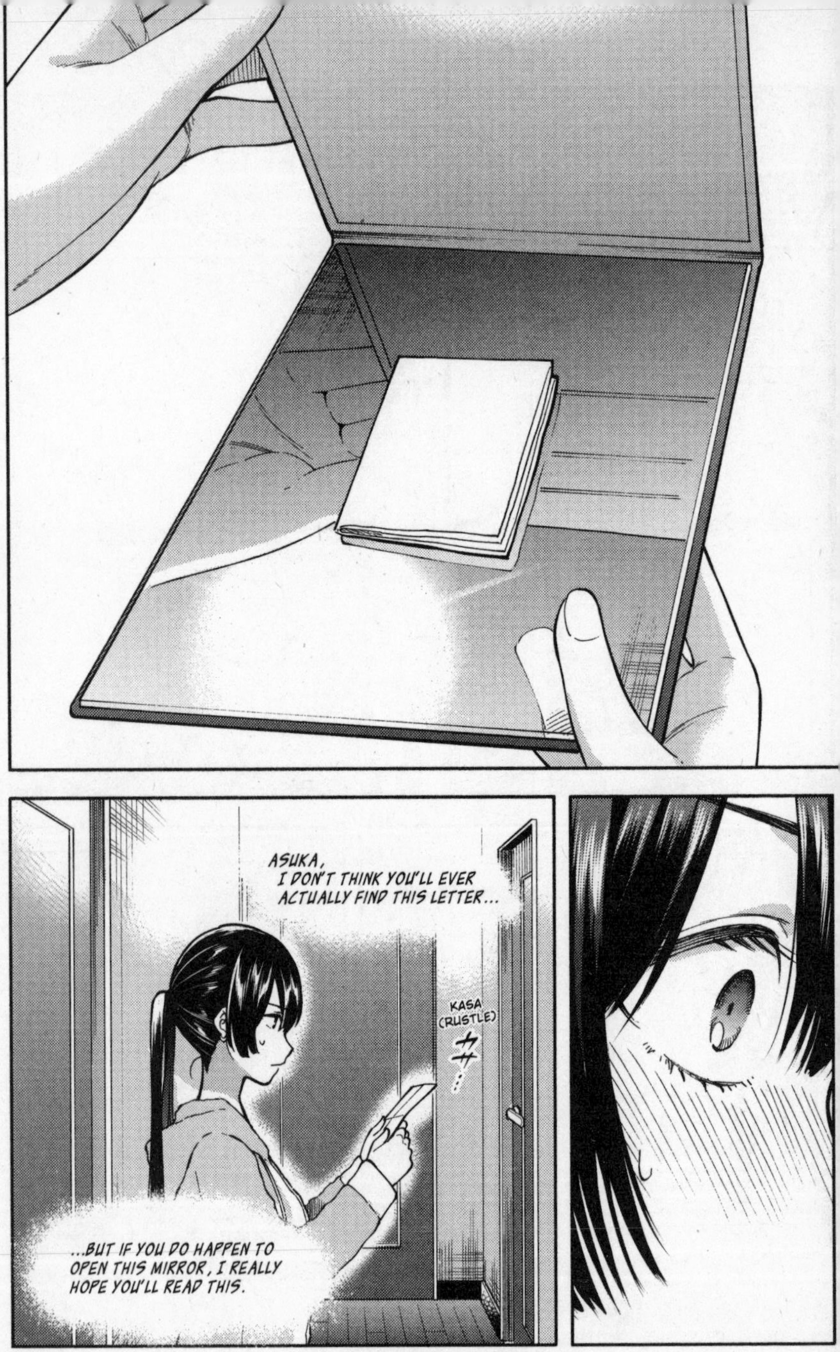
ASUKA, I DON'T THINK YOU'LL EVER ACTUALLY FIND THIS LETTER...
KASA (RUSTLE)
カサ...
...BUT IF YOU DO HAPPEN TO OPEN THIS MIRROR, I REALLY HOPE YOU'LL READ THIS.

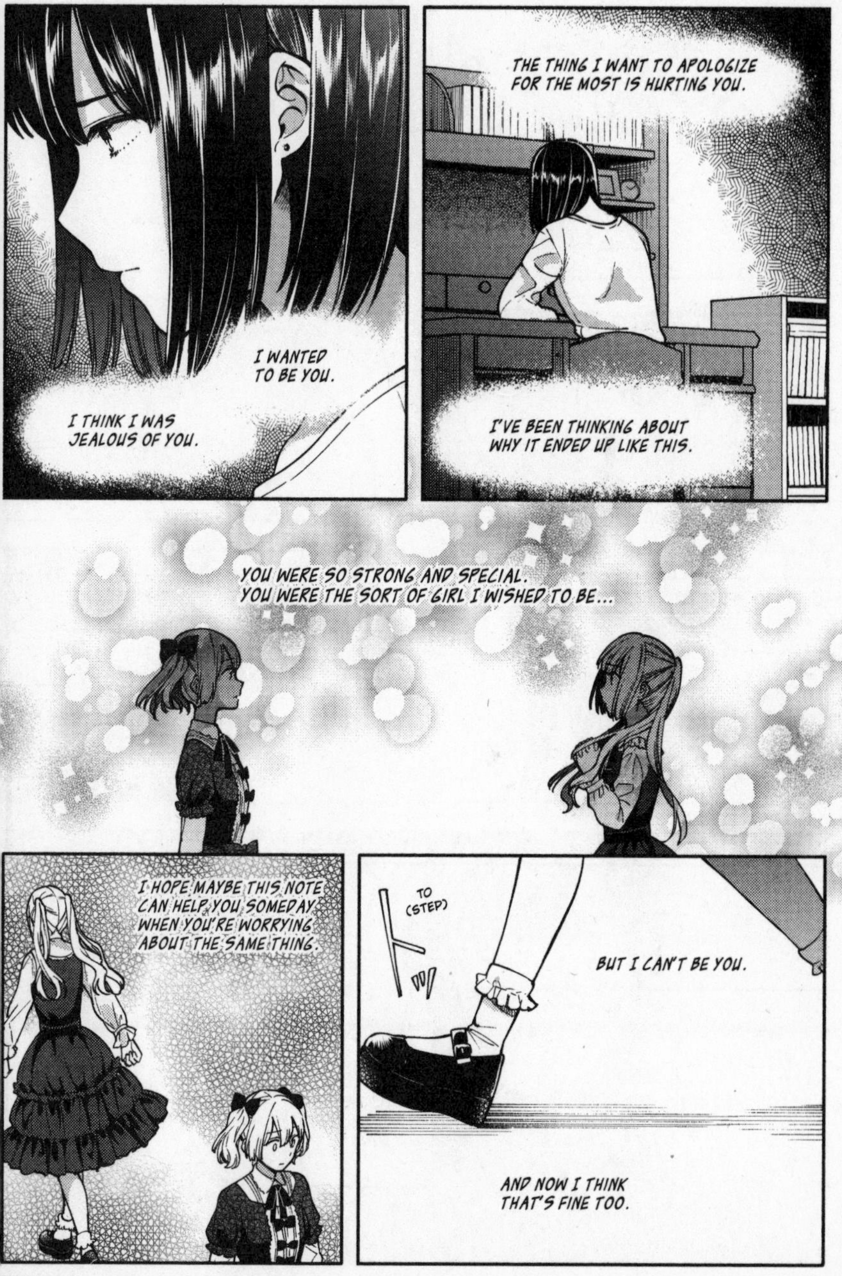
THE THING I WANT TO APOLOGIZE FOR THE MOST IS HURTING YOU.
I'VE BEEN THINKING ABOUT WHY IT ENDED UP LIKE THIS.
I WANTED TO BE YOU.
I THINK I WAS JEALOUS OF YOU.
YOU WERE SO STRONG AND SPECIAL. YOU WERE THE SORT OF GIRL I WISHED TO BE...
TO (STEP)
BUT I CAN'T BE YOU.
AND NOW I THINK THAT'S FINE TOO.
I HOPE MAYBE THIS NOTE CAN HELP YOU SOMEDAY WHEN YOU'RE WORRYING ABOUT THE SAME THING.

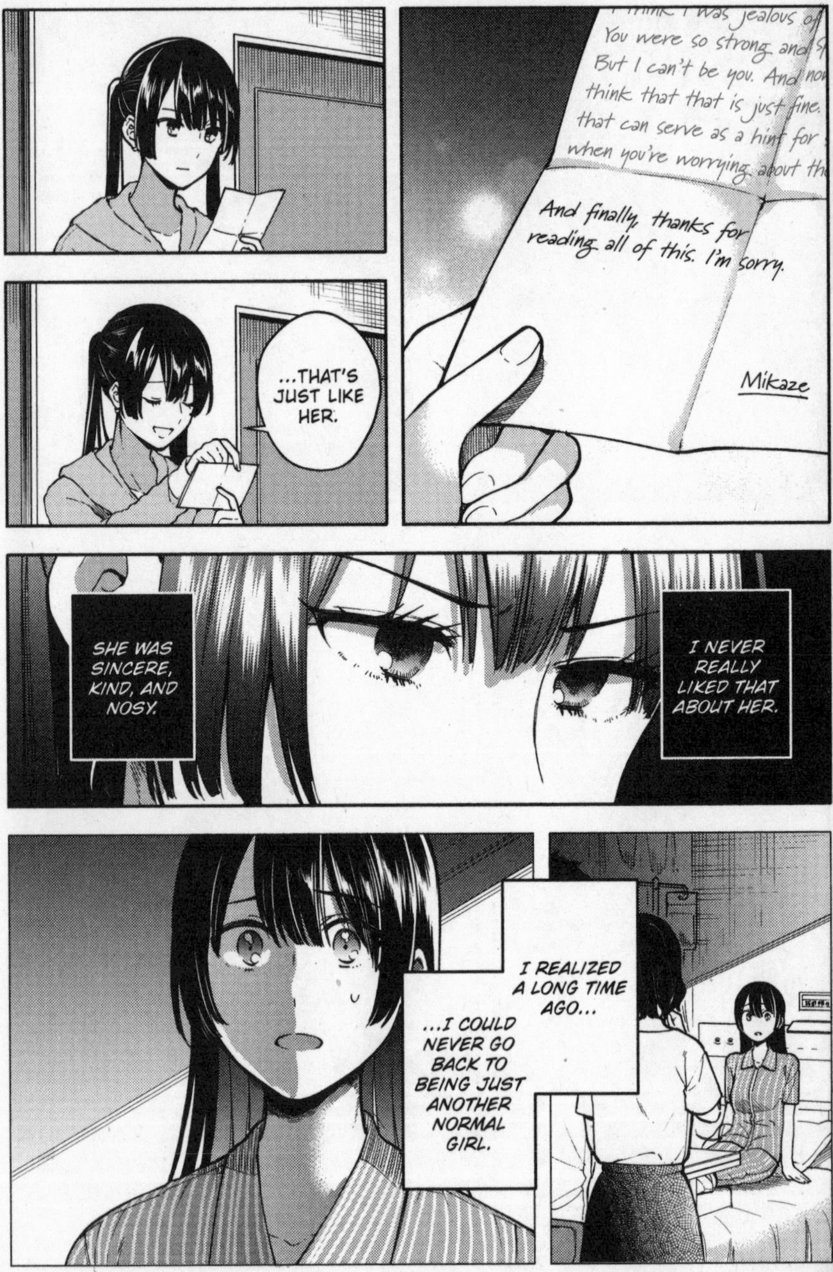
think I was jealous of
You were so strong and
But I can't be you. And now
think that that is just fine.
that can serve as a hint for
when you're worrying about th
And finally, thanks for reading all of this. I'm sorry.
Mikaze
...THAT'S JUST LIKE HER.
SHE WAS SINCERE, KIND, AND NOSY.
I NEVER REALLY LIKED THAT ABOUT HER.
I REALIZED A LONG TIME AGO...
...I COULD NEVER GO BACK TO BEING JUST ANOTHER NORMAL GIRL.

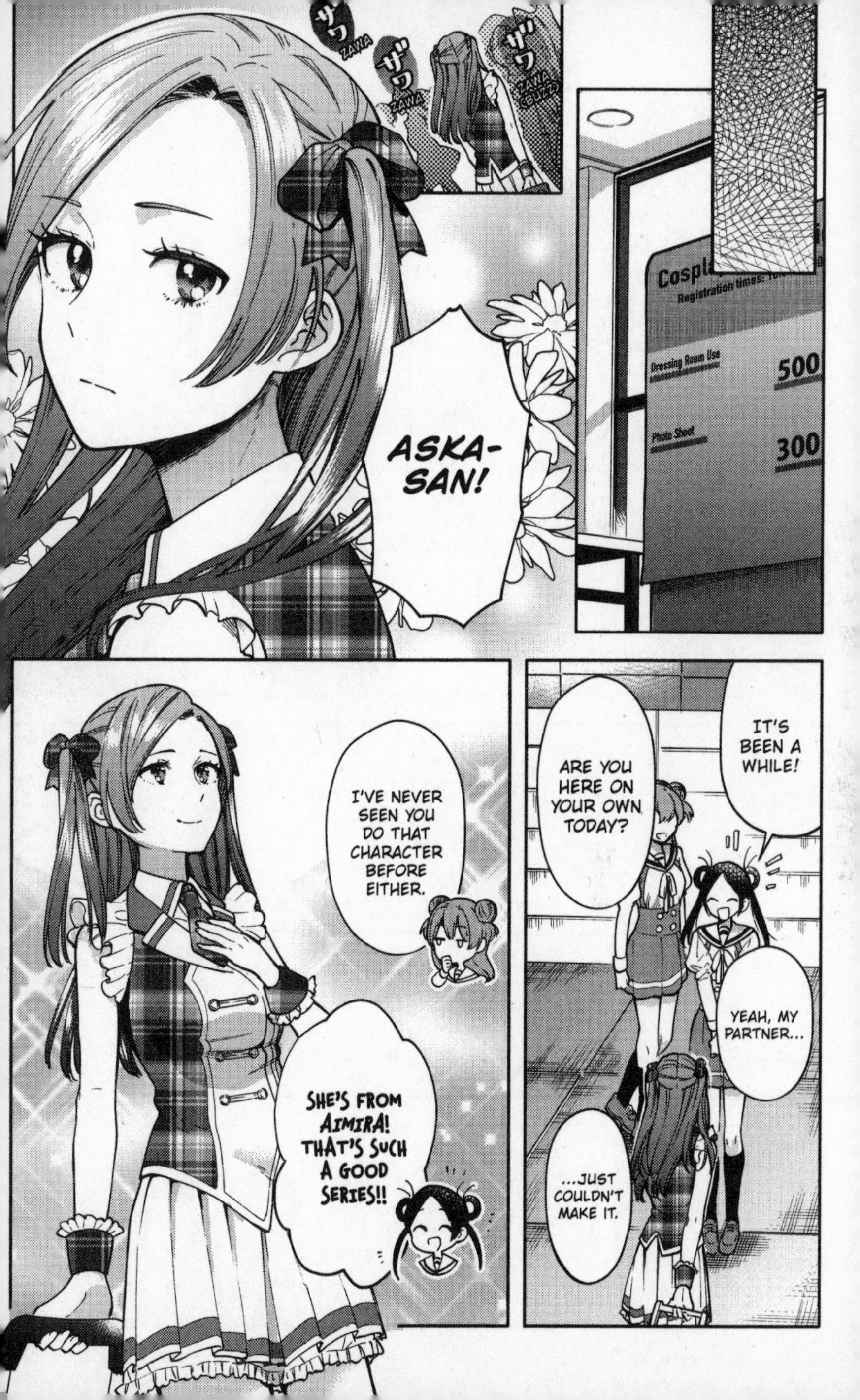
Registration times:
Dressing Room Use
500
Photo Shoot
300
ザワ
ZAWA
ザワ
ZAWA
ザワ
ZAWA (BUZZ)
ASKA-SAN!
IT'S BEEN A WHILE!
ARE YOU HERE ON YOUR OWN TODAY?
YEAH, MY PARTNER...
...JUST COULDN'T MAKE IT.
I'VE NEVER SEEN YOU DO THAT CHARACTER BEFORE EITHER.
SHE'S FROM AIMIRA! THAT'S SUCH A GOOD SERIES!!

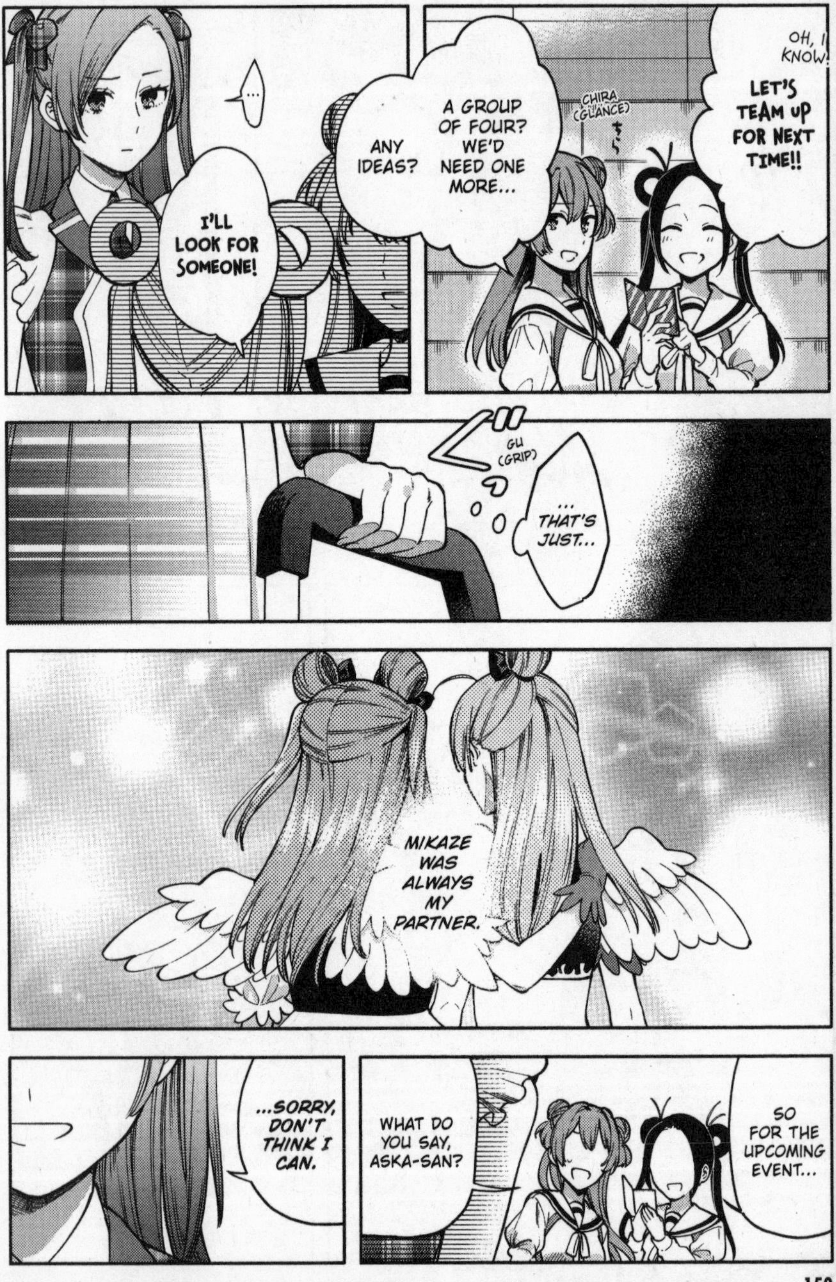
OH, I KNOW!
LET'S TEAM UP FOR NEXT TIME!!
CHIRA (GLANCE)
ちら
A GROUP OF FOUR? WE'D NEED ONE MORE...
ANY IDEAS?
...
I'LL LOOK FOR SOMEONE!
GU (GRIP)
... THAT'S JUST...
MIKAZE WAS ALWAYS MY PARTNER.
SO FOR THE UPCOMING EVENT...
WHAT DO YOU SAY, ASKA-SAN?
...SORRY, DON'T THINK I CAN.

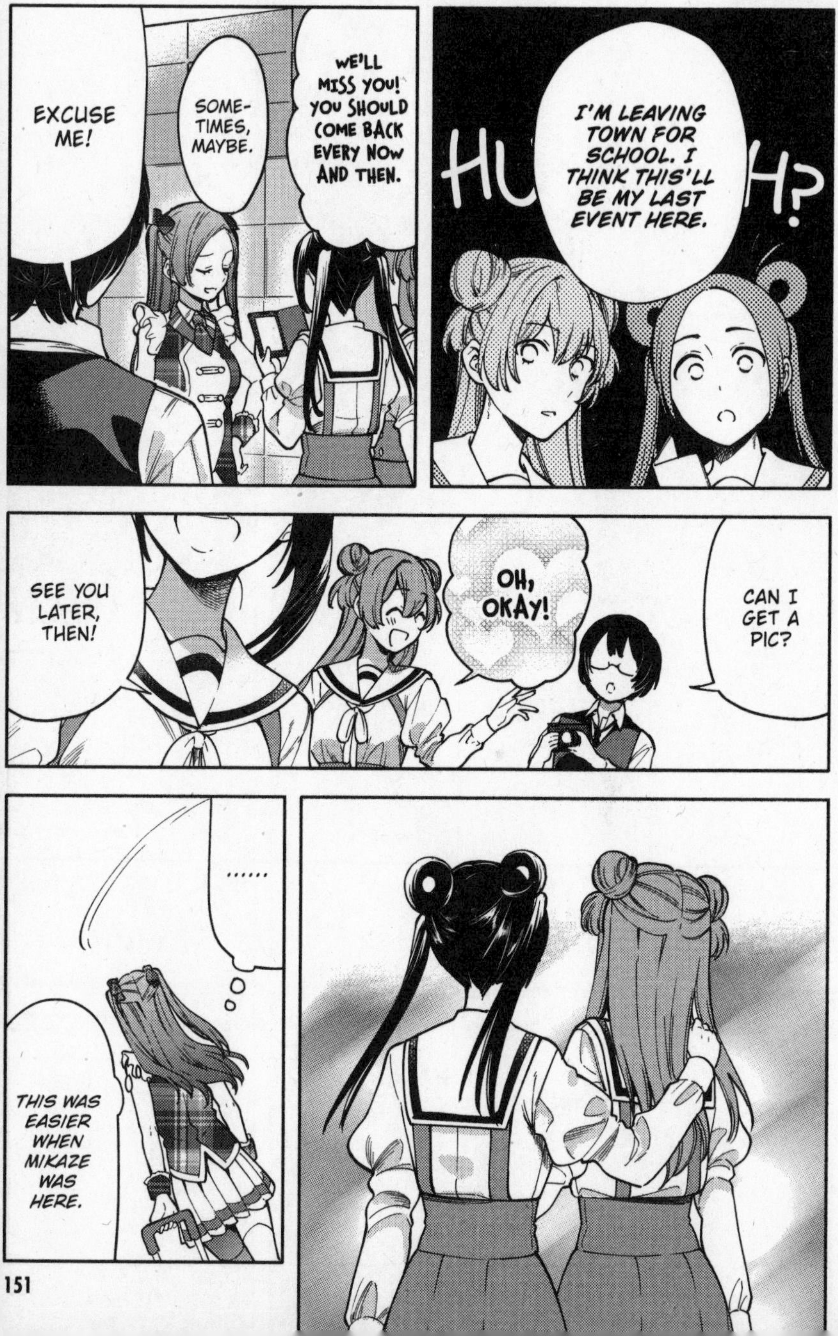
I'M LEAVING TOWN FOR SCHOOL. I THINK THIS'LL BE MY LAST EVENT HERE.
HU H?
WE'LL MISS YOU! YOU SHOULD COME BACK EVERY NOW AND THEN.
SOME-TIMES, MAYBE.
EXCUSE ME!
CAN I GET A PIC?
OH, OKAY!
SEE YOU LATER, THEN!
......
THIS WAS EASIER WHEN MIKAZE WAS HERE.

MIKAZE!!

I WANNA SEE HER.

WRONG PERSON...

...SORRY.

I WANNA SEE MIKAZE.

WHY?

I'M THE ONE WHO DECIDED TO BREAK UP.

SHE'S SINCERE...

...KIND...

...AND NOSY.

AND I...

...ALWAYS—

SIGN: GRADUATION

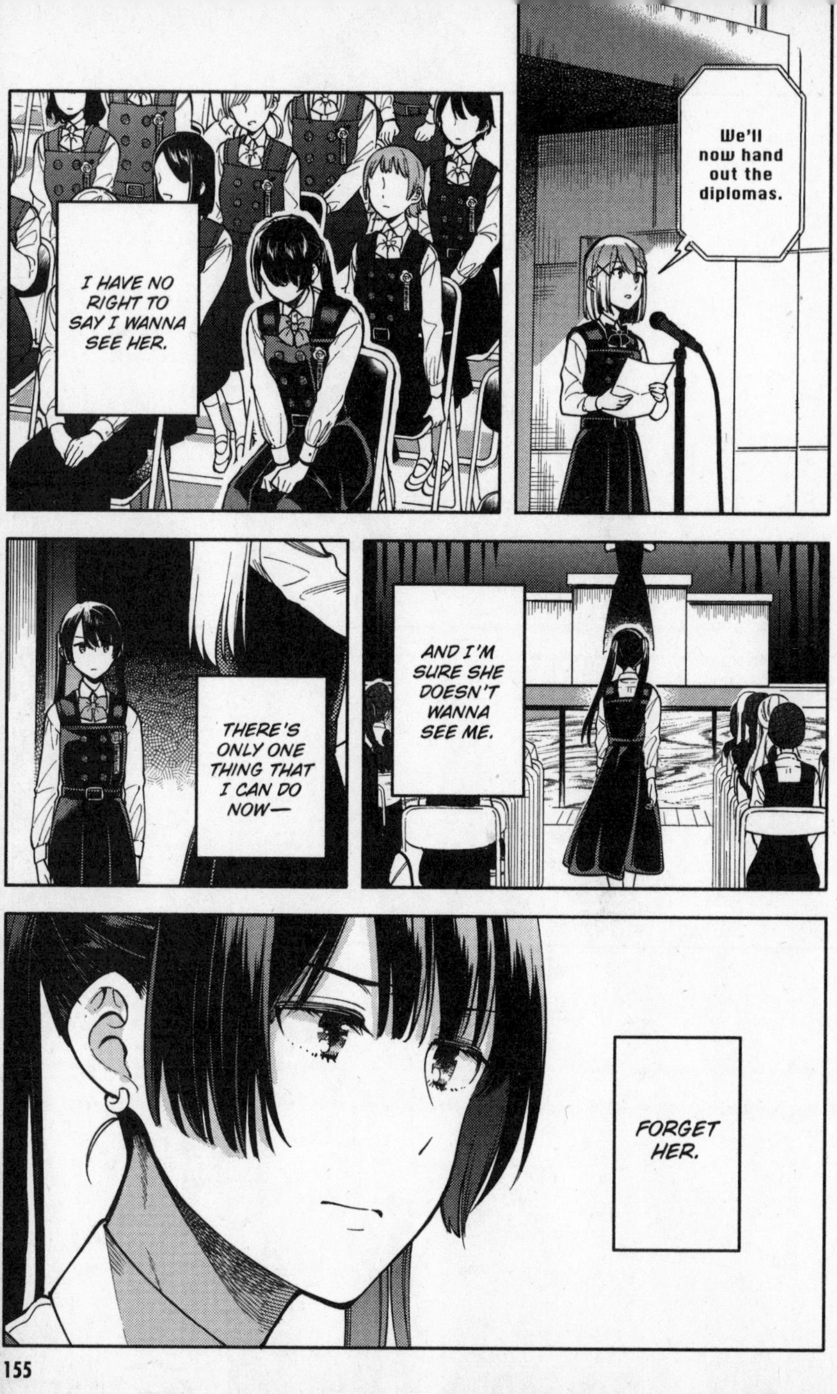
We'll now hand out the diplomas.
I HAVE NO RIGHT TO SAY I WANNA SEE HER.
AND I'M SURE SHE DOESN'T WANNA SEE ME.
THERE'S ONLY ONE THING THAT I CAN DO NOW—
FORGET HER.

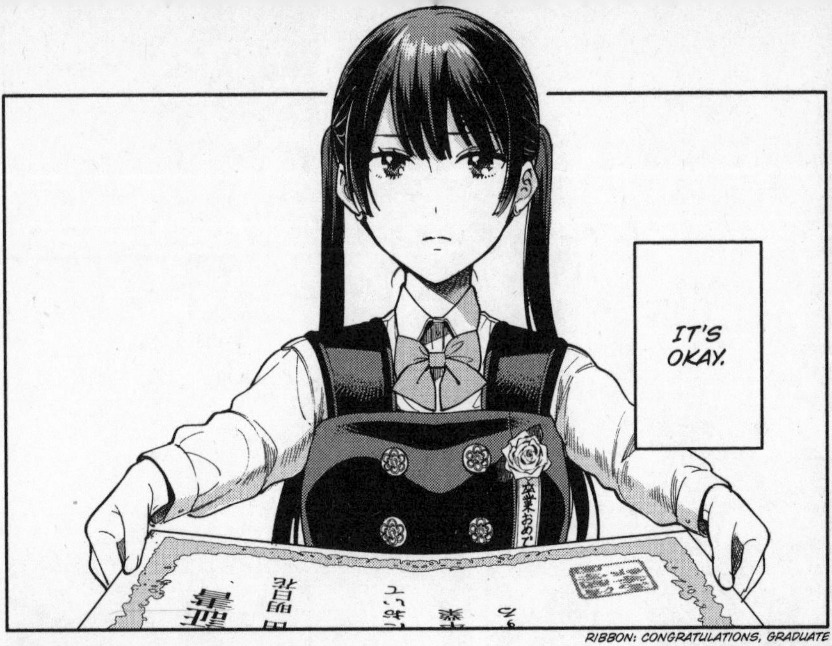
IT'S OKAY.

RIBBON: CONGRATULATIONS, GRADUATE

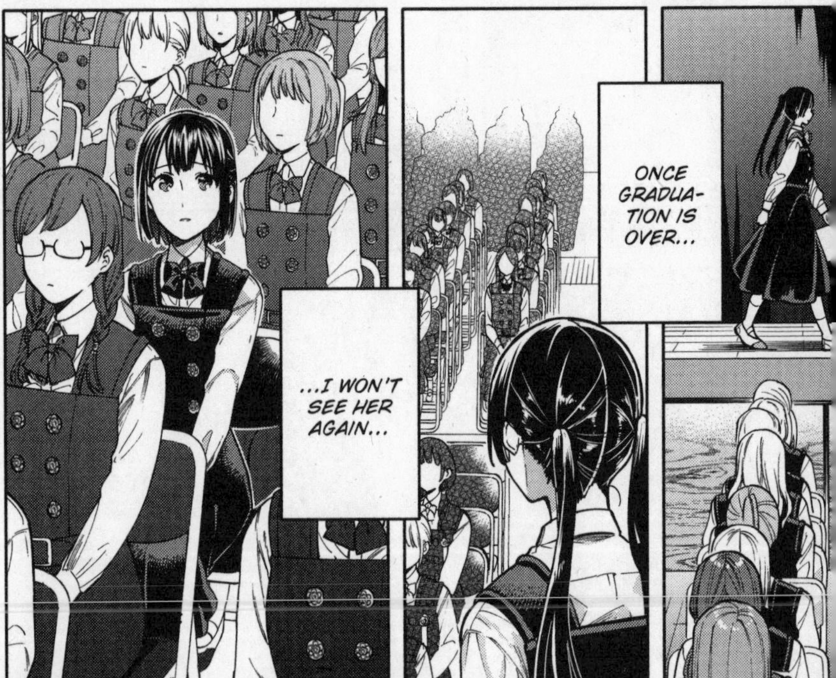
ONCE GRADUATION IS OVER...
...I WON'T SEE HER AGAIN...

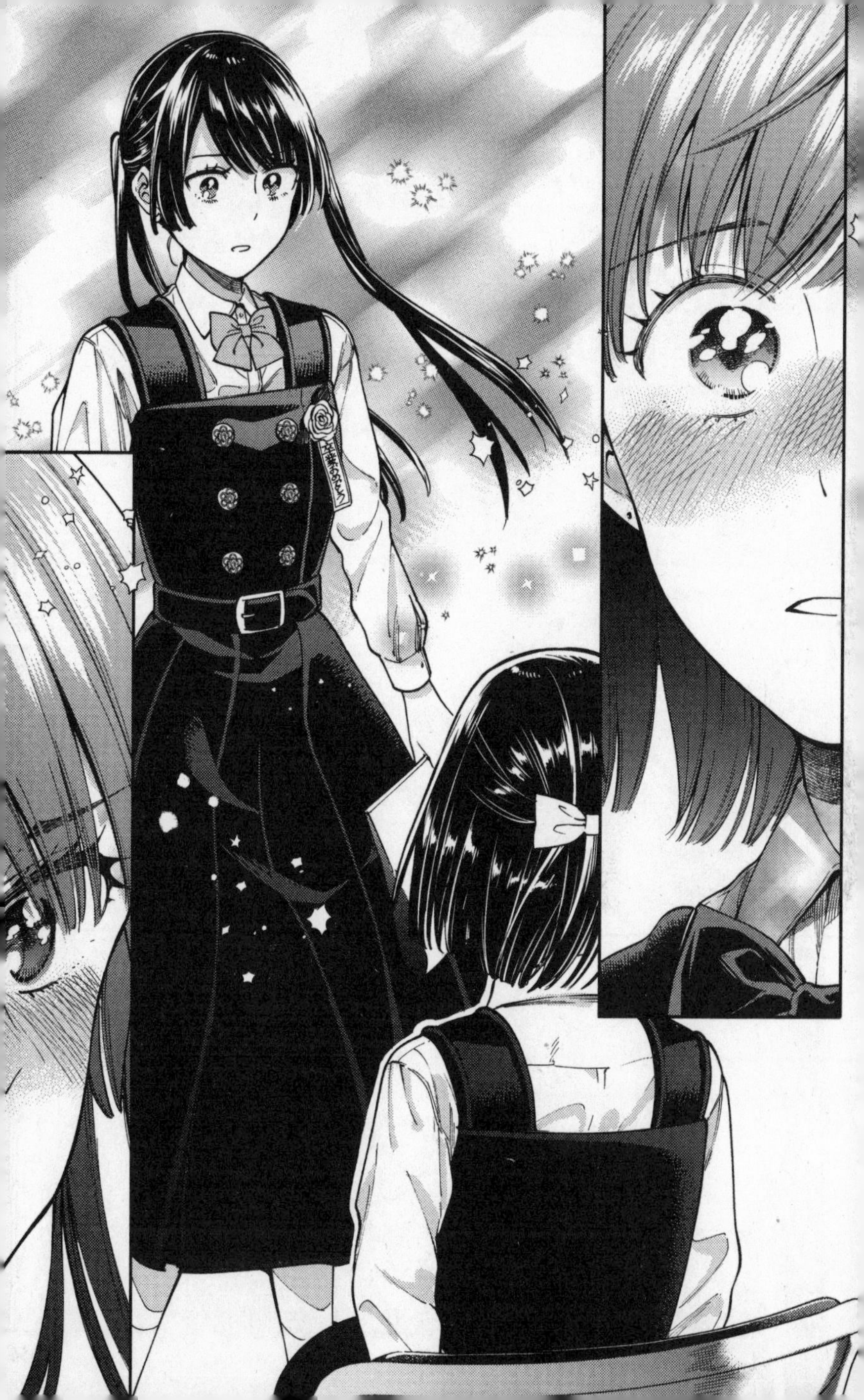
卒業おめでとう

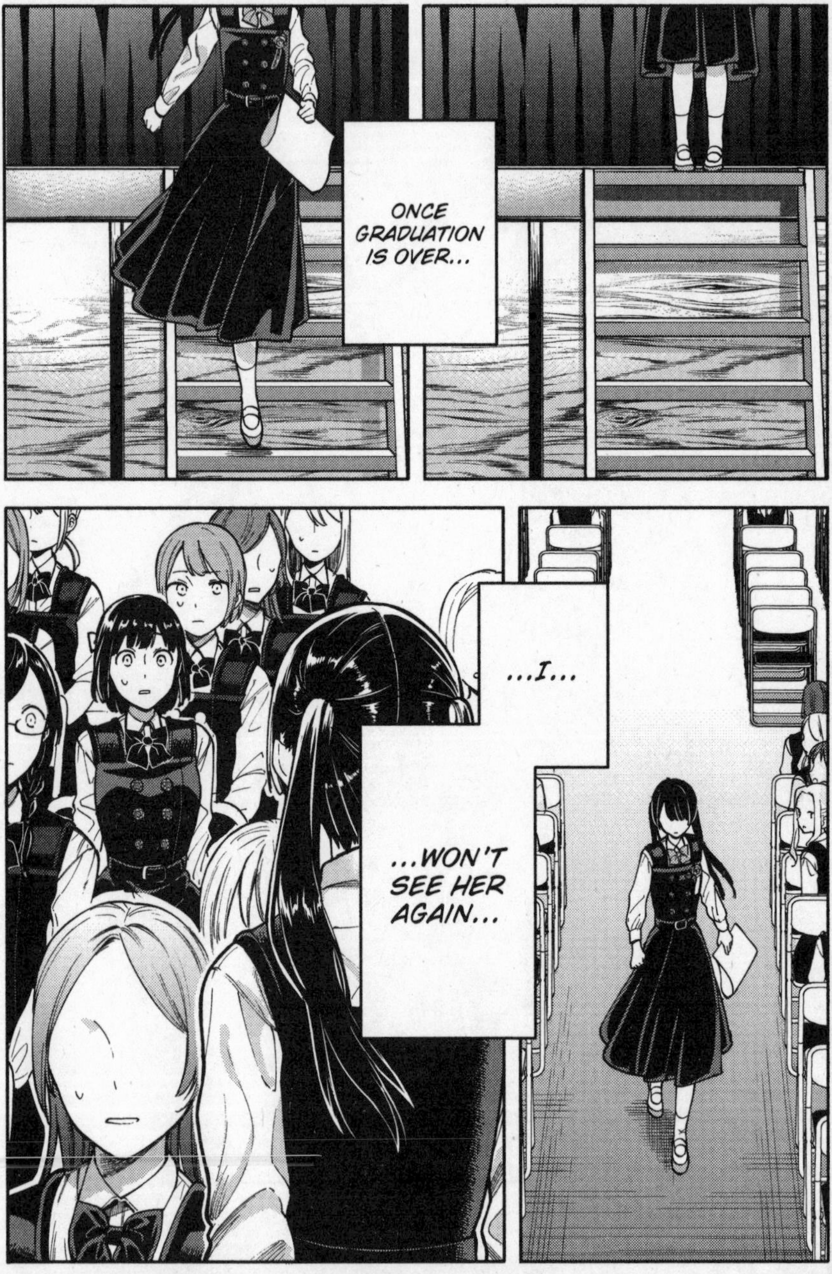
ONCE GRADUATION IS OVER...
...I...
...WON'T SEE HER AGAIN...

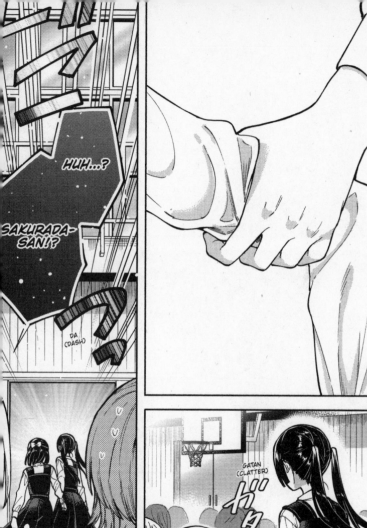

HUH...?

SAKURADA-SAN!?

DA
(DASH)

GATAN
(CLATTER)

A—

ASUKA
...!?

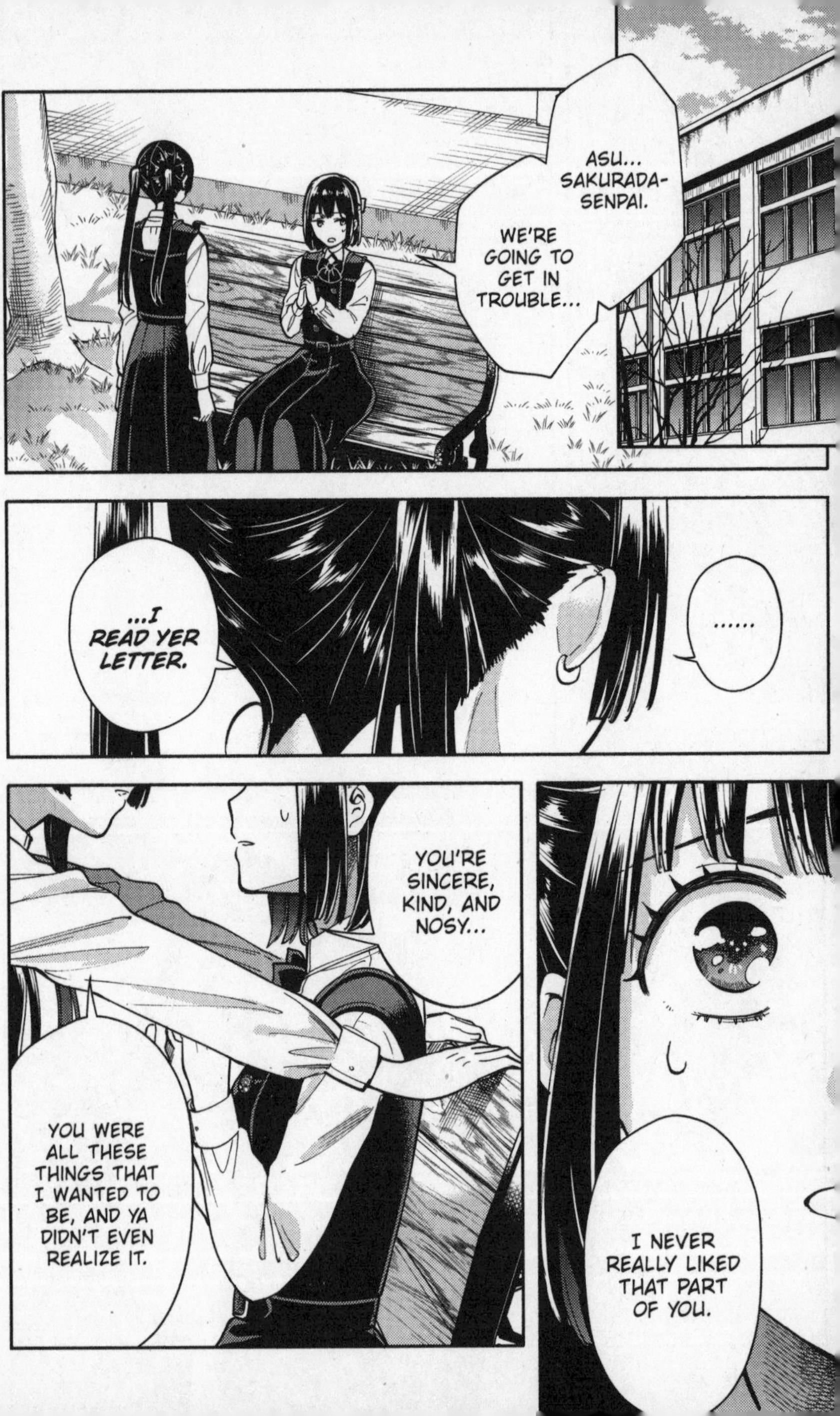
ASU... SAKURADA-SENPAI.
WE'RE GOING TO GET IN TROUBLE...
......
...I READ YER LETTER.
I NEVER REALLY LIKED THAT PART OF YOU.
YOU'RE SINCERE, KIND, AND NOSY...
YOU WERE ALL THESE THINGS THAT I WANTED TO BE, AND YA DIDN'T EVEN REALIZE IT.

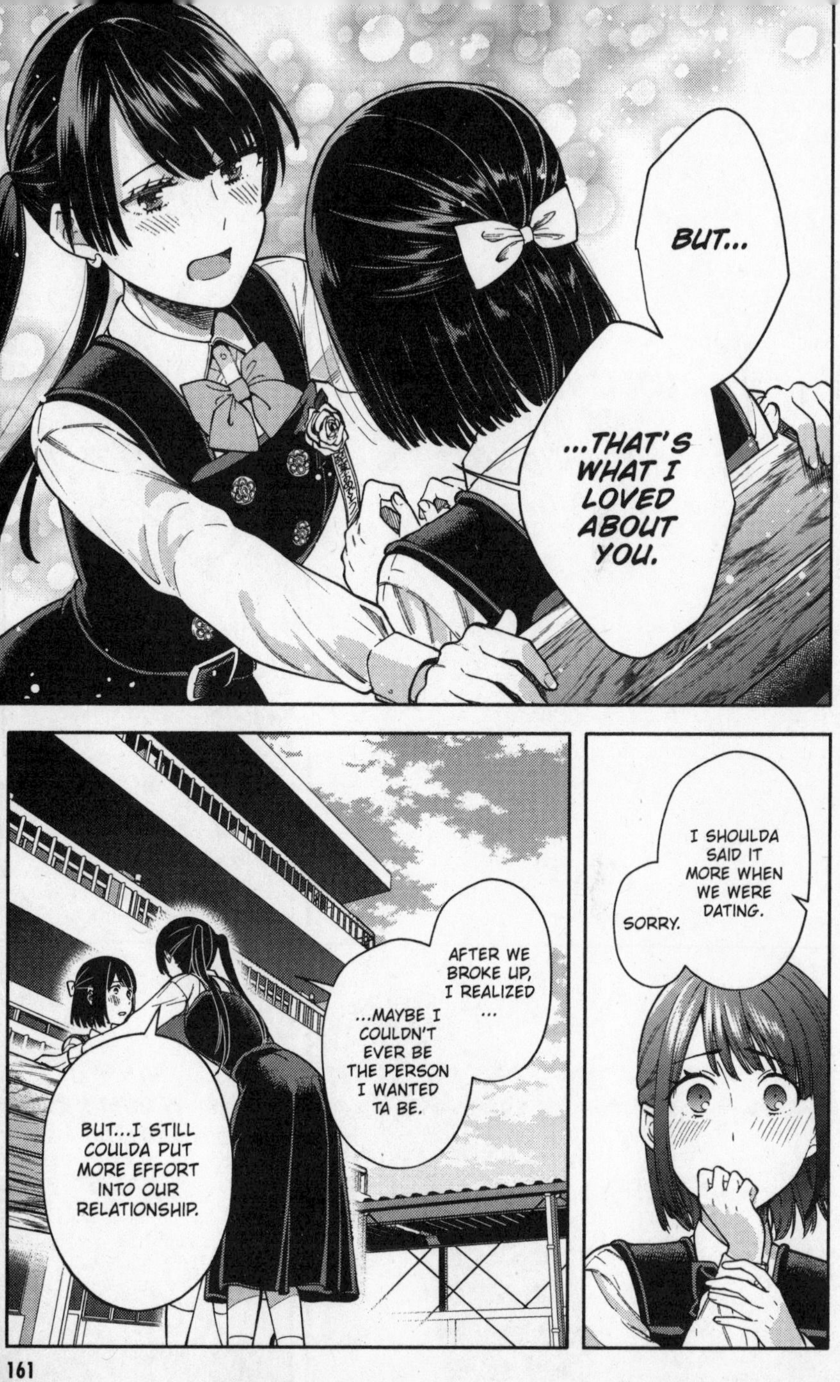
BUT...
...THAT'S WHAT I LOVED ABOUT YOU.
I SHOULDA SAID IT MORE WHEN WE WERE DATING.
SORRY.
AFTER WE BROKE UP, I REALIZED ...
...MAYBE I COULDN'T EVER BE THE PERSON I WANTED TA BE.
BUT...I STILL COULDA PUT MORE EFFORT INTO OUR RELATIONSHIP.

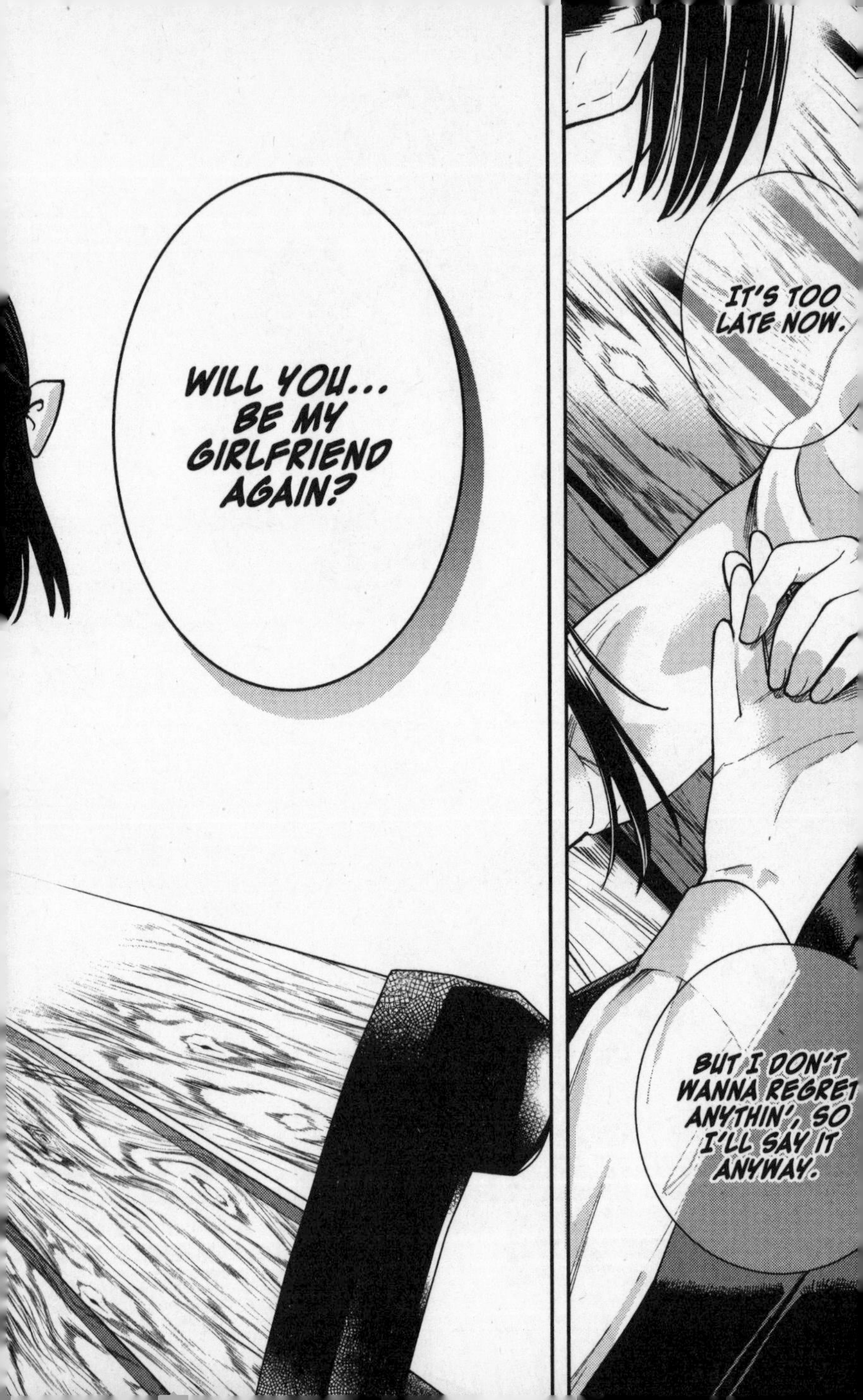
IT'S TOO LATE NOW.
BUT I DON'T WANNA REGRET ANYTHIN', SO I'LL SAY IT ANYWAY.
WILL YOU... BE MY GIRLFRIEND AGAIN?

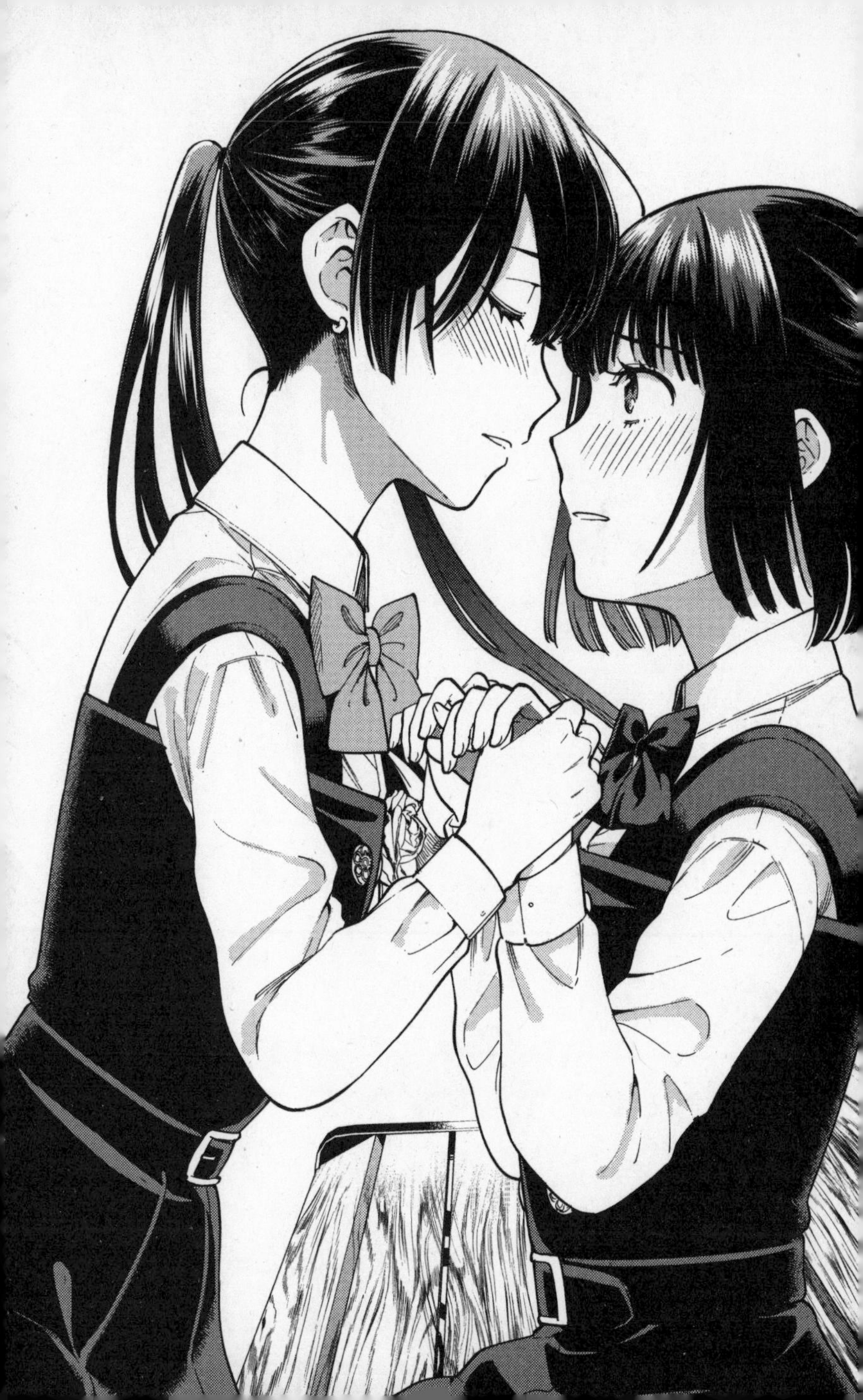

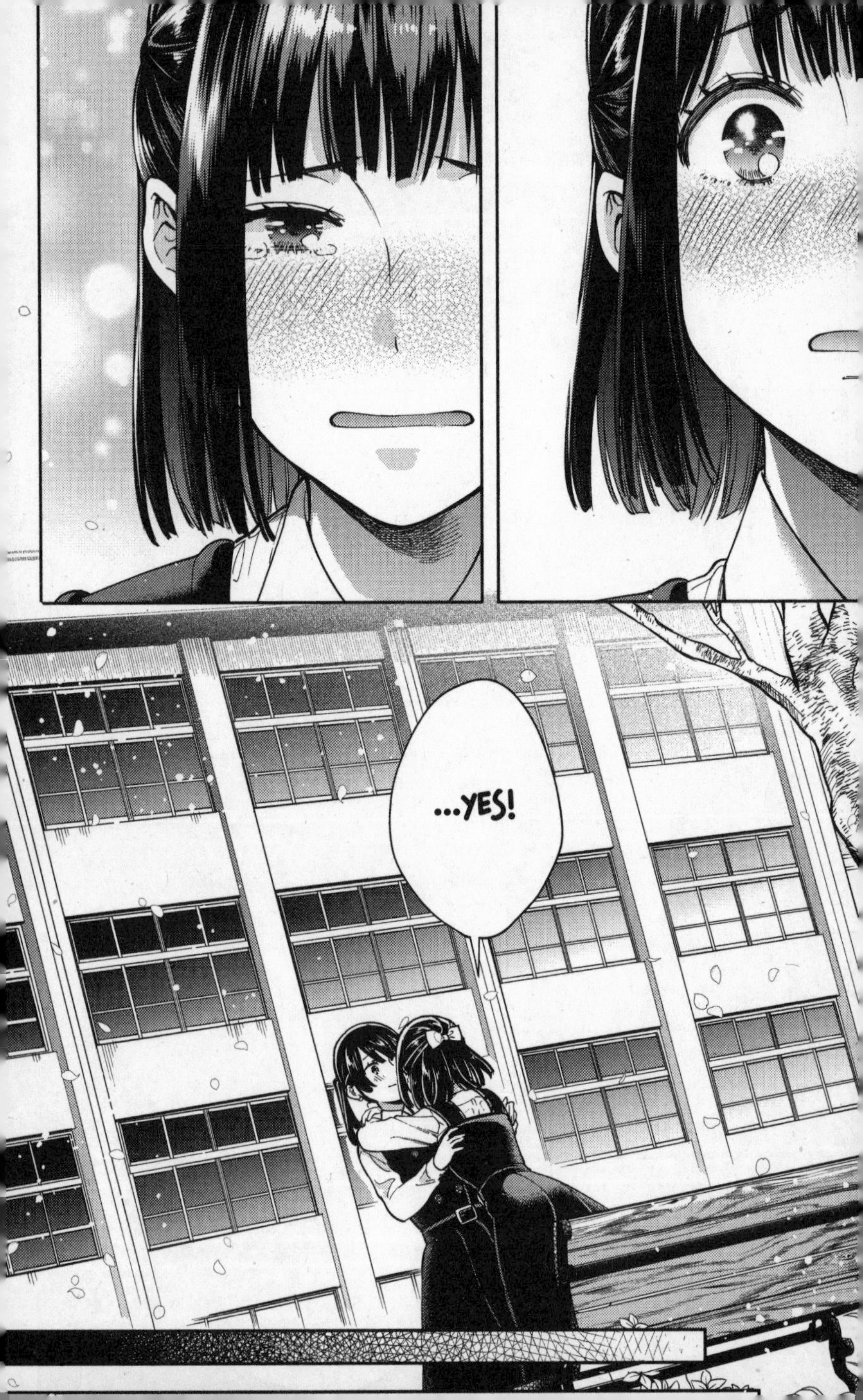
...YES!

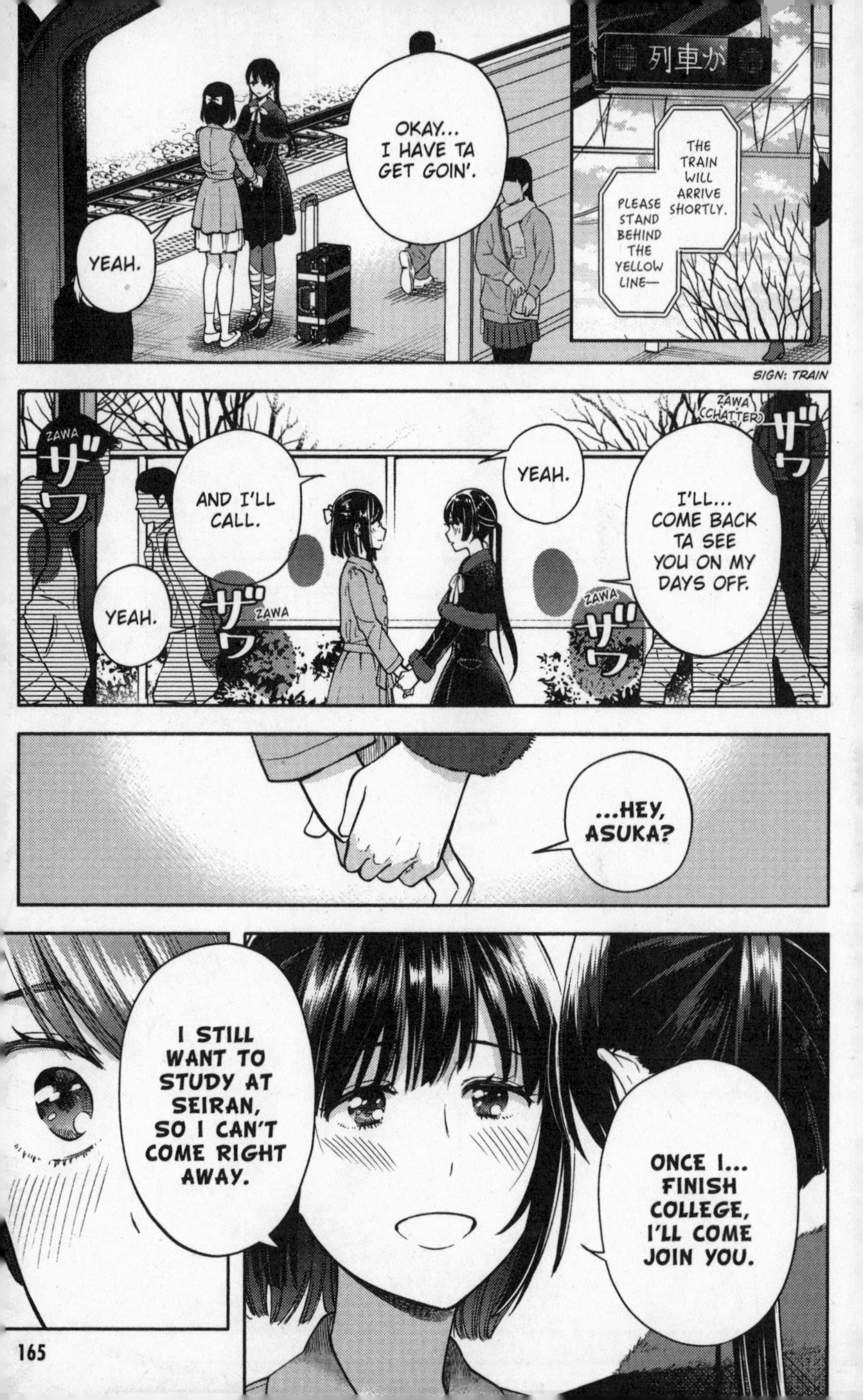
列車が
THE TRAIN WILL ARRIVE SHORTLY.
PLEASE STAND BEHIND THE YELLOW LINE—
OKAY... I HAVE TA GET GOIN'.
YEAH.
SIGN: TRAIN
ZAWA (CHATTER)
ザワ
I'LL... COME BACK TA SEE YOU ON MY DAYS OFF.
YEAH.
ZAWA
ザワ
AND I'LL CALL.
ZAWA
ザワ
YEAH.
ZAWA
ザワ
...HEY, ASUKA?
I STILL WANT TO STUDY AT SEIRAN, SO I CAN'T COME RIGHT AWAY.
ONCE I... FINISH COLLEGE, I'LL COME JOIN YOU.

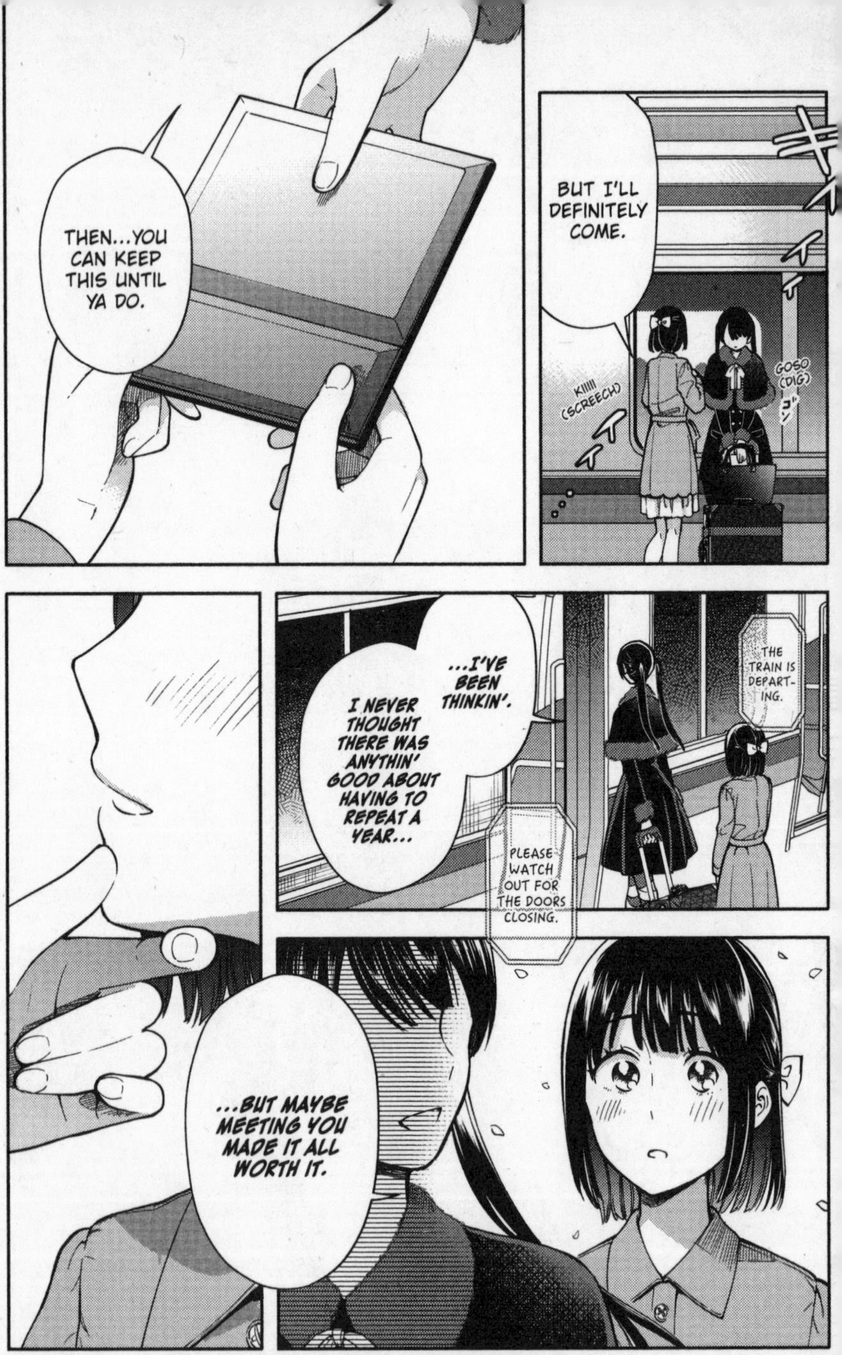
BUT I'LL DEFINITELY COME.
KIIIII (SCREECH)
GOSO (DIG)
THEN...YOU CAN KEEP THIS UNTIL YA DO.
THE TRAIN IS DEPART-ING.
...I'VE BEEN THINKIN'.
I NEVER THOUGHT THERE WAS ANYTHIN' GOOD ABOUT HAVING TO REPEAT A YEAR...
PLEASE WATCH OUT FOR THE DOORS CLOSING.
...BUT MAYBE MEETING YOU MADE IT ALL WORTH IT.

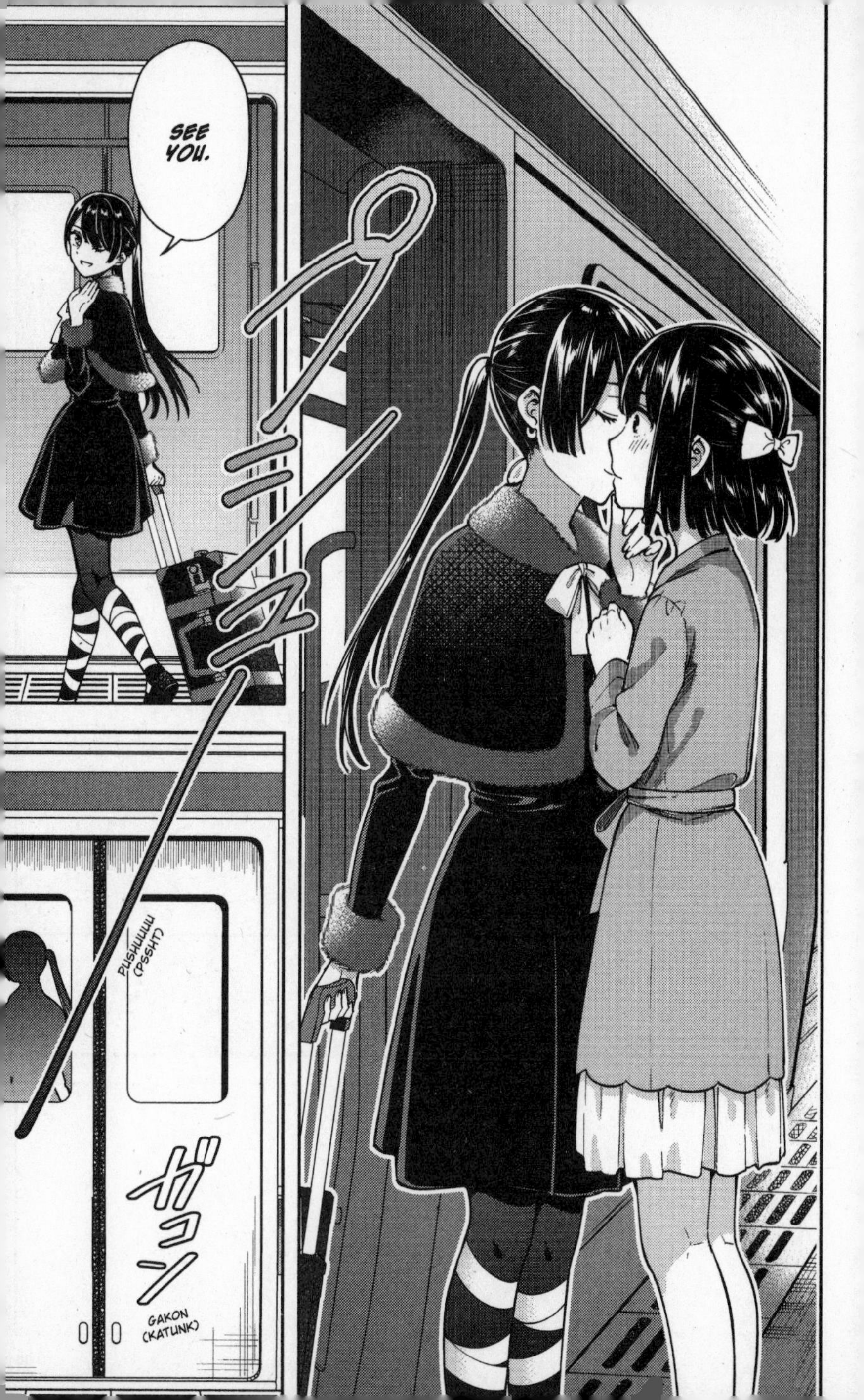
SEE YOU.
PUSHUUUU (PSSHT)
GAKON (KATUNK)

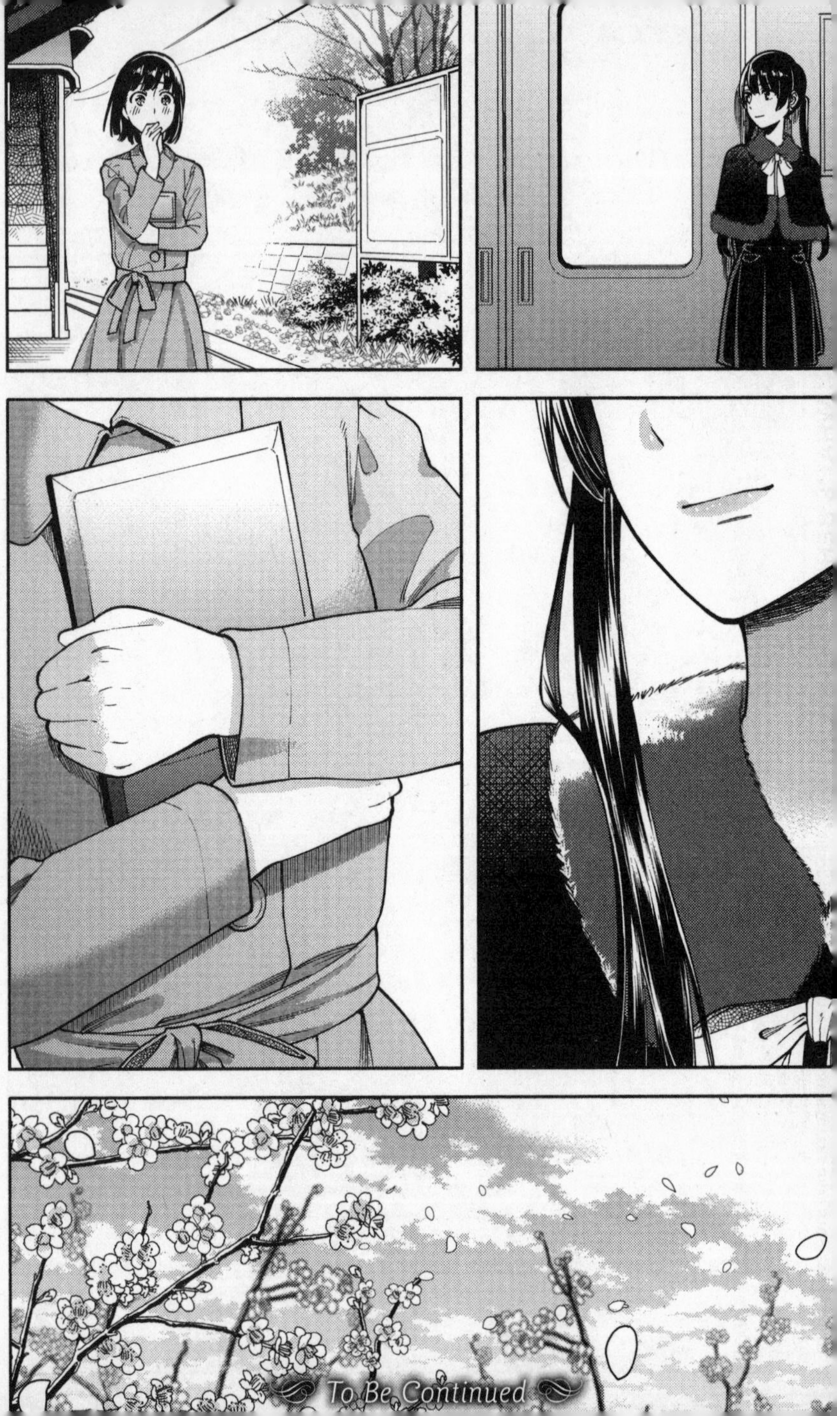
To Be Continued

Starting Now

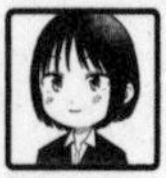

KIDO

AGE TWENTY-FIVE. TEACHER AT SEIRAN. ENJOYS HER WORK.

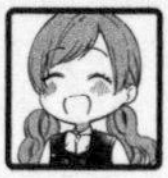

KURADA

HIGH SCHOOL THIRD-YEAR. LAID-BACK.

KISS THEATER: WHAT'S BEHIND THE STORY!? ✶ PEOPLE OTHER THAN THE MAIN CHARACTERS HAVE STORIES TOO. HERE,

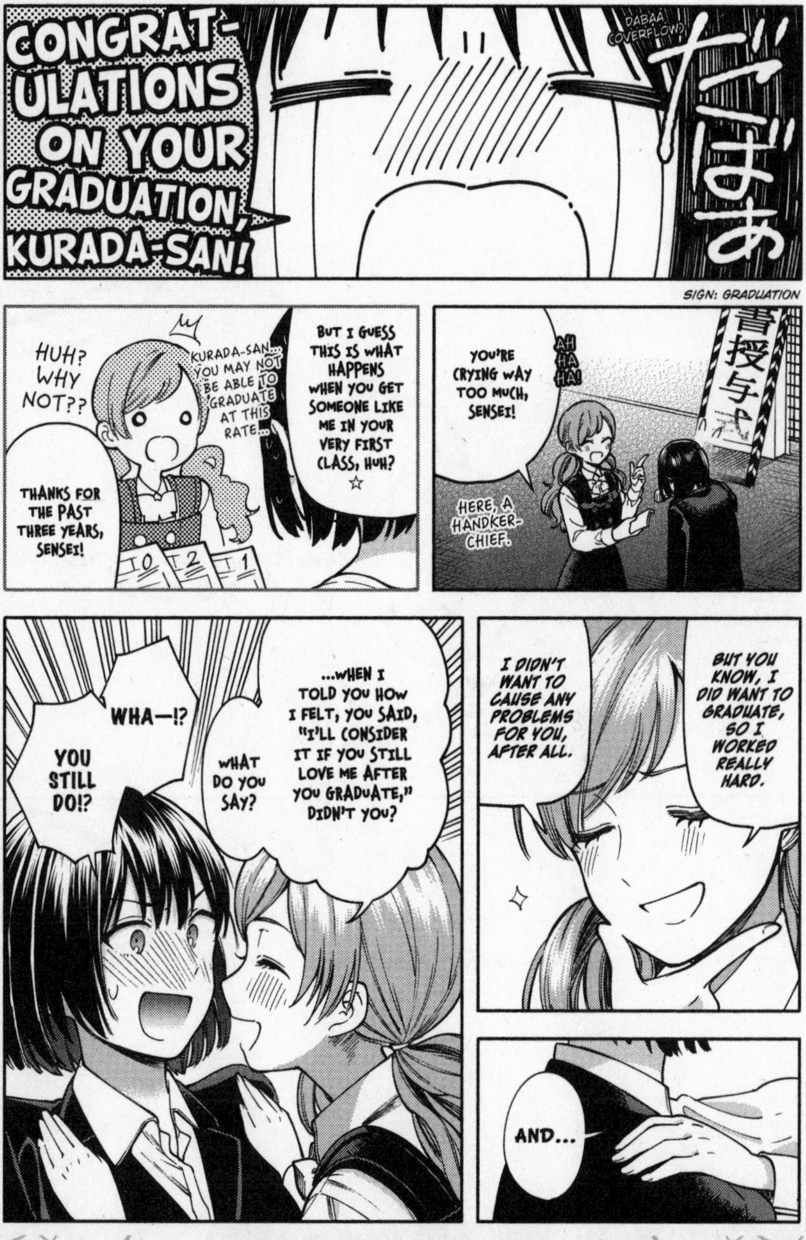

だばあ
DABAA (OVERFLOW)
CONGRATULATIONS ON YOUR GRADUATION, KURADA-SAN!
SIGN: GRADUATION
卒業証書授与式
YOU'RE CRYING WAY TOO MUCH, SENSEI!
AH HA HA!
HERE, A HANDKERCHIEF.
BUT I GUESS THIS IS WHAT HAPPENS WHEN YOU GET SOMEONE LIKE ME IN YOUR VERY FIRST CLASS, HUH? ☆
KURADA-SAN... YOU MAY NOT BE ABLE TO GRADUATE AT THIS RATE...
HUH? WHY NOT??
THANKS FOR THE PAST THREE YEARS, SENSEI!
BUT YOU KNOW, I DID WANT TO GRADUATE, SO I WORKED REALLY HARD.
I DIDN'T WANT TO CAUSE ANY PROBLEMS FOR YOU, AFTER ALL.
AND...
...WHEN I TOLD YOU HOW I FELT, YOU SAID, "I'LL CONSIDER IT IF YOU STILL LOVE ME AFTER YOU GRADUATE," DIDN'T YOU?
WHAT DO YOU SAY?
WHA—!?
YOU STILL DO!?

Kiss and White Lily for My Dearest Girl
Side Stories

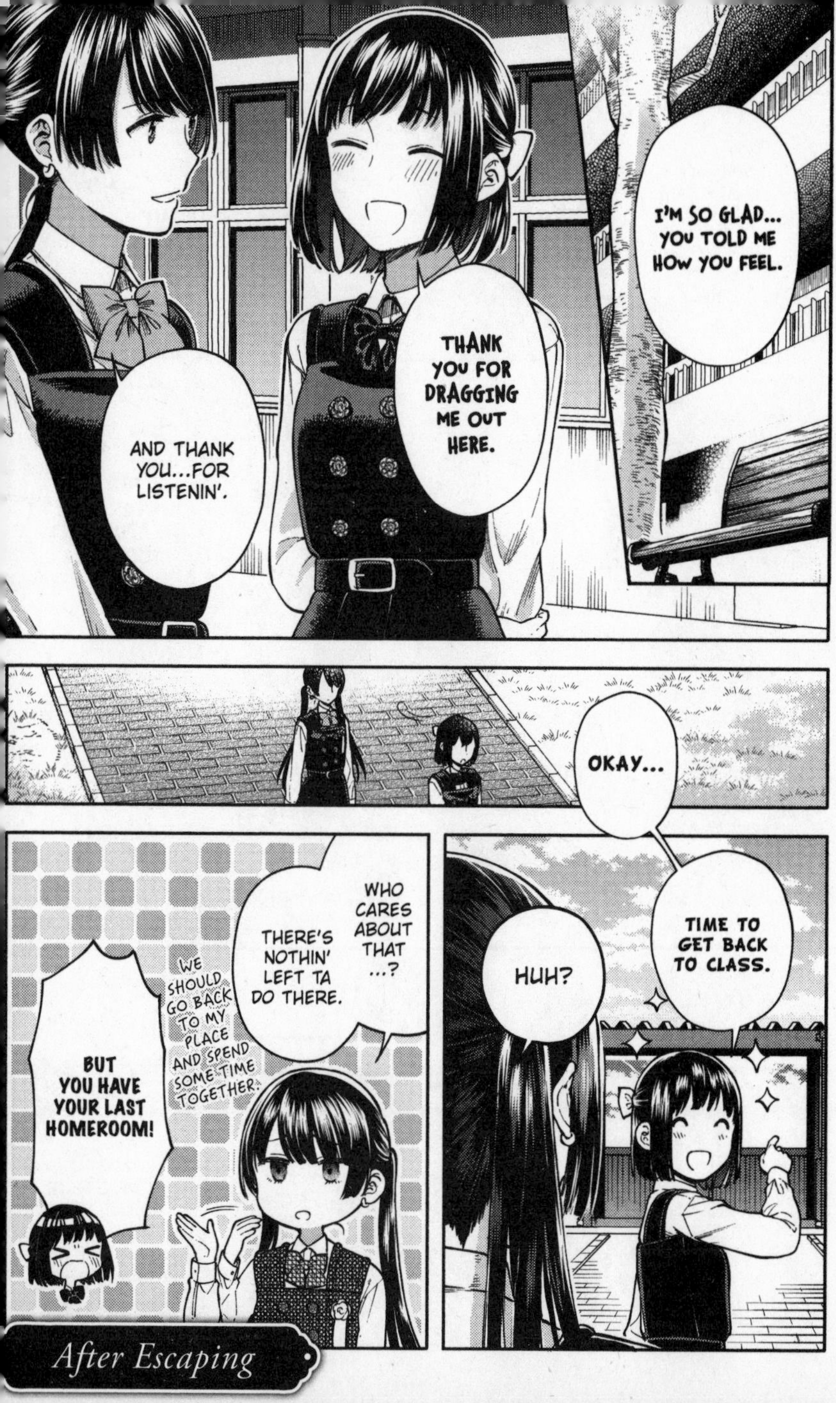
I'M SO GLAD... YOU TOLD ME HOW YOU FEEL.
THANK YOU FOR DRAGGING ME OUT HERE.
AND THANK YOU...FOR LISTENIN'.
OKAY...
TIME TO GET BACK TO CLASS.
HUH?
WHO CARES ABOUT THAT ...?
THERE'S NOTHIN' LEFT TA DO THERE.
WE SHOULD GO BACK TO MY PLACE AND SPEND SOME TIME TOGETHER.
BUT YOU HAVE YOUR LAST HOMEROOM!
After Escaping

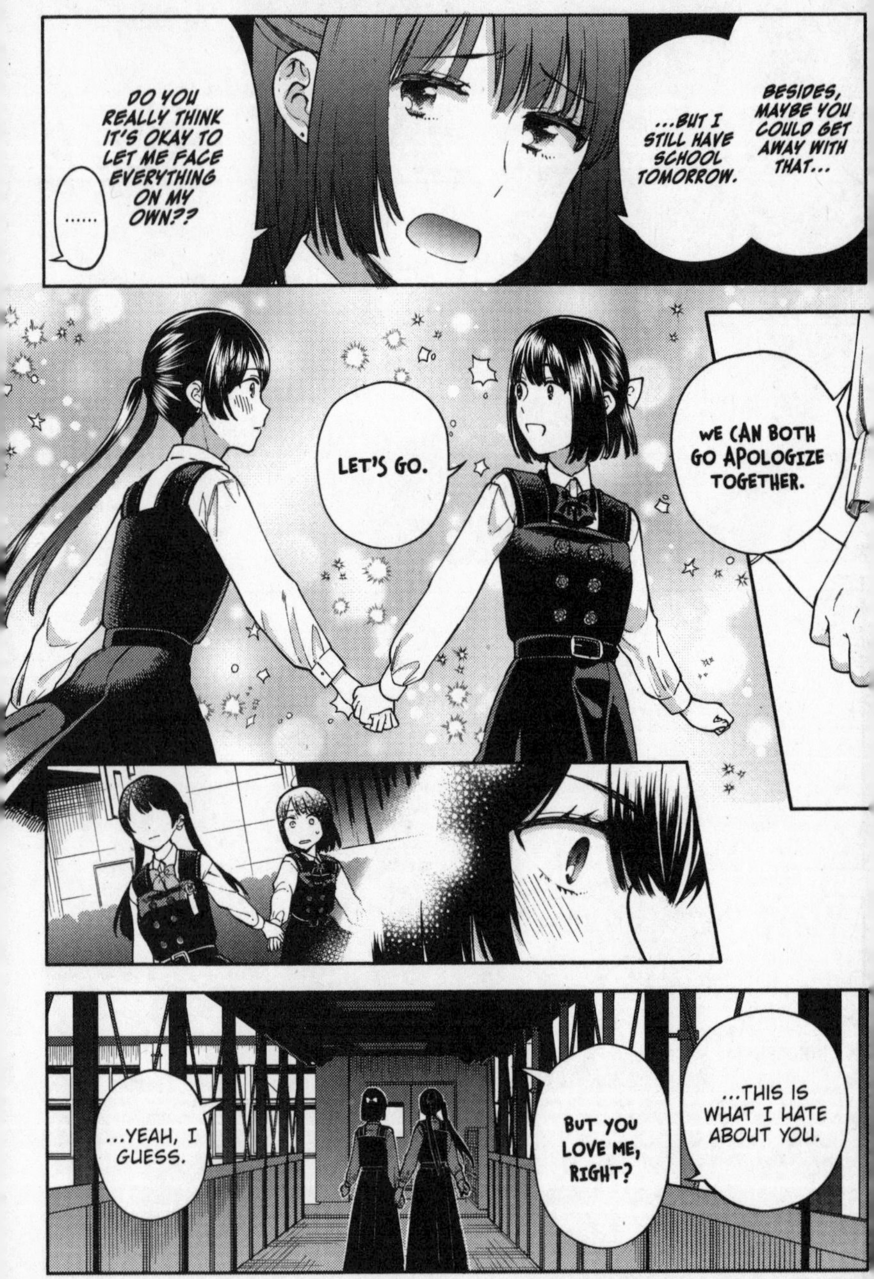
BESIDES, MAYBE YOU COULD GET AWAY WITH THAT...
...BUT I STILL HAVE SCHOOL TOMORROW.
DO YOU REALLY THINK IT'S OKAY TO LET ME FACE EVERYTHING ON MY OWN??
......
WE CAN BOTH GO APOLOGIZE TOGETHER.
LET'S GO.
...THIS IS WHAT I HATE ABOUT YOU.
BUT YOU LOVE ME, RIGHT?
...YEAH, I GUESS.

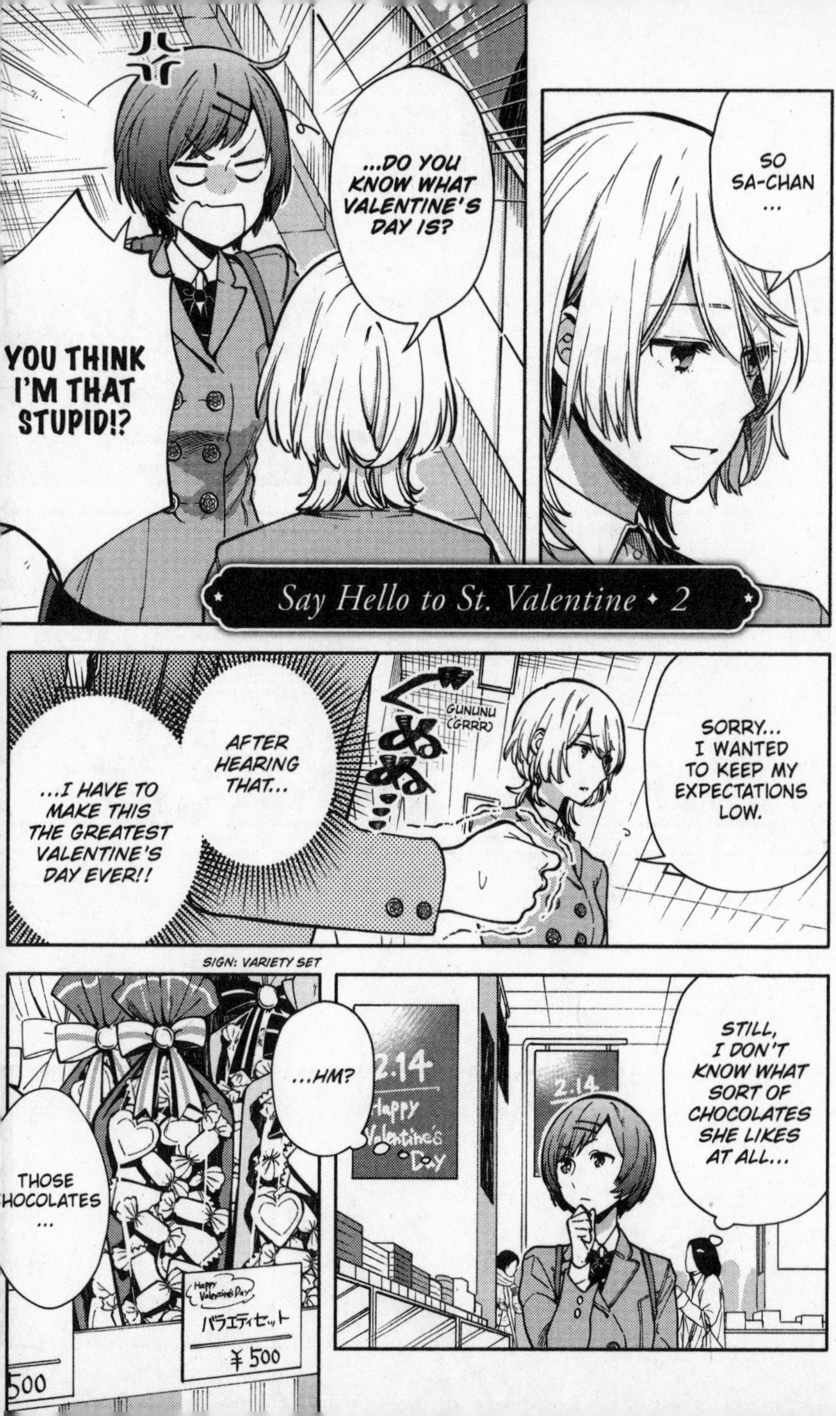
SO SA-CHAN ...
...DO YOU KNOW WHAT VALENTINE'S DAY IS?
YOU THINK I'M THAT STUPID!?
Say Hello to St. Valentine ✦ 2
SORRY... I WANTED TO KEEP MY EXPECTATIONS LOW.
ぐぬぬ…
GUNUNU (GRRR)
AFTER HEARING THAT...
...I HAVE TO MAKE THIS THE GREATEST VALENTINE'S DAY EVER!!
STILL, I DON'T KNOW WHAT SORT OF CHOCOLATES SHE LIKES AT ALL...
2.14 Happy Valentine's Day
2.14
...HM?
SIGN: VARIETY SET
THOSE CHOCOLATES ...
Happy Valentine's Day
バラエティセット
¥500
500

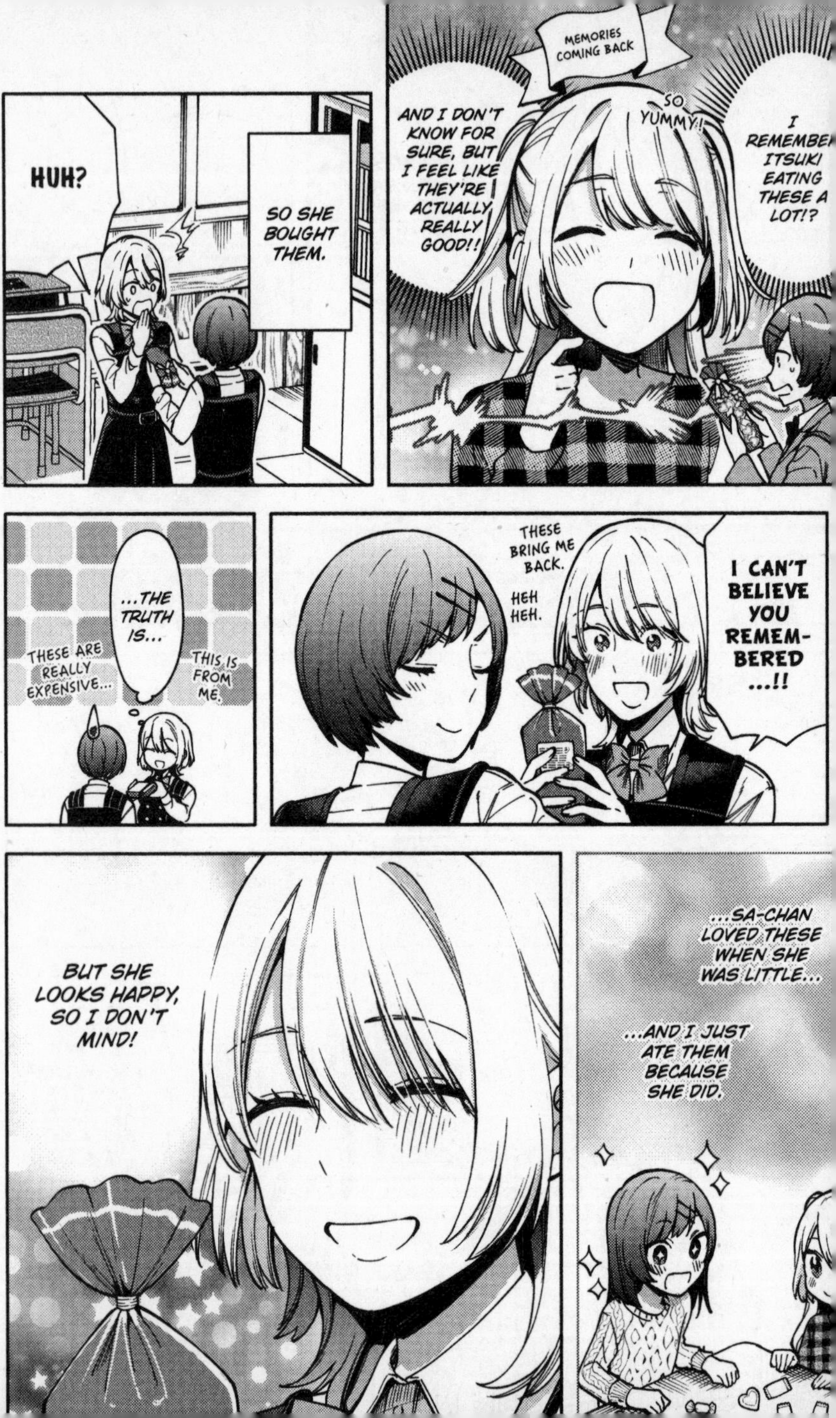
MEMORIES COMING BACK
I REMEMBE ITSUKI EATING THESE A LOT!?
SO YUMMY!
AND I DON'T KNOW FOR SURE, BUT I FEEL LIKE THEY'RE ACTUALLY REALLY GOOD!!
SO SHE BOUGHT THEM.
HUH?
I CAN'T BELIEVE YOU REMEMBERED...!!
THESE BRING ME BACK.
HEH HEH.
...THE TRUTH IS...
THIS IS FROM ME.
THESE ARE REALLY EXPENSIVE...
...SA-CHAN LOVED THESE WHEN SHE WAS LITTLE...
...AND I JUST ATE THEM BECAUSE SHE DID.
BUT SHE LOOKS HAPPY, SO I DON'T MIND!

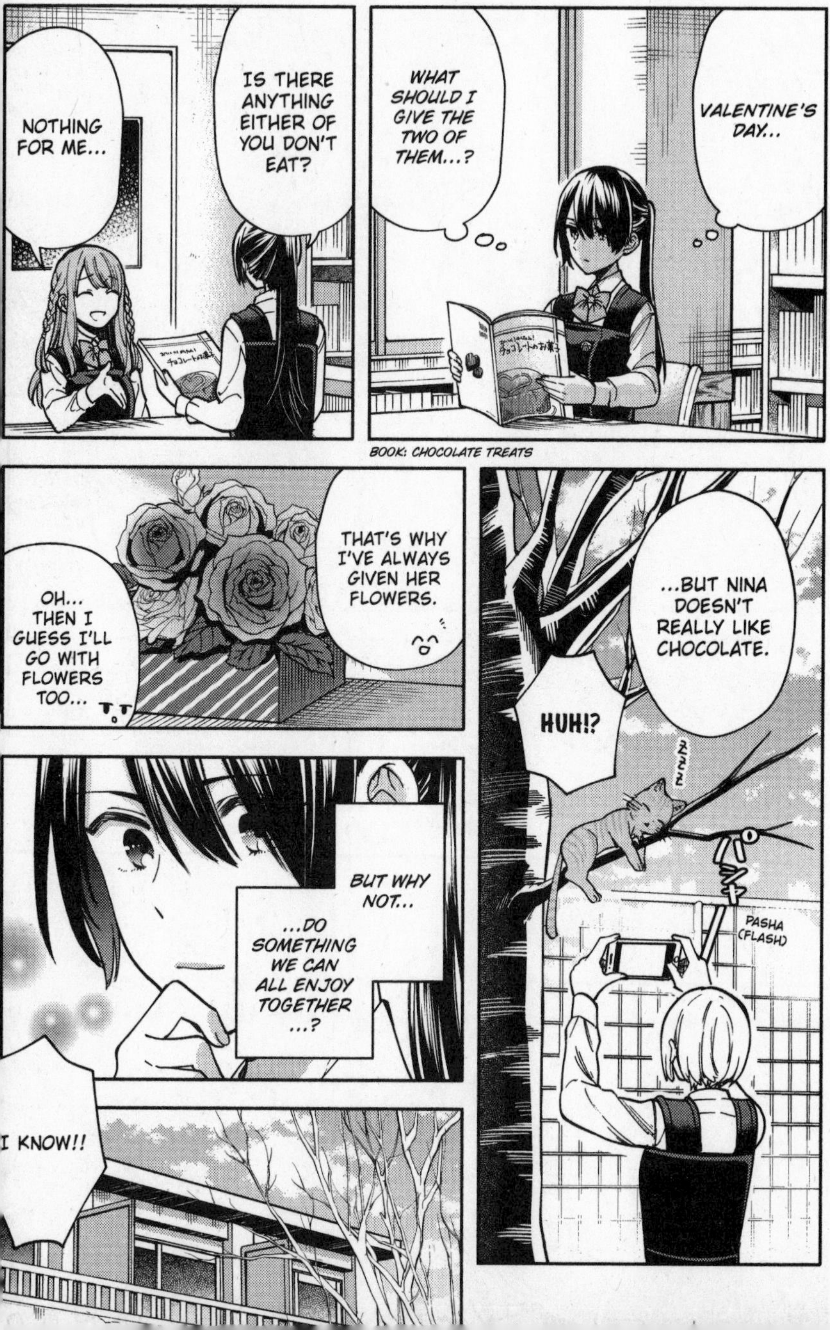
VALENTINE'S DAY...
WHAT SHOULD I GIVE THE TWO OF THEM...?
BOOK: CHOCOLATE TREATS
IS THERE ANYTHING EITHER OF YOU DON'T EAT?
NOTHING FOR ME...
...BUT NINA DOESN'T REALLY LIKE CHOCOLATE.
HUH!?
PASHA (FLASH)
THAT'S WHY I'VE ALWAYS GIVEN HER FLOWERS.
OH... THEN I GUESS I'LL GO WITH FLOWERS TOO...
BUT WHY NOT...
...DO SOMETHING WE CAN ALL ENJOY TOGETHER ...?
I KNOW!!

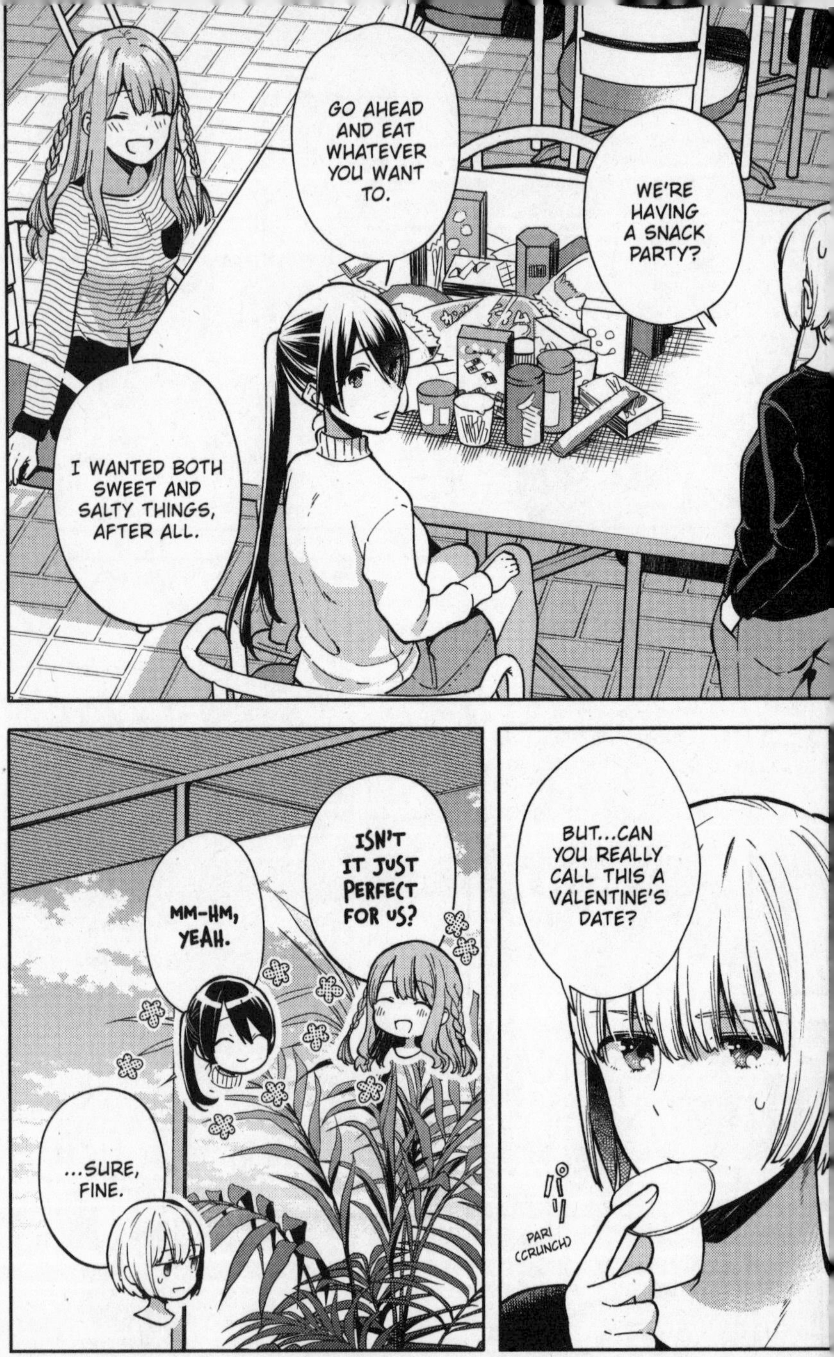
WE'RE HAVING A SNACK PARTY?
GO AHEAD AND EAT WHATEVER YOU WANT TO.
I WANTED BOTH SWEET AND SALTY THINGS, AFTER ALL.
BUT...CAN YOU REALLY CALL THIS A VALENTINE'S DATE?
PARI (CRUNCH)
ISN'T IT JUST PERFECT FOR US?
MM-HM, YEAH.
...SURE, FINE.

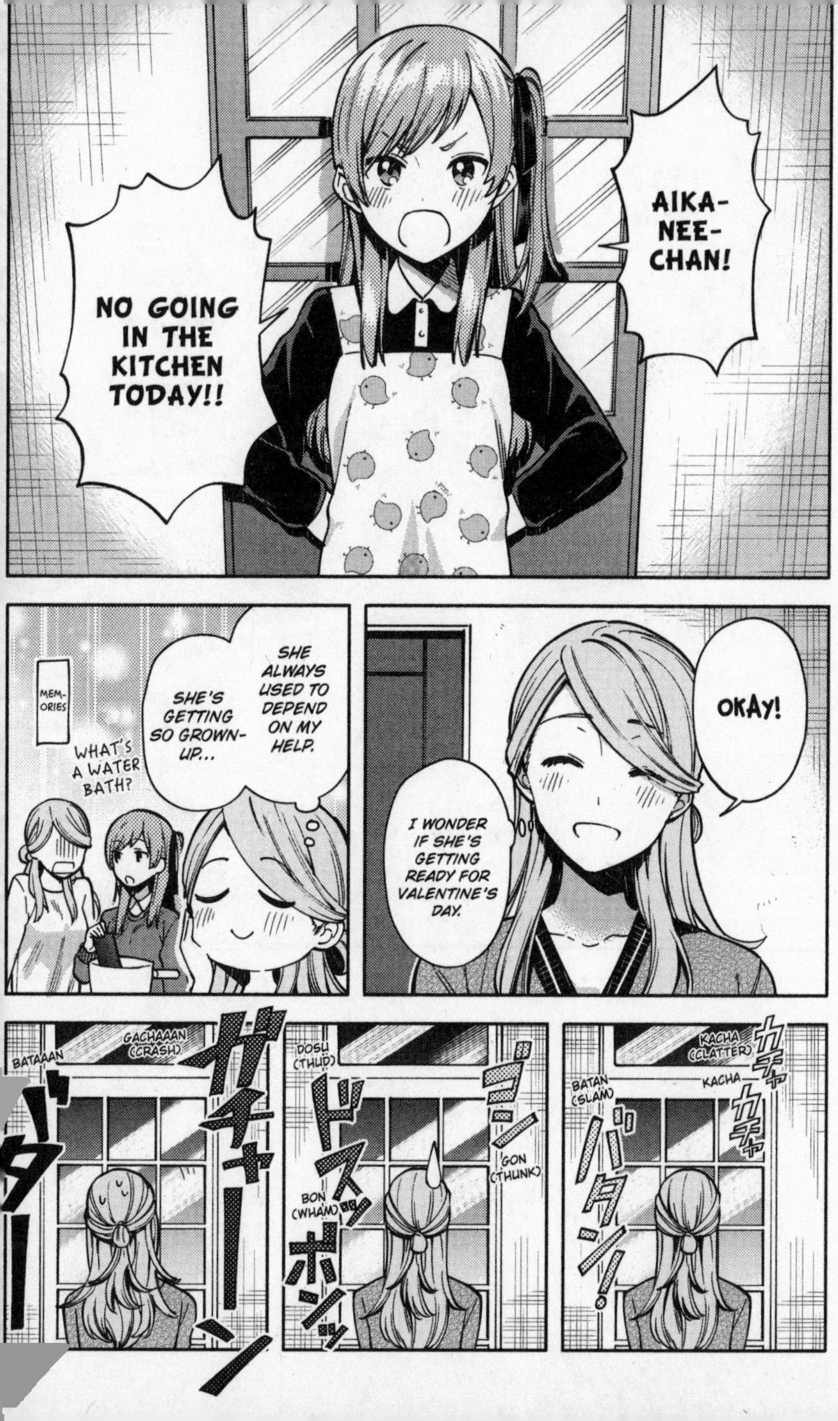
AIKA-NEE-CHAN!
NO GOING IN THE KITCHEN TODAY!!
OKAY!
I WONDER IF SHE'S GETTING READY FOR VALENTINE'S DAY.
SHE ALWAYS USED TO DEPEND ON MY HELP.
SHE'S GETTING SO GROWN-UP...
MEMORIES
WHAT'S A WATER BATH?
KACHA (CLATTER)
KACHA
BATAN (SLAM)
GON (THUNK)
DOSU (THUD)
BON (WHAM)
GACHAAAN (CRASH)
BATAAAN

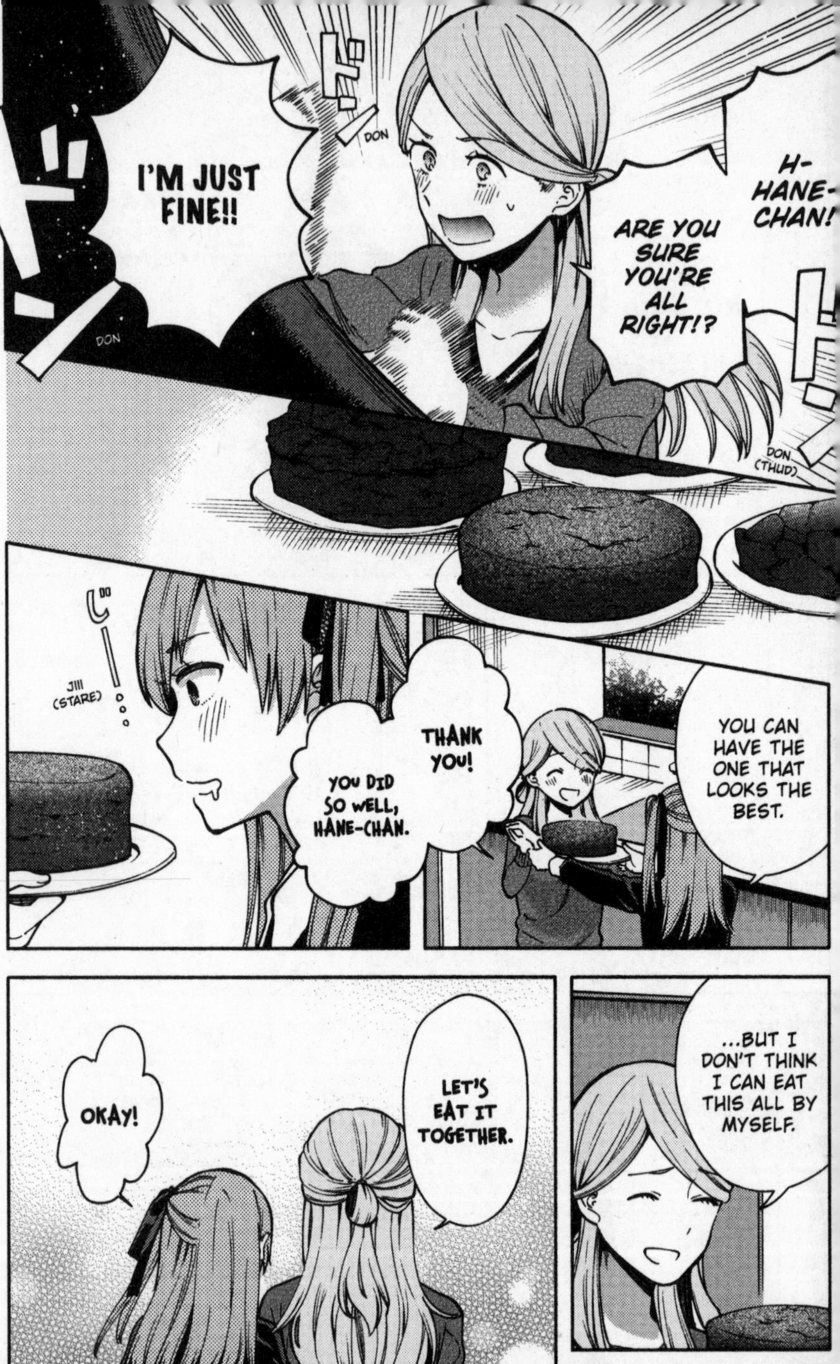
H-HANE-CHAN!
ARE YOU SURE YOU'RE ALL RIGHT!?
DON (THUD)
DON
I'M JUST FINE!!
DON
YOU CAN HAVE THE ONE THAT LOOKS THE BEST.
THANK YOU!
YOU DID SO WELL, HANE-CHAN.
JIII (STARE)
...BUT I DON'T THINK I CAN EAT THIS ALL BY MYSELF.
LET'S EAT IT TOGETHER.
OKAY!

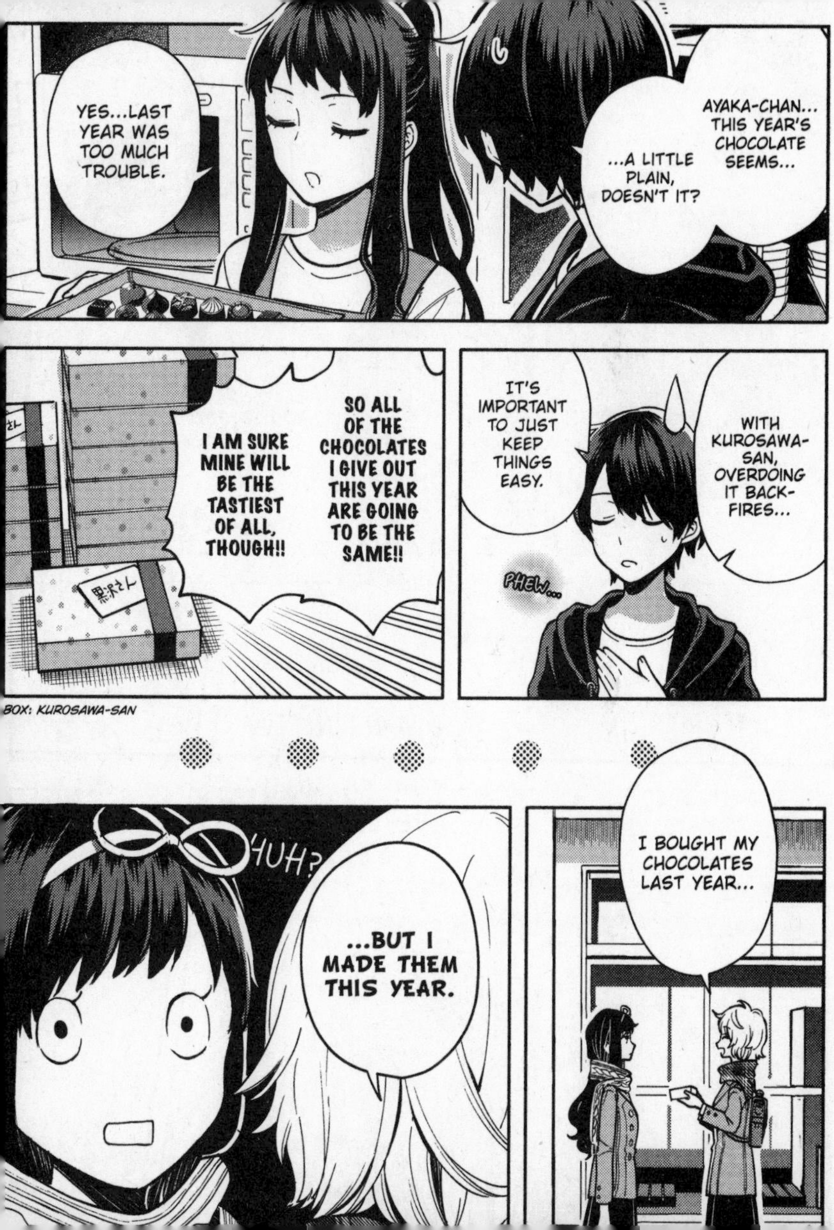
AYAKA-CHAN... THIS YEAR'S CHOCOLATE SEEMS...
...A LITTLE PLAIN, DOESN'T IT?
YES...LAST YEAR WAS TOO MUCH TROUBLE.
WITH KUROSAWA-SAN, OVERDOING IT BACK-FIRES...
IT'S IMPORTANT TO JUST KEEP THINGS EASY.
PHEW...
SO ALL OF THE CHOCOLATES I GIVE OUT THIS YEAR ARE GOING TO BE THE SAME!!
I AM SURE MINE WILL BE THE TASTIEST OF ALL, THOUGH!!
黒沢さん
BOX: KUROSAWA-SAN
I BOUGHT MY CHOCOLATES LAST YEAR...
...BUT I MADE THEM THIS YEAR.
HUH?

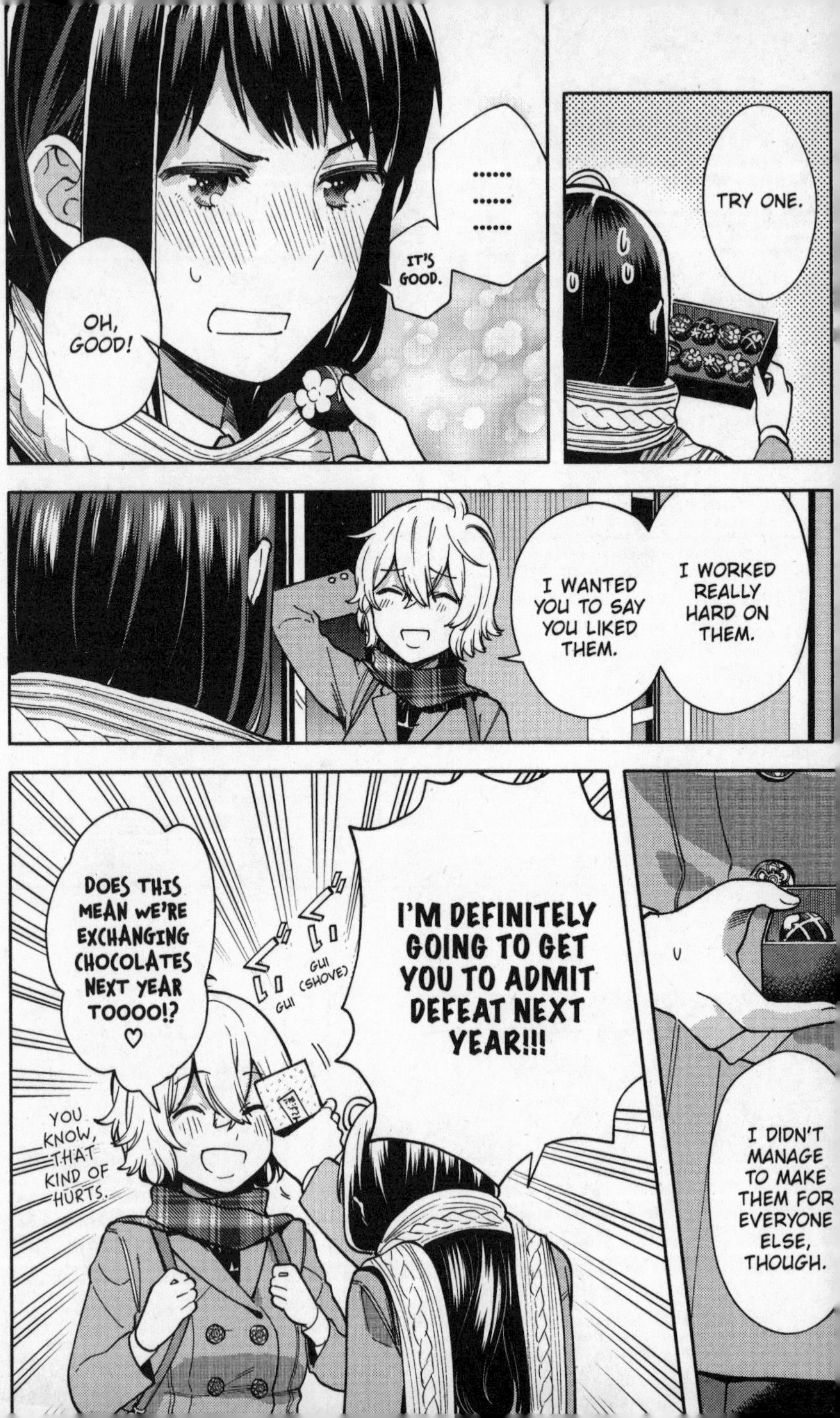
TRY ONE.
......
......
......
IT'S GOOD.
OH, GOOD!
I WORKED REALLY HARD ON THEM.
I WANTED YOU TO SAY YOU LIKED THEM.
I DIDN'T MANAGE TO MAKE THEM FOR EVERYONE ELSE, THOUGH.
I'M DEFINITELY GOING TO GET YOU TO ADMIT DEFEAT NEXT YEAR!!!
GUI (SHOVE)
GUI
DOES THIS MEAN WE'RE EXCHANGING CHOCOLATES NEXT YEAR TOOOO!? ♡
YOU KNOW, THAT KIND OF HURTS.

Afterword

I HAVE NEVER DONE / ANY COSPLAYING BEFORE. / MY NAME IS CANNO. (5-7-5) I'VE BEEN TOLD THAT MOST PEOPLE DON'T USE CARDS THESE DAYS, BUT AS AN OUTSIDER, I THINK THE WHOLE CARD THING WAS A REALLY NICE TOUCH, SO I KEPT IT IN ANYWAY.

ONCE AGAIN, THANK YOU SO MUCH TO EVERYONE IN THE *ALIVE* EDITORIAL DEPARTMENT; THE DESIGNER SEKI-SAN; YUI-SAN, WHO WAS SO HELPFUL; YAMAGUCHI-SAN, WHO HELPED WITH ASUKA'S DIALECT; MY FAMILY; MY FRIENDS; AND EVERYONE WHO CHEERED ME ON AND HELPED GET THIS BOOK OUT SUCCESSFULLY.

SHIRAMINE AND KUROSAWA'S STORY IS GETTING CLOSE TO ITS CONCLUSION. I HOPE YOU'LL STICK WITH ME THROUGH THE END.

CANNO 9

☆ THINGS I UNEXPECTEDLY DIDN'T GET A CHANCE TO DRAW: ASUKA'S STREET CLOTHES ☆

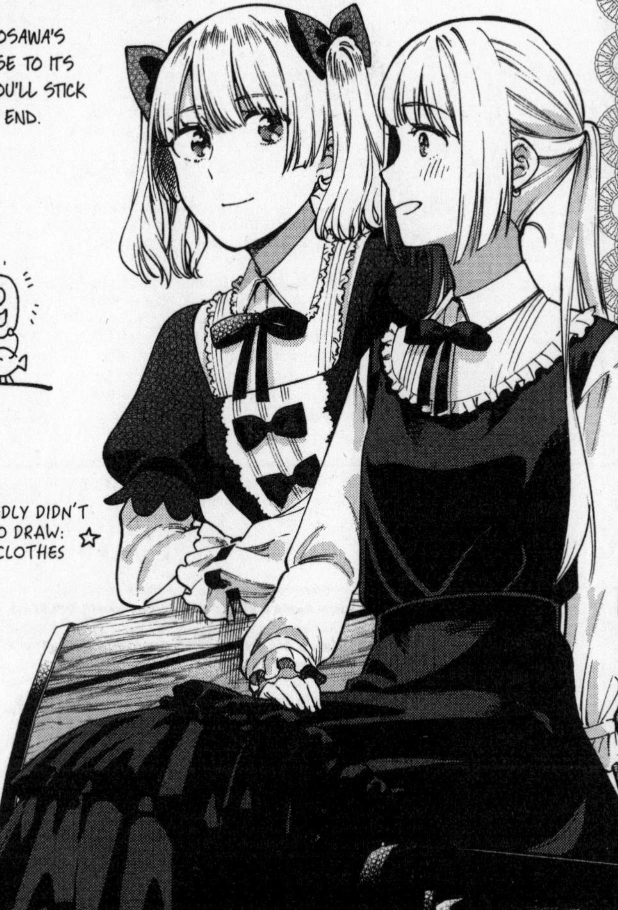

Kiss & White Lily for My Dearest Girl

⑨

CANNO

TRANSLATION: LEIGHANN HARVEY
LETTERING: ALEXIS ECKERMAN

ANOKO NI KISS TO SHIRAYURI WO Vol. 9
©Canno 2018
First published in Japan in 2018 by KADOKAWA CORPORATION, Tokyo.
English translation rights arranged with KADOKAWA CORPORATION, Tokyo
through Tuttle-Mori Agency, Inc., Tokyo.

English translation © 2019 by Yen Press, LLC

Yen Press
1290 Avenue of the Americas
New York, NY 10104

Visit us at yenpress.com
facebook.com/yenpress
twitter.com/yenpress
yenpress.tumblr.com
instagram.com/yenpress

First Yen Press Edition: May 2019

Yen Press is an imprint of Yen Press, LLC.

WOR

Printed in the United States of America